HARVARD HISTORICAL STUDIES

# BISMARCK'S DIPLOMACY AT ITS ZENITH

BY

JOSEPH VINCENT FULLER

New York · HOWARD FERTIG · 1967

First published in 1922

HOWARD FERTIG, INC. EDITION 1967
Published by arrangement with Harvard University Press

*All rights reserved.*

Library of Congress Catalog Card Number: 67-13643

PRINTED IN THE UNITED STATES OF AMERICA
BY NOBLE OFFSET PRINTERS, INC.

TO
ARCHIBALD CARY COOLIDGE

# PREFACE

THIS study of Bismarck's diplomacy covers in detail the period beginning with the interview between the Austrian and Russian Emperors at Kremsier, on August 25, 1885, and ending with the Chancellor's speech in the Reichstag, on February 6, 1888. The period is one of the most crowded with events in Bismarck's entire career as Chancellor. It is marked by two great upheavals in the domain of the Eastern Question and by almost continuously strained relations between Russia and Austria. It witnessed two serious crises in the relations between Germany and France, both occurring in the year 1887. In the course of that same year there were concluded no less than four secret diplomatic agreements involving Germany directly or indirectly. No period is more illustrative of the principles and methods of Bismarck's diplomacy: none since 1871 is more significant for Germany's later history.

At the time this work was undertaken, six years ago, there was practically no documentary material available for the study of the period, beyond the official publications of the parliamentary governments. So much has appeared since then that it is now possible to refer to documents for almost every episode, albeit still incompletely and with important exceptions. From the beginning, I had felt that the accounts of Bismarck's foreign policy given by himself and his German biographers were unsatisfactory; and I had striven accordingly to bring to bear all the other available evidence on the subject. Practically all my early conclusions have been confirmed by the more recently published documents. I am, of course, aware that I shall incur the charge of having cut the new cloth to my old pattern; and such has perhaps inevitably been the case in some degree. Yet more than once, under the impulse of a first impression, I have attacked a mass of fresh material in an effort to work out a different interpretation of Bismarck's policy, only to find myself driven back upon my previous one.

It will be long before the last word on this subject can be said — or, more likely, that time will never come. I can only hope to offer a presentation which will lead to a better understanding of the decisive influence of Germany's great statesman in shaping the course of recent history.

I have one supreme acknowledgement to make — to Professor Archibald Cary Coolidge of Harvard University, for inspiration, advice, and encouragement in carrying out this work, for his unflagging interest in it, and for his indispensable help in obtaining recent material. Most of whatever value this book may possess is due to him; for its defects I accept the sole responsibility. I owe much, also, to Mr. George W. Robinson, whose friendly, careful criticism and experienced aid have made the work presentable after its numerous revisions.

JOSEPH V. FULLER.

MADISON, WISCONSIN,
   October. 1922.

# CONTENTS

## CHAPTER I
                                            PAGE

BISMARCK'S DIPLOMACY AFTER 1871 . . . . . . . . . . . . . 3–16
    Unity of the foreign policy of imperial Germany . . . . . . . . 3
    Hesitation between Russia and England . . . . . . . . . . 4
    The Eastern Question . . . . . . . . . . . . . . . . . . 6
    Bismarck's choice between Russia and Austria . . . . . . . 6
    The League of the Three Emperors of 1881 . . . . . . . . . 8
    Intensive quest of colonies (1884–85) . . . . . . . . . . . . 11
    Bismarck's Continental system . . . . . . . . . . . . . . 12

## CHAPTER II

THE UNIFICATION OF BULGARIA . . . . . . . . . . . . . . 17–54
    Meeting of the Emperors at Kremsier (August 25, 1885) . . . . 17
    The Bulgarian question . . . . . . . . . . . . . . . . . 18
    The *coup d'état* of Philippopolis (September 18, 1885) . . . . . 22
    Serbo-Bulgarian war . . . . . . . . . . . . . . . . . . 36
    Bismarck's misconception of the situation . . . . . . . . . . 48
    Churchill desires an Anglo-German alliance . . . . . . . . . 50
    A patched up peace . . . . . . . . . . . . . . . . . . . 54

## CHAPTER III

THE ABDICATION OF PRINCE ALEXANDER . . . . . . . . . 55–74
    Measures against the German Poles . . . . . . . . . . . . 55
    Strained relations between Germany and France . . . . . . . 57
    Overzealous activity of Prince Alexander . . . . . . . . . . 63
    Italy and the Triple Alliance . . . . . . . . . . . . . . . 65
    Abduction and return of Prince Alexander . . . . . . . . . 69
    His abdication (September 3, 1886) . . . . . . . . . . . . 71

## CHAPTER IV

BISMARCK'S EASTERN POLICY . . . . . . . . . . . . . . . 75–82
    Elasticity of Bismarck's policies . . . . . . . . . . . . . . 75
    Possible courses and their difficulties . . . . . . . . . . . 77
    Indirect blocking of Russia the policy chosen . . . . . . . . 80

## CHAPTER V

THE POWERS AND BULGARIA . . . . . . . . . . . . . . . . . 83–128
    The Hungarians compel Austria to oppose Russia . . . . . . . 83
    Bismarck seeks support for Austria . . . . . . . . . . . . . . 88
    Mission of Kaulbars in Bulgaria . . . . . . . . . . . . . . . 91
    Lord Randolph Churchill . . . . . . . . . . . . . . . . . . 92
    Italy's conditions . . . . . . . . . . . . . . . . . . . . . . 98
    The Egyptian question . . . . . . . . . . . . . . . . . . . 100
    'Two great refusals of alliances' . . . . . . . . . . . . . . . 102
    Salisbury's Guildhall speech (November 9, 1886) . . . . . . . . 106
    Kálnoky's 'middle course' . . . . . . . . . . . . . . . . . 109
    The 'French peril' and the German army bill . . . . . . . . . 114
    Bismarck's double problem . . . . . . . . . . . . . . . . . 119

## CHAPTER VI

BISMARCK AND FRANCE . . . . . . . . . . . . . . . . . . . 129–149
    Bismarck's loyalty to Austria . . . . . . . . . . . . . . . . 129
    Boulangism in France . . . . . . . . . . . . . . . . . . . 130
    Bismarck's speech on the army bill (January 11, 1887) . . . . . 131
    The war scare of January–February, 1887 . . . . . . . . . . 136

## CHAPTER VII

THE TRIPLE ALLIANCE AND ENGLAND . . . . . . . . . . . 150–170
    Renewal of the Triple Alliance (February 20, 1887) . . . . . . 150
    Mediterranean agreement of February–March, 1887 . . . . . . 151
    Military measures of Russia . . . . . . . . . . . . . . . . . 158
    Attempted assassination of the Tsar (March 13, 1887) . . . . . 160
    Crown Prince Rudolf's interview with Bismarck . . . . . . . . 163

## CHAPTER VIII

THE SCHNAEBELE INCIDENT . . . . . . . . . . . . . . . . 171–184
    Unrest in Alsace-Lorraine . . . . . . . . . . . . . . . . . 171
    Arrest of Schnaebele (April 20, 1887) . . . . . . . . . . . . 173
    Arrogant conduct of the German government . . . . . . . . . 177

## CHAPTER IX

THE REINSURANCE TREATY . . . . . . . . . . . . . . . . 185–204
    The League of the Three Emperors nears its end . . . . . . . 185
    Separate treaty between Germany and Russia . . . . . . . . . 186
    Failure of the Egyptian convention . . . . . . . . . . . . . 198
    Campaign against Russian credit . . . . . . . . . . . . . . 202

CONTENTS                                                      xi

## CHAPTER X

FERDINAND OF COBURG . . . . . . . . . . . . . . . . . . 205–224
    Bulgaria seeks a prince . . . . . . . . . . . . . . . . . . . 205
    Ferdinand of Coburg chosen (July 7, 1887) . . . . . . . . . 206
    The 'Bulgarian documents' . . . . . . . . . . . . . . . . 212
    Russia opposed by three Great Powers . . . . . . . . . . . 215

## CHAPTER XI

BISMARCK AND ALEXANDER III . . . . . . . . . . . . . . 225–265
    Germany's Bulgarian policy revealed to the Tsar . . . . . . . 225
    Vain attempts to solve the Bulgarian question . . . . . . . . 233
    Interview between Bismarck and Crispi (October 2, 1887) . . . 237
    Alexander III resents the conduct of Germany . . . . . . . . 241
    The Tsar's visit to Berlin (November 18, 1887) . . . . . . . . 248

## CHAPTER XII

THE TRIPLE ENTENTE OF DECEMBER . . . . . . . . . . 266–302
    Importance of the attitude of England . . . . . . . . . . . . 266
    Letters of Bismarck and Salisbury . . . . . . . . . . . . . . 267
    The question of Belgium . . . . . . . . . . . . . . . . . . 274
    The second Mediterranean agreement (December 12–16) . . . . 275
    The war scare of December, 1887 . . . . . . . . . . . . . . 276
    Russia yields to the triple entente (December 18) . . . . . . . 285
    Further discussion of the 'Bulgarian documents' . . . . . . . 292

## CHAPTER XIII

THE FRUITS OF BISMARCK'S DIPLOMACY . . . . . . . . . 303–325
    The year 1887 termed a 'prophetic year' . . . . . . . . . . . 303
    Publication of the Austro-German treaty of 1879 . . . . . . . 307
    Bismarck's great speech of February 6, 1888 . . . . . . . . . 309
    The situation of Germany in 1885 and 1888 . . . . . . . . . 315
    Failure of Bismarck's policy inevitable . . . . . . . . . . . 321
    Some notes on his successors . . . . . . . . . . . . . . . 322
    Bismarck's diplomacy contained the causes of Germany's downfall  325

## APPENDIX

THE LETTERS EXCHANGED BETWEEN BISMARCK AND SALISBURY IN
    NOVEMBER, 1887 . . . . . . . . . . . . . . . . . . . . 329–335

BIBLIOGRAPHY . . . . . . . . . . . . . . . . . . . . . . 337–352

INDEX . . . . . . . . . . . . . . . . . . . . . . . . . . 353–368

# LIST OF ABBREVIATIONS

B. M. M........Brauer, Marcks, Müller, *Erinnerungen an Bismarck.*
G. B...........*Green Books.* See Italy, in the Bibliography.
G. F. O.........*German Foreign Office Publication.* See *Die grosse Politik der europäischen Kabinette,* in the same.
M. A. Z.........[Münchener] *Allgemeine Zeitung.*
N. F. P.........*Neue Freie Presse.*
P. P............*Parliamentary Papers.* See Great Britain, in the Bibliography.
Y. B............*Yellow Book.* See France, in the same.

# BISMARCK'S DIPLOMACY
AT ITS ZENITH

# BISMARCK'S DIPLOMACY AT ITS ZENITH

## CHAPTER I

### BISMARCK'S DIPLOMACY AFTER 1871

THE foreign policy of imperial Germany is now a closed chapter of diplomatic history. A general survey of the chapter shows it to possess a degree of unity not always attributed to it. *Alter Kurs* and *Neuer Kurs* are, at most, subdivisions of the story. William II, when he took over the pen from Bismarck in 1890, wrote on in a different style, but without breaking the thread of the narrative. "Above all is it false," writes Delbrück, "fundamentally false, to maintain that he struck out an essentially different path from Bismarck's. Everything that he undertook and strove after has its origin, is present in embryo, in the policy of Bismarck. . . . The errors of German policy after 1890 were the results of a change in temperament, rather than in direction."[1]

The idea that a violent revolution in foreign policy accompanied his removal from office was deliberately fostered by Bismarck himself in the course of the controversy with his successors over the dropping of the Reinsurance Treaty with Russia. As a matter of fact, the failure to renew this agreement was not so much the point of departure for a new course as it was the logical outcome of the old. The Tsar Alexander III, it is true, expressed his willingness to renew the treaty in 1890; but he made his advances without enthusiasm, and was rather relieved than otherwise at their failure. "In my secret heart," he noted on the report of the final negotiations, "I am well content that Germany has been the first to refuse the renewal of the treaty, and I do not particularly regret the ending of the entente."[2] The treaty had long

[1] "Kaiser und Kanzler," in *Preussische Jahrbücher*, April, 1920, p. 47.
[2] Serge Goriainov, "The End of the Alliance of the Emperors," in the *American Historical Review*, January, 1918, p. 344.

since become an empty shell, its substance of advantage to Russia sapped away by Bismarck's consistent betrayal of her interests.

Of course, no such conception of the case is to be derived from Bismarck's own presentation of it. His conduct toward Russia is always pictured by him as dictated by absolute loyalty, even when repaid by ingratitude. But it is a notorious fact that from the Chancellor's utterances alone can be constructed no clear, or even truthful, picture of his actual policy. They often conflict with each other and with the facts. Particularly undependable are the explanations and justifications of his conduct of affairs which date from the period after his retirement. The *Gedanken und Erinnerungen* are far from supplying a reliable key to his career, and frequently only confuse and distort the issues. Otto Hammann states the problem well when he writes: "Whoever would come to a true understanding of his statesmanship must recognize the fallibility of his words, which, in the course of his fifty years of political activity, contradicted each other often enough. The enduring verity is to be found in his deeds."[3] It is only by scrutinizing his actions carefully, by weighing his words against his deeds, by bringing the two together in their proper temporal context, that this kernel of verity can be revealed. The result is often highly discreditable to the Chancellor's respect for the truth.

Since the late war this form of criticism has led to some remarkable results. A great controversy has arisen over Germany's fatal hesitation between Russia and England, which ended by assuring her the open hostility of both. In this controversy, the thesis set up by the party which may be called the 'Lichnowsky school' has been that the hesitation was a betrayal of Bismarckian principles of policy, which, if adhered to, would have led Germany into an alliance with England. The champions of this theory do not shrink from taking issue with Bismarck himself, whose bitterest charge against his successors was that they had abandoned his policy in turning their backs upon Russia in order to make friends with England. The case against Bismarck, based upon the contradiction of his words by his deeds, is strikingly put by Eckard-

[3] *Zur Vorgeschichte des Weltkrieges* (Berlin, 1919), p. 18.

stein: "The gentlemen of the Wilhelmstrasse either did not know or had forgotten that, as early as the year 1875, Prince Bismarck had come to realize how great a danger to the German Empire lurked in the rising wave of Russian imperialism and Panslavism, and that, to provide against it, he had striven untiringly for an alliance with England."[4] In support of his assertions, he is able to quote the veteran ambassador, Count Münster.[5] He also relates a number of attempts at an agreement, beginning with the year 1875, and even describes an approach to England in 1887, of which more is made than the facts warrant, as will later be shown.

Where lies the truth in this conflict between Bismarck and his interpreters? In fact, not completely on either side. Bismarck viewed his entire past policy in the light of the controversy which attended the close of his career: the advocates of the theory of the English alliance apply to his whole career the motives which actuated him during a period ending ten years before his dismissal. During the four years previous to 1880, Bismarck unquestionably gave evidence of a desire for at least a close understanding with England; but there is no warrant for assuming that this desire lasted throughout his chancellorship. Circumstances had altered by 1881, and, with them, Bismarck's views.

Furthermore, in explaining Bismarck's motives, Eckardstein

[4] Hermann, Freiherr von Eckardstein, *Lebenserinnerungen und politische Denkwürdigkeiten* (Leipzig, 1919-20, 2 vols.), i, pp. 293-294.

[5] *Ibid.*, i, pp. 296-297. April 14, 1898, Münster to Eckardstein. "Ich weiss es ja, Bismarck hat von jeher ein Bündnis mit England haben wollen. Da er es aber nicht haben konnte, war er bei seinem cholerischen Temperament zeitweise sehr gegen England aufgebracht. . . . Als Lothar Bucher im Auftrage Bismarcks 1875 plötzlich in geheimer Mission in London erschien, um die Möglichkeit eines englischen Bündnisses mit mir zu erörtern, riet ich ihm dringend ab, irgendwelche Schritte in dieser Richtung zu unternehmen, weil ich genau wusste, dass England damals nicht bündnisreif war. Trotzdem erfolgten Schritte, und Lothar Bucher holte sich einen ordentlichen Korb. Das hielt aber Bismarck nicht ab, immer von neuem zu versuchen." The editors of the German foreign office publication, *Die grosse Politik der europäischen Kabinette 1871-1914* (Berlin, 1922, 6 vols.), remark (iv, pp. 3-4, footnote) that no trace is to be found in the archives of this attempt or those in the next two years referred to by Eckardstein. This lack of direct evidence does not wholly destroy the value of the testimony: on the other hand, the editors admit that Bismarck sought an 'Annäherung' in 1876.

proceeds from a false, or at least a doubtful, premise. Fear of Russia was never more than momentarily a dominant motive in shaping Bismarck's policy: the choice between Russia and England did not appear to him the paramount issue for Germany's security. During the early years of the Empire's existence, the Chancellor worried far more about France than about Russia. In France Germany had to face an immediate and acute hostility: with Russia, on the other hand, the ties of friendship were many and close. The friendship of the one cancelled the enmity of the other. When Bismarck ventured, at the risk of war, to play with the idea of rendering France's enmity harmless by interfering with her military reconstruction, he found Russia's friendship less unqualified than he had hoped; but he was still far from judging it valueless. The check of 1875 undoubtedly left behind it a distrust of Russia and a deepened dislike of Gorchakov, but it hardly aroused any consciousness of a Panslavic peril. No serious estrangement from Russia resulted from the incident: that her support against France could not be fully counted on was no reason why she should be driven into France's arms. The approaches to England which were begun in 1875 do not imply that Bismarck had made the choice between her and Russia. He was merely providing for the possibility of Russia's escaping him against his will. Developments dating from that same year, however, finally forced him to make another choice which did cost him Russia's friendship temporarily; so that, under the resulting situation, his advances to England took on the character of an earnest quest of an alliance.

 The choice which gave Bismarck real trouble was that between Russia and Austria. It was forced upon him by the recurrence of the Eastern Question, in which the interests of Germany's two associates in the League of the Three Emperors were fundamentally opposed. Bismarck always maintained that he had honorably put off this choice until he was constrained to make it by Russia's threatening conduct after the congress of Berlin. The fact is that he inclined to Austria's side from the beginning; and he virtually made his decision in her favor in 1876, when he informed Russia that he would not allow either party to suffer a decisive defeat in a trial at arms.⁶ He would promise Germany's neutrality in a conflict between Russia and Austria only in case Russia guaranteed the treaty of Frankfort; and when Russia refused this condition, he left her to take the consequences of an adventure opposed by both Austria and England.⁷ At the congress of Berlin he saw to it that Austria received the compensation promised by Russia in advance — the tenure of Bosnia and Herzegovina — while allowing Russia's gains to be reduced to a minimum.⁸

Although he retained a mask of friendship throughout these transactions, Bismarck felt that their effect upon Russia was serious enough to warrant approaching both her enemies, England and Austria, for alliances. The editors of the documents pub-

⁶ *Gedanken und Erinnerungen*, ii, p. 214. See Felix Rachfahl, "Der Rückversicherungsvertrag, der 'Balkandreibund,' und das angebliche Bündnisangebot Bismarcks an England vom Jahre 1887," *Weltwirtschaftliches Archiv*, July 1, 1920 (pp. 28–31), for an excellent discussion of the significance of this decision and its influence upon the later development of German policy. Rachfahl even goes so far as to state: "so ist die *Balkanpolitik Deutschlands*, wie sie die Mitte der siebziger Jahre durch Bismarck inauguriert wurde, als die causa remota et efficiens der grossen Katastrophe anzusehen, die im Sommer 1914 über Europa hereinbrach."

⁷ Eduard von Wertheimer, *Graf Julius Andrássy* (Stuttgart, 1910–13, 3 vols.), iii, p. 249. See also Hammann, *Vorgeschichte*, p. 23.

⁸ An interesting indication of Bismarck's partiality for Austrian interests in these transactions has lately come to light through the researches of the Danish scholar, Aage Friis, in the Austrian archives, on the subject of the annulment of article 5 of the treaty of Prague. The agreement of Austria and Germany over this measure — frequently mentioned as one of the steps toward the alliance of 1879 — was made public in February of that year as of the date October 11, 1878. It is now established that the treaty of revision was actually concluded in April, 1878, when the question of forcing Russia to submit her treaty of San Stefano to a European congress was at its height. In other words, the 'honest broker' took a slight commission from one of his clients in advance. When Bismarck was later impelled by the affair of the Cumberland-Danish marriage to publish his new arrangement with Austria regarding Schleswig, the date of signature was altered from April 13 to October 11, giving it in appearance an altogether different context. Andrássy's statement to Francis Joseph of the reason for the change was that it avoided the appearance of having accorded to Germany a compensation for Bosnia. A. Friis, "Ophaevelsen af Pragfredens Artikel 5," in *Tilskueren*, February, 1921. How well Bismarck earned his commission is admitted by Hans Plehn in his *Bismarcks auswärtige Politik nach der Reichsgründung* (Munich and Berlin, 1920), p. 136. Plehn's numerous assertions of Bismarck's loyalty to Russia are strangely contradicted by his admission of the intrigues at Berlin which resulted in her isolation and discomfiture.

lished from the archives of the German foreign office deny that Bismarck's advances to England in this case, or in any of the preceding instances, were made with any thought of an alliance in view. The only document from Bismarck's own hand included in their series in connection with this negotiation is a telegram directing Münster to proceed at once to his post at London and ascertain from Lord Beaconsfield "what England's policy will be, if we ... get into trouble with Russia."[9] That such an approach should have been meant to lead no further is, in the nature of things, inconceivable. That it did not, in fact, do so may best be attributed to the passing of the peril which had impelled Bismarck to take the action. Even after Alexander II of Russia had receded from his threatening stand, the negotiations with Austria were pushed to a conclusion; but those with England were dropped. All possibility of their resumption vanished with the displacement of Beaconsfield by Gladstone.

The change of prime ministers in England, coupled with a change of sovereigns in Russia, put an entirely new face on matters. The motives of Bismarck in 1881 are no longer those of 1879. The reconciliation with Russia, which had already begun before the death of Alexander II, culminated in his successor's reign.[10] The tragic circumstances attending his accession to the throne undoubtedly influenced Alexander III to hasten the conclusion of this accord, which would place Russia once more in touch with the conservative elements in Europe's political system.[11] The new League of the Three Emperors was, indeed, far from being a simple return to the old partnership on equal terms.

---

[9] *G. F. O.*, iv, pp. 3–4. September 14, 1879, Bismarck to Radowitz. Also pp. 4–14 for the subsequent despatches of Münster and an instruction through Radowitz to press Beaconsfield for more precise declarations. The English side of the negotiation is set forth in volume v of Buckle's *Life of Benjamin Disraeli* (London, 1920), pp. 486–492.

[10] See *G. F. O.*, iii, chapter xiv, for documents bearing on the origin of this treaty: also Goriainov (*op. cit.*), and J. Y. Simpson, "Russo-German Relations and the Saburoff Memoirs," in *Nineteenth Century*, December, 1917, and January, 1918.

[11] The situation was astutely observed and commented upon by Katkov, who wrote, in March, 1881, in the *Moscow Gazette*: "Why should Russia feel called upon to put herself at Germany's service and act as her guarantor against France, while at the same time abandoning the Turkish heritage to Austria-Hungary? At Berlin they imagine that Russia will find her reward in the support she will receive from

With one of her two associates Germany now possessed a separate treaty of defensive alliance against the other; and a private ministerial declaration preliminary to the renewal of the League provided that relations between Germany and Austria should continue to be governed by the treaty of 1879, without limitation or alteration through the new treaty with Russia.[12]

The tripartite treaty of June 18, 1881, which altered the entire European situation, is almost inexplicable from the Russian point of view.[13] Bismarck's desires were met on practically every point, beginning with the admission of Austria to the partnership. The first article, binding the associated powers to benevolent neutrality in case any member of the combination should be at war with a fourth power, gave to Germany the free hand against France, always hitherto denied her. Yet Russia received no free hand against Turkey in return. On the contrary, the article in question provided that its stipulations should apply to a war against Turkey only in case a preliminary agreement were reached concerning its results — that is, compensation to Austria must be fixed in advance for anything Russia might accomplish. The situation of 1876 was simply reëstablished: Russia had not advanced her cause an inch by the new treaty. At best, she had gained time and security for the maturing of her designs upon Constantinople and the Straits. But she had not, and could not have, the approval of her two associates for those designs. She was only insured against the improbable event of an aggressive policy on the part of Austria-Hungary. Assurance of the attitude of her neighbors in the threatening struggle with England over Central Asia was also an advantage not to be overlooked.[14]

Germany in her struggle with revolutionary propaganda. Do not our friends ask a high price of us for measures which they propose to take in the interest of their own safety?" Quoted by Cyon, p. 130.

[12] A. F. Pribram, *Die politischen Geheimverträge Oesterreich-Ungarns*, i (Vienna and Leipzig, 1920), p. 10. American edition, i, pp. 32–33. See also G. F. O., iii, p. 152. December 22, 1880, Bismarck to Reuss.

[13] The text of the treaty is given in Pribram, i, pp. 11 *et seq.* (Amer., i, pp. 36 *et seq.*).

[14] Strangely enough, this advantage is nowhere mentioned by Goriainov (*op. cit.*) in his discussion of the motives which led Russia to sign and renew the treaty. Yet it seems an obvious consideration, especially at the time of renewal, in 1884.

But the renewal of the league of conservative monarchies against the disruptive forces of the age was undoubtedly the chief gain which Alexander III perceived in the new arrangement.

In entering into this treaty, Bismarck turned his back on England to the extent of pledging a benevolent neutrality to her enemy in Asiatic affairs. Indeed, Bismarck's attitude toward England underwent at this time an almost total change. The conclusion of the Triple Alliance in 1882 placed him at the head of a great Continental combination of interlocking agreements.[15] France lay in the hollow of his hand: it was perhaps natural to expect that he would crush her at the first convenient opportunity. But Bismarck had other plans regarding France. Ever since the crisis of 1875 — or, at least, since the recall of the French ambassador of that period, Gontaut-Biron — a new policy had been taking more and more definite shape. France was being wooed into forgetfulness of her recent injuries. Everything possible was being done to conciliate the late foe — that is, everything short of restoration of what she had lost by her defeat. She was treated as an equal and friend; she was helped to acquire colonial prizes, notably Tunis, as compensation for her losses and as a diversion from dwelling upon them; her ambassadors were taken into the great man's confidence.[16] All this undoubtedly had a purpose beyond

---

[15] Text of the Triple Alliance in Pribram, i, pp. 24 *et seq.* (Amer., i, pp. 64 *et seq.*).

[16] See *G. F. O.*, iii, chapter xx. Also Daudet's series, *La France et l'Allemagne après le Congrès de Berlin: La mission du comte de Saint-Vallier* (Paris, 1918); *La mission du baron de Courcel* (Paris, 1919). Numerous extracts from the despatches of these two ambassadors are printed by Georges Pagès in his section of the "Mémoire sur les responsibilités de la guerre," attached to the *Rapport de la Commission d'Enquête sur les faits de la guerre*, volume i (Sénat, 1919, no. 704). Bismarck's aims are outlined by Courcel in a despatch of January 20, 1885, as: "Assoupir nos souvenirs, détourner nos regards du passé vers un avenir indéterminé, afin de mieux nous habituer aux conditions rigoureuses du présent, nous entraîner ainsi, d'une façon presque insensible, à l'acceptation définitive des faits accomplis en 1815 et 1871, de manière que la France, résignée à ses démembrements successifs et prenant une bonne fois son parti de l'hégémonie militaire et géographique de la Prusse, gravite désormais dans l'orbite du nouvel empire allemand, tel est le programme que le prince de Bismarck suit à notre égard; nous devons lui rendre la justice de reconnaître la franchise et la sincérité entières avec lesquelles il l'expose lui-même. ' Renoncez à la question du Rhin, m'a-t-il souvent répété; je vous aiderai à conquérir sur tous les autres points les satisfactions que vous pouvez désirer' " (p. 196). But Bismarck was left by the French under no illusions as to the difficulties in the way of

the immediate hope of accomplishing by blandishment what bluster had failed to achieve. The ulterior motive is perhaps indicated by the sequel itself.

Under the security of her double set of alliances, Germany pursued the even tenor of peaceful ways for three years; then suddenly disclosed a new development of policy to a startled Europe — and a particularly startled England. This was her intensive quest of colonies.[17] It was accompanied by close coöperation with both Russia and France and a masterly utilization of their disputes with England to Germany's advantage. In Jules Ferry Bismarck found a willing and able collaborator; in Gladstone, an adversary whose discomfiture gave him the keenest pleasure. He made it clear to the British government from the beginning that it had to choose between his friendship and his hostility, and that the former could be purchased at any time by concessions to Germany's colonial desires. "Our friendship *can* be very valuable to English policy," he wrote to Münster at London, on May 5, 1884; and after calling attention to the bearing of Germany's policy upon England's disputes with France and Russia, he added significantly: "We believe, therefore, that our attitude . . . toward England's enemies or rivals is of more importance to English policy than . . . the trade rivalries of German and English firms in distant seas." [18]

Failing to move England by repeated notifications of this kind, Bismarck plunged deeper and deeper into collaboration with her rivals. On August 7, he wrote that he believed "the exclusive efforts of England to attain, as far as possible, the sole dominion over non-European seas will oblige the other commercial powers to form an association among themselves as a counterpoise to the

a permanent solution of his problem. Courcel had made it clear to him that, however intimate might become the relations between the two countries based upon the promotion of immediate mutual interests, the question of Alsace-Lorraine must continue "un domaine réservé."

[17] A discussion of the motives, objects, and methods of Bismarck's colonial policy is beyond the scope of this brief survey of the developments leading up to the situation of August, 1885. This large and important subject is still in need of a full and satisfactory treatment.

[18] *G. F. O.*, iv, pp. 51–52. See also pp. 60, 78, 93–94, for later declarations in the same sense.

English colonial supremacy."[19] He directed that the German ambassador, Prince Hohenlohe, should broach this idea to Ferry. The precedent he called to mind was that of the Armed Neutrality: Napoleon's Continental System is an even better analogy to the combination which Bismarck brought to bear against England in his struggle for Germany's 'place in the sun.'

The acute phase of this contest lasted but a short time — shorter even than Gladstone's tenure of office. The fall of Ferry brought Bismarck's eyes back to Europe: as early as March, 1885, a beginning had been made toward a reconciliation with England. At first the business moved slowly.[20] Bismarck was reluctant to give up his Continental combination, and endeavored to use the rapprochement with England as a threat to force France back into line; but he decided, after a discussion with the French ambassador, that "the fear of 'Revanche' movements and the exploitation of this fear by the existing opposition will prevent any government from maintaining solid relations with us."[21] In abandoning his programme of 1884, he sought only to prevent an embarrassing conflict between France and England from growing out of the animosities it had engendered.[22]

Relations with England were further improved by the change of governments which took place in June. Finding in Lord Salisbury a more congenial personality to deal with than the despised Gladstone, Bismarck felt surer of his ground in passing from the French to the English side. But the protagonists of the Anglophile theory undoubtedly go too far in assuming that the Chancellor's regard for the new prime minister was powerful enough to revive his desire for an English alliance.[23] Without detracting

[19] *G. F. O.*, iii, p. 414.
[20] Lucius von Ballhausen, *Bismarck-Erinnerungen* (Stuttgart and Berlin, 1920), p. 314. On April 27, Bismarck expressed his intention to give England no help in the Indian question.
[21] *G. F. O.*, iii, p. 446. May 25, 1885, Bismarck to Hohenlohe. See also Pagès (Senate Report), pp. 199–200. May 10, 1885, Courcel to Freycinet.
[22] Pagès (Senate Report), p. 202. May 28, Courcel to Freycinet. Lucius von Ballhausen, p. 316.
[23] There are various versions of a remark in this connection. Eckardstein (i, p. 307) speaks of "eine . . . Äusserung Bismarcks, welche er wiederholt in engerer Umgebung getan hat . . .: ' Die Freundschaft Lord Salisburys ist mir mehr wert

from the importance of such personal factors in Bismarck's conduct of policy, it must be pointed out that the reconciliation with England began before the change of cabinets and for other reasons. These very reasons continued to stand in the way of an English alliance. In the same proportion as the hostility of France revived, so also increased the value of the alliance with Russia. With it an English alliance was incompatible, especially in 1885 when the Anglo-Russian rivalry over Afghanistan was reaching a crisis. In that year an Anglo-German alliance was unthinkable.[24] Bismarck's decided preference for the Russian connection is shown by the fact that, in conformity with the League of the Three Emperors, which had been renewed in March, 1884, he threw his support to Russia rather than to England. On April 9, 1885, he wrote to Vienna that an Anglo-Russian war would bring the treaty of 1881 into effect and that he was using his influence to keep Turkey neutral and the Dardanelles closed. He concluded: "If the League of the Three Emperors fails to meet this test, I fear for the reaction upon the internal and external security of the three Empires; but if we hold together, we are unassailable."[25] This attitude was, of course, inspired less by

als zwanzig Sumpfkolonien in Afrika.'" Hammann (*Vorgeschichte*, p. 28, note) gives it as a marginal note to the effect that "das Verbleiben Lord Salisburys auf seinem Posten sei ihm wichtiger als ganz Witu." The *Hamburger Nachrichten* article of February 8, 1891, which gives Bismarck's reply to Caprivi on the subject, renders the marginal note as "England ist für uns wichtiger wie Sansibar und ganz Ostafrika." It is characterized as merely a "Randbemerkung, welche den Zweck hat, übertriebenen oder voreiligen Bestrebungen Schranken zu ziehen." H. Hofmann, *Fürst Bismarck 1890–98* (Stuttgart, etc., 1913, 2 vols.), i, p. 315. This note does not appear among those reproduced in the German foreign office publication.

[24] Moritz Busch, *Bismarck, Some Secret Pages of his History* (London, 1898, 3 vols.), iii, p. 140 (American edition, ii, p. 388; *Tagebuchblätter*, iii, p. 193). On May 31, 1885, Bismarck told Busch: "Our policy must not necessarily be anti-English, but if it were to be English it might prove to be very much against our interest, as we have always to reckon with the Continental Powers."

[25] G. F. O., iv, pp. 113–114. Busch, iii, p. 133 (Amer., ii, p. 383; *Tagebuchblätter*, iii, p. 186), writes, under date of April 19, 1885: "'The Crown Prince's people,' said Bucher, 'are very cross and angry with the Chief because he will not act as mediator at St. Petersburg and help England out of her embarrassment, and because he opposes her schemes at Constantinople. The English have offered the Turks the occupation of Egypt in return for permission to pass through the Dardanelles and the Bosphorus. The Sultan was, however, informed from Berlin and Vienna that

regard for Russia than by regard for German policy, which Bismarck believed was favored by the existence of an enmity between Russia and England. "Germany has no interest," he advised the Emperor, "in hindering Russia from finding the necessary occupation for her army in Asia, rather than in Europe. . . . It is the aim of German policy to bring about between Russia and England hostile, rather than too intimate, relations." [26]

Moreover, since the failure of the transaction with Disraeli, Bismarck had unquestionably been assailed by doubts as to the intrinsic value of an English alliance. Not only could he not afford the breach with Russia which it would entail, but he felt that he could not trust a political system which was so dependent upon public opinion and so liable to sudden overturns. As early as 1882, he had written: "We can only give positive support to English wishes within very narrow limits, unless we are prepared to take up a more hostile position than necessary towards Russia, and to call forth not only in France, but in a great majority of the people of England, the unfounded suspicion that our policy tends to disunite the two great Western Powers and to 'manoeuvre' them into war with each other. The greatest difficulty, however, we encounter in trying to give a practical expression to our sympathies for and our relations with England, is in the absolute impossibility of confidential intercourse in consequence of the indiscretion of English statesmen in their communications to Parliament, and in the absence of security in alliances for which the Crown is not answerable in England, but only the fleeting Cabinets of the day. It is therefore difficult to initiate a reliable understanding with England otherwise than publicly and in the face of all Europe. Such public negotiations . . . would be highly detrimental to most of our European relations." [27]

---

we, too, had a word to say in the matter, and our officers in Stambul would take care that the passage was stopped by torpedoes.'"

[26] *G. F. O.*, iv, pp. 125. May 27, 1885, Bismarck to William I. See also Chlodwig, Fürst zu Hohenlohe-Schillingsfürst, *Denkwürdigkeiten* (Stuttgart, 1907, 2 vols.), ii, p. 358 (Amer., ii, p. 327).

[27] *G. F. O.*, iv, p. 33. September 7, 1882, Bismarck to the Crown Prince Frederick William. The translation is from Edmond Fitzmaurice, *The Life of Lord Granville* (London and New York, 1905, 2 vols.), ii, p. 275. Fitzmaurice describes the

England's friendship might well prove useful in special contingencies; and Bismarck did not fail to cultivate it, within what he considered limits of prudence, in view of such a possibility — which, indeed, was not very long in presenting itself.[28] The maintenance of good relations with England, moreover, served to keep Russia alive to the value of Germany's friendship by holding before her eyes the possibility of a contrary policy.[29] But Bismarck felt very strongly that, in any association with England, he must avoid committing himself to decisive action. "In order to have England's active alliance," he remarked in 1884, "she must be engaged in war before we are and positively require our assistance. If we were to get involved first, we should look in vain for England's aid, even supposing she had the political foresight to realize what dangers she herself would incur by a German defeat."[30] Such sentiments constituted a formidable barrier to an English alliance in Bismarck's latter years.

The choice between England and Russia, then, if it had ever

letter as written by Bismarck to a "highly placed personage." Again, on March 1, 1883, Bismarck told Crown Prince Rudolf of Austria: "England muss für uns freundlich gesinnt sein; ich trachte auch dies Land durch Höflichkeiten zu gewinnen, ihnen zu schmeicheln, denn im richtigen Moment giebt nicht die Vernunft, sondern eine Abstimmung im Parlament die Entschiedung ab." A. F. Pribram, "Zwei Gespräche des Fürsten Bismarck mit dem Kronprinzen Rudolf von Österreich," in *Österreichische Rundschau*, January, 1921, p. 17. For other expressions of his distrust of the English system of government, see K. A. von Müller, "Beiträge zur äusseren Politik Bismarcks," in Brauer, Marcks, Müller, *Erinnerungen an Bismarck* (Stuttgart and Berlin, 1915), p. 263; and *Gedanken und Erinnerungen*, ii, p. 234.

[28] It is only in the sense of such a limited utilization of England that one can interpret correctly the passage quoted by Lucius von Ballhausen (p. 500) from Bismarck's conversation with Francis Joseph, on August 17, 1889: — "Bismarck habe ihm gesagt: Das ganze Ziel und Objekt der deutschen Politik seit zehn Jahren sei, England für den Dreibund zu gewinnen." An analysis of the passage shows it to be much less significant than it at first appears. In the first place, winning England over to the Triple Alliance is not quite the same thing as concluding an alliance between her and Germany. In the second place, a tendency to exaggeration is manifest: one need only point out that the Triple Alliance had not yet been in existence ten years. Finally, the context shows that Bismarck was referring to his use of England in his secret intrigues against Russia after 1885. Therein lies the real importance of the words.

[29] See Hermann Oncken, *Das alte und das neue Mitteleuropa* (Gotha, 1917), p. 48; and Hammann, *Vorgeschichte*, p. 23.

[30] B. M. M., pp. 263–264.

been a real issue in Bismarck's mind, remained so for only a very short time. The importance of Russia's friendship was beyond question, while the value of England's was doubtful. It is true enough that the League of the Three Emperors had flaws. The Central Powers were far from unreserved in their backing of Russia's desires in the Near East; Russia did not mean to allow Germany quite the free hand to which she felt entitled with respect to France.[31] But, in 1885, the alliance stood as one of the proudest of Bismarck's creations, unrivalled by any possible alternative involving England. Taken in connection with the Austrian alliance, the Triple Alliance, and the Serbian and Rumanian alliances, it was an important element in the combination through which Bismarck dominated the continent of Europe. The impending transformation and decay of this elaborate system could not yet be foreseen, although their causes were present at the height of its success.

[31] Nikolai Notovich, *L'empereur Alexandre III* (Paris, 1895), p. 106. The Tsar is said to have remarked to Giers, following the meeting of the allied sovereigns at Skiernewice, in 1884: "Je vous recommande tout d'abord d'observer vis-à-vis de la France une attitude amicale de façon à pouvoir, en temps utile et en cas de nécessité, contracter avec elle une alliance officielle."

## CHAPTER II

### THE UNIFICATION OF BULGARIA

#### I

ON August 25, 1885, the emperors of Austria-Hungary and Russia met in the little Moravian town of Kremsier for a personal exchange of cordialities and some thirty hours of diversion arranged on a more than usually lavish scale. The visit had no other particular importance; for the two sovereigns met under an almost cloudless political sky so far as their own relations were concerned. All the more reason had Prince Bismarck, in his retreat at Varzin, to rub his hands with satisfaction at his success in reconstituting the League of the Three Emperors, which had seemed so hopelessly shattered on the morrow of the congress of Berlin.

Germany herself was not actually represented at the imperial meeting; but there was no question in the mind of Europe as to her presence in spirit. Prince Bismarck had entertained Count Kálnoky, the Austro-Hungarian minister of foreign affairs, only a few days before, at Varzin, and was said to have commissioned him to represent Germany at the conference.[1] The two emperors exchanged cordial telegrams with William I in the course of the festivities; and at their close the Russian foreign minister, Giers, declared in an interview: "You may be sure that, although no representative of Germany is actually present here, Emperor William is with us in spirit just as truly as if he were here himself. When the two Emperors converse together it is quite as if the third were at hand."[2] The very fact that all went off so smoothly,

---

[1] *Times*, August 15, 1885, leading article: "Count Kálnoky has gone to Varzin in order to testify, the week after next at Kremsier, that Germany is there in spirit as well as Austria and Russia. . . . That Count Kálnoky's visit to the North German oracle should be capable of being accepted in lieu of the actual presence of Germany at the Imperial conclave ought to be evidence to Europe of the very satisfactory fact that the three Empires have for the moment no deadly quarrels to appease, or ambitions to indulge."

[2] Interview in *Neue Freie Presse*, August 27, 1885.

and that Bismarck was content to allow his two partners to come together directly, and, indeed, without his participation, argued all the more strongly for the solidity of the reconstituted League of the Three Emperors.

The conversations of the sovereigns were accompanied by conferences between their ministers, with a bearing upon political questions of both general and particular scope.[3] The main subject of their interviews was generally understood to be the attitude of the Central Powers in case Russia should become involved in a war with England over the Afghan boundary question, which was still in an acute stage.[4] This matter was undoubtedly touched upon by the two statesmen in their talk, but hardly at any great length, as Russia had no real intention of pushing her claims in that direction to the point of war. She sought, rather, the help of her associates in avoiding it, and obtained some favorable assurances. Giers was able to state for publication that Russia had hopes of a peaceable solution of the difficulty.[5]

But there was also a matter demanding attention in the Near East. On all hands it was felt desirable that a more definite understanding should be arrived at concerning the immediate future of Bulgaria. By the treaty of 1881, Russia had limited her freedom of action there on the condition that the union with Eastern Rumelia should be recognized, if it came about by force of circumstances.[6] But the cooling of her enthusiasm for that union had by this time reached the point of positive aversion to it under the existing conditions. As the breach widened between Alexander III and his cousin Alexander of Battenberg, the Rus-

[3] Giers told the correspondent of the *Neue Freie Presse*: "Ich leugne nicht dass Conferenzen stattfanden . . . aber was wir bisher besprachen, betraf allgemeine Fragen und nicht specielle. Unsere Politik hat ja eine Basis, auf welcher auch die Erörtererungen dieser Conferenzen sich bewegen." But the correspondent adds, from an Austrian statesman: "Es haben hier Besprechungen über die politische Situation stattgefunden, und keine wichtige europäische Frage ist dabei unerörtert geblieben."

[4] *Times*, August 28. Vienna, August 27. "There are good grounds for believing that this promise related to the securing of Turkish neutrality by Austria in the event of a war breaking out between Russia and England in Asia."

[5] *N. F. P.* interview: "Die Sache steht gut; allerdings sie ist nicht vollendet, aber es geht gut, und ich glaube bestimmt, dass es gut enden wird."

[6] Attached protocol. See Pribram, i, p. 14 (Amer., i, p. 42).

sian government grew more and more anxious to put off the union as long as Prince Alexander remained on the Bulgarian throne. The unfortunate prince had also incurred the dislike of Bismarck, who had become disgusted at his conduct nearly two years before.[7] The German Chancellor now believed him to have fallen under English influence and under the protection of Queen Victoria, who regarded favorably his project of marrying her granddaughter, Princess Victoria of Prussia. Bismarck violently opposed, then as later, this union with a prince so undesirable personally and politically, whose tenure of office he already considered highly insecure.[8] In an interview with the prince, on May 12, 1884, Bismarck had told him: "Germany has no interest in Bulgaria; our interest is peace with Russia. For that reason it is of the greatest importance that Russia should be convinced we are pursuing no interests of our own in the East. But the day a Prussian princess becomes Princess of Bulgaria, Russia will begin to get suspicious and put no more faith in our assurances; so that this marriage would upset my political plans. I will not allow that."[9] Some weeks later, he wrote: "I do not see what danger could arise if the prince should resign his office; on the contrary, I advised him to do so when I had the honor of receiving a visit from him, recommending that he should sell to

[7] Eumène Queillé, *Les commencements de l'indépendance Bulgare* (Paris, 1910), p. 219. Prince Alexander is quoted as saying, on November 9, 1883: "Bismarck affecte une grossièreté outrageante, m'accusant de ' rompre avec les traditions de l'histoire.' Comprenez-vous? . . . Moi non plus. Il ajoute, d'ailleurs, que je suis une bête."

[8] Busch, iii, p. 171 (Amer., ii, p. 411; *Tagebuchblätter*, iii, p. 224). On March 28, 1888, Bucher told Busch: "Princess Victoria . . . was to have been married some time since to the Battenberger, who at that time was still Prince of Bulgaria, but already a tool of English policy. . . . The thought of a marriage was probably suggested by the grandmother in London, who wished to see the position of her servant secured against Russia by an alliance with our Court. The scheme leaked out, and came to the ears of the Chief. Of course he was anything but pleased, and did not conceal his objections from the Emperor, but on the contrary expressed them both verbally and in a statement which I had to prepare. It would show us in a bad light at St. Petersburg, and it was not right to subject a Prussian Princess to the eventuality of a compulsory departure from Sofia. The Emperor recognized this and issued his veto." See also Lucius von Ballhausen, p. 299.

[9] E. C. Corti, *Alexander von Battenberg* (Vienna, 1920), pp. 165–166. According to Alexander's own memorandum of the interview.

Alexander III, for the highest price he could get, the position he owed to Alexander II." [10] As for Austria, she bore the prince no particular ill will, but was not anxious to have the great event in Bulgaria, if it must occur, come about in a fashion which would leave Russia in a bad humor and unwilling to draw the conclusions desired by Austria as affecting Bosnia and Herzegovina.

It was to the interest of all three empires that there should be no further developments in Bulgaria while Prince Alexander occupied its throne. The prince himself was willing to come to an understanding on the point. The insurrection in Eastern Rumelia, prepared long in advance with his approval and probably even with his active coöperation, was not due to be carried out for some months as yet.[11] It would be an unqualified success if, in the meantime, he could effect a reconciliation with the Tsar. He had already discussed the subject of this reconciliation with Kálnoky just before the latter's visit to Bismarck at Varzin.[12] As a result of discussion both there and at Kremsier, an interview was arranged between Giers and Prince Alexander, to take place after the manoeuvres at Pilsen, which the prince had been invited to attend.[13]

As no conflict of interests was involved in any of the subjects which the sovereigns and statesmen of Austria and Russia discussed at Kremsier, no disagreements arose; and they parted with as cordial expressions of friendship as when they met. There was indeed small reason to foresee that within a month they would be at swords' points.

The interview between Prince Alexander and the Russian minister also went off without a hitch. On September 3, Alexander, returning from the manoeuvres, had a final conference with Kálnoky at Vienna.[14] Having learned from him how matters

[10] *G. F. O.*, iii, p. 247. June 23, 1884, Bismarck to Reuss.

[11] Spiridion Gopčević, *Bulgarien und Ostrumelien* (Leipzig, 1886), pp. 303–304; C. Roy, *Souvenirs politiques et militaires de Bulgarie* (Paris, 1887), p. 16.

[12] Adolf Koch, *Fürst Alexander von Bulgarien* (Darmstadt, 1887), p. 204. Corti (p. 187) writes that he asked Kálnoky's intercession with Bismarck.

[13] Arthur von Huhn, *The Struggle of the Bulgarians for National Independence* (London, 1886), p. 35.

[14] *Times*, September 4, 1885. Vienna, September 3.

stood, he went off to visit Giers at Franzensbad. Just how definite were the assurances he gave at this meeting is by no means clear. Bismarck later maintained that the prince, working in the interests of England, had brazenly deceived Russia on this as on every other possible occasion.[15] His conduct, however, is open to a much less dishonorable interpretation. Giers held out some hope of the desired reconciliation. In return, Alexander assured him against the likelihood of any immediate attempt at the incorporation of Eastern Rumelia.[16] Doubtless neither felt that he was binding himself for any great length of time; but both were probably sincere in believing that they had arranged a modus vivendi which would keep the peace while they were waiting for things to take a more favorable turn regarding their respective plans for a final settlement.

So far all had gone well; and there was still nothing in sight to disturb the harmony of the League of the Three Emperors. On September 10, Russia concluded with England the Afghan boundary protocol, which promised to eliminate the nearest threat of trouble from outside. The outcome of the dispute could not have been regarded by Bismarck as an unmixed gain; and there is no evidence of his having lent any effective aid to reaching it. He had kept up appearances as a peacemaker by receiving Lord Rosebery, in the spring, for a discussion of the subject.[17] But if Russia had not been disposed toward a peaceable settlement, it would not have been Bismarck's counsels that brought one about. This annulment of the counterpoise to Russia's Balkan interests did not fall in at all well with his system of checks and balances. In fact, Holstein, who was in a position to pass a competent judgment, once set down the prevention of a collision between England and Russia in Afghanistan as one of the chief mistakes of Bismarckian policy.[18] At the time, this mistake did not appear so serious; for the sudden revival of the Bulgarian question which

[15] Busch, iii, p. 181 (Amer., ii, p. 418; *Tagebuchblätter*, iii, p. 233).
[16] Corti, p. 188, according to Alexander's memorandum; Koch, p. 204; Huhn, p. 36; Hans Klaeber, *Fürst Alexander I*. (Dresden, 1904), p. 152.
[17] Fitzmaurice, ii, pp. 439 *et seq.*; Busch, iii, p. 135 (Amer., ii, p. 384; *Tagebuchblätter*, iii, p. 189).
[18] Hohenlohe, ii, p. 507 (Amer., ii, pp. 462–463).

followed was as little expected by Germany as by her two neighbors who were more immediately affected by it.

## II

All expectations of peace in the Near East, and all the declarations of Prince Alexander at Franzensbad, upon which they were based, were suddenly falsified by the *coup d'état* of Philippopolis, on September 18. The responsibility for the timing of this stroke seems to lie with the Bulgarian nationalists. These men regarded Russia's proposed bargain that they abandon their prince in return for satisfaction of their national desires as an infringement upon the independence of which they were so jealous. In order to anticipate its being forced upon them, they advanced the date of their own design.[19] They did so without consulting the prince, who had been absent from his capital most of the summer. When informed at the eleventh hour of their plan, he strove earnestly to dissuade them from carrying it out and believed he had succeeded. Either they concealed their determination to go ahead, or they found that the movement had gone too far to stop; at all events, two days after his conference with the conspirators, Alexander found himself confronted by an accomplished fact to which he must conform or risk the loss of his crown. After a brief hesitation he placed himself at the head of the national uprising.[20]

The news from Philippopolis was received in Europe with mingled and uncertain feelings. The obvious superficial conclusion was that the whole affair had been engineered by Russia to undo the work of the congress of Berlin; but this conception found lodgment in few responsible quarters, and there only momentarily. The British government, which had not been fully informed of what happened at Kremsier and Franzensbad, seems to have entertained it for about a day. Lord Salisbury, immediately upon receipt of the news of the rising, sent off instructions to the ambassadors at Vienna, Berlin, and St. Petersburg to consult these governments as to the advisability of making "strong representations to the Bulgarian Government

[19] Gopčević, pp. 305–307.
[20] Corti, pp. 191–193, according to Alexander's narrative.

in favour of maintaining the Treaty of Berlin."[21] Although the following day was a Sunday, Paget at Vienna carried out his instructions at once, and was greatly calmed by Kálnoky's replies. The Austrian minister at first stated simply that, until he had received further information, "he could not say more than that he personally was ready to act;" but later on in the same day, he "expressed the opinion that this movement had been organized in Bulgaria, but without the connivance or knowledge of either the Emperor or Government of Russia, whom he believed it would take as much by surprise as it certainly had him."[22]

Bismarck was probably as little deceived as Kálnoky in regard to the responsibility for the untimely event: moreover, he had quite a different opinion from Salisbury's as to the influences which were behind Prince Alexander. He was also informed before long of the reception given the news by the Tsar himself.[23] He advised the British government, as Kálnoky had done, that "any representation to be made to Bulgaria in respect of the revolution in East Roumelia should be made collectively on the part of all Signatory Powers, and the Chancellor deprecates any hasty step by any one Power alone."[24] He remarked to the French ambassador: "Russia has witnessed the explosion, at a moment when she least expected it, of the mines and torpedoes which she herself had planted. Perhaps the Russian government is troubled by the reflexion that, if the Bulgarian principality already proved insubordinate as a single province, a more satisfactory attitude can hardly be expected from a country doubled by the addition of Eastern Rumelia."[25]

By the Monday morning following the insurrection, it is safe to say that the governments of Europe were pretty well informed of the real attitude of the Russian government toward the new situation. Certain journalists of more than ordinary ingenuity

[21] *P. P.*, 1886, lxxv, Turkey no. 1, p. 2. September 19, 1885, Salisbury to Paget.
[22] *Ibid.*, p. 3. September 20, Paget to Salisbury.
[23] *Ibid.*, p. 6. September 22, Malet to Salisbury. Bismarck told Malet of the Tsar's reply to a telegram from Prince Alexander: "It is because I love the Bulgarian nation that I disapprove of what you have done."
[24] *Ibid.*, p. 2. September 20, Malet to Salisbury.
[25] Ernest Daudet, *La mission du baron de Courcel* (Paris, 1919), pp. 210–211.

had connected the event with the meetings at Kremsier and Franzensbad, and even with a visit of the Austrian Emperor to Bosnia.[26] The vast intrigue built up from the correlation of these events was entirely inconsistent with the relations betwen the Tsar and Prince Alexander. A brief consideration, in most cases, sufficed to absolve the Russian government from all complicity in the uprising.[27] But public opinion was hard to convince, once its suspicions had been aroused. The Hungarians found it especially difficult to drop the idea of a great diplomatic plot against the existing balance of nationalities within and without the Dual Monarchy.

One thing was certain: the revolution was an accomplished fact by the time it had come to the attention of Europe. In addition, there could be little doubt that the event was now as irrevocable as it had long been inevitable. Even in Russia, although some journals clamored for intervention to undo all that had been accomplished by the faithless prince and his unscrupulous advisers, cooler heads realized that the Tsar's government was

[26] *Times*, September 21, 1885. Vienna, Berlin, St. Petersburg, September 20. *N. F. P.*, September 20.

[27] *Times*, September 21, leading article and Vienna correspondence. The correspondent, William Lavino, adds his own observations to the report of current opinion: "It may be confidently asserted, however, that the revolution has taken both the Russian and the Austrian Governments by surprise. The meeting at Kremsier, following upon that of Skiernievice, was no doubt the last cause of it, but only because it demonstrated to the Pan-Bulgarian committees of Eastern Roumelia that they had nothing to expect from Russia at present. The arrangement renewed between the Emperors at Kremsier was based on the maintenance of the *status quo* in the Balkans; and there are many reasons why the rising at Philippopolis should, in existing circumstances, be particularly disagreeable to the Cabinet of St. Petersburg. . . . The unification of Bulgaria has been one of Russia's cherished schemes: but it has latterly appeared that Prince Alexander was not the man whom the Panslavists intended to use as their instrument for this purpose, and there is evidence enough that the official Panslavist committees have been doing their utmost to keep matters quiet, both in Eastern Roumelia and in Macedonia." Corti (p. 190) takes issue with this view of the case, maintaining that Russia promoted the whole enterprise deliberately with the design of putting Prince Alexander in the wrong and so bringing about his downfall. This was Alexander's own interpretation of the events — hardly a judicial one. The only evidence cited by Corti in support of the theory is the fact, by no means extraordinary or significant, that the Russian officers in Eastern Rumelia reported the existence of the conspiracy to their government in advance.

powerless to alter the situation, and that all attempts to impose conditions upon the union could only affect the form, not the substance, of the situation.[28]

The Russian government found great difficulty in arriving at any policy whatever. It was almost unthinkable that Russia should now oppose the very things for which she had once fought, and herself enforce the observance of a treaty made against her will. Yet neither could she submit tamely to the triumph of Prince Alexander. To show his disapproval of what had occurred, the Tsar at once recalled all Russian officers in the Bulgarian service, stripping the army down to its captains. But this measure did not affect the international status of the question.[29] The diplomatic attitude finally adopted was one which left all initiative to the other Powers. Russia simply pointed out that their precious treaty of Berlin, imposed at such pains upon Europe, was unquestionably broken, and asked what they were going to do about it.[30] On September 24, Russia put forward the proposition "that the Representatives of the Treaty Powers should meet at once at Constantinople under the presidency of the Doyen, Count Corti, not in a formal Conference, but in order to concert together on the question of the Revolution in Eastern Rumelia, with a view to unity of advice." [31]

The proposition was favorably received everywhere, but for reasons quite unpromising for the fulfilment of Russia's desires. The same governments which had once forced the treaty of Berlin upon her now looked with equanimity upon a breach of that treaty which appeared damaging to her interests. Nevertheless,

[28] Русская Мысль, October 10, 1885, p. 49. Вѣстникъ Европы, October 1, 1885, p. 838.

[29] Luigi Chiala, *Storia contemporanea* (new ed., Turin, 1898), pp. 404–405, makes the statement that, at this time, Russia, "fondandosi sugli accordi presi a Skiernewice, chiese all' Austria-Ungheria e alla Germania la facoltà di occupare temporaneamente la Bulgaria per scacciarne il principe ribelle. L'Austria-Ungheria ... negò il proprio assenso, confidando che la Germania ne avrebbe seguìto l'esempio." The entire context of events points to the unreliability of this unsupported assertion.

[30] С. Жигаревъ, Русская политика въ восточномъ вопросѣ (Moscow, 1896, 2 vols.), ii, p. 252.

[31] *P. P.*, 1886, lxxv, Turkey no. 1, p. 15.

in order that the event should disturb their calculations and combinations as little as possible, they hoped that it could be fitted somehow into the treaty which they had fondly regarded as a settlement of the Eastern Question. A skilful formula might recognize the new development and yet leave all other factors in the situation unchanged.

Austria's acceptance of this point of view was subject to qualifications arising out of her own direct interests in the Balkans. The union itself was a matter of indifference to her; but she was determined that the movement should not extend to Macedonia, the only part of the 'Great Bulgaria' of San Stefano which she was really interested in keeping separate from the Principality. On this score, Kálnoky had displayed great anxiety from the first. On September 22, he informed Paget that "what appeared to him of even more pressing importance was to prevent the revolution from spreading into Macedonia;" that "he had therefore telegraphed to Baron Calice to urge the Sultan's Government, whatever might be their decision in regard to the events in Roumelia and Bulgaria, to take every precaution for the maintenance of tranquility in Macedonia, and to place troops in proper positions to guard that frontier." He wanted the Powers to "warn the Prince and Bulgarian Government that an invasion of Macedonia would not be tolerated."[32] He was also troubled by the demands of Serbia for a 'compensation,' in case the union of Eastern Rumelia with Bulgaria should be recognized.

Another circumstance made the revolution of even more doubtful advantage to Austria. The Bulgarian union was, under the treaty of 1881, to be Russia's *quid pro quo* for the eventual annexation of Bosnia and Herzegovina.[33] As matters stood, Russia regarded the union, no longer as a gain, but as a positive setback to her policy. How then could Austria expect her consent to a com-

---

[32] P. P., 1886, lxxv, Turkey no. 1, p. 6. September 22, Paget to Salisbury.

[33] Pribram, i, p. 14 (Amer., i, p. 42). The matter is not precisely so stated; but both the following clauses are contained in the additional protocol: "1. BOSNIE ET HERZÉGOWINE. L'Autriche-Hongrie se réserve de s'annexer ces deux provinces au moment qu'elle jugera opportun. . . . 4. BULGARIE. Les trois puissances ne s'opposeront pas à la réunion éventuelle de la Bulgarie et de la Roumélie Orientale . . ."

pensation?[34] Still less chance was there that she would admit that Serbia was entitled to anything. Kálnoky found himself in an unpleasant situation. He perceived the impossibility of undoing what had been done and the dangers of any attempt in that direction. He was not displeased at the setback to Russian policy; but he was unwilling to have the blow react unfavorably upon Austria, either through the spread of the revolution into Macedonia or through the damaging of her understanding with Russia.[35] A diplomatic conference opened up a welcome avenue of escape from these difficulties. Austria's ostensible support to Russia's protests might be measured to the point of convincing observers of her loyalty and good will, without preventing an agreement upon some formula that would fix the situation as it stood.

The British government, having no such irons in the fire, had come to a more simple conclusion. Since Russia objected to the union, it must be a good thing which ought to be preserved.[36] That Prince Alexander, who would profit by it, was personally in the favor of the English court and cabinet doubtless played a part in the decision. In a few days the government had lost all interest in the "strong representations" which it had been in such a

[34] H. Friedjung, "Graf Kálnoky," in *Biographisches Jahrbuch*, 1909, p. 363 (*Aufsätze*, p. 334). "Freilich konnte Oesterreich-Ungarn ihre Frucht, die förmliche Einverleibung Bosniens, nicht pflücken, da Russland aus Abneigung gegen den unabhängig gesinnten Fürsten Alexander von Bulgarien die Vergrösserung seines Landes durch Ostrumelien nicht zugeben wollte; und damit entfiel auch die Oesterreich zugesagte Gegenleistung."

[35] *P. P.*, 1886, lxxv, Turkey no. 1, p. 26. His state of mind is indicated in Paget's despatch of September 26. He had just told the Russian Ambassador he would not "put pressure on the Porte to prevent the exercise of the Sultan's Treaty rights, though he would represent that such a course, under present circumstances, would be attended with danger on account of the excitement which a conflict between Turks and Christians would create in Russia, and possibly also in other countries. On the other hand, Count Kálnoky considers a simple acquiescence by the Powers in what has been done to be inadmissible, and thinks that no time should be lost in agreeing upon a protest or a remonstrance to Bulgaria against the violation of the Treaty. He fears it will be impossible to re-establish the *status quo ante*, but he foresees at the same time that agreeing to the union will be productive of risings and disturbances amongst the Serbs, Greeks, and other nationalities."

[36] H. S. Edwards, *Sir William White* (London, 1902), pp. 228–230.

hurry to propose.³⁷ It too was willing to enter a conference for the purpose of devising a new formula, but would hear of no steps which might really endanger the maintenance of what had been accomplished.

These were the attitudes maintained in general by the Powers chiefly concerned in the complicated, hair-splitting negotiations which followed. In this whole affair, Germany played a particularly unassuming rôle. She was not directly interested; and no serious consequences appeared to be imminent. The best means of avoiding them seemed to be to let a solution work itself out which would leave the existing situation undisturbed; and so Germany used all her modest efforts in the interest of harmony and localization of the trouble.³⁸ Only in the admonitions addressed to other Balkan states against attempts to profit by existing disturbances did she take a leading part.³⁹ Bismarck's advice to Austria was that "she should be especially careful to avoid a breach with Russia on account of their respective bosom-children, Serbia and Bulgaria." ⁴⁰

It was practically certain from the outset that the conference of Constantinople, which opened formally on October 4, would prove merely a machine for smoothing over the difficulties of the situation and reconciling it as nearly as possible with the treaty of Berlin. Yet the Powers haggled for weeks over definitions and terms, while Russia, a bit disconcerted at the turn affairs had taken, developed a more and more decided opposition to the recognition of the change. The conference had two main tasks before it. It was expected to produce some form of protest which would save the face of the treaty and console Russia and Turkey, without seriously affecting what had been done. It was also meant to devise a formula which would recognize the change

---

[37] *P. P.*, 1886, lxxv, Turkey no. 1, p. 32. September 28, Salisbury to Paget. Salisbury had just replied to a question from Austria about them: "I said that it was a step which, in my judgment, might have been of value if it had been taken at the very first practicable moment. It had, however, not met with the concurrence of the German Court, and I had not pressed it further. The lapse of a few days had deprived such a measure of any possible utility."

[38] *Ibid.*, p. 102. October 5, White to Salisbury.

[39] *Y. B.*, pp. 35-36. September 26, Courcel to Freycinet.

[40] *G. F. O.*, v, p. 3. September 28, 1885, Reuss to Bismarck.

without altering the letter of the treaty. The British government displayed much more interest in the second point than in the first, suggesting, as the proper way of bridging the gap between the actual situation and the treaty, a "personal union" of the two provinces under the ruler of one of them.[41] Russia was by no means pleased at the suggestion and the sudden readiness to accept the situation which it revealed.[42] England's attitude toward the protest, which Russia regarded as the real purpose of the gathering, was even more disquieting. She had already expressed her disapproval of the event, declared Sir William White, the British ambassador at Constantinople; and "nothing was to be gained by a repetition of this disapproval, which on being reiterated by the Representatives in a formal Resolution, might serve to exclude Prince Alexander, and also encourage Turkey in the belief that they would receive the support of the Powers if they attempted to re-establish the *status quo ante* by force."[43] Any pronouncement that might be taken seriously was therefore out of the question. The declaration drawn up by the ambassadors on October 4 was frankly so framed that it should "simply serve as a means of checking the movement and preventing bloodshed."[44] This declaration, after some further emasculating amendments by Austria, was accepted by Russia as the best that could be got for the moment. On October 13, it was duly presented to the Porte and to Prince Alexander, without exerting any appreciable influence upon the situation. The definite settlement was left to be dealt with by a formal conference.

In preparation for its meeting, Russia took measures to strengthen her hand. Long before the pallid declaration of the ambassadors had been presented, she had perceived that it would accomplish nothing and that no effective steps were to be expected from a common initiative of the Powers. Consequently, Russia turned to her two partners in the treaty of 1881 and opened an exchange of views leading to a special understanding as

[41] *P. P.*, 1886, lxxv, Turkey no. 1, p. 58. October 2, Salisbury to White.
[42] *Ibid.*, p. 73. October 4, Paget to Salisbury.
[43] *Ibid.*, p. 72. October 3, White to Salisbury.
[44] *Ibid.*, p. 77. October 4, White to Salisbury.

the basis for later action.[45] According to the terms of the treaty, Russia's claim for support in demanding a return to the status quo ante was far from strong. The Bulgarian union was not to be opposed by any of the parties; and, although Russia had not foreseen the possibility of being herself affected by this provision, such was now undoubtedly the case. Yet, by making her attitude clear on the matter, Russia could influence greatly the opinions of her two associates, particularly that of Austria. She had only to intimate that recent events had affected her attitude toward the eventual annexation of Bosnia and Herzegovina, in order to make the Central Powers pause and consider the advisability of coming to an agreement. Moreover, Austria still had cause to be concerned over the presence of Bulgarian troops on the Macedonian border; and she was rendered extremely uncomfortable by the increasing restlessness of Serbia.

Russia's approach to her allies was seconded by an assault of the Hungarian Opposition upon the government. On October 1, a bombardment of interpellations was opened in the Hungarian Diet as to the government's intentions regarding the enforcement of the treaty of Berlin, as to the possibility of further violations, and as to the agreements existing with Germany and Russia on the subject.[46] The questions raised at this time and the comments made upon them showed that the Opposition was still animated by the suspicions of the League of the Three Emperors expressed in the preceding year, following the interview of Skierniewice, and by the idea that this secret understanding was somehow to blame for the events in the Balkans.[47] President Tisza took up the defence of the government on October 3. Meeting an allegation that the government had advised Turkey to forego her

[45] *P. P.*, 1886, lxxv, Turkey no. 1, p. 137. October 15, Paget to Salisbury. Kálnoky made a long communication (see below, p. 34) "as the result of the exchange of views between the Cabinets of Vienna, St. Petersburgh, and Berlin upon the mode of proceeding towards a solution of the present situation of affairs in Eastern Roumelia and Bulgaria." Also, Edwards, p. 232 (December 7, 1885, White to Morier). "Up to Oct. 10 or 15, they were favorable here, at Vienna and at Berlin to the personal union. If Russia had agreed the whole thing would have been over by this time. But Nelidoff would not have it so."

[46] *N. F. P.*, October 1, 1885. Publication of the questions put by Szilagyi.

[47] *Ibid.*, October 2. Speech of Szilagyi.

right to armed intervention for restoration of the status quo ante, he stated that the monarchy "recognizes the treaty right of Turkey to uphold and enforce the status quo by whatever forcible means she may see fit to employ; and that right will not be interfered with." But if the right were not exercised, he added, the government recognized a duty "to bring the situation which has come about in contravention of treaties as nearly as possible into harmony with the Treaty of Berlin and with the equilibrium established by that treaty in the Balkan Peninsula." The monarchy would insist, however, that in any event "no single Power was entitled to intervene with armed hand." [48]

Another troublesome point was the query whether the government intended to take advantage of the recent events by annexing Bosnia and Herzegovina or advancing farther into Turkish territory. In raising this question, the Opposition revived the old Hungarian protest against the incorporation of more Slavic territories and the idea that the upheaval which had just occurred was the outcome of a bargain between the Eastern Empires at Turkey's expense. Tisza's reply was a flat denial of any such intentions. Yet he felt called upon to add: "with a view to eventualities imperilling the vital interests of the Monarchy, which we cannot now foresee and may be unable to prevent, we must and will maintain our freedom of decision." These significant words aroused a storm of comment in the house and cries of "Salonica!" from the Left benches.

The ensuing debate was uncommonly lively, even for a Hungarian Chamber; and the answers of President Tisza were accepted only in the face of repeated expressions of dissatisfaction from the Opposition leaders.[49] The government came out with a safe majority; but the tide of criticism was sufficiently strong to make it consider the advisability of listening to Russia's proposals, which corresponded so strangely with those of the Hungarians.

Russia's new project was disclosed to Bismarck by Giers, who visited him at Friedrichsruh on October 7. It was "that the

[48] *N. F. P.*, October 4.
[49] *Ibid.* The edition of October 4 contains a complete report of the debate.

three imperial courts, as soon as they had agreed upon their programme, should make use of the Sultan as a mouthpiece to suggest to the Powers, in the conference enlarged by the addition of Turkey, modifications which would bring the two Bulgarias closer together in their economic and administrative relations without departing from the form of the status quo ante, thus robbing the Serbs and Greeks of any pretext for demanding compensations." Giers explained frankly that he had been obliged to devise this complicated formula because his sovereign, while admitting that some recognition must be accorded to the *fait accompli* in Eastern Rumelia, would not accept the simpler solution of a personal union so long as it would have to be effected through the person of Prince Alexander.

All this was most disquieting to Bismarck, who had been favorably impressed by the British proposal for a personal union as the best means of discomfiting the designs of the Serbs. He was very doubtful about the practicability of the new scheme, but he wrote to the Emperor William: "I did not feel called upon, however, to criticise Russia's policy, believing it better that she should be set right by her own experience and dealings with the other Powers than that *we* should block the road she has chosen as the proper one." He would not undertake to support her policy until she had gained Austria's approval of it. "I believe our interest demands," he wrote his sovereign, "that we should leave Russia and Austria to work out their understanding directly between themselves without taking the initiative, since it does not matter so much to us what they agree upon, provided only they agree. The easiest way is first to let them have their differences out in a *tête-à-tête*, and then to try and arrange the matters upon which they disagree." [50]

The Austrians did not come readily into the understanding. They entertained deep suspicions of Russia's policy and did not wish to see an outcome too favorable for her desires without first making sure of their own interests and those of their protégés, the Serbs, who were clamoring for compensations. Pressure of cir-

[50] *G. F. O.*, v, pp. 13–14. October 9, 1885, Bismarck to William I.

cumstances and the counsels of Bismarck combined to prevail over these obstacles.[51]

The result of the exchange of views among the three governments was apparently an understanding that a return to the status quo ante should be stipulated as a preliminary condition to the final settlement by the conference. The understanding probably did not extend to the settlement itself. The two Central Powers were still of the opinion that the results of the revolution were not to be destroyed; but Russia might hope that, if Prince Alexander and his troops were sent back to Sofia with a sharp rebuke by the Powers, the situation would be so altered as to make the ultimate union acceptable. There was also no agreement as to the means of enforcing obedience if Prince Alexander refused to comply with the Powers' demands. Count Herbert Bismarck told the British ambassador at Berlin "that M. de Giers had been of opinion that the Prince would, under the circumstances, obey the unanimous voice of Europe, and retire to Sophia. Count Bismarck had pointed out to M. de Giers the difficulty of the situation if the Prince refused, and had asked what would happen next. M. de Giers had replied: ' Alors les Puissances aviseront.' "[52] Moreover, Austria and Germany, although bound to press the proposition of the return to the status quo ante, were not obliged unconditionally to see it through the conference.[53]

[51] *N. F. P.*, October 8, 1885. "Erst seit zwei Tagen theilt sich das Dunkel einigermassen, der Geist Bismarck's schwebt wieder über den Gewässern, und man hört endlich eine verständliche Losung, wenigstens so weit die Berliner und Petersburger Politik in Frage kommt. Festhalten am Berliner Vertrage, möglichste Wiederherstellung des früheren Zustandes, Ausschluss der Theorie vom Gleichgewicht auf der Balkan-Halbinsel und der daraus entspringenden praktischen Folgerungen — darin scheint merkwürdigerweise die deutsche mit der russischen Politik sich zu begegnen während bekanntlich die Tisza'sche Interpellations-Beantwortung noch beträchtliche Zugeständnisse an jene Gleichgewichts-Theorie enthielt."

[52] *P. P.*, 1886, lxxv, Turkey no. 1, p. 145. October 17, 1885, Malet to Salisbury.

[53] Corti, pp. 208–209. "Er [Kálnoky] trat mit Russland diesbezüglich in Unterhandlung, und Giers äusserte seine Ansicht, dass schon ein moralischer Druck Russlands genügen werde, um den Fürsten Alexander zur Aufgabe Ostrumeliens zu bestimmen. Kálnoky bezweifelte dies, und beide Staatsmänner kamen nach fruchtlosem Hin und Her überein, vorläufig den status quo als Ausgangspunkt zu behalten, bis die Botschafter in Konstantinopel etwas beschliessen würden." Mohrenheim, at Paris, unquestionably exaggerated the definiteness of the accord, although his testimony is valuable in establishing the fact and its nature.

Once committed to this course, Austria, having more at stake, took her obligation more seriously than did Germany. On October 15, Kálnoky broached the matter to Paget and "laid great stress upon the consideration of the absolute necessity for the Powers to take their stand upon the Treaty of Berlin, and consequently of obliging Bulgaria and Eastern Roumelia to restore things to the condition in which they were before the recent revolutionary movement." The chief reason which he adduced for his insistence, and one which undoubtedly had great weight with him, was the effect of a successful movement of this kind upon the other Balkan peoples, and particularly upon the Serbs. "Unless the treaty were upheld in the case of Roumelia and Bulgaria, it might be difficult to maintain it in that of Servia." Furthermore, Kálnoky "thought it would be difficult to absolve the Prince entirely from all share of responsibility for the part he had, although perhaps unwillingly, taken in recent proceedings." The return to the status quo ante should therefore be imposed upon the Bulgarians; and Kálnoky stated it as his belief, "that a formal summons addressed to them by the unanimous authority of the Powers assembled in Conference would have the desired effect." [54]

All this language had a very disquieting effect upon the British government, which, for confirmation of the sentiments therein expressed, turned to Germany, the arbiter of the League of the Three Emperors. The German government took less seriously its adhesion to the principles enunciated by Kálnoky, being chiefly interested in maintaining the harmony of all the Powers. Count Herbert Bismarck sought to allay England's fears by assuring her

On October 23, Freycinet stated, in a circular despatch: "L'Ambassadeur de Russie vient de me donner spontanément des explications sur le mandat de la future Conférence, au sujet duquel, m'a-t-il dit, les trois Cabinets de Berlin, Vienne et Pétersbourg sont entièrement d'accord. Le premier acte de la Conférence, d'après lui, consisterait, ainsi que la récente suggestion russe le donnait à prévoir, à adresser une sommation au Prince Alexandre pour qu'il ait à se soumettre et à rentrer dans le *statu quo ante*. Le second acte, si le Prince n'obtempérait pas, serait de concerter avec la Porte les mesures d'exécution militaire. Enfin, comme troisième et dernier acte, la Conférence délibérerait sur les modifications qu'il pourrait y avoir lieu d'apporter au traité de Berlin touchant la Roumélie en vue de préserver l'avenir." *Y. B.*, pp. 134–135.

[54] *P. P.*, 1886, lxxv, Turkey no. 1, p. 137. October 15, Paget to Salisbury.

that he considered her interpretation of Kálnoky's proposal exaggerated, and that "the threat is only intended to imply that if he [the prince] resists he will do so at his own risk." [55] Later on he expressed himself as "of the opinion that the proposition that it was the duty of the Powers to maintain the Treaty of Berlin, and not permit its infraction by one of the smaller Powers was unassailable, but he thought that after Prince Alexander had been reduced to obedience, and the dignity of Treaty obligations had been vindicated, the Powers would have a right to examine the situation with a view to seeing what could be done towards meeting the recently declared wishes of the population." He let it be seen clearly enough that Germany had not adhered enthusiastically to the Russian programme and was by no means convinced of its merits. He hoped that England would continue to work with the other Powers, "as he considers a Conference to be the only possible means of restraining all parties interested." [56]

Kálnoky, in all his subsequent conversations, maintained the attitude he had taken on the 15th.[57] It was evident enough that he was considering only the immediate aspect of the case, not its final settlement, and that his views differed from those of the British government, not on fundamental issues, but only as concerned the order of procedure. Yet this difference of opinion was sufficient to delay action for weeks. On November 2, Count Károlyi, the Austrian ambassador at London, informed Lord Salisbury that "he was not instructed to propose a return to the *status quo* definitely, or to exclude a subsequent consideration of the wishes of the populations; that would be a matter for the consideration of the Conference." To which Salisbury replied: "our view was that the method of proceeding should be inverted; that the Conference should be asked, in the first place, in what way it was possible to meet the wishes of the populations, and that questions of procedure could be arranged afterwards." [58] This exaggerated regard for "wishes of the populations" rings

[55] *P. P.*, 1886, lxxv, Turkey no. 1, p. 138. October 17, Malet to Salisbury.
[56] *Ibid.*, p. 145. October 17, Malet to Salisbury.
[57] *Ibid.*, pp. 150, 152. October 17, 20, Paget to Salisbury.
[58] *Ibid.*, p. 199. November 2, Salisbury to Wolff.

somewhat ironically when taken in connection with England's conduct toward this question at the congress of Berlin.

The difference of opinion persisted down to the time when the conference met, on November 5, and marked its first four sessions. At the fourth, on November 12, the lines were clearly drawn. Russia, Austria, Germany, and Italy voted in support of a set of Turkish proposals which would result in the return to a somewhat amended status quo ante; England stood firm for the priority of an inquiry as to the means of meeting the "wishes of the population." France attempted to find a compromise by setting in motion simultaneously the machinery for carrying out both the Turkish and the English proposals, so that the inquiry by the conference would play a part in the final settlement contemplated by Turkey.[59] This was the point which the situation had reached when a new element was injected into it by Serbia's declaration of war upon Bulgaria.

### III

The action of Serbia had long been anticipated, although at first there was some uncertainty as to whether it would be directed toward Macedonia or Bulgaria. The Serbs, like all other Balkan peoples, were not unnaturally indignant that the Bulgarians had overthrown the treaty of Berlin to their own profit while other states remained within that treaty's bounds. They were hungry for a 'compensation' for this aggrandizement of their neighbors, and they did not care particularly at whose expense it should be gained. King Milan felt obliged to place himself at the head of this national movement; and he could be fairly sure of his ground in doing so, because, in the treaty which he had signed with Austria in 1881, the price of the surrender of his country to Austrian exploitation had been a promise of Austrian support in just such an endeavor as that upon which he now proposed to embark.[60] The Serbs, and the Greeks as well, had begun to arm and

---

[59] *P. P.*, 1886, lxxv, Turkey no. 1, pp. 216–220. November 12, White to Salisbury.

[60] Pribram, i, p. 20 (Amer., i, p. 54). Article vii of the treaty of June 28 reads: "Si, par suite d'un concours d'événements dont le développement n'est pas à

to talk of their national aspirations as soon as the Eastern Rumelian revolution took place. The talk became more and more precise and official.[61] The two peoples hoped possibly to attain their desires through the action of the Powers as a reward for keeping the peace; but both, and especially the Serbs, were prepared to go to war if they saw any chance of success by that means.

The Austrian government had shown itself particularly embarrassed by the attitude of Serbia. There could be no doubt of its ability to restrain the Serbs, in spite of the treaty of 1881, if it really determined to do so; but just upon this point it could not make up its mind. Count Kálnoky could not help feeling that Serbia was his pawn in the Balkan game, while Bulgaria was the pawn, if not for the moment of the Russian government, at least, in the long run, of Panslavism. Any gain to Serbia at the expense of Bulgaria seemed, therefore, to the ultimate profit of Austria — a natural calculation, though extremely curious in the light of later developments. On September 27, Kálnoky told the German ambassador that his message to King Milan had been: "He should not stir nor cross the border so long as Bulgaria's violation of the treaty of Berlin has not been consummated. If it should be — if the unification of Bulgaria should be recognized by the Powers — then Austria could not contest the right of her friend, Serbia, to seek for herself a compensation which will restore in some degree the disturbed balance of power in the Balkan Peninsula. This must be brought about, however, through the intervention of the Powers; and Austria-Hungary would intercede with them for her friend, Serbia."[62] Kálnoky did not promise

prévoir aujourd'hui la Serbie était en mesure de faire des acquisitions territoriales dans la direction de ses frontières méridionales (à l'exception du sandjak de Novibazar) l'Autriche-Hongrie ne s'y opposera pas et s'emploiera auprès des autres puissances afin de les gagner à une attitude favorable pour la Serbie."

[61] *N. F. P.*, October 3, 1885. Report of Milan's speech to the Skupchina on the 2d. The policy of his government, he stated, was directed toward "maintaining the status quo ante in the Balkan Peninsula, or making it possible to restore the equilibrium necessary to secure the interests of the various Balkan peoples." Significantly similar language was used next day by Tisza in the Hungarian Diet.

[62] *G. F. O.*, v, p. 5. September 28, 1885, Reuss to Bismarck. See also Corti, p. 200.

Serbia anything definite, nor did he assure her of support in a war. Indeed, he declared to the German ambassador that if King Milan went beyond the advice given him, he would be left to his fate. But next day he qualified this declaration by saying that he could not bring pressure upon Serbia without risking the overthrow of King Milan.[63] The Austrian ambassador at Berlin doubtfully put the question to Herbert Bismarck: "But what shall we do if King Milan starts an advance against our wishes?"[64]

This hesitation was distasteful to Bismarck, whose lack of sympathy with the aspirations of Balkan peoples was notorious, and who strongly desired to avoid further complications. In an interview with the Austrian ambassador on October 1, the Chancellor censured unsparingly Kálnoky's conduct and his whole conception of Balkan affairs. The squabbles of these states among themselves, he asserted, were of minor importance. "These people talk of a disturbed balance of power among the Balkan states," he sneered. "It is laughable: the balance there means the respect of European treaties by each state, and not the proportionate aggrandizement of all of them." And the maintenance of treaties should be the affair of the Powers that made them, not that of the little peoples whose existence they regulated. Encouragement to these in determining their own fate could only lead to serious conflicts of more important interests. "So far as I am concerned," he conceded, "you can unleash the Serbians if you really must, but never upon Old Serbia — at the most, against Bulgaria; for otherwise the spheres of interest of the Western Powers will be threatened, and the situation be made more complicated still." Admitting that Austria must, after all, remain the best judge of her own interests, he concluded with the admonition that, while he would subordinate Germany's action to hers, "I could not join you in a fight, for France would then fall upon us at once, and the rest is beyond foreseeing."[65]

[63] *G. F. O.*, v, p. 7. Postscript to the above.

[64] *Ibid.*, v, p. 9. September 29, memorandum by Herbert Bismarck.

[65] Corti, pp. 204–205. Széchényi to Kálnoky. See also *G. F. O.*, v, pp. 10–12, for Bismarck's observations on this interview and preceding correspondence, as recorded in a despatch to Reuss at Vienna, on October 3.

Kálnoky was at first impressed by this notification, and sought to pass on a similar warning to Serbia. But the principle of patronage of Serbia was too firmly rooted at Vienna to be much shaken by remonstrances from Berlin. The Emperor himself struck out the sharpest sentence from his minister's despatch to Belgrade, leaving it but little more definite than his previous communications.[66] Then, as the effect of Bismarck's words wore off, Kálnoky reverted to his own former ideas on the subject. He took the concept of the balance of power among Balkan states more seriously than did Bismarck; and, while affecting to favor the maintenance of the status quo all round, he could not help feeling that it had been disturbed beyond restoration. The monarchy did not conceal its sympathy with Serbia's claim for compensation and her resolve to take it by force if necessary.[67] She was even allowed to finance her military preparations by a loan from the Länderbank, in which Berlin bankers refused to participate.[68]

Upon one point only did Kálnoky share Bismarck's views of the situation. That was in regard to the direction to be taken by Serbia's effort. There were many reasons why he should prefer that the compensation be sought at Bulgaria's expense, rather than in the Turkish territories to the south, which he regarded as Austria's special preserve. A clash with Serbia would even have the delectable result of calling Bulgaria's troops away from their unpleasant proximity to those regions. So Kálnoky did make it

[66] Corti, p. 206. Kálnoky to Khevenhüller, November 10.

[67] Schulthess, *Geschichtskalender*, 1885, p. 225. On October 31, Kálnoky assured the Hungarian Delegation: "An Serbien wurde thatsächlich keine Aufforderung in dem Sinne gerichtet, dass wir seine Interessen nicht schützen würden, wenn es vor dem Schluss der Konferenz einen Schritt zur Okkupation thue, da wir Serbiens Unabhängigkeit stets anerkannten und respektierten und dem König von Serbien das Recht zukommt, Krieg oder Frieden für sein Land zu machen." The report of the Delegation's Committee for Foreign Affairs declared: "Whatever turn matters may take, the disturbed order of things in the East must be restored by legal means, and, in any case, in such a manner that the wishes of those who have arbitrarily violated law shall in no respect meet with greater consideration than the no less justifiable aspirations of those who have loyally not allowed such aspirations to override their respect for Treaties." *P.P.*, 1886, lxxv, Turkey no. 1, p. 250.

[68] *P. P.*, 1886, lxxv, Turkey no. 1, p. 93. October 9, Wyndham (Belgrade) to Salisbury.

clear enough to Serbia that she must not attack Turkey.[69] With this summons the Serbs cheerfully complied. By mid-October they had decided to direct their attack to the eastward.[70] But King Milan felt safe in returning a flat refusal to Kálnoky's half-hearted request that he demobilize the army which was being concentrated for the stroke.[71] His boldness brought down no retribution on his head.

Bismarck raged at this disregard of his advice. As a last appeal to Kálnoky's reason, he put forward the argument that Austria, by unleashing her Serbs and so antagonizing Russia in a new way, was simply playing England's game.[72] His own reasoning is a little crooked, since England's game was now the confirming of the very Bulgarian union which had aroused the ire of the Serbs; but in any case it was too late to check the course of events. The success of England's game at Constantinople was already assured: the possibility of any concerted action with regard to Bulgaria seemed to have vanished. The natural conclusions were drawn by the Serbs, who were still awaiting the outcome of the deliberations of the Powers, as early in October they had promised to do.[73] A formal recognition of the Bulgarian union might have been accompanied by compensations to other states which would make military action unnecessary: an enforced return to the status quo ante would make it impossible and out of place. But when the conference seemed merely to be letting things drift and arrange themselves, Serbia decided that if she was to get any compensation, the time had come to strike for it. The Russian government had foreseen and sought to avoid this outcome; but its efforts were steadily frustrated down to the very end by the opposition of England to any disturbance of existing condi-

[69] Theodor von Sosnosky, *Die Balkanpolitik Oesterreich-Ungarns* (Stuttgart and Berlin, 1913–14, 2 vols.), ii, p. 79.

[70] P. P., 1886, lxxv, Turkey no. 1, p. 130. October 16, Salisbury to Wyndham. "I saw the Servian Minister this afternoon. I urged upon him the vital importance to his country of a pacific attitude both towards Turkey and Bulgaria. M. Mijatovich spoke as if the danger of war with the former country was much less than it had been. A conflict with the latter seemed to him imminent."

[71] Corti, p. 214.

[72] *Ibid.*, p. 215. November 11, Bismarck to Reuss.

[73] P. P., 1886, lxxv, Turkey no. 1, p. 105. October 8, Paget to Salisbury.

tions.[74] The predictions of Russia were now justified, and the whole situation was dislocated by Serbia's declaration of war on November 13.

The Austrian government alone faced the new situation with a policy ready to apply. As soon as Kálnoky heard of the declaration he telegraphed to Belgrade his good wishes for Serbian success.[75] He had all his arrangements made in advance for converting the Austrian consulate at Sofia into a bureau of military information for Serbia's benefit.[76] He made haste to avert the complications which threatened from the side of Turkey. The Turkish government had declared some three weeks previously that it "would regard an invasion of Bulgaria by Servia as an attack upon the Turkish Empire.'[77] Now, on November 15, Kálnoky authorized Calice at Constantinople to warn the Sultan that "any threat against Serbian soil would bring Turkey into conflict with Austria-Hungary."[78]

In assuming this attitude Kálnoky appealed for support to his ally, Italy, with disconcerting results. Robilant's reply indicated a willingness to join in any action which all the Powers might decide to take toward Turkey, but he grasped this opportunity to assert in startling terms Italy's special interest in the questions involved. On November 17, he sent word to Kálnoky that he was prepared to associate himself with Austria in this case and hoped to continue doing so in the future; but "if, with the development of events, and notably as the result of an armed conflict between Serbia and Bulgaria, new interests and preoccupations arise, it

[74] *P. P.*, 1886, lxxv, Turkey no. 1, p. 215. November 12, Salisbury to Morier. "M. de Staal urged the danger of delay, intimating the fear that nothing could hold back the Servians. I replied that, even if the fact were so, about which some question might be raised, the collision between the Servians and Bulgarians would not be so serious, and would not awaken so much feeling in Europe as a conflict between the Turks and the Roumelians, entered into for the purpose of imposing on the latter a mode of government to which they were averse."

[75] Corti, p. 219. November 14, Kálnoky to Khevenhüller.

[76] *Ibid.*, p. 224. These disloyal activities resulted in the closing of the Bulgarian telegraph service to cipher messages, with consequences later embarrassing to Austria.

[77] *P. P.*, 1886, lxxv, Turkey no. 1, p. 175. October 26, Lascelles to Salisbury.

[78] Corti, p. 218.

seems just and reasonable to reserve our freedom of decision."
He added that Austria could be sure of Italy's support only so
long as "her plans coincide with the requirements of our own special interests." [79] This warning was ominous for the future of the
Triple Alliance, although for the moment the rapid and unforeseen march of events, which rendered any action by Italy unnecessary, prevented its having any effect.

Bismarck was, of course, profoundly disgusted at the entire
trend of developments. His policy of conciliation of conflicting
interests had broken down, owing to his unwillingness to pronounce the deciding word in a Russo-Austrian dispute.[80] Up to
the last moment he had striven vainly to find a way out by rallying to the French proposals of compromise, urging upon the
British government the consideration "that an agreement as to
the course to be followed might put an end to the hostilities between Servia and Bulgaria." [81]

Bismarck's conduct throughout this crisis can be characterized
as little else than culpable inaction. He seemed unwilling to face
the fact that his two imperial allies were on the brink of a serious
rupture. He refrained from utilizing in any positive sense the
arbitral powers that devolved upon him under the alliance of
1881. Instead of entering whole-heartedly into the rapprochement initiated by Russia in October, he arranged merely for an
ineffective support to Russia's ill conceived plan of restoring the
status quo ante. What was needed was a positive solution which
would admit the Bulgarian union, while removing Russia's objection to it by somehow getting rid of Alexander of Battenberg.
Austria might be ' compensated ' if necessary. An agreement on
these lines would not have been easy to bring about, but it was
possible and infinitely preferable to what actually followed. The
opposition of England could have been overcome by resolute

[79] G. B., 1885, p. 2. November 17, 1885, Robilant to Galvagna.

[80] Corti, p. 215. Summary of Bismarck's despatch to Reuss, November 11.
"Immer um die Erhaltung des Friedens besorgt, sagte er die Entente à trois könne
nur währen und die Erhaltung des Friedens verbürgen, wenn dabei der Vorgang
eines von zweien der Mächte auszuübenden Druckes auf die dritte, mit einem Wort
die Majorisierung, sorgsam vermieden würde."

[81] P. P., 1886, lxxv, Turkey no. 1, p. 224. November 14, Salisbury to Malet.

action; for there were still screws to be applied in Afghanistan and Egypt. Instead of devising and pushing through any such solution as this, however, Bismarck allowed the ark of the League of the Three Emperors to drift about in the troubled sea of a general negotiation, with dangerous reefs on all sides, at the mercy of contrary British winds, local Balkan squalls, and fitful gusts of Austrian indecision. It was no time for a policy of all-round conciliation and lulling of the elements. Only a steady breeze and a firm course could now bring the craft safely into port.

The situation afforded cause enough for alarm. Russia was profoundly moved by Serbia's warlike action. Much as the government and the Panslavists hated Prince Alexander, and strongly as they were opposed to a Bulgarian union under him, they were not prepared to see Bulgaria actually reduced in size as the result of a fratricidal war promoted by Austria for her own profit. In the early days of this crisis, when the Bulgarian deputation had visited the Tsar at Copenhagen, he had "warned the Bulgarians of the danger their conduct was likely to bring them into, but said, notwithstanding, that if Bulgaria was attacked, she could count upon Russian intervention." [82] Now the *Moscow Gazette*, the organ of the Panslavists and one of the journals which had led in denunciations of the prince and the *coup d'état*, cried out: "The soil of Bulgaria has been deluged with Russian blood, and the boundaries of Bulgaria have been unalterably and solemnly fixed. To the infringement of these boundaries Russia would be as sensible as to the seizure of any part of her own territory." [83] The success of the Serbian arms might well have led to Russian intervention. Fortunately, the occasion for it did not arise; for, before any of the governments could come to a decision as to its course of action, the Bulgarians themselves had cut the knot of their difficulties with the sword.

The defeat of the Serbian army at Slivnitsa, November 17–19, and its rapid retreat over the frontier, cleared up the situation to a degree, although the counter-offensive of the Bulgarians into Serbia presented a fresh problem. This was the moment for the

[82] *P. P.*, 1886, lxxv, Turkey no. 1, p. 92. October 7, Grosvenor to Salisbury.
[83] *Ibid.*, p. 343. Reported under date of November 22.

Powers to throw aside their hesitations and retrieve the tottering status quo of the Eastern Question before it should collapse altogether. Austria was now more than willing to stop the war which was turning out so disastrously for her protégé: in fact, the Austrian government was appealing in all possible quarters for help in bringing to an end the difficulties which its own rash encouragement of Serbia had brought about.[84] On November 24, Russia responded by a proposal to the Powers for concerted action to stop the hostilities.[85] It was acted upon at once. The representatives of the Powers at Belgrade drew up a collective note demanding an armistice, which King Milan promptly accepted.[86] But in the attempt to communicate with Prince Alexander difficulties were encountered, owing to his absence from Sofia and to the refusal of cipher messages by the Bulgarian telegraph service. The task of getting into touch with the prince was therefore intrusted to the Austrian minister at Belgrade, who was also charged by Kálnoky to add a strong commentary to the note on his own part.[87] The arguments by which he was to support the demand for an armistice were left to his own judgment; but his instructions went so far as to provide: "In case the circumstances require it, Your Excellency will make it quite clear to the prince that he will come into conflict with Austria-Hungary if he does not follow what is now our friendly advice." [88]

The Austrian envoy found Prince Alexander in his camp on November 28, and presented to him first the considerations embodied in the note of the Powers, cautioning him "that he would cause a great war if he continued to advance." When the prince showed himself unimpressed by this and other arguments, Khevenhüller put the situation in more concrete terms by informing him that a further attempt to advance would probably be opposed by Austrian troops. The entrance of the Austrians into Serbia, he added, "would be the signal for the occupation of Bul-

---

[84] Corti, p. 224. Жигаревъ, ii, p. 256.
[85] P. P., 1886, lxxv, Turkey no. 1, p. 308. November 25, Salisbury to Morier.
[86] Ibid., pp. 307, 308. November 24, 25, Wyndham to Salisbury.
[87] Ibid., p. 313. November 26, Wolff to Salisbury.
[88] Corti, p. 228. November 25, 26, Kálnoky to Khevenhüller.

garia by the Russians, a step which would cost him his throne." Alexander saw the point of these remarks and yielded without further parley.[89]

The Austrian government undoubtedly had acted in full knowledge of the probable consequences of its step. The language of Khevenhüller's ultimatum shows that it realized in advance that, as the Russian government hastened to inform it, "once the Austrian troops have penetrated into Serbia, the pact upon which the agreement of the Northern Powers rests will be torn up."[90] The British chargé d'affaires at Vienna wrote that the Austrian threat was "thoroughly intended, and will certainly be carried out if the Bulgarians advance."[91] The effect of the proceeding was neither disguised nor diminished by the belated assurance conveyed to Russia by the Austrian government, in consequence of pressure from Bismarck, that it had no intention of acting upon its ultimatum without a preliminary understanding with Austria's allies.[92]

The threat had its desired effect: the Bulgarians stopped their advance and concluded an armistice, which was kept with some difficulty until final arrangements were made, toward the end of the year, for mutual evacuation of territory. But the Bulgarian victory had also had an unquestionable effect. It was now indeed clear "that the formula, status quo ante, which seemed sufficient at the time of the Serbian threat, no longer meets the demands of the situation since the brilliant military triumph of Bulgaria."[93] The conference of Constantinople ignominiously faded out of existence. At its seventh meeting, on November 25, it was deadlocked as usual by the attitude of Sir William White; and next day Giers declared that his government considered it "as a thing be-

[89] *P. P.*, 1886, lxxv, Turkey no. 1, pp. 341, 361. November 28, December 2, Wyndham to Salisbury. Corti, p. 229.

[90] A. G. Drandar, *Les événements politiques en Bulgarie* (Brussels, 1896), p. 118. The quotation, from a despatch of Giers, is given without date or specific reference. At first sight improbable, it is really quite in accord with Russian policy of the moment. See Corti, p. 230.

[91] *P. P.*, 1886, lxxv, Turkey no. 1, p. 360. November 30, Wolff to Salisbury. Corti, p. 232.

[92] *G. F. O.*, v, p. 25, note.

[93] Вѣстникъ Европы, December 1, 1885, p. 891.

longing to the past." ⁹⁴ The Russian government still had some hope of arriving at a satisfactory solution through the instrumentality of the League of the Three Emperors.⁹⁵ But Bismarck continued to disappoint its expectations by declining to intervene in the difference of opinion prevailing between Germany's two allies.⁹⁶ Finding no support for its views in any quarter, the Russian government had at last no choice but to abandon its opposition to what had taken place in Bulgaria; and, on December 23, it grudgingly admitted "that a return to the *status quo ante* might now prove impossible, and that the union which existed *de facto* might have to be maintained." ⁹⁷ The Turkish government, which had taken advantage of the absence of Bulgarian troops from Eastern Rumelia to send delegates there, with no encouraging results, also announced its readiness "to negotiate with Prince Alexander directly, and to sanction a union in some form or other." ⁹⁸ There was no longer any serious obstacle in the way of a peaceable settlement of the whole Bulgarian situation.

Such a settlement was certainly what Bismarck above all else desired. If he had been annoyed by the revolution of Philippopolis and vexed by the actions of Greece and Serbia, he was now thoroughly enraged by the intervention of Austria. He had not been consulted with regard to the Khevenhüller ultimatum; and he afterwards found no terms strong enough to condemn that step and the whole policy that lay behind it. The

⁹⁴ *P. P.*, 1886, lxxv, Turkey no. 1, p. 371. November 26, 1885, Morier to Salisbury.

⁹⁵ *Y. B.*, p. 324. December 15, Appert to Freycinet. Giers declared: "L'Empereur, dès le principe, s'est placé sur le terrain de l'entente complète des trois Empires; il s'y maintient loyalement et il ne peut aujourd'hui déserter la cause commune."

⁹⁶ *Ibid.*, pp. 338–339. December 19, Courcel to Freycinet. Herbert Bismarck stated: "Quant à présent, le Cabinet de Saint-Pétersbourg persistait dans son programme de rétablissement du *statu quo ante*. A Berlin on attendait patiemment. Quand la Russie et l'Autriche, qui continuaient à échanger leurs vues, seraient parvenues à se mettre amicalement d'accord sur le sort qu'il conviendrait de faire à la Roumélie Orientale, la question aurait fait un grand pas, et l'Allemagne prêterait volontiers son appui au mode de transaction adopté par les deux autres cours impériales."

⁹⁷ *P. P.*, 1886, lxxv, Turkey no. 1, p. 423. December 24, Morier to Salisbury.

⁹⁸ *Ibid.*, Turkey no. 2, p. 22. December 29, White to Salisbury.

correspondence with Vienna which followed was filled with harsh language. Bismarck accused Austria of acting in violation of the treaty with Russia. He warned her that "if . . . the breach with Russia should be brought about by an Austrian advance into Serbia without the preliminary understanding provided for by the treaty, Germany would not consider the case as occasion for a German-Russian war." To the German ambassador at Vienna he added: "In confidence I must admit that I do not yet understand, under the circumstances, what object the Austrian policy of intervention can have in view: the simple assertion of the 'necessity' of this intervention throws no light on it so far as I am concerned." As he saw it, no necessity for military action could possibly arise, even if the Bulgarians pushed on as far as Belgrade, "since the final outcome of the situation depends not upon the Bulgarian successes, but upon the decisions of the Powers." [99]

Bismarck's criticisms of Austria's policy were sound enough in their immediate application, but they seem to be based upon a fundamental misunderstanding of Kálnoky's point of view. This confusion of mind appears in his remarks to Mittnacht, on December 9, and to Busch, on January 5. He told the former: "Kálnoky was deceived from the beginning in thinking Russia was behind the Prince of Bulgaria, who is really more Austrian than Russian. What harm could it do Austria if the Bulgarians marched to Belgrade and if Serbia and Bulgaria formed an independent kingdom under the protection of England? The Austrians ought to wait until they hear the English cannon. The English have the greater interest in the matter, but they keep telling the Austrians theirs is the greater, which the Austrians have come to believe." [100] The last observations are sufficiently acute criticisms of Austrian policy, although the English interest in Balkan affairs was a rather uncertain quantity upon which to reckon.

[99] *G. F. O.*, v, p. 27. December 7, 1885, Bismarck to Reuss.

[100] Herrmann von Mittnacht, *Erinnerungen an Bismarck* (Stuttgart and Berlin, 1904–05, 2 vols.), ii, p. 46. See also Corti, p. 233. Kálnoky took issue with Bismarck's view that the collapse of Serbia would be to Austria's advantage.

Bismarck entertained, both at this time and later, an extraordinarily exaggerated idea of England's part in the Bulgarian affair. In his conversation of January 5 with Busch, he complained: "They ought to know in Vienna that the events in Roumelia are the result of English wire-pulling, and that it is England who supports the Prince." [101] A couple of years later, he made an even more positive statement: "At first he [Alexander of Battenberg] governed in this [the Russian] sense, but he afterwards took up with the English, who wished to create a Greater Bulgaria to serve their purposes, and like Rumania be under obligations to them. It was to be developed into a new Kingdom, which should stand in the way of Russia. That had been planned long beforehand, and the way had been prepared by various measures; but the Prince always tried to dispel any uneasiness by beautifully reassuring speeches and categorical promises. Finally he pledged himself to Giers not to make any change in Eastern Roumelia; and yet shortly afterwards the revolution broke out in Philippopolis, with his previous knowledge and co-operation." [102]

There is practically nothing to support this opinion. The Rumelian revolution forms a pretty straight story in which no traces of English intrigue are to be perceived. If enthusiastic consular officers with Liberal views were inclined to encourage popular aspirations, at least they had no more official backing from their government in so acting than had the Russian functionaries, who were frankly in sympathy with the union in spite of their government's desire to retard it. That the British government had sanctioned Alexander's action in advance is improbable, to say the least. Favorably as Lord Salisbury might regard his sovereign's protégé, quick as he was to see the advantage to England in the accomplished fact, he was not likely to connect himself beforehand with an adventure of such very doubtful consequences. Nor is it likely that the prince should have informed him of what was impending. At the time Alexander was in London, he still considered the revolution a rather remote affair, and

---

[101] Busch, iii, p. 149 (Amer., ii, p. 394; *Tagebuchblätter*, iii, p. 200).
[102] *Ibid.*, iii, p. 181 (Amer., ii, p. 418; *Tagebuchblätter*, iii, p. 233).

he still contemplated the possibility of a previous reconciliation with Russia, for which he made a bid soon afterward on his return through Vienna, and which would hardly have been a recommendation for the project in English eyes. Furthermore, the hypothesis is contradicted by England's precipitate action in urging the other Powers to put pressure upon the prince's government to revoke the action after it was taken. To maintain that this was merely duplicity is no explanation. It was too likely to have some effect upon those Powers already more or less bound to Russia. The British government surely felt no need of thus saving its face, for it showed no embarrassment in reversing this first position once the true state of affairs had become clear. The straightforward interpretation of Lord Salisbury's conduct is the one which best fits the facts as they are known.[103]

It remains to inquire how Bismarck accumulated his misconceptions. In the first place, he had failed from the beginning to take the whole business seriously enough to look into it deeply. All his efforts were directed toward keeping the League of the Three Emperors functioning, confident that a peaceable solution would result, and to restraining Austria's encouragement of Serbia. Then, when blood suddenly began to flow, and when Austria took a hazardous and compromising step without consulting him, he sprang up and looked about for an explanation of this overturn of his calculations. He well knew that Russia was not responsible; while many Russians were loudly blaming England.[104] Their hypothesis seemed perfectly reasonable to him, especially since his encounter with English influence in the matter of Prince Alexander's marriage project. He was ready enough to believe that the prince was moved in all his recent actions by an English intrigue.

The idea did not improve his own opinion of England, nor in-

[103] It is briefly stated by Edwards, p. 228: "England and Russia were equally puzzled by the event, and each Power thought the other responsible for it. The news of the union of the two Bulgarias and of the apathy with which the intelligence was received by the Porte took Lord Salisbury by surprise. But he soon saw that the true policy of England was to support the combination." Corti (pp. 202–203) follows this view of the case.

[104] Жигаревъ, ii, p. 248.

fluence him in the direction of an English alliance. He was given an unexpected occasion at this time to express anew his opinion of such a policy. On December 5, the German ambassador at London, Count Paul Hatzfeldt, reported a conversation with Lord Randolph Churchill, then secretary for India, in which the latter had remarked that "his wish was . . . for an alliance with Germany," adding: "A nous deux nous pourrions gouverner le monde." [105] Although the opinions of this somewhat erratic politician could not be thought to represent any serious tendency in the British government, Bismarck was moved to make a lengthy answer giving his reasons for not entering into the proposition and demolishing Churchill's arguments in its favor.

Bismarck's reasons against an English alliance were no different from those he had frequently expressed before. Hatzfeldt was to say to Churchill "that a lasting alliance with England would require a *law*, which would hardly receive the approval of the English Parliament: otherwise nothing could be accomplished but a ministerial agreement, of which the only result would be that we should serve as relay horses as long as we were needed." Bismarck pointed out that Great Britain and Germany alone could not "govern the world," but that a third partner would be needed, namely, Austria. Great Britain's own interests, he argued, should impel her to take Austria's part against Russia; and he blamed her severely for having "frivolously antagonized Austria." [106]

It was doubtless with reference to this correspondence that Bismarck made the observation: "We could easily transform our relations with England into an intimate understanding if we would sacrifice our Russian friendship for the English — which we have no intention of doing. England has always more to fear than to hope for from Russia; but, in coöperation with Austria and Italy, we could put up a strong defence for her if we retained Russia's friendship." [107] His words, which foreshadow the game he was later to play in abuse of Russia's confidence, also evinced

[105] *G. F. O.*, iv, p. 139. Hatzfeldt to Herbert Bismarck.
[106] *Ibid.*, iv, p. 141. Bismarck to Hatzfeldt.
[107] B. M. M., p. 264.

his determination not to let England stand by while he did the playing.

He urged Kálnoky to go slowly, leaving England, as far as possible, to deal with Russia alone. He also took this opportunity to press for the adoption of a policy of delimiting Austrian and Russian spheres of influence in the Balkans, at least with respect to Serbia and Bulgaria. As far back as June, 1884, he had instructed the German ambassadors in both Austria and Russia to cultivate this idea at the courts to which they were accredited.[108] It had borne no fruit in either case. When Bismarck now undertook to revive it, Kálnoky argued strongly against it. The German ambassador reported his argument on December 9: "If the line separating the two spheres of interest is to be the Serbo-Bulgarian border, he asks, what is to be done about Montenegro? Russia will never give up that position." [109] Bismarck's answer was: "The delimitation I recommend concerns only Serbia and Bulgaria: Montenegro and Rumania continue as they are, unaffected by it. Under this supposition, Austria could view an occasional occupation of Bulgaria by Russia, and the latter, one of Serbia by Austria-Hungary, without disquietude." [110]

The argument continued into the following year, still without result. Bismarck went so far as to warn Austria anew that, if she did not come to some such arrangement, she might find herself engaged in a war in which Germany would not feel obliged to aid her. He told the Austrian ambassador: "loyally and unreservedly as we Germans would back you up if Russia attacked you, we could never contemplate the employment of the German army as an auxiliary force in the extension of Austro-Hungarian influence on the lower Danube." [111]

All this sounds clear and reasonable enough. Bismarck was endeavoring to repair his fault in having permitted the trouble between Russia and Austria to develop to the extent it had attained. His solution, which is propounded here not for the first and by no

[108] *G. F. O.*, iii, pp. 345, 348.
[109] *Ibid.*, v, p. 33. December 9, 1885, Reuss to Bismarck.
[110] *Ibid.*, v, p. 37. December 13, Bismarck to Reuss.
[111] Corti, pp. 244–246. January 14, Széchényi to Kálnoky.

means for the last time, needs to be scrutinized with care. Apparently he cuts very short Austria's expectations of German support in a forward Balkan policy, but in reality he does so only in so far as immediate military help is concerned. Germany retains her benevolent attitude toward the extension of Austrian influence through Serbia and Rumania, the satellites of the Triple Alliance. And even back of her refusal of military coöperation lies the fact of Germany's guarantee against any serious consequences of an Austrian defeat at the hands of Russia. Moreover, Bismarck showed at this time and later that he did not regard the delimitation of spheres of influence as necessarily implying any permanent gain to Russia. "I find it especially hard to understand," he told Széchényi, "why you take every little complication in the Balkan Peninsula so much to heart. If today Russia should undertake a new war against Turkey and push her troops as far as Constantinople, she would only be ripening your harvest for you. With Transylvania and the occupied provinces in your hands, you would have Russia completely at your mercy; and she could not do otherwise than accept whatever conditions you might impose." [112] In other words, the discomfiture of Russia in 1878 might be repeated — perhaps on an even larger scale.

In other communications to the Austrian government Bismarck made it plain that he meant the methods of 1877 to be reproduced, especially as concerned England. Count Herbert Bismarck formulated the advice: "Provided Austria manages to restrain her impatience and conduct her policy from a statesmanlike point of view, she can easily take care of her interests if Russia *first* gets into war with England or only first gets into Constantinople." [113] To a later despatch in similar terms, the Chancellor himself added the prophetic words: "But Austria must never break with Russia, relying solely on German support and without a guarantee of the attitude of the Western Powers. As things now stand in England and France, we might thereby pave the way for a Russo-Anglo-French coalition, in the face of

[112] Corti, p. 246. January 14, Széchényi to Kálnoky.
[113] *G. F. O.*, iv, p. 263. December 7, Herbert Bismarck to Reuss.

which the situation of the allied Empires would be most difficult and the trustworthiness of Italy become doubtful." [114] In this farsighted estimate of probabilities lies the essential difference between Bismarck's policy and that of his successors.

This time Kálnoky followed most of Bismarck's advice; only he declined to admit a Russian occupation of Bulgaria or to show any real enthusiasm for spheres of interest in general. He held back, as suggested, from any serious transactions with Russia until England should get the lines of a settlement laid down. To the great annoyance of Bismarck, England's policy was suddenly disturbed at this juncture by the change of governments early in February, which brought the uncongenial Gladstone back into power. The Bulgarian settlement was in reality facilitated by this change; for the new British government took a less obstinate attitude regarding it, and had less influence at Constantinople with which to back up its policies. Once the chances of profiting by a clash between England and Russia had diminished, the best course left open to the Central Powers was to support all tendencies toward moderation and peace.

Bismarck was now ready to take an active part in the settlement. The advent of an unfriendly government in England impelled him to avoid all further European complications and made him more than ever anxious to see the existing muddle cleared away. He used all his influence to hasten the negotiations both for the peace between Serbia and Bulgaria and for the arrangement of the status of Eastern Rumelia. The former settlement was being delayed chiefly by Bulgaria's claims for an indemnity, which Germany was instrumental in having dropped.[115] When Prince Alexander objected to the periodic renewals of his appointment as governor of Eastern Rumelia, included in the latter transaction, Germany stood with Russia in proposing that the Powers sign the agreement in disregard of the prince's opinion.[116] The treaty, which simply reëstablished peace between Serbia and Bulgaria, was signed at Bucharest on March 3, 1886. The new

[114] *G.F.O.*, iv, p. 246. February, Bismarck to Reuss.
[115] *P.P.*, 1886, lxxv, Turkey no. 2, p. 91. February 10, 1886, Scott to Rosebery.
[116] *Ibid.*, p. 176. March 16, Malet to Rosebery.

arrangement by which the governor-generalship of Eastern Rumelia was intrusted to the prince of Bulgaria was adopted by the reassembled conference of Constantinople on April 5.

The Balkan troubles seemed to be over. Bulgaria was united without disturbance of the other arrangements of the treaty of Berlin. Only the bitterly disappointed Greeks showed themselves refractory about following the advice of the Powers to disarm and accept the situation. Bismarck, with his characteristic indifference to the claims of Balkan nations, advised that they be left simply to take the consequences of any possible rash action, but was finally induced to join in the naval demonstration and threat of blockade which helped bring them to terms.[117]

So peace had been patched up all round. But it was not a peace to be proud of. The situation was more unstable than it had been before the revolt of Philippopolis occurred; and the League of the Three Emperors was correspondingly less secure. Russia could not accept as final a Bulgarian union under Alexander of Battenberg. The Tsar coldly rebuffed his attempt at a reconciliation, in December, in spite of Bismarck's favorable attitude toward such a solution of the problem.[118] The Russian government burned with mortification at its defeat and would not rest until the objectionable prince were got out of the way. Any movement against him could count upon Russian support. But now that the union had been wrought for good or ill, the Powers composing the opposition to Russia's Balkan policy had become doubly apprehensive about Russian influence in Bulgaria. Having administered a setback to it, they had more ground to defend than before, and had become more nervous about defending it. Another crisis was bound to come sooner or later, and it was certain to be more serious than the one just passed.

[117] *Preussische Jahrbücher*, March, 1886, p. 306.

[118] Corti, pp. 238–239. J. F. Baddeley, *Russia in the 'Eighties'* (London, 1921), pp. 267, 270. In two interviews, on December 29, on the subject of this attempt, Count Peter Shuvalov told Baddeley: "Bismarck, with whom he had two long interviews, had even made him proposals based on this supposition;" and "Germany thinks that Prince Alexander acted in a way to forfeit the confidence of Europe but that his subsequent conduct and successes have so strengthened his position in Bulgaria itself that it will be difficult now to get rid of him."

## CHAPTER III

### THE ABDICATION OF PRINCE ALEXANDER

#### I

DURING the early months of the year 1886, in spite of the perils beneath the surface, Germany's relations with Russia seemed to afford no occasion of alarm. The fag-ends of the Balkan crisis were getting tied up one after another; and Russia's essential dissatisfaction with the way matters stood did not visibly affect the situation. The League of the Three Emperors was still intact, having weathered the storm in apparently sound condition. Bismarck did not perceive that all the timbers of his craft had been sprung because it had been left to ride out the gale, instead of being steered into a safe harbor. The next blow would set it leaking at every seam.

The German Chancellor was occupied during these months with matters chiefly of internal significance, but connected in various ways with foreign affairs. One important preoccupation was with the delicate task of arranging his journey to Canossa, assuring himself of as favorable and profitable a reception as possible at the end of his pilgrimage. Papal mediation in the dispute with Spain over the Caroline Islands, the revision of the ' May Laws,' the opening up of new sources of imperial revenue, the renewal of the anti-Socialist laws — all these figured in the complicated intrigue of reconciliation with the Pope and readjustment of the party situation within Germany. Bismarck was also engaged, since the preceding year, in developing a programme of anti-Polish measures in the eastern provinces of Prussia. These measures of internal policy had various implications in the international field, among them an intention on Bismarck's part to strengthen the bonds of the League of the Three Emperors.[1]

[1] Immediately after the speech of December 1 in the Reichstag on this question, Bismarck went to confer with the Russian and Austrian ambassadors. *Regesten*, ii,

Oppression of the Poles was one of Prussia's traditional methods of currying favor with Russia.[2]

On this occasion, it appears that Bismarck overshot his mark, when he carried his campaign to the length of expelling alien Poles and Jews to make room for German colonists. Although the injured persons were of races hated by many Russians, they were, nevertheless, Russian subjects, attacks upon whom must be resented by their government.[3] The resentment did not take the form of intervention in their behalf; but it undoubtedly played its part in influencing the Tsar to issue his ukaz of the following year, directed against German landholding in Russia's western provinces — an act to which Germans still later pointed as a reason for economic measures against Russia. Thus the League of the Three Emperors was weakened in another place. Hitherto, the relations between Russia and Austria had been chiefly damaged: now the seed had been sown of a conflict between Russia and Germany. For the moment that conflict developed no further. Bismarck still looked upon the Russian alliance as his guarantee against a rapprochement between Russia and France.

So far as relations between these last two countries were concerned, matters took a turn most favorable to Bismarck's policies. At the close of the preceding year, the two had shown a tendency to draw closer together than was comfortable for Germany. France's conciliatory conduct throughout the Bulgarian crisis was taken by the Russian government as a mark of friendship, of which it expressed a sincere appreciation.[4] But these promising

p. 383. Cf. Lucius von Ballhausen, pp. 343–344 (April 5, 1886): "Welche grosse Eile eigentlich Bismarck bewegt, den Frieden mit Rom *à tout prix* herbeizuführen, versteht man ebensowenig, wie die heftige Aufnahme der Polenfrage, welche doch in keiner mehr akuten Lage war wie seit Jahren. Ob er grosse europäische Katastrophen drohen sieht? Man muss es fast glauben, denn ohne Grund handelt er schwerlich so. Andere freilich bezweifeln die Planmässigkeit seines Handelns."

[2] See Delbrück, *Bismarcks Erbe* (Berlin, 1915), pp. 151–153.

[3] Вѣстникъ Европы, February, 1886, p. 917. Lucius von Ballhausen, p. 354 (October 17, 1886): "Schweinitz ist der Meinung, dass unsere Ausweisungen russischer Untertanen in Russland viel böses Blut gemacht haben und sicher zu ähnlichen Massregeln gegen die Deutschen später führen werden."

[4] Charles de Freycinet, *Souvenirs* (Paris, 1913), p. 307. A letter written to Freycinet by the Russian ambassador, Baron Mohrenheim, on December 25, 1885, quotes from a despatch from Giers, just received, a passage thanking France for her

prospects were speedily ruined by the French themselves. The pardon of Prince Kropotkin appeared to the Tsar not only as an affront to himself, but as a fresh demonstration of incurable radical sympathies on the part of the French government. The republic was clearly no fit associate for the Russian autocracy. The coolness between the two governments had increased to such a point by March that, when France proposed, in a fashion which gave rise to misunderstandings, to change her ambassador at St. Petersburg, the Tsar declared that no ambassador at all was necessary, and ordered his own representative at Paris to go upon a long vacation.[5] He did not conceal his contempt for the *fichu gouvernement* by the Seine.[6] The campaign for improving Franco-Russian relations begun in April by the brilliant journalist, Katkov, in his *Moscow Gazette*, seemed born under the most unfavorable auspices. It constituted a disquieting element in the situation, but seemed to make little headway against the trend of feeling at court.

So confident was Bismarck of the reliability of the Russian guarantee, that he proceeded to complete the breach with France which had been developing ever since Ferry's fall. Relations with the government of Brisson, his successor, had continued tolerable, although lacking in cordiality. The Chancellor had become more and more doubtful of the results of his policy of reconciliation, concerning which he now spoke with naïve disappointment. In a despatch of September 21, 1885, to Prince Hohenlohe, ambassador at Paris, he commented bitterly on the wave of anti-German attitude in the Bulgarian question, and concluding: "Nous sommes charmés de cette conformité de vues entre nous et le gouvernement français, et nous aimons à espérer que nous continuerons à marcher d'accord."

[5] Ernest Daudet, *Histoire diplomatique de l'alliance franco-russe* (Paris, 1898), p. 186. Alfred Rambaud, *Jules Ferry* (Paris, 1903), p. 402 (May 1, 1886, Ferry to Billot): "Le rappel inutile, maladroit, injustifiable du général Appert a profondément blessé la cour de Russie. Jointe à la grâce de Krapotkine, cette sotte mesure nous a pour longtemps fermé de ce côté tout moyen d'action. A la présentation du nom de B., le czar a mis de sa main, l'annotation suivante: 'Ni B., ni personne.' Et il a ajouté qu'il n'avait pas besoin d'ambassadeur; qu'un simple chargé d'affaires suffirait pour un pays 'qui va droit à la Commune.'" See also *G. F. O.*, vi, p. 97.

[6] Prince N. N. Golitsyn, "Lettre au 'Figaro' sur les théories de Katkow," republished by *Edinburgh Review*, January, 1888, p. 153 See also *G. F. O.*, vi, p. 99. According to Schweinitz, the phrase was *ignoble gouvernement et canailles*.

feeling which had swept over France at the time of his dispute with Spain. He complained: "Fifteen years of friendly advances in all fields of policy, with the *single* exception of Alsace, could not suffice to bring about any change or moderation in this feeling."[7] The transfer of Prince Hohenlohe from the embassy at Paris to the post of governor of Alsace-Lorraine marked the inauguration of a new regime of severity in the Reichsland, based upon distrust of French policy.[8] Then in the French elections of October, the majority became so divided over the question of retaining Ferry's colonies that the Conservative groups were enabled to make large gains. The Radicals' propaganda against the Ferry policies and the Conservatives' tendency toward an Orleanist reaction were equally disturbing to Bismarck.[9] To the French ambassador he bitterly denounced the general revival of the spirit of revenge.[10] On November 28, he expressed his feelings publicly in the Reichstag, telling Germany and the world: "We have so far had the good fortune to live in peace and good relations with the government of France. But we cannot say the same of the French political parties; and recent occurrences . . . have shown, to our regret, that in all parties the leading organs regard demonstrations of hostility to Germany, and of a determination to take revenge when the moment arrives, as the best arguments for influencing public opinion in the elections."[11]

[7] *G. F. O.*, iii, p. 452. See also Lucius von Ballhausen, p. 319.

[8] Pagès (Senate Report), p. 216. On September 30, 1885, in taking leave of Freycinet, Hohenlohe remarked: "Je pars pour Strasbourg avec appréhension, car je sens bien qu'on se fait en Allemagne des idées qui vont me gêner beaucoup. J'aurais voulu gouverner tranquillement et avec douceur. Mais l'on me poussera aux mesures énergiques, parce qu'on croit que la population est devenue plus difficile, plus hostile. On redoute les excitations qu'elle reçoit de ce côté, où il y a une recrudescence des idées de revanche."

[9] *B. M. M.*, p. 258. "Nur kein Orleans," he exclaimed, "solange er nicht unabwendlich von selbst kommt. Dass die Republik zur Anarchie führt, muss nicht verdunkelt werden."

[10] Daudet, *Courcel*, pp. 193–195. "Aucun de vos partis dans ses programmes électoraux n'a osé désavouer le principe de vos revendications et se déclarer partisan d'une acceptation finale des faits accomplis. J'en dois conclure qu'il existe une pensée commune à la nation entière. . . . Je ne peux avoir la sécurité que la France ne cherchera pas à profiter de la première secousse qui se produira en Europe . . . pour nous attaquer et compromettre l'oeuvre du traité de Francfort."

[11] *Reden*, xi, p. 263.

The new year brought with it a new government in France, where the Brisson ministry had been tottering since the elections of October. Its overthrow, by a moral defeat on the question of holding Tonkin, signified a more decided reaction than ever against all that Ferry had stood for.[12] A timely rally of some fragments of the old majority, however, checked this reaction, enabling Freycinet's government of 'republican concentration' to take over the reins of power. No abrupt change in foreign policy then occurred, although the new government roundly asserted its acceptance of the country's pronouncement against recent tendencies.[13] Bismarck's commentary was: "In colonial matters we must not take too much in hand at a time, and we already have enough for a beginning. We must now hold rather with the English, while, as you know, we were formerly more on the French side. But, as the last elections in France show, every one of any importance there had to make a show of hostility to us." [14]

Although there was still no real cause for quarrel between Germany and France, the press of both countries had gradually reassumed its old acrid tone of mutual recrimination and picking of controversies. At first the Orleanists were the chief target for abuse from the German side.[15] When these princes overreached

[12] The issues were strongly brought out in the debate of December 24, 1885, in the Chamber of Deputies. To Spuller's "En France l'honneur n'a jamais été un mot," Clemenceau rejoined: "M. Spuller, je vais vous répondre. Votre honneur s'est trouvé blessé quand, dans cette Chambre, des hommes ont demandé d'évacuer Tonkin: voulez-vous me dire ce que vous avez ressenti, et si votre honneur n'a pas tressailli quand vous avez lu une dépêche signée ' Jules Ferry,' dans laquelle, le jour même où nous avons appris l'échec de Lang-Son, le cabinet français implorait ' le précieux concours ' de M. le prince de Bismarck?" Wild demonstrations against Ferry followed the reading of the telegram in question from the Yellow Book. *Journal officiel*, December 25. The government resigned after a proposal to evacuate Tonkin had been defeated by only four votes.

[13] *Journal Officiel*, January 16, 1886. Ministerial declaration to the Chamber: "S'il est un point sur lequel le suffrage universel se soit exprimé sans équivoque c'est sur la direction à donner à nos affaires extérieures. Il attend que la France ait une politique digne et pacifique, et qu'elle concentre ses forces sur le continent. . . . Il ne veut plus de ces expéditions lointaines. . . ."

[14] Busch, iii, p. 154 (Amer., ii, p. 398; *Tagebuchblätter*, iii, p. 204).

[15] *M. A. Z.*, March 24, 1886. Berlin, March 22. "Die offiziöse und inspirirte Presse ist in jüngster Zeit mit besonderem Eifer bemüht, alle Anzeichen unversöhnlicher und kriegerischer Stimmung französischer Parteiführer oder doch franzö-

themselves with their Portuguese marriage and were stricken by the republic's decree of expulsion, only the German newspapers in all Europe refrained from attacking the measure. One grievance was gone; but meanwhile German public opinion had fixed upon a new incarnation of the ' French peril.' This was General Boulanger, minister of war in Freycinet's cabinet—a personality at first unknown, except as a self-advertising though amenable subordinate, but very soon to mount the wave of his ill-starred popularity. Bismarck himself took a leading part in building up the legend of his mysterious power, his sinister designs, and his formidableness to Germany. Without any particular reason, unless that of finding a bogy with which to menace public opinion, he dragged the French minister of war into the conclusion of his speech on the brandy monopoly, on March 26. The spectre he called up was that of a France rushing to war under the red flag of Socialism; and he introduced Boulanger into this picture by seizing upon certain expressions of which that general had made use in defending the conduct of the French army toward the strikers at Decazeville. "Today," Bismarck told the Reichstag, "the French army stands facing the labor unrest in Decazeville. We do not know whether to lay more emphasis upon the fact that it is holding that unrest in check or upon the ministerial declaration that the soldier of today is the worker of yesterday, and the worker of today, the soldier of yesterday. We do not know who will finally emerge victor in these troubles in France." [16] The allusion was unmistakable, and was widely commented upon. It was the beginning of that element in Boulanger's popularity which arose from the belief that, since he was the man who was hated and feared by Bismarck, he was therefore the man for France.

sischer Pressorgane gegen Deutschland zu sammeln und die deutsche Leserwelt auf dieselben aufmerksam zu machen. Namentlich wird auf deutschfeindliche und kriegsdrohende Absichten der Orleans hingewiesen. . . ."

[16] *Reden*, xi, p. 365. The passage from Boulanger's speech referred to runs: "Est-ce que nos ouvriers, soldats d'hier, auraient à redouter quelque chose de nos soldats d'aujourd'hui, ouvriers de demain? . . . peut-être à l'heure où je parle, chaque soldat partage-t-il avec un mineur sa soupe et sa ration de pain." *Journal officiel*, March, 1886, p. 441. Chambre, March 13. Interpellation on Decazeville strike.

Bismarck, for his own part, was often glad of a foreign danger to hold over the heads of the Opposition at home, and did not scruple to foster this development of French chauvinism, which had the further merit of discrediting France in the eyes of Russia. The campaign was taken up by the German press, and was materially aided by the publication in France of an optimistic review of French military prospects, entitled *Avant la bataille*, and by the energetic programme of army reform into which the new minister of war had at once plunged.[17] And the attacks continued, despite the remonstrances of the French government and the opinion of the German ambassador at Paris that France's assurances of peaceful intentions were well meant and serious.[18] The *schwarze Punkt* on the political horizon, of which the Chancellor spoke at

[17] The *Norddeutsche Allgemeine Zeitung*, on April 19, reprinted a Berlin letter from *Politische Correspondenz*, of Vienna, listing the causes for alarm at developments in France as follows: "das vor kurzem in Paris erschienene Buch ' Avant la bataille,' das auf Grund officieller Mittheilungen veröffentlicht worden sein soll; die Thatsache, dass die Regierung gewissermassen eine Prämie auf den Chauvinismus gesetzt hat, indem sie hervorragende Mitglieder der Patriotenliga, Männer wie Paul Bert und den Abgeordneten Thiessen, mit guten Stellungen bedacht hat; gewisse Aeusserungen des Kriegsministers General Boulanger und anderer hoher Offiziere, welche die Runde durch die französische und durch die ausländische Presse gemacht haben; zahlreiche Anzeichen endlich dafür, dass alle Parteien in Frankreich, von der äussersten conservativen bis zur extrem radicalen, in einem Gefühle, dem des Hasses gegen Deutschland, innig verbunden sind." Also, *M. A. Z.*, July 8 (Berlin, July 5). "In officiösen Kundgebungen ist in den letzten Monaten wiederholt darauf hingewiesen worden, dass Deutschland durch den Gang der französischen Politik in hohem Grade verstimmt sei. Namentlich dem neuen Armee-Organisationsplan des Generals Boulanger wurde in dieser Hinsicht eine besondere Bedeutung beigelegt und angedeutet, dass, falls derselbe zur Ausführung gelangen sollte, Deutschland gezwungen sein würde, auch seinerseits eine weitere Verstärkung der Armee eintreten zu lassen. Die dem französischen Kriegsminister ergebene Presse hat sich dieser Kundgebungen bemächtigt, um für die Ideen des Generals Propaganda zu machen."

[18] Pagès (Senate Report), p. 223. March 26, 1886, Courcel to Freycinet. Courcel warned Herbert Bismarck that the language of the German press was creating "une méfiance vague qui peut devenir dangereuse un jour." Count Herbert only replied that the dangers being pointed out were real. Cf. Lucius von Ballhausen, pp. 346–347 (April 22, 1886): "Graf Münster besuchte mich und äusserte sich sehr beruhigend über die Lage in Frankreich. Man fürchte sich da sehr vor uns, und Freycinet habe ihm wiederholt versichert, solange er im Amt sei, wäre an Krieg nicht zu denken. . . . Hier müsse man natürlich stets bereit sein, aber den Krieg nicht provoziren. Die Franzosen täten es sicher nicht."

the beginning of 1886, had, by the middle of the year, become an appreciable shadow.[19]

He saw in its growth no cause for serious anxiety. Germany's position appeared secure. France was still isolated and satisfactorily at odds with both England and Russia. These two, in their turn, had fallen out with each other anew. The question of Afghanistan was in abeyance; but Russia provoked England to great irritation, in July, by her closure of Batum, which she had declared at the congress of Berlin she intended to keep a free port. No one could prevent her from changing her mind on the subject, especially since the treaty of Berlin had been tampered with in far more serious respects. Certainly Bismarck had no thought of disputing her right to do so; for the English rivalry was one of his holds upon Russia. This incident served to keep the ill humor between the two countries from dying away.[20]

Bismarck was very far, at this time, from seeking an English alliance in place of his Russian one. Thoughts on England's supposed responsibility for the Bulgarian troubles still occupied his mind.[21] The return of Gladstone to power during the first half of the year had revived his personal animosity and his desire to thwart British policy wherever he could do so through others. Any satisfaction he may have felt at Salisbury's recovery of office in June was tempered by the new demonstration of the insecurity of British governments in general. He was willing enough to keep direct relations between England and Germany on an amicable footing. He even concluded, in the summer of 1886, three new

[19] Newton, *Lord Lyons* (London, 1913, 2 vols.), ii, p. 369. July 13, 1886, Lyons to Rosebery. "Certainly it comes round to one in various ways from Germany that war is very generally expected, or at all events talked of there. The accounts current in Germany of supposed French provocations look as if there was a party there trying to work up hostile feeling against France. An alliance between France and Russia seems to be the bugbear. I don't see symptoms at present of any war spirit in this country."

[20] A very brief *Blue Book* was issued on the subject in 1886. England had evidently little ground or desire for making a real diplomatic incident.

[21] Lucius von Ballhausen, p. 340. March 22, 1886. "Se. Majestät: Es sehe im Osten wieder bedenklich aus, der neue Konflikt mit dem Sultan und dem Fürsten von Bulgarien sei bedenklich. . . . Bismarck meinte, er könne nicht glauben, dass die Königin Viktoria so mutig sei, den Konflikt aus Familieninteresse zu schüren. Se. Majestät meinte: Das glaube er doch!"

colonial agreements, affecting Zanzibar, Southwest Africa, and the Guinea Coast.[22] All this was in accordance with his intention, expressed to Busch, of holding in colonial matters rather with the English than with the French. But the League of the Three Emperors still overshadowed European politics to the extent of excluding any general combination with England.

An opportunity to bring about such a combination — in the very form favored by Bismarck of an Anglo-Austrian accord — was afforded by Lord Salisbury, who remarked to the German ambassador, on August 13, that England was too weak in military power to keep the peace in the Near East alone, and would welcome an understanding with Austria for the purpose.[23] But Bismarck believed at the moment that the Eastern Question could be taken care of by other means, and feared that Austria might be made a catspaw. He confined himself to advising Salisbury that if Great Britain needed troops to maintain her interests in the Near East, she should subsidize the Turkish army.[24]

Bismarck's assurance that peace would be kept in the Near East without England's help was not due to any lack of causes of trouble there. The Bulgarian question obstinately refused to stay quiet. Apparently settled in the spring, by midsummer it was once more set stirring through the overzealous activity of Prince Alexander. Once given his inch of legal standing in Eastern Rumelia, the prince proceeded to take his full ell of liberty in disregarding the limitations of the treaty of Berlin. Deputies from the newly acquired province were called to the Great Assembly of the principality; and the factitious separation of the two territories was in every way treated as nonexistent. The Powers looked upon these developments with concern, since they tended to disturb the delicate balance between the treaty terms and the *fait accompli* of September.[25] Russia, although

[22] Edward Hertslet, *The Map of Africa by Treaty* (London, 1909, 3d ed., 3 vols. and maps), iii, pp. 874–881.
[23] *G. F. O.*, iv, p. 266. August 13, Hatzfeldt to Bismarck.
[24] *Ibid.*, iv, p. 268. August 20, Berchem to Hatzfeldt.
[25] See p. 138 of *Revanche-Idee und Panslawismus* (1919), edited by Wilhelm Köhler (vol. v of the series *Zur europäischen Politik*, edited by Bernhard Schwertfeger). July 4, 1886, despatch of Count Errembault de Dudzeele, Belgian minister

especially disgusted at them, took no overt action. The goal of her policy was now the upsetting of Prince Alexander from his throne.[26] The Russian government was even giving signs that, in the future conduct of its Balkan policy, it would not pay overmuch attention to the League of the Three Emperors, which had proved of so little value in the foregoing year.[27]

The problem of keeping Russia in line was one of the most serious which confronted the leading statesmen of the two Central Empires in their summer conferences of July 22–24, at Kissingen, and August 9–10, at Gastein. Despite the controversies of the previous year, and Bismarck's sharp criticisms of Kálnoky, the Austro-German alliance remained firm, as the backbone not only of the League of the Three Emperors, but of Bismarck's whole international system. These yearly interviews demonstrated its solidity and helped fix its attitude toward pending questions and toward the outlying combinations. One question debated at this particular period, as it had been since the formation of the alliance, was apparently that of rendering it more intimate by a customs and military union — a proposition never acceptable to Austria.[28]

But foreign affairs formed, after all, the chief topics of discussion at these interviews. The ties with Russia were being loos-

at St. Petersburg. "La séparation définitive de la Roumélie Orientale de l'Empire Ottoman serait un commencement d'exécution de ce démembrement; c'est pourquoi l'on s'efforce de retenir le Prince Alexandre d'une démarche qui ôterait à cette province son apparence de vasselage. Au fond, nul ne tient à l'integrité de la Turquie, mais chacun veut la garantir par précaution contre le voisin, et la Russie en particulier parce qu'elle s'aperçoit que toute dépouille arrachée à cet Empire n'ayant jusqu'à présent profité qu'à ses rivales, le plus sage est de conjurer le partage de la Turquie jusqu'au moment propice pour le faire tourner à l'avantage de la Russie . . . En conséquence de ce qui précède, il faut s'attendre à voir les cabinets de St. Pétersbourg, de Vienne et de Berlin agir avec assez d'ensemble pour imposer le maintien du *status quo* à la Porte et au Gouvernement bulgare."

[26] Кнгаревъ, ii, p. 267.

[27] *Zur europäischen Politik*, v, p. 145. August 7, 1886, Count de Jonghe d'Ardoye wrote from Vienna: "Depuis les événements de Bulgarie la Russie tout en ne cherchant pas à reprendre ouvertement encore sa position prépondérante à Sofia, trouve que la triple alliance paralyse sa politique dans la presqu'île des Balkans, et sans s'en détacher, déjà témoigne qu'elle n'est pas disposée à laisser porter atteinte sérieusement à sa politique traditionnelle en Orient."

[28] *Ibid.*, pp. 162–163. December 27, 1886, Jonghe's despatch.

ened. That fact probably did not worry Kálnoky unduly; but to Bismarck it was of grave importance. An agreement was, therefore, reached to assure the maintenance of the League of the Three Emperors by offering no opposition to Russia's design of eliminating Prince Alexander.[29] Beyond his disappearance, the future could not be determined.

Another troublesome problem which presented itself concerned the renewal of that other auxiliary combination, the Triple Alliance, due to expire in the following spring. Since 1883 it had been regarded as undependable by both Central Powers.[30] It had shown itself so in the recent crisis. Yet neither minister was willing to let it lapse; and a decision was arrived at in their interviews that the existing relations should be maintained unaltered.[31] This was, unfortunately, not going far enough to meet the case; for a statesman was now at the head of Italian affairs with a policy designed to place his country in an international position far different from that of 1882.

Ever since the advent to power of Count Robilant, in October, 1885, it had been a foregone conclusion that Italy was not to be kept in the Triple Alliance without the extension of some further advantages to her interests. Robilant's private secretary has

[29] *Zur europäischen Politik*, v, p. 146. August 23, 1886, Jonghe: "C'est alors qu'en présence des dangers que présenterait la rupture de l'alliance, ont eu lieu les entrevues de Kissingen et de Gastein. Après un mûr examen de la situation l'on a reconnu que mieux valait laisser reprendre à la Russie son rôle dominant en Bulgarie que d'exposer l'Europe aux dangers d'une nouvelle conflagration en Orient. Ce serait ainsi à Gastein que le Prince Alexandre aurait été sacrifié au maintien de la paix." Later in the year, Karavelov, who resigned from the Bulgarian Council of Regency, alleged publicly, in a Tyrnovo newspaper, that such an agreement had been reached, giving as its immediate occasion the discovery by the Imperial governments of an intrigue between Alexander and the Rumanians for support to an insurrection in Macedonia in return for the cession to Rumania of the Rushchuk-Varna frontier strip. *Times*, November 29 (Vienna, November 26). Corti (p. 258) states that Alexander did visit Rumania in June for the purpose of negotiating a rapprochement. On November 27, Szögyény answered an interpellation in the Hungarian Delegation on Karavelov's story by denying all the allegations involving the Austro-Hungarian government. *N. F. P.*, November 28.

[30] Pribram, "Zwei Gespräche des Fürsten Bismarck mit dem Kronprinzen Rudolf von Oesterreich," in *Oesterreichische Rundschau*, January, 1921, pp. 16–17. Conversation of March 1, 1883.

[31] Pribram, *Geheimverträge*, i, p. 173 (American ed., ii, pp. 47–48).

written that, at the outset, he declared the scope of the alliance must be enlarged: "The Triple Alliance does not guarantee us on the sea: there is need of establishing intimate bonds of friendship with England, which will be useful, not to us alone, but also to our two allies." In order to obtain the satisfaction of her desires, he believed, Italy must avoid displaying the eagerness with which she had rushed into so unproductive a treaty. She must remain aloof and pursue vigorously her own interests. Then, "after a year of this policy, the renewal of the alliance will be sought of us; and without effort we shall obtain what today would never be conceded." [32]

Events in their later courses had played into Robilant's hands. The cooling of relations between Germany and France, together with the rise of the Bulgarian crisis, brought home to both Bismarck and Kálnoky the importance of the Italian connection. From the first, the Chancellor held out hope to the Italian ambassador, Launay, that the treaty would be made more advantageous and that relations with England would be improved.[33] Robilant received these overtures coolly, leaving to Germany the initiative in carrying them further.[34] One of Robilant's first proceedings after his assumption of office had been, accordingly, to communicate to Kálnoky his complaint that the alliance in its existing form did not give sufficient support to Italy's interests.[35]

There followed Italy's declaration of independence as to her action in the Serbo-Bulgarian war, which uncovered hitherto unconsidered interests in the Eastern Question. The speedy clearing up of this crisis left Italy's declaration without immediate effect; but a new issue had been raised upon which satisfaction must ulti-

[32] Raffaele Cappelli, "La politica estera del conte di Robilant," in *Nuova Antologia*, November 1, 1894, p. 6.

[33] Francesco Crispi, *Politica estera* (Milan, 1912), pp. 129–130 (*Memoirs*, ii, p. 161). The latter phrase refers to the only bit of substantial evidence we have on this important aspect of the negotiation before the account of Bismarck's conversation with Malet on February 1, 1887. It is significant that Robilant should have felt an organic connection to exist between the Triple Alliance and the desired rapprochement with England, and that he should have called upon Germany to intercede for him with the British government.

[34] Chiala, p. 466.

[35] *G. F. O.*, iv, p. 181. October 10, 1885, Reuss to Bismarck.

mately be given. No steps were taken toward doing so, once the first Bulgarian crisis was out of the way. Indeed, negotiations looking toward a renewal of the Triple Alliance lagged generally. Robilant showed no haste to press them. He declined the initiative, displayed indifference, and even intimated a possibility that he would let the alliance drop.[36] Bismarck, on the other hand, showed no inclination to make the display of eagerness which the Italian government seemed to require. He refused to assume the appearance of bringing pressure upon Vienna, and told Launay that "Germany was only secondarily interested in the prolongation of the treaty."[37]

The coolness of the Italian government toward Austria and Germany was accompanied by a cultivation of good relations with France, apparently in pursuance of the design to live on good terms with all its neighbors. Robilant took up the matter of a treaty of navigation between the two countries, in suspense since 1881, and pushed it to a conclusion in the treaty of April 30, 1886, which was quickly approved by the Italian Parliament. To his discomfiture, the treaty was rejected by the French Chamber on July 13. The attempt at a rapprochement ceased abruptly with a decree submitting French vessels in Italian ports to the general port dues; and relations went henceforth from bad to worse.

The Italian statesman, nevertheless, kept out of the series of little interviews which Bismarck arranged with his colleagues of allied states during the summer of 1886. The hints dropped to him from Berlin and Vienna, after the encounters of July and August, to the effect that the two Empires desired a simple renewal of the existing agreement, were met by a firm statement that the treaty could never be renewed *tel quel*, and by suggested modifications which were found rather stiff in both capitals.[38]

[36] Chiala, p. 471. In June, 1886, replying to Launay's suggestion of a little visit to Gastein, Robilant wrote: "Le prince de Bismarck a fait de belles phrases sur mon compte quand je suis venu au ministère, mais en dehors de cela il n'a pas remué le petit doigt pour accentuer un rapprochement plus pratique vers l'Italie. . . . Décidément l'Italie est fatiguée de cette alliance inféconde et je ne me sens pas l'envie de la forcer à la renouveler . . . Si le chancelier désire lui entâmer des négociations dans ce sens, il n'a qu'à prendre lui l'initiative, et à nous faire connaître ses pensées."

[37] Pribram, i, p. 173 (American ed., ii, p. 47).     [38] Chiala, pp. 474-475.

Even more significant than Robilant's absence from the ministerial colloquies of that summer was the fact that no interview took place between Bismarck and Giers, although the latter was no further away than Franzensbad, and although he had been seeing the German Chancellor at least once a year ever since 1882. Their failure to meet at this opportunity may be partly ascribed to the effects of the great blow in Katkov's campaign struck by the leading article of the *Moscow Gazette* on July 31. This article inveighed bitterly against Russia's submissiveness to German dictation in an alliance which had never worked otherwise than to her own disadvantage. It compared the annual visits of Giers to Bismarck with the mediaeval pilgrimages of the Muscovite princes to the Golden Horde, and urged a policy of freer relations with other countries whose interests might lie closer to those of Russia — particularly with France.[39] Although it brought about no revolution in Russian policy, the general effect of the article was a little that of a bombshell; and the Russian minister may well have waited for the smoke of it to blow away before proceeding in his old paths. The semiofficial German and Russian press hastened to inform the European public that the failure of his visit had no connection with this article or with any change of policy on the part of the Russian government, and that, at any rate, the meeting was only delayed.[40]

[39] Élie de Cyon, *Histoire de l'entente franco-russe* (2d ed., Lausanne, 1895), pp. 153–154. The article is also reprinted in full in the *Nouvelle Revue* of August 15, 1886.

[40] *M. A. Z.*, August 7, 1886. Berlin, August 5. "Eine Aenderung in den Beziehungen der drei Kaisermächte zu einander wird von kundiger Seite entschieden in Abrede gestellt. Beweis hierfür ist die Kaiserbegegnung in Gastein und der Besuch des Erzherzogs Karl Ludwig von Oesterreich in Peterhof. Der Aufschub der Reise des Hrn. v. Giers ist durch Familienangelegenheiten veranlasst worden. Hr. v. Giers wird sicherlich mit dem Fürsten Bismarck im Laufe der nächsten Wochen zu sprechen Gelegenheit nehmen, und sollte es nicht dazu kommen, so braucht man desshalb nicht an politische Gründe zu glauben." Brussels *Nord*, August 7, 1886. "M. de Giers vient de quitter Pétersbourg pour se rendre à Franzensbad, où il va pour se soigner sérieusement et non pour s'occuper de politique. Vraisemblablement, il verra M. de Bismarck. . . . Mais si cette entrevue n'a pas lieu, cela ne troublera pas la paix européenne, et ne nuira pas aux bons rapports entre les trois empires."

## II

The deferred interview between Bismarck and Giers took place in an atmosphere troubled by a new Bulgarian crisis. During the night of August 20–21, Prince Alexander of Bulgaria was set upon by a group of officers, forced to sign a paper which they intended as an abdication, and carried off in a carriage to Rakhova on the Danube. He was at once shipped away in his own yacht to Reni on Russian soil, and thence, under Russian guard to assure his safety, over the Austrian border to Lemberg, which he reached on the 27th. The conspiracy was of purely domestic origin, arising out of various causes of dissatisfaction among the Bulgarian army officers.[41] It was doubtless encouraged by Russian officials, but cannot be called a plot of the Russian government, favorably as the news was received in official circles. The report of the event was as unexpected and as unwelcome to Europe as had been the news of the revolution of Philippopolis less than a year before. The Eastern Question was reopened; and there was grave danger that all the labor of reconciling conflicting interests would have to be gone through with again.

This time Bismarck grasped the situation at once and personally took it in hand — all the while proclaiming loudly his complete lack of interest in the matter.[42] One of his first steps was to pay his promised visit to Giers at Franzensbad, where the two were closeted together for a good part of the two days of August 26 and 27. The substance of the conclusions at which they arrived is not difficult to divine.[43] It was obvious that the

[41] С. Горяиновъ, "Разрывъ Россіи съ Болгаріей въ 1886 году," in Историческій Вѣстникъ, January, 1917. Corti, pp. 260–262.

[42] *P. P.*, 1887, xci, Turkey no. 1, p. 110. August 28, 1886, Malet to Iddesleigh. Berchem told Malet that Bismarck continued to say, "that Germany is not primarily interested in the events passing in Bulgaria, that its efforts will be reserved for the preservation of peace, which does not appear to be in danger at present."

[43] The statement given out by Giers on August 30 is not particularly enlightening as to what took place. He told a correspondent: "In der Entrevue, wobei Bismarck Österreichs Interesse nicht minder warm als dasjenige Deutschlands vertreten hätte, sei der Grundsatz des Zusammengehens der Ostmächte erneut befestigt worden. Wenn Bulgarien ruhig bleibe, seien ernstere Krisen zunächst nicht zu besorgen. Russland denke im Falle der Erhaltung der Ordnung nicht an die Okkupation. . . . Die Hauptschuld an den Ereignissen habe weniger Fürst Alexander als

time had come to get rid of the prince of Battenberg, whom Bismarck had called, a few months before, "the main hindrance in the way of a satisfactory settlement of the Bulgarian question." [44] An understanding had just been reached with Kálnoky on the subject.[45] Yet it was also clear that the means by which this end had been attained would not do. The act of violence must be recalled and an orderly form of abdication contrived. Events had taken a turn which rendered such action possible; for the loyalists had speedily regained the upper hand in Bulgaria and were urging the prince to return. This return was to be facilitated, and the further disposition of the affair placed in the hands of the Tsar.

The return journey of Prince Alexander from Lemberg to Rushchuk was, accordingly, an unclouded triumph; and among the foremost figures at his reception on Bulgarian soil was the Russian consul. The omen seemed favorable. The prince and the consul were soon deep in a lengthy interview as to what should be done next. The consul held out hope that the future attitude of his government would be unprejudiced and encouraged the prince in the idea of placing his fate in the hands of the Tsar.[46] The result of this interview was the well known telegram of Prince Alexander to Tsar Alexander, placing his crown at the disposal of the sovereign of the country to which he owed it. As this step had been planned in advance, the Russian government was prepared

England, welches ihn benützte. Giers bestritt, dass Bismarck dem Fürsten die Rückkehr angeraten haben könnte. Vorläufig sei die Hoffnung auf Erhaltung des Friedens berechtigt." *Geschichtskalender*, 1886, p. 392.

[44] Busch, iii, p. 149 (Amer., ii, p. 394; *Tagebuchblätter*, iii, p. 200).

[45] Edwards, pp. 242–243. August 27, 1886, Iddesleigh to White. "From my conversation with the German and Austrian representatives, I gather that they would rather prefer that the Prince should not come back again. ' If he does not return,' said Count Hatzfeldt, ' matters will be easily arranged; but if he does, there will be difficulties from the side of Russia.' "

[46] Corti, p. 273; Baddeley, p. 281. That the intrigue was the work of Giers, without the participation of the Tsar, is indicated by the anecdote of Baddeley (p. 283): "The Tsar was furious: ' How could a Russian Consul dare to go in uniform to meet the fellow? — scratch him off the list! scratch him off! scratch him off!' De Giers mildly ventured to remonstrate, pointing out that this petty *chinóvnik* had really done Russia a great service by putting Alexander in a position that left him no choice but to abdicate. With great difficulty the Emperor was at last brought to say: ' Well, he may stay on at Rustchuk.' "

with its reply. Vlangali and Jomini, the representatives of Giers at St. Petersburg, drew it up, but not in terms strong enough to meet the approval of the Tsar, who finally sent off a stinging answer of his own composition.[47] This answer had at least the merit of being quite unmistakable in meaning, and could only be followed by the prince's abdication. Any possible hesitation was cut short by his finding the Austrian and German consuls significantly on the side of the Russian in demanding that no executions of conspirators follow his return.[48] The abdication followed on September 3, the prince leaving the government in the hands of a council of regency composed of the three nationalist leaders, Stambulov, Mutkurov, and Karavelov.

There was no stopping the course of these events; and only England made any attempt at it. The Italian government simply announced that it would await the outcome of the conference between Bismarck and Giers, then quietly acquiesced in the resulting situation.[49] Kálnoky at first affected reticence and a favorable attitude toward the return of the prince, but, after the exchange of telegrams with the Tsar, declared no action was called for, especially "since it was also now evident that it would not be supported by Germany." [50]

[47] Hohenlohe, ii, p. 393 (Amer., ii, p. 350). See also Cyon, p. 158. To the prince's submissive statement—"La Russie m'ayant donné ma couronne . . . c'est entre les mains de son Souverain que je suis prêt à la remettre"—the Tsar replied: "Je ne puis approuver votre retour en Bulgarie. . . . Je m'abstiendrai de toute immixtion dans le triste état de choses auquel la Bulgarie a été reduite, tant que vous y resterez. Votre Altesse appréciera ce qu'elle a à faire." *P. P.*, 1887, xci, Turkey no. 1, p. 136.

[48] *Preussische Jahrbücher*, October, 1886, p. 405. *P. P.*, 1887, xci, Turkey no 1, p. 182. September 22, 1886, Scott (Berlin) to Iddesleigh. "Under present circumstances, a summary sentence or execution would undoubtedly provoke reprisals on the part of the opponents of the party now in power at Sophia; these reprisals might even be taken in other States of the Balkans, and European complications might ensue the consequences of which it would be impossible to foresee. This was the nature of the advice which Herr von Saldern had been instructed to give when the counter-revolution took place and Prince Alexander returned to the Principality." Also, Kálnoky, in the Hungarian Delegation, November 13. *M. A. Z.*, November 16, 1886. The German consul general had instructions to regard the prince's return as only a visit of a few days, and, accordingly, did not even trouble to call on him. Corti, p. 275.

[49] *P. P.*, 1887, xci, Turkey no. 1, pp. 103, 150. August 27, September 8, 1886, Lumley to Iddesleigh.

[50] *Ibid.*, pp. 107, 129. August 28, September 3, Paget to Iddesleigh.

The attitude of Bismarck was the determining factor in the whole situation. He consistently discouraged England's ardor. The British government, which had freely expressed its opinion in favor of the prince's return to Bulgaria, and had even urged the Porte to summon him back, finally proposed that the Powers extend to him a "frank and open support." [51] Bismarck simply replied that he could not advise England to proceed with the project, "feeling, as he does, certain that such an attempt would not succeed." He was further "of opinion that, though Prince Alexander was placed upon the throne of Bulgaria by the Great Powers, it is not incumbent upon them, either conjointly or separately, to maintain him there." [52] Shortly after the abdication, he announced "that it is now open to the Great Powers to take the Bulgarian question into consideration, Prince Alexander's abdication being taken as a point of departure, and the Chancellor would be willing to entertain a proposition with this object in view." [53]

In the face of this firm attitude of the German government no contrary action was possible, despite the obvious dissatisfaction of England and the reluctance of Austria. Kálnoky followed Bismarck's lead closely throughout the development of this affair. He announced to the Austrian diplomatic corps that a strong policy on England's part might enlist his support, but that he would not take the initiative in one.[54] He cut short Sir Augustus Paget's explanations of the inferiority of England's interest in the case by the remark: "Then I don't understand why you are so anxious to push us into a fight." [55] In the communications between England and Austria at this juncture is already visible the outline of the situation later wittily described as one "in which Austria declares that she would be delighted to take the first step, as Lord Salisbury proposes, if Lord Salisbury will begin by taking

---

[51] *P. P.*, 1887, xci, Turkey no. 1, pp. 112, 96, 127. August 30, 25, September 2, Iddesleigh to Malet, to Thornton, to Malet and Paget.

[52] *Ibid.*, pp. 128–129. September 3, Malet to Iddesleigh.

[53] *Ibid.*, p. 139. September 7, Malet to Iddesleigh.

[54] Corti, p. 271. August 27, Kálnoky, circular despatch.

[55] *Ibid.*, p. 271.

the second." [56] At this time neither took any real step at all, though both had to face a general popular sympathy with Prince Alexander, now loudly expressed by the same Hungarians who could find nothing bad enough to say about him a year before. Indignation at the events in Bulgaria and alarm lest the situation work out to the advantage of Russia were filling the newspapers of both countries, and even those of the Opposition parties in Germany.[57]

In the midst of this agitation Bismarck stood unmoved. He let it be known that he regarded the disappearance of Prince Alexander as the contrary of an 'untoward event.'[58] All his controlled newspapers kept up a steady fire in support of this position.[59] It is worth noting, however, that, at the same time these organs were already calling upon England as the Power whose duty it was to stand forth in the first rank against a possible Russian advance.[60]

[56] Sir Charles Dilke, *The Present Position of European Politics* (London, 1887), p. 23.

[57] In his speech of January 13, 1887, before the Reichstag, Bismarck quoted a number of extracts from these press utterances. *Reden*, xii, pp. 256–265. Two examples may suffice: *Freisinnige Zeitung*, August 25: "Wenn die Unterwerfung unter den Willen des Czaren den Weltfrieden bedeutet, so mag das richtig sein. Aber es gibt eine Grenze, wo diese Unterwerfung aufhören muss, und dieser Grenze nähern wir uns um so mehr, je mehr die russische Herrschsucht und der Panslavismus durch Erfolge auf der Balkanhalbinsel zu neuen Abenteuern für immer weiter gesteckte Ziele ermuntert werden." *Germania*, September 1: "Wir glauben also, ein grosser Moment ist jetzt wieder einmal für den deutsch-österreichischen Bund gekommen — die Versperrung der Strasse nach Konstantinopel gegen Russland ist möglich."

[58] *Preussische Jahrbücher*, October, 1886, p. 408.

[59] *M. A. Z.*, August 24, quotes from a recent article in the *Kölnische Zeitung*: "Für den deutschen Standpunkt sei es angezeigt, heute wieder eines Wortes eingedenk zu sein, welches Fürst Bismarck in einem kritischen Moment des Berliner Congresses aussprach: 'Meine Herren! Wir sind hier nicht versammelt, um über das Glück der Bulgaren zu berathen, sondern den Frieden Europa's zu sichern.'"

[60] *Nationalzeitung*, August 23, referring to the stopping of Russia's advance: "Diese Aufgabe fällt entweder England im Verein mit der Pforte und den dortigen nach Selbständigkeit verlangenden Bevölkerungen zu, oder sie fällt Niemandem zu." *Kölnische Zeitung*, August 23, waxed sarcastic. "England aber — doch wer spricht heute noch in solchen Fragen von England? Man ist in Europa einig, dass England in die politischen Rechnungen nicht höher eingestellt werden darf als Holland. Wer seit zehn Jahren England als eine Grossmacht in Rechnung zog, hat sich betrogen. Vielleicht hat auch Fürst Alexander diesen Fehler begangen . . . lassen." Again, August 31, the *Kölnische Zeitung*: "Wenn nun die Kriegspartei im grossen Reiche

The note thus sounded, and pretty continuously harped upon thereafter, foretells Bismarck's double game.

> des Ostens einen Schlag ausführt in einer Region, deren Verteidigung die Sache ganz anderer Mächte wäre, da ruft die radikal klerikale Opposition, Deutschland solle die Kriegslust des östlichen Nachbars auf sich ziehen, womit es zugleich dem westlichen Nachbar das Signal zum Versuch der so heiss ersehnten Revanche gibt. . . . Und wenn Deutschland die Last des russisch-französischen Krieges auf sich genommen hätte, wie würde es dann mit der englischen Hilfsbereitschaft stehen? Es wäre der grösste Schaden und läge die stärkste Selbsttäuschung darin, bei einer ernsten deutschen Gefahr auf irgend einen Grad englischer Hilfe zu rechnen. Wenn England den, wie es scheint, unaufhaltsamen Fortschritt Russlands im Orient hemmen will, so mag es den Versuch unternehmen, die mohammedanische Welt widerstandsfähig zu machen, aber es mag Deutschland mit der Zumutung verschonen, den Expansionsdrang der herrschenden Klassen in Russland auf sich abzulenken."

## CHAPTER IV

### BISMARCK'S EASTERN POLICY

THE principles which guided Bismarck in dealing with the situation as it presented itself at the beginning of September had not yet assumed the character of a rigid policy. Indeed, at no stage of his career are his actions to be interpreted according to any pre-arranged and inelastic plan. With certain precise ends of national interest ahead, he had always several ways in view by which to reach them, and never allowed one road to be closed to him until success was assured by another, never hesitated to change from one to another if circumstances rendered it advisable. Herein lies in large part the secret of his success, and, at the same time, the difficulty of understanding his motives and of reconciling his own frequently contradictory explanations. His conduct during the second Bulgarian crisis is only to be explained as not determined by any fixed policy, but as a course carefully steered according to a clear comprehension of the ends to be reached among a set of exceedingly difficult circumstances. His policy remains for months in a fluid, elusive state, and takes definite shape only when the end is in sight; yet such as it then emerges, it can be seen to be consistent from the beginning, although always subject to one or more alternative possibilities.

The ends that Bismarck sought were, as always, fairly simple. The dominant position of Germany in international politics, which she had held since 1871, was to be maintained. The Austrian alliance was to remain the basis of that position, as it had been virtually since 1876; and the interests of Austria were accordingly to be furthered to the greatest extent which other factors would permit.[1] Good relations with Russia, only second in

[1] The feeling which had led Bismarck to sign the ministerial declaration of 1881, recognizing the priority of the Austro-German Alliance over the League of the Three Emperors, had led him again, in 1883, to desire the renewal of the Alliance ahead of that of the League. His words to Crown Prince Rudolf of Austria, in their interview

importance to those with Austria, were to be kept as far as possible unimpaired. These were the fundamental principles by which Bismarck guided himself. The Bulgarian problem as such was the least important element in his calculation.

The situation was probably as difficult as any with which Bismarck was ever called upon to deal. The Bulgarian question was reopened and must now be boldly faced. Further temporization was useless: the solution might as well be sought once and for all. The question reopened was in reality that of the reëstablishment of Russian influence in Bulgaria and its possible extension even farther — perhaps to Constantinople itself. The problem of Germany's attitude toward this possibility was a grave one, since it involved directly the interests of her ally, Austria, and ultimately, as many Germans, not altogether excluding Bismarck, realized, her own.

On the immediate issue, the elimination of Prince Alexander, Bismarck's decision was firm and direct. He disliked the prince personally and regarded him as the chief source of trouble. He would not lift a finger in opposition to Russia for the sake of Alexander of Battenberg: on the contrary, he contributed his influence to getting the prince out of the way. But once gone, he must be replaced; and it was most unlikely that the replacement could be effected to the equal satisfaction of Russia and Austria and the national party in Bulgaria itself. The probability was that this last element, which Russia believed did not represent the true feeling of the mass of Bulgarians, but which was strongly intrenched in power, could only be induced to accept a Russian choice by the application of force. But the reappearance of Russian, or even Turkish, troops in the Balkans would be the signal for a tremendous and irresistible outburst in the Peninsula and in

---

of March 1, 1883, reveal his supreme regard for the treaty of 1879. The Crown Prince reported. "Er meinte, der Friede und die Zukunft beider Staaten sei auf dieser Allianz begründet, welche die einzige Garantie giebt, wirksamen Widerstand gegen die auswärtigen Feinde und die im Innern aller Länder so stark auftauchenden republikanischen Tendenzen leisten zu können. . . . In diesem Bündnis liegt die Zukunft Europas. . . . Das eine ist sicher, unser Bündnis steht fest und hierin sehe ich das grösste Glück und werde immer daran arbeiten es für *alle* Zukunft dauernd zu befestigen." Pribram, *Oesterreichische Rundschau*, January, 1921, pp. 15–16.

Austria-Hungary, followed almost inevitably by a great European war. In the face of such a disastrous possibility, Germany must pick her way with great caution.

Three possible courses of action presented themselves. Germany might support Austria unreservedly from the start, announcing boldly that she would be on her ally's side in the event of war. She might espouse Russia's claims and persuade Austria, for a consideration, to concede them. Or she might keep in the background, letting Austria go ahead on her own responsibility, only endeavoring to assure her the support of some other combination, not openly including Germany, which in the end would balk Russia of her desires.

The first course was inconceivable as long as Bismarck stood at the helm of the German ship of state. He was never swayed by the vision, which had already gained a considerable following in Germany, of a great struggle between Slav and Teuton of which Constantinople should be the prize. He was not wholly incapable of taking such a broad and imaginative view of the future. The idea was sufficiently familiar to him. He had even considered it as a remote possibility worth providing against without going out of his way to do so.[2] But as a guiding principle of immediate

[2] Hohenlohe, ii, p. 302 (Amer., ii, pp. 276–277). July 15, 1880, a letter from Hohenlohe to the Crown Prince, repeating Bismarck's views on the project of sending Prussian officers as instructors to Turkey. "Auch sei der Einfluss, den wir damit in den türkischen Ländern erhielten, nicht zu unterschätzen. . . . Es könne uns nützlich sein, auch die Türken zu Freunden zu haben, soweit es unser Vorteil gestatte. . . . Wenn in Russland der Chauvinismus, Panslawismus und die antideutschen Elemente uns angreifen sollten, so wäre die Haltung und die Wehrhaftigkeit der Türkei für uns nicht gleichgültig. Gefährlich könnte sie uns niemals werden, wohl aber könnten unter Umständen ihre Feinde auch unsre werden." Both Oncken (p. 52) and Hammann (*Vorgeschichte*, pp. 38–41) attribute to Bismarck much more far reaching views than these, basing their conclusions upon the account of an interview between Bismarck and St. Vallier published in 1884 by Robolsky, in his *Bismarck, Zwölf Jahre deutscher Politik 1871–1883*. In this conversation, dated in 1879, Bismarck is said to have urged France to enter a continental alliance for the purpose of preventing an Anglo-Russian partition of Turkey. The numerous despatches from Saint-Vallier and his successor, Courcel, printed by Pagès, bear out the impression of Bismarck's policy given by this interview. On July 17, 1881, Saint-Vallier wrote: "Dans cette redoutable question du partage de l'empire ottoman, le prince de Bismarck voit avant tout un des éléments importants devant peser lourdement dans la balance de la grande lutte des races slave et ger-

action, it was very foreign to his practical, everyday views of *Realpolitik*. Moreover, he was always opposed to surrendering Germany entirely to the direction of her ally, as must inevitably result from severing all relations between Berlin and St. Petersburg.³ His whole conception of German policy depended upon avoiding any such surrender to either of his neighbors. The 'honest broker' might surreptitiously favor Austria upon occasion, but he had no intention of giving up his advantageous position as a broker to join forces openly with one of his clients.

Not the least serious of his objections to so doing was the consideration that such a course would certainly precipitate the Franco-Russian alliance which it was his lifelong struggle to prevent, and possibly involve England and even Italy against him. In the event of an appeal to arms, such a course would at least bring upon Germany the dreaded war on two fronts. He never faltered in his determination to live up to his guaranty of Austria's existence as a Great Power. He realized full well, despite his reiterated denials of Germany's obligation to espouse Austria's Balkan interests, that she could not escape defending in the long run any interest which Austria deemed vital enough to make the occasion of a war. In a crown council of May 23, 1888, he told the Emperor Frederick: "We could not look on passively if Austria got into a war with Russia, even though our *casus foederis*

manque. Il regarde cette lutte comme inévitable dans un avenir plus ou moins éloigné; il s'y prépare militairement et politiquement, et il n'est pas un de ses familiers qui ne sache combien cette perspective est l'objet de ses préoccupations. L'Autriche sera son satellite dans ce duel de races dont l'issue décidera de l'Empire de l'est européen; il l'a préparée de longue main à ce rôle, et il est parvenu à la compromettre de telle sorte que, le voulût-elle, il ne lui serait plus possible d'y échapper." Senate Report, p. 179. Courcel expressed similar views in a despatch of February 22, 1882. *Ibid.*, pp. 181–182. M. Pagès bases his own interpretation of Bismarck's policy upon these statements of men whom he qualifies as "informés et clairvoyants." A survey of their despatches, however, raises doubts as to whether they were either. Some of Saint-Vallier's opinions appear especially fantastic, as for instance, when he writes, on March 31, 1880, of Bismarck as having "avec tant de peine rompu l'alliance des trois empereurs pour en expulser la Russie et réduire l'Autriche à son rôle actuel de satellite." *Ibid.*, p. 176. The exaggerated and distorted character of some of these reports appears to be the result of attributing to Bismarck many current conceptions of policy with which he was actually very little in sympathy.

³ *Gedanken und Erinnerungen*, ii, p. 252.

were not fulfilled. We should be obliged at first to *faire le mort*, play dead, but not so long as to allow Austria to be destroyed." [4] But he would do all in his power to avert such an embarrassing situation by restraining Austria's impetuosity: above all, he would avoid taking the initiative in forcing a final solution of the Balkan problem.

The second course, that of concessions to Russia accompanied by compensations to Austria, brought into consideration the policy of a line of demarcation between the Russian and Austrian spheres of influence in the Balkans. This was a policy by which Bismarck set great store. He had strongly urged it upon Kálnoky at the close of the preceding year. He revived it in this new crisis and clung to it long after it had been definitely rejected by both the powers concerned. Yet just how much he meant by it must remain questionable.

The whole object of these endeavors was to obtain an arrangement which would satisfy Austria-Hungary and safeguard her interests and her position as a Great Power without obliging him to oppose openly the Russian advance. But that any such arrangement could be made to the permanent satisfaction of Russia was a practical impossibility. The final reckoning would be only postponed by an understanding confined to Bulgaria and Serbia. The further implications of his policy had been explained to Kálnoky as early as 1883. "If we should find," wrote Bismarck, "that Russia was working round to the plan of making the collapse of Turkey an object of our alliance, we could always refuse our coöperation, and, if necessary, hinder the execution of unacceptable projects, only not too hastily." And again — "The injuries that Austro-Hungarian interests might incur outside the Bosnian-Serbian region are certainly great enough not to be permanently accepted; but the Porte, Rumania, and England would be still more directly affected." If no mutually acceptable arrangement proved possible, he concluded: "my political vote would be for letting Russia go her own way on her own responsibility and without apparent control, until other Powers become so alarmed as to require our support." [5]

[4] Lucius von Ballhausen, p. 442.
[5] *G. F. O.*, iii, pp. 300, 295. September 15, 11, Bismarck to Reuss.

But the outcome which Bismarck thus indicated as the result of a postponement of the issue was also possible of realization at an earlier stage. If the point at which Russia might be stopped was the point at which other powers entered the field against her, she might, by bringing in the other powers sooner, be kept out of Bulgaria entirely. Such a result was what Austria-Hungary really desired, rather than any partition agreement of doubtful value and assured fragility. This third possible course of action, the indirect blocking of Russia's progress, had, in fact, the most to recommend it. It was the method employed with success at the time of the Russo-Turkish war and the congress of Berlin, to the profit of Austria, without any commensurate Russian gain. By engineering it skilfully, Germany could serve all Austria's interests and yet avoid breaking with Russia. She would thus keep France and Russia apart and maintain her own very advantageous position as the mutual friend of both Russia and Austria. If Bismarck could only get Austria to show some signs of conciliation while he worked out his scheme, he might repeat for her the peaceful victory of 1878.

The power most eligible for the position of Austria's ally was England, the enemy of her enemy, Russia, and her own former partner at the time of the congress of Berlin. But in order to induce England to play this part, it was necessary that Germany should conceal her own hand and assume an attitude of indifference, taking no chances with England's fondness for letting others do her work for her.[6] Moreover, England could not be counted upon to move rapidly in either a diplomatic or a military sense; and Austria must take great care not to rush matters, but so to manoeuvre that the initiative should come from England's side.[7] Another power to be ranged on Austria's side was her

---

[6] Lucius von Ballhausen, p. 500. August 17, 1889. "Bismarck habe ihm [Francis Joseph] gesagt: Das ganze Ziel und Objekt der deutschen Politik seit zehn Jahren sei, England für den Dreibund zu gewinnen. Das sei nur möglich, wenn Deutschland immer wieder seine Indifferenz gegen die orientalische Frage betone. Geschähe das nicht, brouilliere sich Deutschland deswegen mit Russland, so werde England behaglich still sitzen und sich nur die Kastanien aus dem Feuer holen lassen."

[7] Ibid., p. 442. Bismarck's exposé in the Crown Council of March 23, 1888.

partner in the Triple Alliance, Italy — and even more important than Italy's own support was the influence that might be exerted through her upon England, owing to the common interests of the two states in the Mediterranean. But of Italy her allies could not be sure unless important concessions were made in revising the treaty of 1882. One of Italy's desires was for some effective backing of her interests in the Mediterranean, which had been touched upon only in a general and inoperative clause of the original treaty.[8] Austria would be most unwilling to take any such obligation upon herself, while England was just the power to do so. By bringing about an agreement between Italy and England, therefore, Bismarck might serve the double purpose of reaffirming the loyalty of an unreliable ally and of bringing definitely within his controlled system of alliances the other power he would like to see acting at the side of Austria in the Near East.

One aspect of Bismarck's policy in thus seeking to develop an anti-Russian entente among the other powers still requires explanation. Apparently he never allowed the Austrian government any real insight into the possibility of such a development. He gave Kálnoky to understand that his acceptance of Russia's claims in Bulgaria was sincere and that Austria had only to make the best of a bad bargain. Instead of hopes, he kept only fears before the eyes of the Austrian statesman. The tone of his communications was always that Germany's support was strictly limited, that a real danger existed from the side of France, and that the maintenance of existing ties with Russia and with Italy was a matter, not of manoeuvring for advantages, but of life or death.[9] The explanation of this attitude is probably largely personal. Bismarck had not overmuch confidence in Kálnoky's discretion. His opinion of the Austrian minister's ability had fallen especially low since the Serbo-Bulgarian war. The behavior of

"Österreich dürfe gegen Russland nicht eher losschlagen, als bis England aus seiner Passivität herausgedrängt sei und seine Interessen im Orient aktiv betätige, bis seine Kanonen im Bosporus knallten wie im Krimkrieg."

[8] Pribram, i, p. 25 (Amer., i, p. 66). In article i. — "Elles . . . se promettent en outre leur appui mutuel dans la limite de leurs propres intérêts."

[9] See *G. F. O.*, v, chapters xxxii and xxxiii; also Pribram, i, pp. 172, 192 (Amer., ii, pp. 52–53).

such an undependable colleague could be better regulated by keeping him in the dark, and even in a little anxiety, than by admitting him to foreknowledge of a policy still uncertain as to outcome and requiring great delicacy of manipulation to bring to a successful conclusion. The policy is no less real and continuous for the fact that Bismarck kept all its threads strictly in his own hands and concealed its entire development as far as possible by putting forward the alternatives. It must always be kept in mind in following the later developments of this crisis.

# CHAPTER V

## THE POWERS AND BULGARIA

### I

THE possibilities of the situation have been outlined as they presented themselves to Bismarck at the moment of Prince Alexander's abdication. With that factor out of the way, the question immediately to be faced was how far Russia would go in asserting her claims to a special voice in the settlement which was to follow. For the moment this issue did not take acute form. The Russian government gave comforting answers to the request of the Porte that no foreign intervention take place in the principality.[1] Bismarck hastened to impress upon the Turks and all others the eminently satisfactory character of these assurances.[2] In its final form, as it reached Constantinople, the Russian reply was not without some qualification, but at least it indicated no desire for immediate action.[3] The Austrian reply to the same request, on the other hand, went further than was called for, and no doubt further than was welcome to Bismarck; for Kálnoky added to his assurances against intervention on the part of his own government, the statement "that it hopes and is persuaded there will be none on the part of any other Power. Such intervention would be contrary to its views."[4] He thus placed himself from the start squarely in opposition to the idea that Russia had any special right to take a hand in Bulgarian affairs.

[1] *P. P.*, 1887, xci, Turkey no. 1, pp. 147, 154. September 7, 9, 1886, Morier to Iddesleigh.

[2] *Ibid.*, p. 153. September 9, Scott to Iddesleigh. Bismarck had told the Turkish ambassador "that the Sultan ought to be satisfied with the distinct and satisfactory assurances given by the Russian Government that it had no intention of intervening in Bulgaria, and Germany had certainly no such intention."

[3] *Ibid.*, p. 165. September 19, Thornton to Iddesleigh. "The Russian reply further states that . . . Russia will not interfere, nor will she occupy the country unless disturbances should take place in it and force her to do so."

[4] *Ibid.*, p. 152. September 9, Paget to Iddesleigh.

This opposition was dictated much less by Kálnoky's personal convictions than by the demands of the Hungarian element of the Dual Monarchy. The government had placed before the country, through a semi-official article in the *Presse* on September 7, a policy quite along the lines of Bismarck's suggested compromise with Russia. It proposed, in fact, seeking compensations after the manner of Andrássy, in 1877.[5] This feeler was met by the Magyars, as might have been expected, with a storm of protests and demands for decisive action against Russia.[6] Obliged to yield to the force of this current, Kálnoky formulated his policy accordingly, as was indicated in his assurances to Turkey on the 9th. But the Hungarian press, and even part of the Austrian, did not stop with assertions of the Dual Monarchy's interests: it went further, bitterly criticized the alliance of 1879, and railed at Germany for not springing to the defence of those interests now

[5] *Presse* (Vienna), September 7. "Wir glauben dass die allem Anscheine nach zuwartende Haltung des Grafen Kálnoky zum mindesten dieselben Vorzüge aufweist, wie die Politik des Grafen Andrássy, der 1877 sehr gut daran gethan hat, die Russen ruhig nach Plewna und nach San Stefano marschiren zu lassen. Die bevorstehende Position Russlands in Bulgarien ist uns gewiss so unangenehm, als den Panslawisten die Occupation Bosniens durch Oesterreich-Ungarn, aber es kann eben auf der Balkan-Halbinsel nicht immer nur das geschehen, was unserer Monarchie angenehm und bequem ist, so wenig ja nur das immer geschieht, was Russland frommt und behagt. . . . Aber weil wir von der Politik Oesterrich-Ungarns wünschen, dass sie nur das Erreichbare vertrete, um so entschiedener glauben wir fordern zu dürfen, dass das Wiener Cabinet in dem Masse, als die jüngste Action Russlands Erfolge aufweist, nichts versäume, was in der Macht einer gesunden und kräftigen Compensations-Politik liegt."

[6] *Pester Lloyd*, September 8. "Sollten aber die Dinge nach der Entfernung des Fürsten Alexander dort eine Wendung nehmen, welche für unsere Interessen bedrohlich erscheint, dann werden wir einer solchen mit dem Aufgebot all unserer Kraft entgegentreten müssen, und es gibt keine Art der ' Abfindung,' welche uns an der Erfüllung dieser Pflicht der Selbsterhaltung hindern könnte." *M. A. Z.*, September 11. Aus Oesterreich, September 9. Report of Deputy Horvath's speech to his constituents: "With regard to the threatening extension of Russian influence, a line of demarcation between the Russian and Austro-Hungarian spheres is something not to be thought of. . . . The Hungarian nation knows very well that the establishment of Russia's power on the lower Danube means the endangering of the monarchy and its most vital interests. I hold it natural and justifiable that the Hungarian nation should exert so much pressure upon its legislative and diplomatic organs that, if the time ever comes when diplomatic action no longer suffices to safeguard its interests — which I can hardly believe possible — they would not shrink back even from war."

that they were threatened.⁷ A lively newspaper campaign ensued between these journals and Bismarck's controlled press, the latter consistently maintaining that Austria was acting in a fashion quite contrary to her own interests, which demanded no such uncompromising stand, but rather a conciliatory policy toward Russia.⁸ So serious did the conflict become that Bismarck felt called upon to descend personally into the arena with two dictated articles in the *Norddeutsche Allgemeine Zeitung*. The first of these, appearing on September 25, was directed against the Austro-Hungarian newspapers which had criticized the working of the Austro-German alliance.⁹ The second, on September 27, was a violent attack upon Alexander of Battenberg, whom the Hungarians sought to defend.¹⁰

⁷ *Pester Lloyd*, September 8. "Die Freundschaft mit Deutschland ist für uns von überaus hohem Werthe, aber sie wird uns nie der Verpflichtung entheben können, für unsere Interessen selber zu sorgen." *N. F. P.*, September 7. "Die öffentliche Meinung in Oesterreich . . . hat aber nicht geglaubt, dass das deutsch-österreichische Bündniss in einem entscheidenden Augenblicke nicht mehr Wirkung äussern würde, als dass Russland unbehindert ganz Europa seinen Willen auferlegen könne."

⁸ *Norddeutsche Allgemeine Zeitung*, September 7. "Fürst Bismarck konnte unbedenklich seine Ueberzeugung von der Bedeutungslosigkeit Bulgariens für Deutschland aussprechen, weil er mit den befreundeten Kaisermächten *cartes sur table* spielt." To which the *Neue Freie Presse* replied, on the 11th: "Der deutsche Reichskanzler, sagt die Norddeutsche Allgemeine Zeitung, spielt mit offenen Karten. Zugestanden, aber er hatte bei der diplomatischen Partie, welche jetzt gespielt wird, die Vorhand, und er hat Russland die Honneurs und Oesterreich die leeren Blätter gegeben. Muss sich da nicht bei uns das dringende Verlangen regen, er möge noch einmal und besser mischen." *Kölnische Zeitung*, September 24. "Auf die Dauer aber darf es [Oesterreich] das Vertrauen haben, dass auch auf der Balkan-Halbinsel die Natur der Dinge sich stärker erweisen wird, als die übertriebenen Gelüste des Panslawismus. Oesterreich braucht desshalb selbst in Bulgarien keine Politik der gränzenlosen Nachgiebigkeit zu treiben; es gesteht einfach zu, dass nach dem vorigjährigen Septemberputsch das Gleichgewicht auf der Balkan-Halbinsel zu Ungunsten Russlands aus dem Lot gegangen war, und dass Russlands Wunsch, dasselbe wieder einzurenken, eine gewisse Berechtigung hat. Sollte Russland aber jemals Miene machen, in jenen Interessenkreis hinüberzugreifen, den Oesterreich mit vollem Bedacht für sich abgesteckt hat, dann wäre es immer noch Zeit, die Panslawisten daran zu erinnern, dass sie da eine Frage anrühren, die nur dadurch gelöst werden kann, dass die Völker zum Waffentanze in die Arena herniedersteigen."

⁹ B. M. M., pp. 345 *et seq.*
¹⁰ *Ibid.*, pp. 349 *et seq.*

Bismarck's own policy at this time in regard to the further development of the Bulgarian question is indicated in a despatch of September 13 to the ambassador at Vienna: "As for our programme, for which I am striving to win the approval of the other two imperial courts, I can only recommend an agreement whereby Austria recognizes the Russian influence in Bulgaria, and Russia, the Austrian in Serbia."[11] He had laid this programme before Giers in a second interview at Berlin, on the 7th, and the latter had given it at least his verbal indorsement.[12] Prince William was also instructed to propose it directly to the Tsar on the occasion of a visit of ceremony at Brest-Litovsk, and even to extend the suggestion by repeating Bismarck's often expressed assertion of willingness to see the Russians go as far as Constantinople. The young prince was much disconcerted by Alexander's haughty answer: "If I wish to have Constantinople, I shall take it whenever I feel like it, without need of permission or approval from Prince Bismarck."[12a] This rebuff did not discourage the Chancellor as to the prospects of his scheme of a partition; for, in his despatch on the 13th to Reuss, he wrote: "The conversations between His Royal Highness Prince William and the Emperor Alexander give me reason to expect that Russia's explicit assent to such a mutual engagement can be obtained."

The concluding sentence of this despatch refers to an element in the situation which already threatened to upset all Bismarck's calculations—the parliamentary Opposition in Hungary. It was all very well for him to assert the "impossibility of subordinating the foreign policy of a great country like the German Empire to the humors and fractions of a parliament, whether German or Hungarian." Kálnoky was unable to share this fine disregard; and, through his actions, the Hungarian Diet was bound to influence Bismarck also in the end.

Parliamentary pressure upon the Austro-Hungarian government was, indeed, not long in making itself felt. On September

[11] *G. F. O.*, v, pp. 62–63.

[12] *Ibid.*, v, p. 62. September 9, Bülow to Bismarck.

[12a] "Memoirs of the Kaiser," in the *New York Times*, September 24, 1922. The writer's comments on the incident show a complete lack of understanding of the nature of the negotiation in which he was engaged.

18, two sweeping interpellations were brought into the Hungarian Chamber of Deputies, involving the government's Balkan policy and its relations with both Russia and Germany.[13] These were supported by the Opposition leader, Count Apponyi, who himself brought in a third one, on the 24th, flatly accusing Germany of betrayal.[14] A fourth attack, on the 29th, finally drew an answer from the government, delivered next day by the premier, Count Tisza. "In agreement with the ministry of foreign affairs," he stated, "I hold that . . . the monarchy, while repudiating all designs of expansion or conquest, should employ all its efforts and influence to encourage the development of those [Balkan] states and prevent their falling under any foreign protectorate or permanent influence not provided for in the treaties. . . . The government stands firmly by its repeatedly expressed opinion that, under the existing treaties, unless Turkey should assert her rights, no power is entitled to undertake any single-handed armed intervention or to set up any protectorate in the Balkan Peninsula." Upon the subject of the German alliance he was more reserved, saying only: "With Germany we stand today upon the same footing as always; and for that very reason we must not doubt that together we can defend our common vital interests without endangering the general peace."[15] The concluding words indicated that the government was not counting upon Germany's support in any policy of challenging Russia to an armed conflict. The Opposition expressed some discon-

[13] *M. A. Z.*, September 21. Pest, September 18. Interpellations by Horvath and Iranyi. Horvath's speech contained the sentence: "It is a vital issue for us that we should promote the formation of independent, self-sufficing states in the East; and the whole weight of our power should be thrown into the scale for their maintenance. Any diversion from this policy will sooner or later avenge itself heavily."

[14] *Ibid.*, September 23. Aus Oesterreich, September 21. Apponyi: "We must cast our entire strength into the scale to prevent the policy of encouraging Russia's lust for expansion from being carried any further." September 26 (aus Oesterreich, September 24). Apponyi, in presenting his interpellation: "I solemnly affirm that the tendency on Russia's part to subdue Bulgaria completely to her will, which conflicts directly with the interests of our monarchy, has been supported throughout by German diplomacy. . . . Our own national interests, as well as the standing of our monarchy as a Great Power, exclude the possibility that the expansion of any single Great Power should be permitted in any part of the Balkan Peninsula."

[15] *M. A. Z.*, October 3, 1886; *Geschichtskalender*, 1886, p. 247.

tent, but on the whole had reason to congratulate itself upon having convinced the government of the impossibility of making any concessions whatever to Russia.

In spite of the unpromising trend of events in Austria-Hungary, Bismarck persisted in his efforts, both with that country and with Russia, to arrive at an amicable settlement.[16] "Unhappily," he told the new French ambassador, Herbette, "I do not find much response at St. Petersburg. That would not be so inconvenient if only I could succeed in calming the irritation of our friends at Vienna. And I would surely have been able to do so, if they did not have to reckon with Hungary, with the parliamentary system, and with the press."[17] It was a difficult situation for an 'honest broker' to be in.

While thus striving to hold back Austria from a complete defiance of Russia, Bismarck never lost sight of the alternative policy to that of concession and conciliation, which was that of building up a strong enough combination to make Austria's effort successful without his aid. A foreign office memorandum dated September 23, for the information of the ambassador at Vienna, contains the following observations on the situation in Austria-Hungary: "If . . . there is any intention of pursuing a policy of the Battenberg kind . . . without us and at their own risk . . ., such a policy would be accompanied by our most sincere wishes for its success; but, in His Highness's opinion, we could not take part in it. Such a policy might, rather, count upon the support of England. But, according to the views of the Imperial Chancellor, Austria will be sure of this support only if she waits until England takes the initiative in a break with Russia." The memorandum also repeats Bismarck's advice, given "openly and honorably," against such a course, and his assertion that Germany is not bound by her treaties to support it, but makes the significant admission: "if this policy should miscarry, it is always from us, rather than from England, that Austria can expect succor."[18]

At this moment, however, it was most unsafe to go ahead with any calculations based on British support, because of the division

---

[16] Pribram, in *Österreichische Rundschau*, January, 1921, p. 59.
[17] Daudet, *Ferdinand*, p. 82.    [18] G. F. O., v, p. 125.

of opinion on foreign policy existing within the British government. The cabinet in general was inclined to follow in the footsteps of Beaconsfield, but was retarded by the doubts of one of its strongest members, Lord Randolph Churchill. The brilliant new chancellor of the exchequer was by no means a blind devotee of the foreign policy of the former leader of his party. He opposed any over-energetic action in the East, and even favored a further development of the understanding with Russia reached in the Afghan boundary settlement.[19] He had disapproved of the government's ineffective attempt at support of Prince Alexander, writing Salisbury, on September 4: "I do most earnestly trust that we may not be drifting into strong and marked action in the East of Europe."[20] On September 15, he wrote to Lord Salisbury that, in a conversation with the Russian ambassador: "I hinted at an understanding with Russia by which she should give us real support in Egypt, abandon her pressure upon Afghanistan, in which case she might settle the Balkan matters as she would — or rather, as she *could*!"[21]

Such a point of view was as far as could possibly be from that which Bismarck would have liked to see England assume. Fortunately for him, it was also too extreme for the rest of the cabinet; and the Russian understanding, at least, had no prospect of going through. Yet even without it, Churchill was still a good way from falling in with Bismarck's ideas. His own alternative to the understanding was an anti-Russian policy in which England should go hand in hand with Germany — the very course which Bismarck was determined not to pursue.

Although there was little hope of persuading Germany thus to come out openly in opposition to Russia, Churchill was given leave to try. So great was his importance to the Unionist party that Lord Salisbury, waiving departmental distinctions, allowed him to conduct personally this matter of purely foreign affairs. On September 24, he had an interview with the German ambassador, Count Hatzfeldt, in which he stated his point of view, offered

[19] W. S. Churchill, *Lord Randolph Churchill* (London and New York, 1906, 2 vols.), ii, p. 155.
[20] *Ibid.*, p. 156.   [21] *Ibid.*, pp. 157–158.

simply as a member of the House of Commons. "Any anti-Russian policy," he said, "which involved England taking the lead ostensibly on the side of Turkey, either about Bulgaria or even Constantinople, would probably place the Unionist party in great peril, might fail to receive the support of the constituents, and would be savagely assaulted. An anti-Russian policy, however, in which Austria took the lead supported by Germany, we could . . . well fall in with, and hold our own easily in the House of Commons." Hatzfeldt made the equally frank and flat reply: "That is all very well; but what will be wanting will be Germany's support of Austria. Our eyes are riveted on France." So anxious was Churchill to impress the German government that he went on to declare that England's loyal and thoroughgoing support of Germany and Austria against Russia "would seem to entail logically action on our part, diplomatic or otherwise, against France if she tried to be nasty." [22]

Even this incautious offer failed to move Bismarck from his position. "Do not fall in with him!" he wrote on the margin of Hatzfeldt's despatch. "He will have the same scruples as today, and show less haste, when others precede him." And again: "If England does not take the lead, Austria will be foolish to count upon her. If Churchill hesitates with Austria and Turkey at his side, how should Austria bell the cat alone?" [23]

Any reconciliation of the views of Churchill and Bismarck was clearly impossible; but Salisbury was not ready to break with his powerful and popular colleague by finally vetoing his policy. He refused to admit that England could withdraw herself from the Eastern Question to the extent of declining to act when the Russians actually moved.[24] But for the moment he put off any decisive action which might commit England to any course in advance. Some action was, naturally, inevitable as the question continued to unfold itself, and it tended always in the direction of the traditional anti-Russian view; but fortunately for a cabinet of divided counsels, the development of affairs was not taking so serious a turn as to demand an immediate decision.

[22] Churchill, ii, pp. 158–159. Compare Herbert Bismarck's account in *G. F. O.*, iv, p. 272.

[23] *G. F. O.*, iv, p. 273.     [24] Churchill, ii, pp. 159–160.

## II

The Russian government had decided to make its action in Bulgaria as little extraordinary as possible. Instead of naming a special commissioner, it gave to the representative sent to bring about a readjustment merely the regular office of diplomatic agent and consul general. The representative chosen, General Kaulbars, brother of the former Bulgarian minister of war, was said by the *Journal de St. Pétersbourg* to be instructed "to study the situation, and, by his counsel, to assist the Bulgarians in putting an end to the present crisis in their affairs." This was surely not a formidable step on Russia's part. Upon his arrival in Sofia, the general urged three measures upon the provisional government: (1) The immediate raising of the state of siege; (2) The immediate release of all persons implicated in the recent conspiracy; (3) The postponement of elections to the National Assembly.[25] The Bulgarian government replied that it accepted the first point, but was unable, without violating the laws and the constitution, to comply with the other two. It also appealed for the support of the Powers in maintaining this decision, asking that they "use their influence to prevent any demands being addressed to the Bulgarian Government with which it is impossible for them to comply without violating the Constitution."[26] The anti-Russian regency, of which Stambulov was the head and front, was playing a risky game; but there were powerful influences operating in its favor, if only they could be brought effectively to bear. It endeavored to commit the other Powers to opposition to Russia as far as possible in advance.

The British government was the first to move. On September 29, Lord Iddesleigh wrote: "This reply has the concurrence of Her Majesty's Government."[27] On the previous day, he told the Russian ambassador that the proceedings of General Kaulbars "seemed to partake of the character of an intervention in the internal administration of the country."[28] On the 30th, he sent out a circular despatch, declaring the government to be "strongly of

---

[25] *P. P.*, 1887, xci, Turkey no. 1, p. 183.
[26] *Ibid.*, p. 184. September 28, 1886, Lascelles to Iddesleigh.
[27] *Ibid.*, p. 184.     [28] *Ibid.*, p. 185.

opinion that the Great Powers should give their earliest attention to the condition of the country, and should offer to the Bulgarian Government such advice as they think calculated to meet the exigencies of the case." [29] These pronouncements made clear the attitude of the British government, although they did not quite commit it to independent action. The reserved nature of all replies to its circular soon showed it the need of circumspection.

Nevertheless, Lord Randolph Churchill found that the steps taken went much too far. On the 30th, he wrote Lord Salisbury: "What is the reason for this apparently isolated and certainly most risky action? . . . Have we any right to express approval in so pointed and uncalled for a manner, without at the same time letting those poor Bulgarians know that beyond the merest diplomatic action we cannot go? . . . We shall never get joint action while Iddesleigh keeps rushing in where Bismarck fears to tread. . . . Our action with Austria means war with Russia. Our action with Austria and Germany means peace. But I feel sure that our present niggling, meddling, intriguing, fussy policy is gaining for us the contempt and dislike of Bismarck every day." [30] In his reply, on October 1, from Puy, Lord Salisbury made the divergence of opinion quite clear. "A pacific and economical policy," he wrote, "is up to a certain point very wise; but it is evident that there is a point beyond which it is not wise either in a patriotic or party sense — and the question is where we shall draw the line. I draw it at Constantinople. . . . I am afraid you are prepared to give up Constantinople: and foreign Powers will be quick enough to find that divergence out." [31]

On the next day, Churchill made at Dartford the greatest political speech of his career, and in it he felt obliged to incorporate a declaration of government policy toward the existing international crisis. He announced England's determination to support the freedom and independence of Bulgaria. Yet he was careful to emphasize his opinion that, however great were England's interests in the Bulgarian question, she should leave the initiative to others; that, if she must act, she should do so in agreement with

---

[29] *P. P.*, 1887, xci, Turkey no 1, p. 186.
[30] Churchill, ii, pp. 160–161.   [31] *Ibid.*, p. 162.

the whole Triple Alliance, not with only one or two of its members; and that she should not abandon hope of a settlement by peaceful means.³²

This speech, in its general lines, seemed the complement of the one recently delivered by Count Tisza; but it had characteristics of its own which were only too apparent and which robbed it of any enthusiastic reception by the Bismarckian press in Germany.³³ The true sense of the speech is further made evident by

³² Churchill, ii, pp. 166–168. *Times*, October 4. "It has been said by some, and even by persons of authority and influence, that in the issues which are involved England has no close or material interest. Such an assertion would appear to me to be far too loose and general. The sympathy of England with liberty and with the freedom and independence of communities and nationalities is of ancient origin, and has become the traditional direction of our foreign policy. . . . A generation ago Germany and Austria were not so sensitive as they are now to the value of political liberty . . .; but times have changed, and it is evident from the speech of the Hungarian Prime Minister on Thursday that the freedom and the independence of the Danubian Principalities and of the Balkan nationalities are a primary and vital object in the policy of the Austro-Hungarian Empire. . . . As Lord Salisbury said at Manchester in 1878, ' the Austrian sentinel is on the ramparts,' and we cannot doubt that the liberty-giving policy of the Treaty of Berlin will be carefully and watchfully protected. Whatever modification this great fact may enable us to make in our foreign policy, whatever diminution of isolated risk and sole responsibility this may enable us to effect, you may be certain of one thing — that there will be no sudden or violent departure by Her Majesty's present Government from those main principles of foreign policy which I have before alluded to. . . . There are Powers in Europe who earnestly and honestly desire to avoid war and to preserve peace, to content themselves with their possessions and their frontiers, and to concentrate their energies on commercial progress and on domestic development. There are other Powers who do not appear to be so fortunately situated, and who, from one cause or another which it is not necessary to analyze or examine, betray a regrettable tendency towards contentions and even aggressive action. . . . Should circumstances arise which from their grave and dangerous nature force the Government of the Queen to make a choice, it cannot be doubted that the sympathy, and if necessary even the support of England will be given to those Powers who seek the peace of Europe and the liberty of peoples, and in whose favour our timely adhesion would probably and without the use of force, decide the issue."

³³ *Nationalzeitung*, October 5. "Die kriegerischen Worte, welche, wie es scheint, in Folge eines Missverständnisses der Tisza'schen Erklärung, Lord Randolph Churchill in einem englischen Städtchen am Sonnabend gesprochen, kommen *post festum*. Lord Churchill scheint sagen zu wollen, wenn Oesterreich die Waffen erhebe, werde es den Beistand England's erhalten. . . . Man wird dort [in Wien] den plötzlichen Muth des feurigen Schatzkanzlers von England einigermassen komisch finden, der, übrigens in wenig autoritativer Form, einen Beistand verheisst, den der Gang der Dinge überflüssig gemacht hat."

another letter to Lord Salisbury, written on the following day, in which Churchill says: "You must not think that I in any way disagree from what you urge about Constantinople. It is only that I have a great doubt whether the particular method and scheme of policy which was carried out at the time of the Crimean War, and again to a great extent in 1876–78, is the best. I doubt whether the people will support that method; and it seems to have this enormous disadvantage, that it enables Austria to lie back. We can, I think, perfectly defend Constantinople by going in for the independence of Bulgaria; and we can best obtain that independence by persuading Austria to take the lead." [34]

It was quite clear that until Churchill's influence should be eliminated from the English cabinet, an anti-Russian combination in the shape desired by Bismarck was out of the question. The German Chancellor, therefore, continued along the other road which he had marked out from the beginning as an alternative — that of conceding as much as possible to Russia's interests, while attempting to hold Austria back on terms favorable to her. His only official step in the Bulgarian affair had been a caution addressed to the regents, similar to that given to Prince Alexander, against any hasty executions.[35] He placed this action on the ground of interest in the general peace; but it was also calculated to create a favorable impression in Russia. The tone of articles in his controlled press was continuously in Russia's favor, although by October these were reduced to playing only upon the worn string of invective against Alexander of Battenberg. The unfortunate prince had now become harmless enough so far as Bulgaria was concerned, although there was still some talk of his reëlection; but he continued to irritate Bismarck and the Em-

[34] Churchill, ii, pp. 162–163. These opinions were not concealed from the Austrians. Count Kinsky wrote Kálnoky on October 3 that Churchill had used the words: "We cannot stir if Austria does not take the initiative. It is Austria's affair to take the task upon herself: we cannot do it in her place." Corti, p. 285.

[35] *P. P.*, 1887, xci, Turkey no. 1, p. 182. September 22, Scott to Iddesleigh. "I have the honour to state that Count Bismarck explained to me that the advice which Herr von Thielmann had been instructed to give to the Provisional Government at Sophia had certainly been given in consequence of a communication from the Russian Government; but that it referred only to executions, and not to trials of the conspirators."

peror by the airs he was giving himself in his Prussian general's uniform and by his irrepressible aspirations to the hand of Princess Victoria.[36] To the English note of September 30, asking common action in Bulgaria, Germany simply returned no answer.

Bismarck's discouraging attitude toward Austria kept Kálnoky and his colleagues from straying too far from the path of caution and conciliation of Russia. Tisza's speech had threatened a departure from that path, but in fact had made it easier to follow by lulling Magyar opinion for at least a time. When the English note came, Kálnoky was able to resist temptation, and to reply that, "while agreeing in the general principles therein expressed," he was "nevertheless disinclined to give advice to the Bulgarian Government on any specific point, and referred to M. Tisza's recent speech as being a full and clear enunciation of Austrian policy, which he believed would have an effect at Sophia as well as elsewhere." He "went on to say that, in his opinion, things were tending towards a compromise between the Bulgarian Government and General Kaulbars, and that this might possibly be marred by the other Powers supporting the Bulgarian Government in opposition to Russian demands."[37] The unskilful and ineffective handling of the situation by General Kaulbars made possible the maintenance of this benevolent attitude toward his activities.[38]

England's own early indiscretion was followed by a most cautious avoidance of the initiative. Wavering between the counsels of Churchill and Salisbury, the government's course was uncertain and confused. Repeated hints at an understanding were given to the Austrian ambassador at London. A vaguely phrased memorandum was sent to Vienna stating that, while England admitted an interest in the defence of Constantinople, she could

[36] Hohenlohe, ii, p. 394 (Amer., ii, p. 362). Corti, pp. 291, 280. Bismarck drove the Crown Prince to abandon his advocacy of Alexander's project by a threat of resignation.
[37] P. P., 1887, xci, Turkey no. 1, p. 189. October 2, Paget to Iddesleigh.
[38] Жигаревъ, ii, pp. 275–280. His circulars to the Russian consuls, his efforts with the regents, his speaking tour of the country had all proved failures, which damaged rather than advanced the cause he represented.

not move in the matter unless assured of support from Germany or Austria.[39] Filled with distrust of the influence of Churchill, Bismarck advised against paying any attention to these advances, and wrote on the margin of the report regarding the memorandum to Vienna: "Man hofft nur Oesterreich und uns anzuputschen."[40]

Kálnoky's conversion to Bismarck's point of view was, for the time being at least, so complete that he had already rebuffed this advance. His answer was that England's declaration of interest in the affairs of the Near East might have affected the situation greatly if it had arrived earlier, but that now he could only give it a Platonic approval. "Austria's relations with Russia are just now excellent," he added, according to the report of the German ambassador; "and he felt some assurance in hoping that through these relations a way would be found out of the existing difficulties."

The suspicions of British policy upon which the caution of Bismarck and Kálnoky was based were amply confirmed by the activities of Churchill. Soon after the delivery of his speech at Dartford, the chancellor of the exchequer left England on a mysterious Continental tour which included Berlin and Vienna. This trip seemed at the start to be of immense political importance.[41] It was carried out, however, in apparently the most harmless fashion, involving nothing more serious than visits to shops and theatres, and, so far as newspaper reporters could discover, leading to not a single encounter with a foreign statesman. The affair remains a mystery, but could hardly have been quite so innocuous as it looked.[42] One secret meeting did take place with a subordinate official in Vienna, which Churchill himself afterwards re-

[39] *G. F. O.*, iv, pp. 276–278. October 4, Reuss to Bismarck.
[40] *Ibid.*, iv, p. 278.
[41] *Times*, October 7. Berlin, October 6. "We were even informed that his lordship was coming here on an express invitation from Count Herbert Bismarck, and that after exchanging civilities with his host he would make a pilgrimage to Varzin in the company of the British Ambassador, with the view of discovering on what terms England could secure the co-operation of the German Powers in the task of combating the aggressive policy of Russia."
[42] Winston Churchill treats the trip through Germany and Austria as purely a pleasure tour.

counted to the German ambassador at London. He had given out the declaration, he stated, "that England could not act alone, but that, in case Austria were to make at Petersburg a categorical declaration (he used the word 'ultimatum') against the advance of the Russians into Bulgaria, she would give it her unconditional support." [43] What answer he received, if any, and what else he may have attempted was not disclosed. At all events, Lord Randolph returned less communicative on foreign policy than before. At a political rally in Bradford on October 26, he answered a bellicose resolution in very peaceable words.[44] In his main speech he reiterated his previous declarations, but gave the impression that they were rather those of his colleagues than his own, and left all further pronouncements to Lord Salisbury in the coming Guildhall speech.

What Lord Randolph Churchill had apparently ascertained on his travels, perhaps even through his failure to receive an invitation to Varzin, was that no hope existed of getting Germany to take active part in any anti-Russian combination, and that the Austrian government would seek to follow rather than to precede England. His own belief, as then and later expressed, seems to have been that, under the circumstances, England ought to steer entirely clear of Continental complications.

Bismarck could only give way to the logic of this situation, although he showed signs of wishing to do otherwise. When Churchill once put his proposal in the form "that England is

[43] G. F. O., iv, p. 279. October 26, Hatzfeldt to Bismarck.
[44] Times, October 27. The resolution read: "that Her Majesty's present Government will pursue the patriotic policy of Lord Beaconsfield in guarding British interests in the East from the aggression of Russia." Churchill's reply was: "There is no doubt that the policy of Lord Beaconsfield with regard to the interests which the British Empire possesses in the East will, as a general rule, be a guide to the present Government, so far as the changed circumstances of the condition of Europe will admit of such a policy being followed. . . . It is quite possible that the most prudent and statesmanlike course for us to adopt and follow at the present moment is to watch very closely and carefully the state of things which are now taking place in Europe, and abstain from committing ourselves to any positive line. . . . If such a deplorable state of things should take place as the breaking out of war between the Great Powers of Europe, it does not necessarily follow that our interests are so vitally critical in these matters that we should allow ourselves to be involved in these wars."

willing and able to go forward with Austria, if Germany only comes *tacitly* into the agreement," Bismarck ventured the marginal comment: "no objection." [45] But the idea was not pursued further at this time.

### III

While England was thus restrained by Churchill from taking the course Bismarck had laid out for her, Italy was being similarly restrained by Robilant.[46] Bismarck was resolved not to meet Churchill's views; but, since the emergence of the new Bulgarian crisis, he had become very favorably disposed toward those of Robilant. Unhappily, he found trouble in persuading Kálnoky to look at matters in the same light.

In espousing Italy's claims to modifications of the treaty of 1882, Bismarck had at first striven to repeat his former tactics, summed up in the phrase, "the road to Berlin lies through Vienna." At the close of September, he was still trying to direct Launay along that road. Yet he was also striving discreetly to create a favorable reception at the Austrian capital for Italy's demands for support in her Mediterranean policy.[47] When the Italians persisted in refusing to follow the old humiliating path, he assumed the rôle of go-between, transmitting to Vienna the proposals brought out in his negotiations at Rome. These were that Italy should have a guaranty against a French occupation of Tripoli and a voice in any arrangement of spheres of interest in the Balkan Peninsula between Austria and Russia.[48] Kálnoky

---

[45] *G. F. O.*, iv, p. 281.

[46] Chiala, pp. 429–430. The attitude which Robilant took toward the Bulgarian question was strikingly similar to Bismarck's. It is expressed in a despatch of October 8, 1886, to the chargé d'affaires at London: "Non conviene infatti dissimularci che le potenze, riunitesi a congresso nel 1878, mentre credettero limitare notevolmente le conseguenze delle vittorie russe, non intesero però intieramente escludere una particolare influenza della Russia in Bulgaria, che a quelle vittorie deve la sua esistenza politica . . . L'Italia è bensì grandemente interessata alla conservazione della pace ed al mantenimento dello *statu quo* in Oriente, ma non ha interessi politici in giuoco diretti negli affari speciali della Bulgaria."

[47] Pribram, i, p. 175 (American ed., ii, p. 49).

[48] *G. F. O.*, iv, pp. 186–189, 191. October 5, Keudell to Bismarck; October 15, Herbert Bismarck to Reuss. Pribram, i, p. 175 (Amer., ii, pp. 49–50). October 19, Reuss to Kálnoky.

raised strong objections against the first proposition, if intended to go further than "moral and diplomatic support," and against the second, unless it should open the way to an "eventual Italian coöperation against Russia." [49] This cool reply showed Bismarck that he must do more than act as messenger between Rome and Vienna: he must support the Italian claims by arguments of his own. While putting the most acceptable interpretations upon Robilant's demands, he pointed out to Kálnoky that the consequences of a refusal to meet Italy's conditions might even go so far as the bringing about of a hostile combination embracing Italy, France, and Russia.[50] His observations carried the expected weight at Vienna, especially as Kálnoky would soon be called upon to define his policies before the Hungarian Delegation, and must have more certainty of Bismarck's support than was indicated by this difference of opinion. He therefore hastened to inform Bismarck that he would have no exception to take to the proposals as now presented. Only he feared that the Italian claims in the Near East might become excessive and prematurely definite.[51]

This dragooning of Austria into acceptance of Italy's conditions was accompanied by a new form of pressure upon England impelling her in a similar direction. A screw that could always be turned upon England was that of French jealousy of her position in Egypt; and Bismarck had not yet separated himself so far from France as to find himself unable to influence her sentiments. The Egyptian question had been reopened even before Churchill returned from his travels, to the further unsettlement of the young statesman's ideas upon British policy.

The French themselves opened up for Bismarck the opportunity to play them off once more against England in the familiar manner. Before the end of September the German ambassador at Paris reported that the French government was making advances toward a resumption of the policy of Ferry, and that the newly

[49] Pribram, i, pp. 176–177 (Amer., ii, pp. 50–51). October 23, Kálnoky's notes on his conversation with Reuss. Cf. G. F. O., iv, p. 196. October 22, Reuss to Bismarck.
[50] G. F. O., iv, pp. 200–201. October 30, instructions to Reuss.
[51] Pribram, i, p. 179 (Amer., ii, pp. 53–54). November 3, Kálnoky to Reuss.

appointed ambassador to Berlin, Herbette, would bring a definite request for support in the Egyptian question. Count Herbert Bismarck wrote that, while the Chancellor did not think it wise to enter upon such a policy, the French proposals would be "not sharply declined, but evasively answered." [52] In his interview with Herbette on November 12, all the Chancellor would promise in response to his proposal for support was an 'abstention bienveillante.' [53] He also expressed a dangerous approval of coöperation with Russia. The French felt sufficiently encouraged about his attitude to renew their attempts to pin England down to a date of evacuation. By the middle of October all the French newspapers had taken up the discussion; and a formal summons to evacuate was being freely mentioned as a possibility. Informal advances were even made to British statesmen. Count d'Aunay, consul general to Egypt, then in France, visited Lord Salisbury at Dieppe and told him that the French government meant business.[54] On October 19, he called upon Churchill, whose travels had by this time brought him to Paris, and urged strongly that the British government fix a definite date, however remote, for the evacuation. To this Lord Randolph steadily refused to listen.[55] But the French would not give up: they were blindly playing Bismarck's game.

Bismarck himself had not the slightest intention of doing more than permit the French to go on fooling themselves. In a despatch sent to London on October 16, he assured the British government that it could count on his support in the Egyptian question and all other matters of dispute with France as long as Germany's colonial claims received satisfactory treatment. And on this score he had no complaint to make, the tedious negotiations concerning Zanzibar being brought to a conclusion before

[52] *G. F. O.*, vi, pp. 137-138. September 28, Herbert Bismarck to William I.
[53] *Ibid.*, vi, p. 152.
[54] *Times*, October 19. Paris, October 18. "It was said, in fact, and people have repeated it to me in various quarters, that Comte d'Aunay informally, and even, if you will, amicably, intimated to Lord Salisbury that France could not indefinitely see England in Egypt, without seeking to ascertain the length of her stay, and that the French silence would not be prolonged beyond the commencement of the English session."
[55] Churchill, ii, pp. 172-174.

the month was out. At the same time, German diplomacy was supporting the negotiations of Sir Henry Drummond Wolff at Constantinople for the Egyptian convention, which was signed on October 24.[56] This convention defined England's tenure in Egypt as somewhat that of a 'leaseholder' — in accordance with a suggestion once made by Bismarck.[57] The Chancellor at one time made the observation, which was duly transmitted to London, that he would not stand in the way of a friendly accord between England and France, for the significant reason that "a counterpoise to Russia's arrogance, which may become uncomfortable, would not be unwelcome to him."[58] But the remark can hardly be taken as more than a passing speculation prompted by the increasing difficulties besetting Bismarck's path. The most advantageous course for him to pursue in the situation so opportunely created by France was to keep before England's eyes the French threat to her Mediterranean interests, thus demonstrating practically the wisdom of entering a combination which would safeguard those interests, while at the same time inflicting a check upon Russia for which Germany need incur no responsibility.[59]

The Chancellor's skilful use of the Italian and French factors in the situation thus tended to advance his projects, while circumventing the unwelcome activities of Churchill. Italy was made

[56] H. Drummond Wolff, *Rambling Recollections* (London, 1908, 2 vols.), ii, pp. 284–287.
[57] *Reden*, xi, p. 61. Speech of March 2, 1885.
[58] *G. F. O.*, iv, p. 156. October 22. Memorandum by Count Rantzau.
[59] *Times*, October 12. Stillman's article from Rome on the 9th shows Bismarck's propaganda permeating the Italian press. "The alliance pointed to, clearly enough, by the *Popolo Romano*," he writes, "is that between England, Italy and Austria, and, so far as England is concerned, the guarantees which Italy might receive are that France shall not be allowed to take possession of Tripoli, with the implication that if the *status* of the African shore is to be disturbed, Italy shall be allowed to occupy it. . . . What is of importance to know to-day is if England is ready to enter into an alliance with Austria, Italy, and the Balkan States to exclude Russian occupation of Bulgaria, and until this question is cleared up we are in no position to form any anticipation as to the results of the present crisis. I have long ago pointed out that the interests of peace required that Germany should not enter into any such combination, and without her the alliance indicated ought to suffice to keep the peace."

the central point of a combination involving both Austria and England. The French were induced to create a diversion that would force England in the right direction. But the raising of the Egyptian question had another timely effect upon France herself. It enhanced the value to her of good relations with Germany and rendered her correspondingly less susceptible to the attractions of a Russian entente, for which the circumstances were otherwise favorable.

Early in the following year, Sir Charles Dilke made the remarkable statement: "In October last two great refusals of alliances took place. France, I am told, declined a formal alliance with Russia, and Austria declined an alliance with Great Britain, although in both cases we ought to use the phrase ' declined with thanks.' "[60] The writer's sources of information were sufficiently respectable to entitle his words to great consideration, but in neither case is it possible to put one's finger upon a definite offer of alliance. Both possibilities were in the air. The English advances to Austria were fairly obvious: those of Russia to France, less so, although numerous reports were current in diplomatic circles of secret approaches begun as far back as September or August. Freycinet himself later gave the German ambassador an account of such an approach.[61] This story was doubted by the ambassador at St. Petersburg and flatly denied by Giers.[62] It is safe to say, however, that there was always a certain amount of intrigue going on with the French in the twilight zone of official diplomacy, and that some special activity of the sort apparently took place about this time. The one solid fact in the situation was the Tsar's decision to renew the exchange of ambassadors between the two countries. In each case the refusal, which could have been no more formal than the offer, was largely due to the influence of Bismarck. At the same time that his apparently pro-Russian stand on the Bulgarian question kept Russia from going far in her advances to France, his dallying with the Egyptian question kept France from any step which would separate her

[60] *Present Position*, p. 16.

[61] *G. F. O.*, vi, pp. 93–95, 97. October 1, 7, November 5, Münster to Bismarck.

[62] *Ibid.*, vi, pp. 100, 105–106. November 9, Schweinitz to Bismarck; December 24, Bülow to Bismarck.

definitely from Germany. In the case of Austria, his counsels of moderation restrained her from committing herself to anything in the nature of Churchill's policy, while his own attitude prevented any agreement involving Germany directly. The refusal of the English offer by Germany, of which Dilke does not speak, is here the deciding factor.

So the month of October passed away without bringing about any definite alignment of the Powers on the Bulgarian question. Russia had taken only indecisive steps. Austria and England had each come out separately in opposition to any effective ones, although the latter showed more disinclination to take the initiative. Germany persisted in an attitude of indifference professedly favorable to Russia. France remained outside, hoping to profit by the disturbance in other quarters. Italy also maintained an attitude of reserve, Robilant showing no inclination to play Bismarck's game for nothing.

In the meanwhile, the affairs of Bulgaria became more and more disturbed. The mission of General Kaulbars had proved a hopeless failure. The Great Assembly was called and elected against his advice; and the elections had gone very badly against the pro-Russian party. The Russians alleged that fraud and intimidation had been freely employed by the party of the regency. Moreover, elections had been held in Eastern Rumelia; and delegates were sent from there to the Assembly, in complete violation of the treaty of Berlin. In consequence of these facts, the Russian government informed all the Powers, on October 24, that "we cannot recognize the validity of the decisions of an Assembly which we consider to be illegal." [63] The question of the arrested conspirators was also becoming more acute as their trial was put off from day to day. General Kaulbars openly stated that if they were summarily executed, his government "would be obliged to take extreme measures, as they would consider that act as a direct provocation to Russia." [64] Excitement mounted, and rioting became frequent. On October 28, Russia officially announced the despatch of two warships to Varna for the protection of Russian

[63] *P. P.*, 1887, xci, Turkey no. 1, p. 240.
[64] *Ibid.*, p. 246. October 27, Lascelles to Iddesleigh.

lives and property there. Two days later, General Kaulbars informed the Bulgarian government that if within three days it had not taken measures to stop "the vexations to which the subjects and partizans of Russia were subjected," he and his staff would take their leave.[65] The Bulgarians returned a conciliatory answer and asked for specific cases, whereupon Kaulbars, while refusing to go into details upon matters so notorious, modified his ultimatum to the effect that he would leave upon the occurrence of the next act of violence.[66] So Russia had brought on a crisis, but had not yet committed any overt act.

## IV

The situation at the beginning of November could not have been more unfavorable in Kálnoky's eyes for an encounter with the Magyar parliamentarians — and the Delegations had been summoned for the 4th. Russia's attitude, threatening yet still undecided, might easily be affected by his declarations of policy. He must be cautious and yet firm enough to satisfy the Hungarians. To meet the latter requirement required some courage; for, to all appearances, he stood alone. England was holding off from any decisive commitments. With Austria's allies, Germany and Italy, relations were far from satisfactory. Although Kálnoky had signified his willingness to accept modifications in the treaty of the Triple Alliance, he had not yet learned Robilant's exact demands. Bismarck had so far made him feel only uncomfortable pressure toward accepting these in full, and misgivings as to the extent of German support in the Eastern difficulties. An attempt made on November 6, through the chargé d'affaires at Berlin, to obtain some modification of Germany's attitude by protesting that the demarcation of spheres of interest was to Austria's disadvantage met a firm rebuff from Herbert Bismarck.[67] In his statements regarding the situation and his own policy, he must limit himself to ground of which he felt reasonably sure; and that was still rather narrow territory.

[65] *P.P.*, 1887, xci, Turkey no. 1, p. 251.
[66] *Ibid.*, p. 256. November 2, circular despatch from Giers.
[67] *G. F. O.*, v, pp. 143–144. Herbert Bismarck to his father.

When the Delegations were opened the government showed what might be considered a proper attitude toward the emergency by asking an increase of funds for military expenditure; but every one realized that it could not escape a heavy attack upon its Eastern policy. The Hungarians announced their determination to clear up the discrepancies between its words and actions.[68] The opening speeches of both premiers evinced a willingness to go to war rather than yield a jot to Russia in the Balkans.[69] These speeches could not have been made without the previous knowledge of Kálnoky; but he was simply unable to prevent them, although he made an effort to attenuate their meaning by newspaper articles.[70] The speech from the throne, which followed, was as colorless and pacific as such utterances usually are.[71] Public opinion in the Austrian half of the Dual Monarchy did not rally enthusiastically to the declarations of its spokesman in the Delegation, appearing fairly well satisfied with the speech from the throne; while that in Hungary showed itself stoutly back of its representative's words, accusing the government and its supporters of faintheartedness.

[68] *Pester Lloyd*, November 4, 1886. "Es wird Aufgabe der Delegationen sein, Klarheit in diese Verhältnisse zu bringen und die Harmonie herzustellen zwischen den Versprechungen der Regierung und den Thatsachen, zwischen dem, was das Cabinet als sein Programm ausgibt und dem was es duldet."

[69] *M. A. Z.*, November 7. Dr. Smolka, Austrian premier: "Ob aber der Friede auch für die nächste Zukunft wird erhalten werden können? Eine Frage welche sich einer zutreffenden Beurtheilung unsererseits zwar entzieht, welche aber angesichts der schwierigen äusseren Verhältnisse, wie sie sich zu gestalten begonnen haben, eine ernste Beunruhigung wachzurufen geeignet ist." Count Tisza, Hungarian premier: "The peoples of the monarchy, and especially the Hungarian citizens, justly insist that the vital interests of the monarchy in the East must be defended at any cost, even at that of an armed conflict."

[70] *Presse* (Vienna), November 5. "Selbst Dr. Smolka dachte wohl kaum an eine unmittelbare bevorstehende Action. . . . Wir glauben daher aussprechen zu dürfen, dass übermässige Besorgnisse nicht am Platze sind, und dass es voreilig wäre, wenn man an das plötzliche Hervorbrechen eines Conflictes glauben würde."

[71] *Times*, November 8. "The recent events in Sofia have brought about a fresh dangerous crisis, the development of which and, I trust, its pacific solution occupy at the present moment the full attention of my government. . . . The excellent relations on which we stand with all the Great Powers . . . justify the hope that, notwithstanding the difficult situation in the East, it will be found possible, while safeguarding the interests of Austria-Hungary, to preserve the blessings of peace to Europe." Also *Geschichtskalender*, 1886, p. 256.

Bismarck could see more trouble coming and but little chance of escape, except through the caution of Kálnoky. He did well to make known his wish that Germany be kept out of the discussion as far as possible. On November 7, the *Norddeutsche Allgemeine Zeitung* expressed the opinion that the speeches of the two premiers would not affect the sound policy of the government. Next day, it expressed strong approval of the speech from the throne and joined the Emperor in hoping that Austria's interests could be preserved without endangering the general peace.

The increasingly critical aspect of the Bulgarian situation and the determined attitude of the Hungarians impelled the Austrian government to push more actively the progress of its rapprochement with England while the parliamentary struggle was still going on. Kálnoky hurried back from Pest to Vienna for a talk with Sir Augustus Paget, who left at once for London. The project of an understanding for the purpose of frustrating Russia's designs was freely spoken of.[72] Nevertheless, matters had developed no further by the 9th of November, when Lord Salisbury delivered his speech at the Lord Mayor's banquet.

The prime minister had two main questions of foreign policy with which to deal — the two being much more closely connected than was apparent. The first one he took up was that of Egypt, in regard to which the French had been showing themselves increasingly importunate. The matter of evacuation had been pressed by the French ambassador. Freycinet had even discussed it with the other Powers and found Russia and Turkey willing to support him, Germany and Austria non-committal, Italy in opposition. On November 7, the *République Française* had published a complete account of these informal negotiations, beginning with the d'Aunay interviews. The question was thus put squarely and publicly before the British government; and Lord Salisbury was obliged to deliver a firm reply. He did so, stating that no date could possibly be set for the evacuation, which was to be determined by accomplishment within the country and not by pressure from outside powers.[73]

[72] *N. F. P.*, November 8.
[73] *Times*, November 10.

Turning to Bulgaria, he reviewed the course of events there, beginning with the "midnight conspiracy" of officers "debauched by foreign gold," which had brought down Prince Alexander; and continuing with the efforts of Russia "to save those men from the doom they had justly merited," and her further "encroachment upon the rights of a free and independent people." Yet his conclusion was hardly in tune with this fiery invective against Russian policy. The responsibilities which England had assumed under the treaty of Berlin, he said, were corporate, not isolated: "The duties which fall upon England, not on account of our own interests but as a member of the European confederacy, she will perform in concert with the other Powers of the European confederacy, but she will not accept the duty of maintaining these obligations on behalf of others who do not think it necessary to maintain them for themselves." The others who were so backward in asserting their rights he indicated to be Austria and Turkey. Perhaps his most significant pronouncement was the sentence: "The opinion and judgment of Austria must weigh with enormous weight in the councils of Her Majesty's Government, and the policy which Austria pursues will contribute very largely to determine the policy which England will also pursue." He concluded by saying, like the Austrian Emperor, that for the present he saw "no cause for apprehension that the blessing of European tranquillity will be disturbed."[74] The speech was, in Bismarck's view, an improvement over Churchill's in that it evinced a willingness to act with Austria alone and did not require the coöperation of the entire Triple Alliance; but it showed no disposition to move faster than Austria herself did, and indicated that the understanding was as yet incomplete.

Within the Dual Monarchy there was a general feeling that Great Britain had definitely declined the initiative.[75] The Hungarians showed a strong disposition to take the lead thus proffered, relying upon what were after all pretty definite as-

[74] *Times*, November 10.
[75] *M. A. Z.*, November 13. Vienna, November 11. "Man hat eben hier sowohl als in Pest nicht übersehen, dass aus der Rede Lord Salisbury's hervorgeht, es sei ein Mitthun Englands nur dann zu erwarten, wenn Oesterreich vorangeht."

surances of support.[76] Bismarck's press, while making the most possible out of Salisbury's declarations, still threw its greatest weight on the side of a peaceful understanding on the basis of the League of the Three Emperors.[77]

When Count Kálnoky came, on November 13, to make his exposition of foreign policy before the budget section of the Hungarian Delegation, he gave evidence of accord with the views then being pressed by Bismarck. He insisted upon the peaceful settlement of disputes with Russia as the fundamental object of his policy, minimizing the seriousness of the existing situation. He admitted the existence of certain limitations upon the German alliance, but affirmed its solidity as a final resort. He expressed confidence that Germany would support the Austrian cause within the limits of prudence imposed on her by circumstances.[78]

[76] *Pester Lloyd*, November 11. "Schwerlich konnte jemand erwarten, dass eine Allianz unserer Monarchie mit England ohne weiteres werde herzustellen sein; aber eine förmliche Allianz hat ja auch auf dem Berliner Congress so wenig bestanden, dass England theils mit der Pforte, theils mit Russland separate Unterhandlungen führte. Die Entente der beiden Mächte — Oesterreich-Ungarn und Grossbrittanien — über die cardinalen Punkte der Politik genügte jedoch bereits, um unter Assistenz Deutschlands und unter thätiger Theilnahme Italiens eine Constellation herzustellen, der sich Russland beugen musste. . . . Es kann nicht zweifelhaft sein, dass einer offenen Aggression Russlands eine Gruppirung der Mächte folgen würde, welche derjenigen des Jahres 1878 weder an Kraft, noch an Erfolg nachstehen musste. So vorsichtig die Besprechungen Lord Salisbury's auch seien, dieselben dürfen in ihrem Werthe doch nicht unterschätzt werden."

[77] *Politische Correspondenz*, Berlin, November 12. "Diejenigen welche in der Natur der orientalischen Fragen etwas tiefer eingedrungen sind, werden sich dadurch, dass eine solche Frage mit allen ihren Schattenseiten und Schwierigkeiten wieder hervorgetreten ist, keineswegs verblüffen und sich auch nicht in der Ueberzeugung irre machen lassen, dass bei dem Schwergewichte der thatsächlich friedlichen Absichten der drei Kaiser eine friedliche Lösung sich ermöglichen lassen wird. . . . Das Berliner Cabinet glaubt, dem Frieden nicht besser dienen zu können, als indem es sich dem ernsten und aufrichtigen Bestreben widmet, divergirende Anschauungen auszugleichen, zwischen widerstreitenden Interessen zu vermitteln und Missverständnisse aus dem Wege zu räumen."

[78] *Times*, November 15. "It is only natural that two great States of such extent . . . should have also some interests not common to both, and lying without the sphere of interest of one or the other. There are no obligations to protect these interests. . . . Relations such as exist between Austria-Hungary and Germany are then only called into practical force when the absolutely united interests of both countries are concerned. . . . The continuance of each country as a strong and independent Power forms for both an important interest. In the present state of

Prince Bismarck, he said, had "made his advice and mediation felt . . . in the most loyal and advantageous way for the peace of the world and for our own interests. On this point there exists between the two Cabinets not the slightest want of harmony, but only the utmost friendliness and mutual confidence." He indicated England as the immediate reliance in case of actual trouble.[79] In defining the limits of such trouble, he declared that, "even a temporary single-handed occupation of Bulgaria by foreign troops, without the previous consent of Turkey and the other Powers, would be a violation of the treaties which in our opinion is not admissible." As to the extent of Russian control which might be permitted in the final settlement, he could "only say that any appropriation of the self-governing powers of the autonomous principality, or anything approaching a protectorate would not be admissible." After replying to several questions, he reiterated his conviction that "a middle course must be found," and declared that, "in the definitive settlement of the Bulgarian situation Russia's coöperation is unquestionably essential." [80]

This last declaration characterized precisely Kálnoky's diplomatic method and defined the issue between him and the powerful predecessor who now came forward as his critic. Count Andrássy, the signer of both the treaty of Berlin and the alliance with Germany, was at this moment opposing the policy of the understanding with Russia in the press, in the council chamber, and in Parliament. A memorial to the Emperor argued strongly for direct action against Russia in Bulgaria, based simply upon

Europe, Germany's present position without the powerful Austria-Hungary at her side is scarcely conceivable. . . . In this sense the community of the position of Germany and Austria-Hungary is more unshakable than if it were based only on the clauses of treaties." *Geschichtskalender*, 1886, p. 259.

[79] *Times*, November 15. "Our relations with England are at present of special interest, . . . and I attach much value to the declarations of English statesmen in the present question, since they show that a profitable change of views has taken place in healthy public opinion. . . . The identical view held in England on the important European questions now under discussion, the identity of important interests and the wish for the maintenance of peace, permit us to hope that England will also join us if it should come to a question of intervening for the maintenance of the Berlin Treaty and the legal status created by it." *Geschichtskalender*, 1886, p. 260.

[80] *M. A. Z.*, November 16. *Geschichtskalender*, 1886, pp. 260–261.

German support and in full confidence that the only outcome would be Russia's peaceful submission. According to the views expressed by the former minister, the foundation of Austro-Hungarian foreign policy, as laid by him in the German alliance, was a finished work, upon which the structure of eastward expansion could be solidly reared without need of further additions. Understandings with Russia, such as he himself had had recourse to before the German alliance was reached, were thenceforth to be rejected as building material which could only weaken the edifice. Recent policy, he maintained, had almost undone his work by reintroducing this harmful element. "If the congress of Berlin," he wrote, "excluded Russia from the Balkan Peninsula, my successors have brought her back again." He refused to admit any doubt that the policy of exclusive dependence upon Germany was practicable. "If it was possible," he argued, "to bring Bismarck to sign a treaty which assured us of Germany's coöperation without our having to accord full reciprocity as regards France, it should be ten times easier to hold him to the obligation after his signature." Bismarck's favorite project of partitioning the Balkan Peninsula he repudiated as absolutely as he did the policy of yielding to Russia which seemed its only alternative, on the ground that such an outcome meant eventual war.[81]

Andrássy's whole criticism of Kálnoky's policy really turns upon the question, whether or not Bismarck could have been brought to accept any other. Upon this point Andrássy's argument, based upon a single success on his own part, breaks down. Despite Bismarck's preference for the Austrian alliance when it came to an enforced choice, he never meant to cut the 'wire to Russia.' He would do all in his power to avoid taking the side of Austria openly in a dispute, knowing that the inevitable consequence would be a rapprochement between Russia and France. He would come out decisively in favor of his chosen ally only

---

[81] Friedjung, in *Biographisches Jahrbuch*, iii, p. 364 (*Historische Aufsätze*, p. 335). Cf. Wertheimer, iii, p. 329: "Ich befürchtete und befürcht noch, dass uns diese unnatürliche Kooperation in ihren Konsequenzen früher oder später, aber sicher vor folgende Alternative stellen wird: entweder Verzichtleistung auf unsere natürliche Machtsphäre oder Zweiteilung der Macht auf der Balkanhalbinsel und als Folge davon: Krieg."

when she was threatened with actual material injury which could not be prevented otherwise. Andrássy's solution, then, really meant war, which he professed it would avert.

Kálnoky, better informed of the real state of affairs than his predecessor, could, however, make but a feeble reply to this brilliant criticism. His main answer to the formidable memorandum was a statement pointing out that Andrássy owed all his own successes, in the days preceding the *Zweibund*, to a policy of conciliating Russia; but he made it without explaining why a different course was still not possible. Kálnoky did assert, however, that there were limits upon his conciliation of Russia to which he would firmly adhere.[82] Such had been his defence before the Emperor and such was now the sense of his speech to the Delegation. But his critic, still refusing to leave him in peace, resumed the attack in public.

On November 15, the Hungarian Opposition journal, *Pesti Naplo*, published a leading article attacking the Russian understanding and urging the government to take a strong initiative in regard to Bulgaria.[83] In the session of the following day, Andrássy personally took the floor with a speech of criticism along the same lines as this article and his recent memorandum. He had left the Dual Monarchy's foreign policy solidly based upon the German alliance, he stated: but "from the day it became apparent that the point of departure for our policy, especially in the Eastern Question, should be first of all an understanding with Russia, our alliance with Germany could no longer continue what it originally was." Now, "the troublesome task of continual arbitration between the two allies must weigh more and more heavily upon Germany every day," interfering with the proper working of her alliance with Austria. "The fault is to be found,"

[82] Friedjung, in *Biog. Jahrb.*, iii, p. 364 (*Aufs.*, p. 336). "Diesen Einwendungen begegnete Kálnoky durch die Erinnerung an die Tatsache, dass auch Andrássy seine Erfolge durch Vereinbarungen mit Russland vorbereitet hatte, vorerst durch das seit 1871 gepflegte sogenannte Dreikaiserbündnis und später durch die Abmachung von 1876 . . . Kálnoky versicherte übrigens, dass, wenn Russland sich je über die Verträge hinwegsetzen sollte, es auch ihm an Festigkeit in der Abwehr nicht fehlen werde."

[83] *M. A. Z.*, November 17. Article quoted.

he concluded, "not in any lack of good will on Bismarck's part, but in the very nature of the triple relationship and in the conception of it which impels us to wait for others to do what we should do, to speak as we should speak." His interpretation of the nature and application of the German alliance is highly significant: "I believed I ought to say all this in order to demonstrate the falseness of the view that the bond between the two states is less advantageous to both parties than had been expected. It is my personal conviction that, so long as our policy in Balkan matters directly concerning us is based upon a programme consistent with the interests of the monarchy and the peace of Europe, . . . we can count under all circumstances upon the coöperation of our German ally." [84]

Andrássy's real purpose in making this attack is not clear. He could hardly have hoped to persuade Kálnoky into altering his course and trying to force Bismarck's hand after matters had gone as far as they had. Even if all the advice had been sound, a responsible minister might well have hesitated to follow it. Austria's recent venture in taking the initiative — the Serbian business — had not brought encouraging results. Kálnoky would surely prefer henceforward to conduct himself as Bismarck desired he should do. Whether the ex-minister finally recognized the uselessness of the argument or not, he ended by abandoning his position without further debate.[85] Kálnoky, in his reply, made no reference to Andrássy's observations regarding the German alliance, and only met the criticism of his statement about the necessity of consulting Russia by the lame explanation that he "had in view, naturally, only the fact that Russia, like all the other signatory powers, had to take part in this work." Nevertheless, Andrássy declared his doubts satisfied, and said he had no desire to make difficulties for the government.[86]

---

[84] *M. A. Z.*, November 19. *Geschichtskalender*, 1886, pp. 262–263.

[85] Bismarck's opinion, expressed on the 15th, was: "Andrassy habe jetzt Kalnoky beseitigen wollen, es sei aber nicht geglückt. Von dem phantastischen ungarischen Parlament könne man keine vernünftige auswärtige Politik erwarten." Lucius von Ballhausen, p. 356.

[86] *M. A. Z.*, November 19.

On November 18, before the Austrian budget section, Kálnoky made some statements that more nearly met Andrássy's criticisms of his policy. The German alliance, he asserted, had suffered no alteration since 1879, "either in its fundamental basis or in its extent and effectiveness." Having an "entirely different character" from the Russian understanding, it remained unaffected thereby.[87] The Austrian government thus showed itself fully committed to Bismarck's view of the case and fully confident that what he advised would bring results in the end.

German comment upon these declarations, and indeed upon the whole Bulgarian situation at this time, was exceedingly sparse, and, for the most part, unenlightening. However, the *Kölnische Zeitung* published, on November 15, a weighty article approving Kálnoky's stand. It declared that "the boundaries of the German-Austrian alliance are wide enough to permit Germany to live in peaceful relations with Russia while Austria, in concert with England, restrains the insolence of Panslavism." It defended the policy of peaceful understanding with Russia, asserting that the alliance "would mean war and not peace if it bound Germany to oppose Russia and so forced the Tsar to dip for favors in the witches' caldron by the Seine." Bismarck's unrivalled statesmanship assured an arbitration which would satisfy Russia's just claims in Bulgaria without war. But any attempt on Russia's part "to answer the evolving Anglo-Austrian understanding by a Franco-Russian . . . would set in motion a whole forest of bayonets."[88] The last point was made with proper sharpness; for Bismarckian policy was just then in a situation demanding sharp action. Having practically cut off all prospect of good relations with France, the chancellor must trust solely to his influence upon Russia to keep these two apart.

[87] *M.A.Z.*, November 21. *Geschichtskalender*, 1886, p. 264. The speech is first misplaced and given as of the session of the 13th, then repeated in part under its proper heading.

[88] Lucius von Ballhausen (p. 357) records similar opinions to these under the date of November 16. He even goes so far as to make the somewhat over-hasty statement: "Klar wird daraus, dass es Bismarck gelungen ist, England in den Vordergrund zu bringen und stark gegen Russland engagiert zu haben."

## V

By mid-November, the road to good relations with France was indeed closed. The agitation over Egypt, incited to distract the British government, had been under way hardly a month when it died down, owing to Bismarck's refusal to meet France's demands for support. Having served his turn, it was killed off as soon as the French government attempted to convert his hints into serious assurances. On November 10, the Royalist organ, *Le Français*, sarcastically announced: "The courteous refusal which M. Herbette's overtures have received at Berlin coincides with the Marquis of Salisbury's declarations at Guildhall, and leaves no doubt that the only result of the Machiavellism of the Quai d'Orsay has been to facilitate the rapprochement between the London cabinet and the German Empire." On the same date, Hohenlohe records that a confidant of Grévy approached him on the subject of an entente and was rebuffed on the ground that Germany could never meet France's conditions.[89]

After a brief interruption, the German press had readily recurred to its chronic recriminations against France's incorrigible lust for revenge. The annoyance of the German government at France's refusal to accept the treaty of Frankfort as final was, moreover, transforming itself into a real disquiet at the increase of French military strength. The reforms of 1875, which had nearly led to a new war, had left France formidable but still in a position of inferiority to Germany. Those now undertaken by Freycinet and Boulanger threatened to give her an ultimate superiority. The project of reducing the term of service from five to three years would make possible the training of increased numbers of recruits. The Lebel rifle, with its smokeless-powder cartridge, and the new explosive, melinite, would establish a superiority of

---

[89] Hohenlohe, ii, p. 401 (Amer., ii, p. 368). Paris, November 10. "Der Advokat Reitlinger, ein Vertrauter Grévys, mit dem ich in einer Prozessangelegenheit zu verhandeln hatte, erbot sich, mit mir über die Bedingungen einer Annäherung, einer Allianz zwischen Frankreich und Deutschland zu sprechen. Ich lehnte es ab, da ich zu solchen Verhandlungen nicht kompetent sei. Auch bemerkte ich ihm, ich wisse sehr wohl, dass die Franzosen eine Allianz mit Deutschland unter Bedingungen anstrebten, die ihnen Deutschland nun und nimmermehr gewähren könne. Darauf zog er ab."

armament. The reorganization and reëquipment of the army would probably require years to effect; but the outlook appeared far from rosy to German eyes.

German military authorities had begun seriously to calculate the chances of Germany's being passed in the race if something were not done. Their first measure must be an effort to keep ahead. Accordingly, the ministry of war prepared a new seven-year army bill, raising the active force to a figure consonant with the population of the empire at the period.[90] The increase of the army at a rate to keep pace with the growing population and wealth of the nation was a cardinal point in Bismarck's system. This particular increase was not excessive; and the time for renewing the law of 1880 was anticipated by only a year. That the army must be kept as far as possible out of the Reichstag's control by long-term appropriations was another axiom of policy. Apart from the French peril, there were reasons enough for the bill as it was presented and for making every effort to push it through. The peril itself gave him a lever for doing so, and had not improbably been cultivated by him partly with such a purpose in mind. There must be a bogy of foreign danger to flourish before the eyes of the Reichstag in order to make the measure acceptable. Under the existing circumstances, Russia could not well be employed in this rôle, while France had become admirably fitted to play it.

All Germany's military leaders did not share in the general alarm. On November 16, the acting chief of the general staff, Count Waldersee, sent a very cool-headed survey of the situation to Bismarck. He discounted the rumors of impending war which came from the military attaché at Paris, and gave it as his opinion that all the military considerations in the case were against the probability of a French attack. He described the development of the French army as in every way far behind the German, but

[90] The proportion between active army and total population established by article 60 of the imperial constitution was 1 to 100. As the population of the empire in 1887, based on the figures of the census of December, 1885, was about 47,000,000, there was nothing extraordinary in the proposal to raise the army figure to 468,000. The strength fixed in 1880, for the period ending March 31, 1888, was 427,000.

offered no observations on the future.[91] It is to be noted that these views of Waldersee, although Bismarck signified his approval of them, did not hinder the government from proceeding with the new army bill.

Behind the obvious considerations in favor of its course lurked others more sinister still, influencing the military authorities and, despite his professions to the contrary, even Bismarck himself. If the war propaganda stirred up to impress the country should precipitate an actual conflict, the result (it was felt) would be gain rather than loss; for the inevitable war might then be waged under conditions relatively more favorable than those of a later period. The minister of war stated that everything was ready for a speedy victory and that an immediate war would be highly advantageous.[92] If, then, the Reichstag should not respond to the government's pressure, there would be every reason for forcing the issue, since the maintenance of the existing ratio between French and German strength would have been made practically hopeless. With all these possibilities in view, Bismarck did not shrink from aggravating the situation by stirring up popular passions.

On November 22, the new bill was passed by the Bundesrat. Next day, the *Kölnische Zeitung* opened the campaign designed to terrify the Reichstag into concurrent action. The same inspired journal which, ten days before, had warned Russia against any relations with Germany's western neighbor now stated: "It is only a question of time, measurable by years or half-years, before the old struggle must be resumed. . . . The probability appears slight that, without a new trial of arms, the conviction can be impressed upon France that Germany's success springs from fundamental causes."

The strained situation brought about by this press campaign against France coincided most inconveniently with a new crisis in Russia's relations with Bulgaria. On November 10, the Assembly at Tyrnovo had unanimously elected Prince Waldemar of Den-

---

[91] *G. F. O.*, vi, pp. 153–154. This is the only document printed bringing out the views of the military authorities on this situation.

[92] Lucius von Ballhausen, p. 355.

mark, brother-in-law of the Russian Emperor, to the Bulgarian throne. But the prince at once declined the honor, under persuasion of the Russian government, which did not desire a sovereign of quite such high connections for this refractory people. The Sobranie thereupon dissolved, leaving full powers in the hands of the regency. Soon afterward, General Kaulbars involved himself in a final dispute with the provisional government, and, on the 20th, left the country, severing diplomatic relations on the part of his own government. The only practical effect of his mission had been the ruin of the Russian cause in Bulgaria. The golden opportunity to revive it had passed; and it must henceforward sink lower day by day.

This severe setback to Russia's prestige was very painfully felt at St. Petersburg. Already most disquieting reports were coming from the German representatives there. Counsellor von Bülow was told: "The Emperor is exasperated by the situation, furious against Austria, and much irritated against you too." [93] When Count Peter Shuvalov endeavored to defend Bismarck from the somewhat vague accusations brought against him, the Tsar replied: "Yes, but when we ask anything of Bismarck, he doesn't do it." [94] The court was more than ever riddled by political intrigues, with the Panslavist and pro-French clique rather in the ascendant. Its leading protagonist, Katkov, was getting more and more into the Tsar's confidence every day, while Giers, the champion of the German alliance, was losing favor and in danger of dismissal. Under these circumstances, no great importance could be attached to a reassuring despatch sent out by Giers on November 23, explaining the outcome of the Kaulbars mission, and asserting that his sovereign sought only the welfare of Bulgaria and would continue to pursue it "by peaceful means, without departing from treaties so long as they are respected by the other Powers." [95]

One of the most disturbing facts about the situation was that no one knew what Russia now wanted to do — least of all, the Russians themselves. An occupation of Bulgaria was spoken of,

[93] *G. F. O.*, v, p. 68. November 15, Bülow to ?
[94] *Ibid.*, v, p. 73. November 16, Schweinitz to Bismarck.   [95] *Ibid.*, v, p. 89.

even a direct attack upon Austria. In preparation for some vaguely conceived action against Russia's existing allies, attempts were made to enlist new ones — attempts as ill-regulated and planless as Russia's foreign policy of the moment in general. It was one of these which brought about the curious imbroglio in regard to the protection of Russian interests in Bulgaria after the breach. The details of this extraordinary tangle are almost impossible to unravel. Negotiations were apparently being carried on through at least three, and perhaps four, Russian agencies at once — Kaulbars at Sofia, Nelidov at Constantinople, the foreign office, and, it was said, the Tsar himself. At all events, propositions were made to both Germany and France for taking Russian subjects under the protection of their consuls. Neither government displayed much enthusiasm about the proffered honor; and Freycinet seems to have communicated with Bismarck before making his reply to the request.[96] The outcome, reached only after a week of complicated negotiations, was a division of the task. Germany assumed it in Bulgaria proper: France, in Eastern Rumelia.

Associated with this clumsy advance on Russia's part was another, better calculated to win France's favor and destined to develop seriously in the following year. The earliest reports of advances in the preceding months had contained mention of an offer of Russian support in the Egyptian question. Bismarck had actually expressed approval of such a course in his interview with Herbette, although he himself was supporting England and less than a month previously had given the British government to understand that he would favor an Anglo-French understanding on the matter as a counterpoise to Russia. At all events, Russia now stepped into the place which Germany had declined to fill. At the same time that Kaulbars was handing over the archives at Sofia to the French consul, Nelidov was backing up the French ambassador at Constantinople in a protest against any private arrangements between Turkey and England as to the future of Egypt.[97] Welcome as was this support, it led to no immediate im-

[96] H. Galli, *Les dessous diplomatiques*, Paris (1894?), p. 30.

[97] *Times*, November 22, 1886 (Constantinople, November 20); *L'Univers*, November 23 (Varna, November 21).

provement of relations, owing to England's delay in opening new negotiations on the subject. So Russia's efforts in the direction of France strengthened her position but little. A tentative approach to Italy yielded even less result.[98]

No better prospect was opened by the fall of Freycinet, on December 3; for the collapse of his government was generally attributed to disapproval of his modest declarations of November 27 respecting Egypt and the Far Eastern protectorates.[99] Although the final crash came over a question of internal administration, it marked in reality a new reaction against the heritage of Ferry. There was nothing to be gained, then, at the moment by offers of coöperation in the field of colonial policy. The Russian government again gave up its attempt to draw closer to France.[100]

## VI

The approach of a crisis in Germany's relations with France at the very moment when the Bulgarian question was entering upon a new and dangerous phase put before Bismarck a double problem of appalling difficulty. All the previous accomplishments of his policy in both Western and Eastern Europe were at stake. A way out of his predicament might have been found by sacrificing either Austria's position in the Balkan Peninsula or Germany's position in Alsace-Lorraine, but he was determined to yield nothing on either hand. It is upon a judgment of the wisdom and statesmanship displayed in this determination that any

[98] Golitsyn, *Edinburgh Review*, January, 1888, p. 153.
[99] *Journal officiel*, Chambre des députés, session of November 27, pp. 2012-13. "A mon sens jamais la France ne doit se faire à l'idée que l'Egypte puisse passer définitivement entre les mains d'une grande puissance européenne. . . . il serait impolitique et peu conforme à la dignité de la France et à sa considération dans le monde, de renoncer aux acquisitions qu'elle avait faites, de sorte que notre devise a été, prenant le héritage tel que nous le recevions: Rien de moins! rien de plus!" The answer to these declarations was a vote of 269 for and 245 against the Annam-Tonkin appropriations.
[100] *Times*, December 29, 1886. Vienna, December 26. "Respecting Bulgarian affairs, M. Clemenceau admitted that there had been some coquettings between Russia and France. . . . 'Russia, in fact, chucked France under the chin, and France did not repel the advance. But she did not encourage it, and nothing serious was intended on either side.'"

criticism of his subsequent diplomacy must be based. Taking it as a starting-point, the obvious course to follow was the one he chose.

Since the disturbing elements in the situation, as Bismarck had created and maintained it, were France and Russia, the natural process of diplomacy was to build up a combination of all the other Powers against these two. With this process, which was already in operation, Bismarck continued more energetically than ever, though for reasons which he held to be important he would still not enter openly into that aspect of the combination which was directed against Russia. As far as France was concerned, the reasons which had led him, two years before, to include her in a system designed for the discomfiture of England had now disappeared, and he was quite willing to reverse the combination, only holding back from too close relations with England on his own part. These reservations make his diplomacy tortuous and confusing; but its ends remain clear.

A fairly good outline of Bismarck's policy is found in a marginal note on a document dated January 3, 1887. It runs: "Our interest calls for: Italy's support for ourselves against France and for Austria against Russia . . . ; as eventual *pis aller*, a dual alliance with Italy against France alone, with Italy's benevolent neutrality in dealings between Austria and Russia . . . . That in such dealings Austria should be strengthened by the support of Italy and, eventually, of England, is also to our interest; for they will not lightly go to war with Russia, and if they only oppose her and keep her occupied, that will assure peace for a long time to come."[101]

As matters stood toward the close of the year 1886, there were necessary to complete Bismarck's combination two Powers of which he could not be sure, Italy and England. Negotiations with the former had been at a standstill throughout the preceding month, pending the transmission to Vienna of Italy's proposed amendments to the treaty of the Triple Alliance. When this was finally accomplished through Herbert Bismarck, on the 1st of December, the proposals justified Kálnoky's worst fears both as

[101] *G. F. O.*, iv, p. 228.

to their extent and as to their definiteness. The first proposal was for an article providing that, while all parties should coöperate in maintaining the status quo in the Turkish territories bordering the Adriatic and Aegean Seas, any occupation of regions there by Italy or Austria-Hungary in consequence of action by a third Power should be undertaken only after a preliminary accord based upon the principle of compensation. Another addition was designed to safeguard Italy's negotiations with England regarding Egypt against any impairment by the policy of her allies. The final proposal was for the full backing of the Central Empires in any hostilities which might be undertaken by Italy against France in Europe or in Tripoli in consequence of French aggression against Tripoli or Morocco.[102]

The price for Italy's adhesion to the policy of the Central Powers was indeed a heavy one; but Bismarck must needs make an effort to pay it. He had by this time broken definitely with France and opened the press campaign which preceded the submission of his army bill to the Reichstag. The importance of Italy's position in his system of alliances increased as the chronic threat of war with France approached possible realization. Moreover, Italy was the bond by which he hoped to attach England to his system, both as a factor of importance in a French war and as a member of the triple combination in restraint of Russia by which Austria's interests might be conserved without his own direct intervention. He could not do otherwise than assure Robilant of his best efforts in behalf of the proposals.[103]

While awaiting the decision, Robilant measured his support of the anti-Russian combination with great nicety. He expressed sufficient approval of the views of Austria and England to indicate his preference for their side, yet maintained a certain reserve and continually laid emphasis upon Italy's special interests. On the 28th of November, following upon the declarations of Salisbury and Kálnoky, he defined his own position in a speech before the

[102] G. F. O., iv, p. 205.
[103] Chiala, p. 477. December 1, 1886, Launay to Robilant. "J'ai lieu de croire que le Chancelier apportera l'esprit le plus bienveillant et le plus conciliant dans l'examen du projet du traité, et que dans la mesure du possible il s'emploiera à exercer une bonne influence à Vienne."

Chamber of Deputies. In the whole Bulgarian matter, he said, "our conduct is based clearly upon the Treaty of Berlin. . . . The prince must be acceptable to Bulgaria and must be chosen by the Bulgarian Assembly. . . . The election must then obtain the sanction of the Sultan and the approval of all the Powers." [104] So much was commonplace and committed him to little. He continued, for the benefit of the foreign statesmen who sought his support: "But, gentlemen, at the same time, we have not lost sight of the general interest (which is ours in particular) that the peace of Europe should not be disturbed by a question in which we do not find ourselves directly involved, but which would become of the greatest importance to us if it should ever lead to a conflict between two or more Great Powers, or to separate accords between them." [105] Italy's position was sufficiently clear. Her allies must make her an equal partner in their dealings — and even assure her certain advantages besides.

The demands proved to be more than Austria could swallow, although Bismarck accompanied them with a strong recommendation for their acceptance, declaring that he found in them nothing prejudicial to Austria's interests.[106] Kálnoky objected both to the commitment of Austria in Mediterranean issues and to the restriction of her freedom of movement in the Near East.[107] He was forced to give way by Bismarck's threat to close with Italy alone.[108] However, he sought to modify the Near Eastern clause by extending its application to the Balkans as a whole and by eliminating the principle of compensation. He further urged that Italy's promise of a benevolent neutrality in the event of war with Russia be converted into one of armed support.[109] Bismarck argued strongly and repeatedly against the proposed extension of the Balkan clause on the ground that it implied a sort of guarantee of the status quo, which he maintained Germany could not enter

---

[104] Chiala, p. 444.      [105] *Ibid.*, p. 446.

[106] G. F. O., iv, p. 204. December 1, Herbert Bismarck's memorandum.

[107] *Ibid.*, iv, pp. 211–212. Reuss to Bismarck. Pribram, i, p. 185 (Amer., ii, p. 59).

[108] Pribram, i, p. 185 (Amer., ii, p. 60). December 13, Tavera to Kálnoky.

[109] G. F. O., iv, pp. 213–219. For the last of these proposed amendments, see Pribram, i, pp. 186–188 (Amer., ii, pp. 61–62). December 20, Kálnoky to Széchényi.

into, since she recognized Russia's special right to intervene in Bulgaria. He even revived his unaccepted theory of the line of demarcation.[110] The Chancellor seems to have feared a trap which would have committed him to something, and to have overlooked the consideration that such a check upon Austrian zeal might have its uses. The condition that Italy pledge herself to an active part in war with Russia displeased him for the opposite reason that it would give Austria too many active partners, since she could already count on Serbia and Rumania. Robilant also refused to consider the Austrian amendments.[111] A deadlock set in which was not broken until well on into the year 1887.

Negotiations with England were also at a standstill. The dealings of the German ambassador continued to be mainly with Churchill, who was able to keep the government's policy tied up, but could not make formal and official proposals in the line of his own views. These were expressed by him, on December 4, as: "If Austria, with Germany's tacit backing (*connivence*) takes a decisive stand on the Eastern Question, England will join her, throwing her whole weight into the scale."[112] The displeasing feature of this programme was still, as Kálnoky shrewdly remarked, that "Austria is to take the first step." Salisbury talked of bolder measures — of a declaration to Russia that England could not remain indifferent to any hostile move against Austria, which Bismarck approved in a marginal note as "the practical way."[113] But Salisbury could not move without Churchill, who found such suggestions far too strong. Already foreseeing a breach with his chief, Churchill, wrote him the somewhat misleading letter of December 22, which was published after his resignation. In this letter he said: "A wise foreign policy will extricate England from Continental struggles and keep her outside of German, Russian, French or Austrian disputes. I have for some time observed a

[110] *G. F. O.*, iv, pp. 219, 222–223. Marginal notes. See also B. M. M., pp. 247–249.

[111] *G. F. O.*, iv, p. 226. January 3, Herbert Bismarck's memorandum of a conversation with Launay.

[112] *Ibid.*, iv, p. 285. December 5, Hatzfeldt to Bismarck.

[113] *Ibid.*, iv, pp. 288–289.

tendency in the Government attitude to pursue a different line of action which I have not been able to modify or check." [114]

Churchill may have felt himself being beaten by this time, but it was still a long while before English policy could throw off his hampering influence. The discussion with England, like that over the renewal of the Triple Alliance, dragged fruitlessly on into the following year.

Churchill was the great stumblingblock in the way of the fulfilment of Bismarck's whole design. Kálnoky would have displayed much less captiousness about the terms of the bargain with Italy, if he could have been sure that the adhesion of England would be thrown in. Reuss wrote from Vienna, on December 14: "If an agreement could be reached between England, Austria, and Italy for a common attitude on the Bulgarian question, Kálnoky believes, with Churchill, that it would have a great effect upon St. Petersburg and that a satisfactory solution of the existing difficulties would probably result." [115] But lack of confidence in Churchill blighted this entire conception of policy.

Bismarck was doing his best to make the Italian alliance more worth while to both Austria and Germany by attaching to it the coöperation of England. Toward the end of November Robilant had conveyed to Herbert Bismarck a letter stating that, in case of war, Italy would be able, besides defending her own frontier, to send 200,000 men, "either over the Alps to the aid of Germany on the Rhine, or through Austria against Russia." [116] The answer of the German government was: "Italy's military force would be much more important and valuable if it could be brought to bear *in alliance*, or at least in community of action, *with England*." The Italian government was advised "to make energetic efforts in this direction with Lord Salisbury." [117] But the current of diplomacy thus set in motion could reach no results until Churchill's opposition was overcome or got out of the way.

As long as the great design remained so far from fulfilment, Bismarck was obliged to move very cautiously with respect to

[114] Churchill, ii, p. 239. *Times*, January 28, 1887. Hansard, 3d series, cccx, col. 69.
[115] G. F. O., iv, p. 289.   [116] *Ibid.*, iv, p. 208.
[117] *Ibid.*, iv, pp. 224–225. December 27, memorandum by Herbert Bismarck.

Russia, endeavoring to calm the irritation caused by her failure in Bulgaria. This had become especially difficult, as Bismarck no longer had any positive plan on which to base a policy of conciliation. His old idea of a line of demarcation had been practically abandoned since the middle of November, when he had written on the margin of an unfavorable report from St. Petersburg: "Austria has just as little desire for a line of demarcation; it is, therefore, better that we should give up this idea and silently let it drop. Peter Shuvalov can be told that we no longer attach any importance to it, since *both* the interested parties are opposed to it."[118] When Bismarck brought up the idea again in his controversy with Austria over the proposed Balkan clause of the Triple Alliance, it no longer possessed any validity or real meaning. That Germany regarded the line as a *fait accompli*, as he wrote that she did, was no solution of the problem in the eyes of either Russia or Austria.

Moreover, Austria was beginning to break away again from the conciliatory course to which she had for a time adhered. About the 25th of November Kálnoky had made at Constantinople a proposal that the affairs of Eastern Rumelia, still in the hands of a Turco-Bulgarian commission, should be turned over to a body representing the signatories of the treaty of Berlin, a step which Bismarck stigmatized as an infraction of both public and private treaties.[119] In consequence of his remonstrances, Kálnoky altered his proposal, but only to the extent that he put it in the form of a warning to the Sultan to take no action concerning Bulgaria without first consulting the friendly Powers.[120]

Bismarck protested vehemently against Austria's course, which went quite contrary to the one he himself was attempting to follow. On December 2, he had composed a carefully phrased despatch to St. Petersburg asserting his recognition of the fact that "the prepanderance of Russian influence in Bulgaria is in accord with the spirit of existing treaties," and assuring the Russian government that he would place no obstacles in the way

[118] *G. F. O.*, v, p. 75.
[119] *Ibid.*, v, pp. 145–146. December 3, Herbert Bismarck to Reuss.
[120] *Ibid.*, v, p. 148, note.

of its efforts to reëstablish that influence.[121] This was not much of an assurance, but Bismarck proceeded to back it up by advising the Porte in favor of coöperation with Russia in Bulgaria.[122] This action was the exact antithesis of that being taken by Kálnoky at the same time.

The Russian reply asked a still greater service, namely, that Bismarck should use his influence with the other governments to assure their acceptance of the Sultan's proposals in regard to Bulgaria.[123] Bismarck replied that Russia was going beyond all right in asking him thus to bring pressure upon Austria. The memorandum of December 14 contains the additional observation, significant for the subsequent events: "On our part, we have never expected Russia to intercede at Paris for our desires, nor to endeavor to calm the *revanche* agitation among the French, although it must be clear to Russia that we would be freer to act politically in her favor if our relations with France were more secure." [124]

Having taken steps to plant this idea in the Tsar's mind, Bismarck proceeded to give another inexpensive demonstration of his good will by having his son, Herbert, advise the Bulgarian deputation, then canvassing Europe for candidates to their throne, that they had better come to terms with Russia and accept her candidate.[125]

The Tsar Alexander III had from the first responded warmly to these friendly overtures. On December 8, he remarked to the German ambassador: "I certainly do not wish to disturb the peace, and I know that the Emperor William will do everything to preserve it; I count upon him and Prince Bismarck." [126] He

[121] *G. F. O.*, v, p. 85.
[122] *G. B.*, 1889, Bulgaria, p. 43. December 6, 1886, Launay to Robilant. "Le comte de Bismarck ferait néanmoins entendre à ce diplomate [the Turkish Ambassador], que dans les limites du traité de Berlin, l'Allemagne prêterait volontiers son appui a tout accord entre la Turquie et la Russie, et qu' à cet effet il y aurait lieu de conseiller la Sublime Porte d'user son influence légitime dans la principauté pour obtenir une modification partielle de la régence."
[123] *G. F. O.*, v, p. 91. December 9, Giers to Shuvalov.
[124] *Ibid.*, v, p. 97.
[125] *Ibid.*, v, p. 159. December 19, 1886, memorandum by Herbert Bismarck.
[126] *Ibid.*, v, p. 92.

had complained, however, of the conduct of Austria. Before Bismarck's suggestive despatch of the 14th had been communicated to him, he sent Count Peter Shuvalov on a special mission to Berlin with instructions to declare solemnly that Russia had not the slightest intention of intervening in Bulgaria unless Prince Alexander should return, in which case he would occupy the country at once, regardless of the consequences. Shuvalov had no instructions bearing upon Bismarck's hints about support of Germany against France, but he took it upon himself, when the despatch containing them was shown him, to state that the Tsar would willingly subscribe to anything Germany might desire in that quarter, in return for an assurance that she would agree to the eventual 'closing of the Straits,' which was Russia's aim in the Near East.[127]

These personal assurances from a diplomat so thoroughly committed to the policy of the German alliance as Count Shuvalov were of no final significance as regarded the Tsar's own sentiments; nevertheless, they encouraged Bismarck to go forward in the dangerous course he had entered upon of stirring up public opinion over the probability of a Franco-German war. The immediate occasion for this agitation was the putting through of the new army bill; but its potential consequences, as has been pointed out, were numerous and far reaching. If they were pushed to the extent of risking hostilities with France, the attitude of Russia must, indeed, be reckoned with. The diplomatic combination against her was still too far from completion to risk any flouting of her wishes. Austria was, accordingly, called sharply to order by a communication in harsh terms stating: "We regard a French war as a near eventuality and wish, therefore, to avoid with all possible care a simultaneous war with Russia." It was even stated, in disregard of the opinions expressed a month before by Count Waldersee, that "the French army is at present stronger than ours."[128]

It was under these circumstances that the German government

[127] *G.F.O.*, v, pp. 160–161, 212–214. January 6, 1887, memorandum by Herbert Bismarck.
[128] *Ibid.*, v, p. 149. December 16, memorandum by Count Rantzau.

prepared for its contest with the parliamentary Opposition. On December 13, in discussing with Lucius von Ballhausen the prospects of the new bill in the Reichstag, Bismarck ventured to observe: "It might even be a good thing if they should reject the military proposals and so give occasion for a dissolution. The danger of a war with Russia is just now less than ever, since we are in complete accord with respect to Bulgaria. The Austrians have been pursuing a foolish policy; and he [Bismarck] is obliged to stand between them and the Russians as between two quarrelsome dogs which would leap at each other the moment he unleashed them. They would surely do so if we got into a war with France; while the Russians would also hardly suffer us to annihilate France completely. Yet he is certain of the Emperor, though mishaps are of course possible." [129]

[129] Lucius von Ballhausen, p. 359. On the same date he wrote to the minister of war, General Bronsart von Schellendorff: "Für unsere gesammte politische Stellung würde das Verharren der Opposition bei der ursprünglichen Gegnerschaft und die dadurch bedingte Auflösung das Nützlichste sein, es ist aber mit unserem Pflichtgefühl nicht verträglich, diese Wendung anzustreben." Letter published in *Deutsche Allgemeine Zeitung*, April 2, 1922.

# CHAPTER VI

## BISMARCK AND FRANCE

### I

THE year 1887 was one of greater and more prolonged strain in relations between France and Germany than any since 1871. On two occasions war seemed very near, and it might well have come about but for the restraining influence of complications in the East, which would have given it a wider scope than Bismarck was prepared to consider. There were not wanting suspicions that he was deliberately manoeuvring toward a conflict and would have brought it on if he could have satisfactorily accounted for Russia — that his conciliatory policy in that quarter was designed to gain the Tsar's consent to the execution of his plans against France. Yet there is no reason to suppose he had any intention of sacrificing Austria's interests in the Balkans to such a scheme. His conciliation of Russia always stopped short of injury to Austria. His support of Austrian policy on the two alternative lines already discussed — the partition agreement with Russia and the construction of an Austro-Anglo-Italian entente against Russia — remains constant. If Russia and Austria were to be prevented from coming to blows, it was only to be done by a settlement which should conserve Austrian interests intact. This essential loyalty to the Austrian ally must not be lost sight of in following the actions and utterances of the German Chancellor through the early months of the year.

At the beginning of the year he believed that he had amply secured the interests of his ally, for the moment at least, by his recent efforts to pacify the Russians and reconcile them anew to the peaceable, if slow and unfruitful, course of diplomatic negotiations. He felt free to give his undivided attention to the quarrel with France. The very change of governments which had lately interfered with Russia's attempt at a rapprochement with France on the basis of the Egyptian question had at the same time given new occasion for hostile comments by the German press. If it meant a new reaction against Ferry's colonial policy, it meant also a new reaction against his system of intimate relations with Germany. Moreover, in the ministry formed by Goblet, the now formidable Boulanger retained his post; and in this fact German newspapers found confirmation of their worst fears as to the growth of the spirit of revenge.[1] In vain the new minister of foreign affairs, Flourens, instructed the ambassador at Berlin, on December 14: "There has been no change in the foreign policy of the government of the republic. I have, therefore, no new instructions to give you. What I ask of you is to make it felt by your attitude and language that the ministerial crisis . . . is to have no effect upon our diplomatic relations with the other Powers, and particularly with Germany."[2] In vain the German ambassador, Count Münster, again confirmed these assurances by his reports on conditions and the state of public opinion in France, even crediting Boulanger with peaceful intentions.[3] Bismarck impatiently dubbed him 'optimist,' and devoted himself to rebutting his arguments. When Münster incorporated a long, reassuring survey of the situation in a personal report intended for the Emperor, the Chancellor took him sharply to task, beginning his despatch with the words: "If His Majesty and the federated governments shared the views developed . . . therein, the imperial government would hardly be in a position to present and uphold with conviction the military proposals it has made to the Reichstag."[4] The report was not presented to the sovereign.

Instead, Bismarck threw all his energy into measures of military preparation. On December 24, he wrote a long letter to General Bronsart von Schellendorff, the minister of war, asking his professional opinion on the advisability of hastening the re-

[1] *M. A. Z.*, December 8, 1886. Berlin, December 5. Freycinet (p. 364) makes the comment concerning the crisis of the 3d, "De ce jour date l'ouverture de la période appelée communément ' le boulangisme.' "

[2] Pagès (Senate Report), p. 219.

[3] *G. F. O.*, vi, pp. 156–160. December 20, 21, 30, Münster to Bismarck.

[4] *Ibid.*, vi, p. 163. January 4, 1887, Bismarck to Münster.

ëquipment of the entire army with the improved rifle which had recently been adopted. If the change was essential to Germany's victory in the next war, he said, no financial sacrifice should stand in the way of its immediate completion. "As regards the question of time," he wrote, "war *may* break out in the coming summer, although the probability is greater that it will be postponed for a year or more." [5]

The new army bill came up in the Reichstag on January 11. The government opened the debate in the traditional manner by attempting to plunge it into an atmosphere of imminent war. Old Field-Marshal von Moltke was brought forward to sound the ominous note. "If the demands of the government are refused, gentlemen, then I believe we shall quite certainly have war," was the solemn warning he uttered.[6] This was the stock phrase of the militarist justifying his doctrine of ' armed peace '; but a weight of special meaning lay behind it in view of the motives which had inspired the government to bring in the bill at this time. The warlike tone was taken in deep earnest by the military authorities, absorbed as they were in the doubtful competition of armaments with France.[7] Bismarck followed Moltke with a speech in which he elaborated on the field-marshal's theme of the danger to peace and outlined for the benefit of Germany and the world at large his general position and policy in regard to foreign affairs.

He began his exposition by eliminating any argument as to danger on the eastern frontier, and turned the attention of his auditors forcefully and repeatedly toward France. "If we had to reckon only with our relations in the East," he informed the deputies, "they would require no such exposition. But with regard to France it is quite otherwise." Of course, he went on to assure them, "We shall never attack France under any circum-

[5] *Deutsche Allgemeine Zeitung*, April 16, 1922.  [6] *Reden*, xii, pp. 173-174.
[7] *Zur europäischen Politik*, v, pp. 167-168. January 28, 1887, report of Count van der Straten Ponthoz (Berlin): "L'insistance du parti militaire pour une guerre immédiate révèle aussi la signification des paroles du Maréchal de Moltke . . . La pensée du Maréchal et des Généraux est que l'Allemagne devra se hâter d'entreprendre la guerre avec son armée encore fortement organisée, plutôt que de s'exposer à devoir faire plus tard cette même guerre avec une armée affaiblie par l'abandon de son budget septennal."

stances." But war must be expected. "My conviction is that we have to fear it through French aggression — whether in ten days or in ten years is a question I cannot answer. That depends entirely upon the duration of the present government in France."

The assembly was earnestly assured of the reality of the danger of a French attack. "It is possible any day," Bismarck asserted, "that the tiller may pass into the hands of a French government whose entire policy is nourished by the *feu sacré*. . . . Or the duel between ourselves and France may be precipitated whenever France becomes stronger than we, either through alliances or through the superiority of her armament." As an afterthought, he added as still another possibility, "the case that, as under the third Napoleon, foreign enterprises should be made safety-valves for the internal situation." The outcome of such a war he professed to regard as extremely doubtful, unless Germany made every preparation in her power. "I must say in this connection," were his words, "we have to face the possibility of defeat in such a war. I am not fearful enough to predict it; but no one can deny the possibility."

In conclusion, the Boulanger scarecrow was dangled before the assembly. "If Napoleon III," ran the Chancellor's warning, "undertook against us a great and difficult war which cost him his throne — in no way constrained from without, but simply because he believed it would strengthen his government within — why should not General Boulanger, for example, attempt the same thing if he came into power?"[8] The words found a vehement echo both in Germany and in France, where they proved the best possible advertising for the brummagem hero of the 'Patriots.'[9]

Deeming his development of the 'French Peril' sufficient to convince his hearers of their duty to vote the army bill, the Chancellor devoted the other portions of his speech to a justifica-

[8] *Reden*, xii, pp. 184 *et seq.*

[9] Freycinet, p. 369. "Ces paroles eurent en France un retentissement extraordinaire. Le Boulangisme prit naissance. Le général était, de par M. de Bismarck, sacré l'homme de la revanche. . . . On peut se demander si M. de Bismarck, dont tous les éclats étaient calculés, n'avait pas voulu appeler sur la France les troubles et les dissensions qui la paralysèrent pendant près de trois années."

tion of his Eastern policy, defending himself against the charges, pressed chiefly by Windthorst, of having sacrificed Germany's own interests and her treaty obligations to a culpable friendliness for Russia.

Germany's own interests, he insisted, were not involved in the Bulgarian question at all. The stir it had made in the country reminded him only of Hamlet's inquiry, "What's Hecuba to him?" Bulgaria was no more to Germany than Priam's wife to the player. The bones of the Pomeranian grenadier were once more rattled in derision of those who worried about Eastern affairs. He would see to it that Germany was never led astray by any such trifling considerations into damaging the important friendly understanding with Russia.[10] Yet he stoutly maintained that Austria had been neither betrayed nor ignored in the development of German policy. The bond between the two allies was very nicely defined in the sentence: "Our relations with Austria are based upon the consciousness on the part of both of us that the unimpaired existence of each as a Great Power is a necessity for the other." Still, he must add, "there are certain specific Austrian interests for which we cannot commit ourselves"; and vice versa. Austria's Balkan interests, he inferred, were just as much outside the scope of the alliance as Germany's colonial enterprises. "Whatever interests Austria has in Constantinople, Austria alone must judge: we have none there — I repeat it." [11] The declaration sounded categorical and complete; yet one has only to look back to the introductory sentence regarding the essential community of interests, which closely resembles the previous Austrian pronouncements, to observe a certain qualification — the fact that

---

[10] *Reden*, xii, p. 183. "Es ist uns vollständig gleichgültig, wer in Bulgarien regiert, und was aus Bulgarien überhaupt wird, — das wiederhole ich hier; ich wiederhole Alles, was ich früher mit dem viel gemissbrauchten und todtgerittenen Ausdruck von den Knochen des pommerschen Grenadiers gesagt habe: die ganze orientalische Frage ist für uns keine Kriegsfrage. Wir werden uns wegen dieser Frage von Niemand das Leitseil um den Hals werfen lassen, um uns mit Russland zu brouillieren. Die Freundschaft von Russland ist uns viel wichtiger als die von Bulgarien und die Freundschaft von allen Bulgarenfreunden, die wir hier bei uns im Lande haben."

[11] *Ibid.*, pp. 216–217.

Austria was operating under a guarantee of security which Bismarck had no intention to diminish.

The Chancellor enlarged upon the difficulties of his position, acting at once as *Anwalt des Friedens und Friedensadvokat*, holding the balance between Russia and Austria in the interest of the peace of Europe.[12] Peace, and only peace, he affirmed, was the object of Germany's policy in the East. Nevertheless, he did not close his speech without a hint at the desirability of a stronger policy on the part of other Powers. "England can fight Russia," he remarked, *à propos* of nothing but his cherished alternative to the policy he publicly professed, "without herself having to fear any serious damage at the hands of Russian forces. . . . But for us the case is very different." [13]

Thus is the exposition of policy complete. With France Germany stands in a relation of deliberately chosen hostility. German diplomacy is interested in holding off Russia from taking the French side. Yet the affected regard for Russia's interests in Bulgaria covers a secure guarantee of Austrian interests and a determination to serve them in the long run. If an arrangement like that of 1877 will not meet the needs of the situation, a combination like that of 1878 is to be expected.

The speech made the impression upon Europe which Bismarck's utterances could always be counted upon to produce. The forcible candor of his expressions carried conviction of his sincerity into most quarters. Official Russia and the 'Western' wing of opinion accepted his declarations upon the Eastern Question at their face value, finding an explanation in his powerlessness to follow any other course.[14] The Panslavists, through

[12] *Reden*, xii, p. 184. "Wir laufen dabei Gefahr, dass wir in Oesterreich und noch mehr in Ungarn als russisch bezeichnet und in Russland für österreichisch gehalten werden. Das müssen wir uns gefallen lassen; wenn es uns gelingt, den eigenen Frieden und den Europas zu erhalten, so wollen wir uns das auch gern gefallen lassen."

[13] *Ibid.*, p. 262.

[14] Вѣстникъ Европы, February, 1887, p. 859; Corti, p. 293. The matter was taken up by a special council at St. Petersburg, at which the chief of the general staff, General Obruchev, argued against accepting Bismarck's assurances and for joining France in a war upon Germany; but Giers and the party of the German alliance carried the day. January 23, 1887, Wolkenstein to Kálnoky.

their apostle, Katkov, expressed other views, but laid the blame for Russia's betrayal to her own stupidity.[15] The danger of a war between Germany and France was generally taken seriously, though opinions differed, naturally, as to the responsibility for the threat. The fact that the German publications dwelt upon the peril constantly, displaying increasing vehemence in their denunciations of France, was a consequence mainly of the Reichstag's refusal to adopt the government's military programme unless the period of its application were cut from seven years to three. The issue had been referred to the country; and propaganda must be made to influence the elections. France got more and more attention in the German press; Bulgaria, less and less. It was assumed that Germany's peaceful counsels had prevailed in regard to that problem, and that both Russia and Austria had decided to be reasonable.[16]

As far as Russia was concerned, this assumption was sufficiently justified by the attitude of Alexander III. When Bismarck's despatch of December 14 was at last read to him, on the 4th of January, he declined, indeed, to go into the references to France, but he expressed great satisfaction with the declarations respecting the Bulgarian question. He also spoke of the *entente intime* with Prussia as the "pivot of his policy," only regretting that state's decision to ally herself with Austria.[17] Bismarck's speech further reassured him. The Chancellor was able to inform the other German courts: "My statement has had its intended effect on both sides. The Emperor Alexander is, for the time being, calmed and contented, and no mistrust or resentment has been aroused against us in Vienna." [18]

But if the effect produced by the speech upon the state of feel-

[15] Katkov wrote in the *Moscow Gazette*: "It can be seen what a pitiful rôle our diplomacy has been playing in subordinating Russia to the ally of our enemy. Germany is closely bound to Austria, and Austria is crowding Russia out of the East by damaging her most vital interests. Austria could never have competed with Russia so boldly and, alas! so successfully if she had not been supported by Germany. That is why the latter finds herself forced to play the doubtful and equivocal rôle of posing at once as *procureur* and *avocat* of the peace." Cyon, p. 214.
[16] *Preussische Jahrbücher*, February, 1887, p. 173.
[17] *G. F. O.*, v, pp. 115–116. January 5, 1887, Bülow to Bismarck.
[18] *Ibid.*, v, p. 118.

ing in the Austrian capital could not be called one of mistrust, it was at least one of misgiving. This was as Bismarck desired, for he was extremely anxious at this moment to restrain Austria from any conduct irritating to Russia. His marginal comments on a report, describing the mental attitude of the Emperor Francis Joseph as 'depressed,' were: "That was necessary; better than if it were adventurous." [19] Kálnoky was even displaying a readiness to renew the treaty of the League of the Three Emperors.[20] Under these circumstances, Bismarck felt justified in pushing the development of the French 'war scare' with new vigor.

## II

The dissolution of the Reichstag had hardly been announced when the German newspapers began accumulating evidence of hostile designs on the part of France. The whole course of developments from then on is strongly reminiscent of the events of 1875. First came the piling up of minor incidents — items concerning French purchases of horses, of acids used in the manufacture of explosives, of lumber for the construction of temporary barracks in garrison and frontier towns. A touch of almost comic relief was later provided by an article suggesting that these new constructions were designed as quarters for the famous 'fourth battalions,' which had figured so largely in the crisis of 1875. Prohibitions upon the export of horses were proclaimed by Germany, Austria, and Russia. In a note of December 22, approving the recommendation of the minister of war for the German regulation, Bismarck had written: "A general prohibition on the export of horses, provided it is at all justified, would also have a useful parliamentary effect and . . . would bring home the situation in a properly comprehensible light to the voters in the event of new elections." [21] In a despatch to the chargé d'affaires at Paris, the Chancellor remarked: "The imperial government is considering the question of calling the French government's attention to the seriousness of measures which are likely to mislead the

---

[19] *G. F. O.*, v, p. 153.
[20] *Ibid.*, v, pp. 215–217. January 7, 17, Reuss to Bismarck.
[21] *Deutsche Allegemeine Zeitung*, April 16, 1922.

people as to the unquestionable desire of both governments to maintain peace." [22]

A rumor of this formidable intention, published in the London *Daily News*, led to the panic of January 24 on the Paris Bourse — the first of a series of such crises affecting the French and German stock exchanges in rapid succession. The rumor developed that Germany was about to ask explanations of France's military measures. It was denied by the *Norddeutsche Allegemeine Zeitung*; but the denial was followed in the same column by a communication from Lorraine to the effect that local opinion there had reached the "firm conviction that there will soon be war."

Bismarck was neglecting no means of confirming this conviction. On January 22 Hohenlohe had come to interview his chief on the advisability of certain local measures in Alsace-Lorraine. "I asked Bismarck," he writes, "if he approved of my proceeding against the French officers. He replied that he quite approved, only he thought it would be necessary to reintroduce the system of compulsory passes. This would emphasize the existing separation and alienation and react usefully upon the elections. Bismarck thinks it likely that war will break out at no distant date. He says that Boulanger may make a *coup d'état* at any moment, and then cause a rupture. The concentration of troops on the frontier, the mobilization, is forcing similar measures upon us." [23] Similar utterances were reported to the Belgian minister at the same period.[24] It appears from a conversation reported by him

[22] *G. F. O.*, vi, p. 167. January 22, Bismarck to Leyden.
[23] Hohenlohe, ii, p. 404 (Amer., ii, p. 371).
[24] *Zur europäischen Politik*, v, pp. 166–167. January 28, 1887. Count van der Straten Ponthoz reports, as received from a sure source, a conversation in which Bismarck discussed the situation: "Les conjonctures présentes ont beaucoup de gravité. Le Chancelier se défend d'en exagérer les perils pour intimider les électeurs. Comme il l'a dit dans ses récents discours au Reichstag, il prévoit qu'une guerre entre l'Allemagne et la France est inévitable. . . . Devant cette certitude d'une nouvelle guerre le parti militaire demande avec énergie qu'elle soit entreprise sans tarder, lorsque la France n'a pas complété encore la réorganisation de son armée. . . . L'ajournement de la guerre qui n'empêchera pas la guerre, diminue les chances de succès de l'Allemagne. Il y a pour le Chancelier une très grande responsabilité à résister aux généraux qui poussent à une guerre immédiate." Bismarck's apologists are able to cite many utterances voicing their hero's aversion to the doctrine of 'preventive wars'; but he appears to have deviated from these opinions on more

that, as in 1875, Bismarck was allowing himself to be swayed by the military alarmists and was again playing with their idea of a 'preventive war' to take France before she should be ready to begin. The party in favor of such a decision was numerous, powerful, and determined. The crown prince adhered to its views.[25] It was a force in the state which the Chancellor could not possibly ignore.

The opinion that war was near was shared by most observers. The London *Times*, on January 25, voiced a well considered conclusion that the danger was real and that it was in great part attributable to Bismarck. "We have not disguised our conviction," ran the leading article, "that the existing relations of the European Powers are painfully strained, and that this tension cannot be indefinitely prolonged without the risk, if not the certainty, of a collision. . . . If Germany, under the guidance of Prince Bismarck, were free to deal only with the French Government, it is quite conceivable that, in spite of all pacific protestations, an appeal would again be made to the arbitrament of the sword."

Before the close of the month, it was beginning to look as if the threat of war had passed the bounds of mere election propaganda

than one occasion. The most notorious one was in 1875, as to which I may refer to my article, "The War-Scare of 1875," in the *American Historical Review*, January, 1919. Much new material has come to light since the publication of this article; but I feel that its general conclusions stand, although they are attacked by Hans Herzfeldt in his *Die deutsch-französische Kriegsgefahr von 1875* (Berlin, 1922). Final judgment on the affair still awaits the publication of Goriainov's article, which has been found, but not yet printed.

[25] *Videant consules ne quid respublica detrimenti capiat* (Cassel, 1890), p. 38. "Diese Sachlage war denn auch in zahlreichen Kreisen erkannt, und diese Kreise drängten zu einem tapferen Entschluss; das Bemühen dieser entschlossenen Männer ist nicht an das Tageslicht der Oeffentlichkeit getreten. Zweifellos jedoch ist es, dass der damalige Kronprinz diese Ansicht vertrat, und aller Grund liegt zu der Annahme vor, dass auch der Chef des Generalstabs dieselbe theilte und seinen berechtigten Einfluss in diesem Sinne geltend machte. Von dieser Zeit hauptsächlich stammt die wieder auftauchende und stets geläugnete Annahme einer politischen Unterströme die zum Kriege dränge. . . . In diesem Sinne hat ohne Zweifel eine politische Unterströmung bestanden die sich im Gegensatz wusste zu unserer officiellen Politik; ob auch im Gegensatz zum Fürsten Bismarck muss dahingestellt bleiben." This anonymous pamphlet attracted widespread attention when it was published, and was criticized much more on the ground of indiscretion than on that of inaccuracy.

and had come to express a serious intention on Bismarck's part. *Pester Lloyd* affirmed that such was the case. "In Berlin," it asserted, "a war between Germany and France is, as a matter of fact, regarded as more probable than would be inferred from the information accessible to the general public. The views expressed by the newspapers to the effect that the reports concerning French armaments are merely circulated by the semi-official German press for electoral purposes are erroneous. . . . The Imperial Chancellor is represented to have added that the statements in question were no electoral manoeuvres, but a warning and a cold *douche*, which was only turned on with less force this time in order not to give provocation. It would, however, be made stronger should necessity arise. . . . In view of this state of affairs Germany was compelled to consider whether it was expedient to await inactively a French attack."

The Belgian minister at Berlin went even further. He informed his government: "It seems quite evident that Prince Bismarck, by handing over the East to Russia's predominance, has assured himself of the Tsar's non-intervention in any action Germany may take on the Rhine. It would be rash to affirm that the Chancellor has decided to go to war with France; but there is every indication that he foresees a situation which will compel him to do so. The thing may come about at any moment. He is prepared for it, and he is preparing public opinion as well." [26]

The French government had at once taken measures to avert more serious developments by conveying assurances to Bismarck that Germany's apprehensions were groundless. On January 25, the minister of foreign affairs, Flourens, instructed Herbette to offer explanations proving that the supposed preparations for war were greatly exaggerated. He was not to permit the personality of Boulanger to be involved in the discussion. "But," concluded Flourens, "you may say that in our country it is not the minister of war who decides between war and peace, and that the firm resolution of the whole government, including the Chambers, which represent public opinion, is to keep the peace." [27] On the

---

[26] *Zur europäischen Politik*, v, p. 168. January 28, 1887.
[27] Pagès (Senate Report), p. 226.

28th, Herbette reported that he had talked with Bismarck, who had repeatedly declared that Germany had no intention of attacking France, but had received the reciprocal assurance on France's part, together with the accompanying explanations, "with a certain air of polite incredulity." Bismarck had, as Flourens feared, centred his complaints upon the person of the minister of war. "What I apprehend," he said, "is the accession of General Boulanger to the presidency of the council, or even of the republic. In that case, there would be war very shortly." [28]

This shift of objective in the German campaign from a question of actual measures to one of personalities made it only the more dangerous. The sacrifice of a minister would be an even more humiliating concession than an explanation of armaments. Yet the new form of attack was pursued with redoubled vigor. It was taken up by the Berlin *Post*, which, as it had done in 1875, furnished a climax to the crisis. Its article of January 31, 'Auf des Messers Schneide,' created almost the same stir as the memorable, 'Ist der Krieg in Sicht?' War was inevitable, was the burden of its croaking, and General Boulanger, the villain of the plot. "The impression left on the minds of all observers," it concluded its review of the situation, "is that the armaments of France are being pushed forward with feverish energy. General Boulanger has it no longer in his power to lead the French people back into the path of peace, or, if he attempted it, he would have to quit his post, burdened with the reproach of having led France to the brink of a great peril." A second panic on the Bourse ensued. In writing of it to the *Times*, Blowitz added the observation: "I venture to say that if Prince Bismarck, in his first speech, . . . had not specially and by name designated General Boulanger, if

---

[28] *Ibid.*, p. 227. Lucius von Ballhausen (p. 366) gives Bismarck's account of the interview: "Er erzählte von einer langen, am Tage vorher mit Herbette gehabten Konversation, worin ihn dieser über Boulanger's Stellung und Einfluss zu beruhigen versucht hat. Bismarck habe ihm erst Relief gegeben, indem er ihn erwähnte u. s. w. Bismarck erwiderte: *Boulanger c'est la guerre*. Einmal an der Spitze, kann er gar nicht anders, die Verhältnisse würden sich stärker erweisen als sein Wille, wenn er den überhaupt hätte, Frieden zu halten. Bismarck hat offenbar Herbette stark eingeheizt, und man hat den Eindruck, als ob sich die Sachen jetzt wieder friedlicher gestalteten. Freilich sprach Bismarck im selben Atem von der Möglichkeit des Ausbruchs des Krieges in den nächsten Wochen."

he had not made him the ostensible object aimed at by Germany, the General would probably have already fallen. It was by describing him in this way that Prince Bismarck wounded the national self-love of France, which could not thenceforth permit the overthrow of a War Minister so clearly alluded to."

The belief that war was at hand was spreading in the best informed circles. It had found a footing at Vienna.[29] On February 3, the Berlin stock exchange shared in the panic which had been sporadically shaking the Bourse at Paris for the past ten days. The occasion was a report of Bismarck's intention to place before the Prussian Landtag a project for a loan to cover the first expenses of the military programme which was being held up by the dissolution of the Reichstag. Lucius von Ballhausen's opinion of this proposal had been: "A measure which will have the effect of a thunderclap. It seems hardly credible that Bismarck should take this decisive step as a mere electoral manoeuvre. It means war! At least it will be looked upon here as the first move toward war." [30] The proposal was not made after all, as the crisis had passed before the time set for it; but the mere rumor of it had all the effect Lucius had prophesied. Following the panic which resulted, the Italian embassy at Berlin, which had hitherto taken a hopeful view of the situation, went over to the camp of the pessimists. The only diplomat in Berlin who seems to have persisted in believing that there was nothing in the whole chorus of alarms beyond electoral tactics was Sir Edward Malet, representative of the oldest parliamentary government.[31]

The opinion of the British ambassador was not shared by his countrymen at home. The disturbed condition of Europe for the

[29] *G. F. O.*, vi, pp. 170–172. February 4, 1887, Reuss to Bismarck. February 1, report of Count Wedel, military attaché. "Graf Kálnoky glaubt an einen Krieg zwischen uns und Frankreich, er glaubt auch, dass derselbe von militärischer Seite gewünscht wird, weil man ihn auf die Dauer für unvermeidlich halte und daher die gerade jetzt für uns günstigen Chancen benutzen möchte." See also *Zur europäischen Politik*, v, p. 170. Bismarck's contention that there was no military party in Germany in this sense (see the same, vi, p. 181) is not convincing. Moreover, he contradicted himself damagingly on this point in his interview of March 17, with Crown Prince Rudolf (*infra*, pp. 163–164).

[30] *Bismarck-Erinnerungen*, p. 366. Cabinet session of January 30.

[31] *Zur europäischen Politik*, v, p. 173. February 11, van der Straten Ponthoz.

past month and more had led to a great deal of discussion in England as to the policies she should follow in case more serious complications arose, and especially as to the attitude she should take toward a violation of Belgian neutrality. The sudden crisis in relations between Germany and France brought this discussion to a head in a noteworthy letter signed ' Diplomaticus,' published by the *Standard* on February 4. It was accompanied by a leading article generally believed officially inspired, approving the doctrine that England was bound by neither interests nor obligations to defend Belgium against invasion. The pronouncement was regarded as so definite and authoritative that Sir Charles Dilke, in his later articles on international politics, treated England's abandonment of Belgium as a settled question.[32]

With the appearance of this article, it was Belgium's turn to take alarm. The Belgian government had already become disquieted by the discussions in England, but had received highly reassuring declarations from English representatives. Now, seeing itself abandoned just as the situation was growing most critical, it renewed its appeals for assurance of protection with redoubled vigor, approaching not only England, but the other guarantors of Belgian neutrality as well. The results of these inquiries were so little encouraging that the government deemed new measures of defence immediately necessary and entered upon a programme for fortifying the line of the Meuse.[33] Leaving

[32] *Present Position*, pp. 322–324. See also Sanger and Norton, *England's Guarantee to Belgium and Luxemburg* (London, 1915).

[33] *M. A. Z.*, December 3, 1887. Brussels, December 1. "Als nach der Auflösung des deutschen Reichstags im Januar die Möglichkeit eines deutsch-französischen Krieges in bedenkliche Nähe gerückt war, richtete die belgische Regierung zwei Noten an die europäische Grossmächte. Die eine derselben war an das Cabinet von St. James gerichtet und enthielt die Anfrage, wie sich das Ministerium Salisbury zu den officiösen englischen Presskundgebungen gegen den Schutz der belgischen Neutralität verhalte. Die zweite Note ging an alle Garantiemächte ab und sprach den Wunsch aus, dieselben möchten die feierliche Versicherung abgeben, dass sie eine Verletzung der belgischen Neutralität gegebenen Falles mit Waffengewalt verhindern werden. Die Antworten . . . lauteten so zuversichtlich, dass die Regierung schon im März die . . . Maasbefestigung decretiren liess." See also Schwertfeger, *Der geistige Kampf um die Verletzung der belgischen Neutralität* (Berlin, 1919). A controversy arose over this incident in 1917. On March 14, the British government officially stated that the *Standard* article had been instantly repudiated through the

aside the vexed question of England's actual intentions regarding Belgium, the fact which stands out in all this discussion is the evident feeling in both countries that the danger of war was pressing and real.

That danger went on increasing. Early in February, while the atmosphere was stormy with rumors of the proposed Prussian military loan, the German command assembled 72,000 reservists in Alsace-Lorraine, ostensibly to receive instruction in the use of the new magazine rifles. Legitimate as was the excuse, the measure was unquestionably a most dangerously provocative one to take under the circumstances. Boulanger's demand for countermeasures was restrained by President Grévy; but the French minister of foreign affairs hastened to the German ambassador to ask an explanation of the extraordinary proceeding. The situation of a few days before was neatly reversed. France was now making the very demand she had so resented on Germany's part, and was by so much putting herself in the wrong. Count Münster's reply to the questions of Flourens was moderate, but well calculated to take advantage of the situation.[34] He gave the official reason for the calling out of the troops. "He added that 25,000 more would be called for the same reason, but that, under the existing circumstances, the German government, if it wished to make trouble, would have much more cause to complain of the hasty constructions on our eastern frontier and of the immoderate language of General Boulanger. Without presenting any formal demand or explicit ultimatum, Count Münster dwelt upon the necessity of our getting General Boulanger out of the ministry if we really wished to avert the complications which seemed to be

minister at Brussels. The *Norddeutsche Allgemeine Zeitung*, on August 19, printed a reply based on researches in the Belgian archives. The actual files of despatches were said to have been removed; but enough fragments were patched together from notebooks, registers, and letters to show that, while definite assurances had been given in January, the tone of England's representatives in February was decidedly that Belgium must shift for herself. Only the transactions with England are dealt with by the writer; but from the title, ' 1 England,' appearing at the head of an extract from an inventory of conversations, it may be concluded that other Powers were consulted too.

[34] Pagès (Senate Report), pp. 227–228. February 7, Flourens to Herbette.

impending."[35] The parallel with the later Delcassé incident is too deadly to be missed.

Germany's plan of campaign appeared to be taking shape with startling clearness. France's nerves had been unstrung by persistent nagging. She was already taking false steps. The attack was becoming centred upon Boulanger, the hothead and popular hero of the cabinet. War was as close as it had ever been during the crisis of 1875: the slightest word or act on either side might upset the trembling balance. The telegraphic correspondence of the German financier, Bleichröder, which was somehow tampered with by the French, indicated that Germany was deliberately forcing upon France the choice between Boulanger's dismissal and war.[36] The same correspondence gives a clew to the reason why the whole storm, just as it seemed on the point of breaking, suddenly blew over with no damage done. One of Bleichröder's telegrams stated that, while Germany was fully prepared to strike, she was waiting on assurances as to the attitude of Russia.[37] Again, as in 1875, the maintenance of peace in Europe depended upon Russia's word. And again the French government had lodged its appeal at St. Petersburg in advance.

Toward the end of January, Flourens had imparted to the Russian ambassador his anxiety at the turn affairs were taking, assuring him of France's intention to do all in her power to keep the peace.[38] A similar communication was made through the French ambassador at St. Petersburg.[39] Flourens also confided to Julius Hansen, private counsellor of the Russian embassy, his fear that Germany intended to make some formal representation

[35] Émile Flourens, *Alexandre III.* (Paris, 1894), pp. 311–312.

[36] Newton, ii, p. 384. "Messages came through Bleichröder and members of the *haute finance* in Paris, who expressed the opinion that if Boulanger remained in office, war with Germany was certain."

[37] Pagès (Senate Report), p. 229. February 12, Flourens to Herbette. "On a saisi une dépêche de Bleichroeder, dans laquelle il dit que la guerre est décidée et que, pour nous la déclarer, l'Allemagne n'attend qu'une chose, c'est que la Russie ait promis sa neutralité."

[38] Goriainov in *American Historical Review*, January, 1918, p. 331. According to Goriainov's account, Flourens made the damaging admission that "France would not attack Germany unless the latter were strongly engaged elsewhere."

[39] Daudet, *Alliance*, p. 213.

on the subject of France's alleged armaments.[40] But he was wise enough to interfere with the ill advised attempt of Boulanger to send a personal letter to the Tsar — a project which would have resulted in more harm than good.[41] The accounts of still other communications with the Tsar may be disregarded: Flourens's official measures sufficed to acquaint him with the state of affairs.[42] When Mohrenheim reported to his government that what France desired was moral support in case a demand for disarmament were made, the Tsar wrote on the margin of the despatch that she should have it. But Giers's official reply was that the apprehensions of Flourens appeared to him exaggerated, as Bismarck had always assured Russia that he would not attack France. He added that the surest way to put France in real danger would be to let Bismarck suspect her of any private dealings with Russia.[43]

What Bismarck was waiting for was some further action on certain proposals which Count Peter Shuvalov had made to him in a conversation on January 10, just the day before his inflammatory speech in the Reichstag. Following up his own suggestion made to Count Herbert Bismarck a few days before, inspired by the German despatch of December 14, the Russian diplomat had submitted to the Chancellor a draft of a Russo-German treaty. The basis of this agreement was that, in return for Germany's

[40] Hansen, *Mohrenheim*, p. 28.

[41] Both Baron Beyens, the Belgian minister, and Lord Lyons, the British ambassador, reported this incident in despatches dated, respectively, February 8 and February 18 (*Zur europäischen Politik*, v, p. 171; Newton, ii, p. 387). According to their accounts, the story of the occurrence was told by Madame Flourens during a visit to the daughter of the German ambassador, Count Münster. When Flourens heard about the letter he had made a lively scene in the council of ministers, threatening to resign if it were sent. The project was disapproved and abandoned. See also *G. F. O.*, vi, p. 176, note.

[42] Flourens, in his life of Alexander III (pp. 312–313), wrote: "Par une voie confidentielle et sûre, il fut fait part directement à l'empereur Alexandre III de l'imminence du danger. Le Tsar fit répondre aussitôt qu'il allait employer toute son autorité à amener un dénouement pacifique." Cyon (p. 225) tells of a personal letter written by President Grévy.

[43] Goriainov, *loc. cit.* The date, January 22, is given for Giers's despatch, without specifying whether it is Russian or Gregorian style. The context of events makes it almost certainly the former — that is, February 3 by the calendar of Western Europe.

friendly neutrality toward an attempt to close the Straits, Russia would observe the same friendly neutrality "dans tout conflit qui pourrait surgir entre l'Allemagne et la France."[44] With Bismarck's eager approval, Shuvalov had returned to press this proposal at St. Petersburg.

After a month or so had passed, however, without his hearing any more of the matter, Bismarck began to grow doubtful of any practical results from this advantageous proposition. According to several accounts, the German ambassador, about the 6th of February, called for a definite decision on it and was rebuffed.[45] No confirmation of these statements is to be found in the published documents of the German foreign office: if the ambassador mentioned the matter, it would appear that he acted without specific instructions. On the 17th, Bismarck wrote him: "Your Excellency was informed by the Russian ambassador, on your latest visit to Berlin, of the discussions between Count Peter Shuvalov and myself a few weeks ago about a Russo-German agreement. Since there has been no further word concerning Shuvalov's proposal, I conclude that it was unsuccessful, and that we may not count upon Russia's willingness to go into it. There is no need to bring up the matter, as to do so would give the impression that our need of such an agreement is more urgent than Russia's, and would be misinterpreted."[46]

There was also, by this time, little doubt as to what Russia's attitude would be toward a Franco-German war. In the early days of February, Russian newspapers were generally proclaiming that she could not permit a decisive defeat of France. Through Kálnoky came reports that Giers himself had used similar language.[47] There was, then, for these further reasons, no need to

---

[44] *G. F. O.*, v, pp. 214–215.

[45] *Figaro*, October 29, 1887. Cyon, pp. 198, 234. The second reference is to a passage from Cyon's diary under date of February 10, 1887, repeating the story as told him by Katkov in person. André Mévil, *De la paix de Francfort à la Conférence d'Algésiras* (Paris, 1909), p. v, introduction. Hansen, *Mohrenheim*, pp. 30–31. Daudet, "Le règne d'Alexandre III," in *Revue des deux Mondes*, May 15, 1919. Corti, p. 294. Salisbury, according to letters to Queen Victoria which she communicated to Prince Alexander, believed that something of the sort took place.

[46] *G. F. O.*, v, p. 218.

[47] *Ibid.*, v, p. 219. February 10, Reuss to Bismarck. Passage quoted in a despatch

ask a final decision on the Shuvalov proposals. As Bismarck wrote at the close of the month, the silence concerning these was rendered doubly significant by "the attitude of even the *officious* Russian press toward us, which differs only in form, but not in spirit, from that of the private professionally fanatic sheets." [48] In fact, the inspired *Nord* of Brussels was using language which, a few days before, had been that of only the most ardent Panslavists.[49] Through all possible channels it was made known to Europe in general that the attitude of the government was "that Russia need not hasten the solution of the Bulgarian question, but has to fix her attention chiefly on near eventualities in the direction of the Rhine, which are destined to become the principal factors in the solution of the Bulgarian question." [50] After the clouds had blown over, the conservative 'Western' review, *Viestnik Evropy*, gave a reasoned and rather enlightening summary of what had occurred. Russia had declined a disreputable bargain, the proposal of which cast doubts upon the sincerity of all Germany's peaceful professions. The conclusion as to Bismarck's intentions was that he had meant, in addition to influencing German public opinion, to coerce France into getting rid of her objectionable minister of war and into a reduction of her programme of armaments.[51]

from Schweinitz, February 21. Bismarck's marginal note to the effect that France was also necessary to Germany as a "maritime counterpoise to England," further elaborated in a despatch of February 25 to Schweinitz (vi, pp. 177–178), is no convincing evidence of peaceful intentions. He added, significantly: "so wird sich im nächsten Kriege, wenn wir siegen, eine schonende Behandlung empfehlen, gerade wie Österreich gegenüber 1866." All this was calculated to reassure Russia as to the consequences of leaving him a free hand.

[48] *G. F. O.*, v, p. 220. February 28, Bismarck to Schweinitz.

[49] Katkov wrote in the *Moscow Gazette* on February 3: "The policy of Berlin is manipulating the events in the East in such a way as to drag us into them and distract our attention. But all these projects will fail. Russia wishes first of all to keep close watch on what happens in the West, knowing very well that the East will not escape her. The Eastern troubles are instigated elsewhere: they are phenomena and not causes. Perhaps Russia will prefer to occupy herself rather with the causes than with the phenomena." Cyon, pp. 230–231.

[50] *Nord*, February 20. See also *Times*, February 21 (St. Petersburg, February 17); and *Politische Correspondenz*, February 17, St Petersburg correspondence.

[51] Вѣстникъ Европы, March, 1887, pp. 398–399.

The conclusion is charitable. Bismarck would doubtless have been quite satisfied with such a result; but the probability is that he was considering a much more far-reaching solution — that, as in 1875, he was prepared to go to the length of war if circumstances had proved favorable and if France had withstood his pressure to the extent of making it the only way of accomplishing his ends. When circumstances turned against him, he wasted no laments over lost opportunities, but carefully covered all traces of having looked for any. One object he had attained: the elections of February 21 gave the government a solid majority for its army bill. The future was that much more secure at least. Yet Bismarck let it be understood that he did not consider the danger passed for good: the crisis was subject to revival at any time.[52] This attitude was disquieting; but the consequences of a defeat at the polls had been even more terrifying to contemplate.[53] Happily, the campaign of propaganda, fraught with danger as it was, had so roused public opinion that the result was never very much in doubt. With the parliamentary victory, this first crisis of 1887 had come to an end.[54]

From Bismarck's dealings with France and Russia at this time, from his own words and the opinion of contemporaries, the impression distinctly emerges that something extraordinary was

[52] *Zur europäischen Politik*, v, p. 174. February 11, van der Straten Ponthoz: "Les dispositions pacifiques du chancelier ne modifient pas ses prévisions à l'égard de la France. Dans sa récente visite à l'Ambassade d'Angleterre, il a renouvelé à Sir Edward Malet ses déclarations faites au Reichstag, de ne pas attaquer la France. Il en prenait l'engagement en homme d'honneur, et cependant il était certain, a-t-il dit, que le Général Boulanger déclarerait la guerre à l'Allemagne, aussitôt que le pouvoir serait dans ses mains. Le chancelier se montre pacifique, mais il ne désarme pas complètement."

[53] *Ibid.*, v, p. 177. February 18, Errembault de Dudzeele (St. Petersburg): "De l'avis unanime du public russe, si les élections parlementaires de l'Allemagne sont favorables au Prince de Bismarck, l'éventualité d'une guerre franco-allemande n'aura pas disparue pour cela de l'horizon, mais si le Chancelier au contraire éprouve un échec, elle deviendra certaine." Cyon, p. 235. Katkov expressed similar opinions to Cyon during the latter's visit of February 12–13, but went to the length of adding that Russian military authorities expected Bismarck also to forestall a possible attack from that side by taking the offensive in the East.

[54] Chiala (p. 465) quotes a telegram from Herbette on March 12, following the passage of the army bill by the Reichstag: "L'orage est passé; tout est tranquille. On peut fermer les parapluies et ouvrir les parasols."

afoot. That impression is strengthened by still another development. The crisis with France coincides with the moment of Bismarck's final energetic effort to put through the negotiations with Italy and England. By a sudden and ingenious combination of moves he effected at once England's entanglement with the Triple Alliance and a renewal of that compact upon terms which steadied Italy's shaky loyalty. Success came just in time to help him out in a war with France, had it occurred, though only after the immediate possibility of it had died away.

# CHAPTER VII

## THE TRIPLE ALLIANCE AND ENGLAND

### I

THE parliamentary victory on the military question was supplemented almost at the same time by the diplomatic victory of the renewal of the Triple Alliance. Throughout the crisis of early February the issue in this field had remained in doubt, despite the fact that this crisis had stimulated Bismarck to new efforts and had substantiated the peril, which he held before Kálnoky's eyes, of a conflict with France. The Austrian government had, in fact, rebelled against the Chancellor's bullying, which had culminated in his speech of January 11. In an interview with Reuss on the 16th, Kálnoky had taken back all his offers of concessions to Italy. If Austria was to get no support at all in maintaining her interests against Russia in the Near East, he declared, she must firmly decline to go out of her way to back up Italian interests against France in the Mediterranean.[1] Even the Balkan agreement he now proposed to limit to a simple engagement to notify of impending action.

The outlook for an understanding seemed desperate, when Bismarck produced a new solution. Robilant was induced to accept the happy idea of splitting up the responsibility for what he desired. He was brought to demand of Austria acceptance only of the Balkan clause, and to content himself with an engagement from Germany alone for support in the Mediterranean.[2] This

---

[1] G. F. O., iv, pp. 233–234. January 16, 1887, Reuss to Bismarck. Pribram, i, p. 193 (Amer., ii, pp. 67–68). January 17, 1887, Reuss to Bismarck. Kálnoky observed: "Je offenbarer die Tatsache für Freund und Feind wird, dass Österreich-Ungarn für seine unleugbaren Interessen an seiner Südostgrenze allein einzutreten haben wird, je mehr unsere Gegner hierin eine Ermunterung, unsere Freunde eine Entmutigung erblicken werden, desto mehr müssen wir bedacht sein, uns in keinerlei Verbindlichkeiten einzulassen, welche uns ausserhalb unserer Interessensphäre engagieren."

[2] G. F. O., iv, p. 241. January 27, Bismarck to Reuss.

partition of engagements narrowed the issue to a proposition acceptable to Austria. Kálnoky admitted as much, yet still proposed conditions. The status quo in the Balkans must include Austria's occupation of Bosnia and Herzegovina, the annexation of which should entail no obligations. The principle of compensation for other gains must never involve the Trentino. Italy should bind herself to take part in a Russian war.[3] When Robilant objected to the last condition, unaccompanied by an Austrian pledge against France, it was dropped. For the rest, Bismarck, just then in the most acute throes of his crisis with France, labored furiously to bring matters to a conclusion before hostilities should break out. He succeeded in reconciling these differences only after the possibility of a war had been eliminated by other considerations.

The sudden success encountered by Bismarck's idea of freeing Austria from responsibility for the Mediterranean guarantee was made possible only by the success of another plan which placed the greater part of that obligation on England's shoulders.[4] Negotiations with England had been making reasonable progress since the resignation of Lord Randolph Churchill at the beginning of the year. More than one factor was involved. Besides giving support to Italy in the Mediterranean, England must be enlisted actively in the opposition to Russia in Bulgaria. As a direct gain from her adhesion to the Triple Alliance, England might expect its support in putting through the second convention with Turkey regulating England's tenure of Egypt and the terms of evacuation, which Sir Henry Drummond Wolff had been sent to negotiate at Constantinople.

On the Bulgarian matter, the English government had reached

[3] Pribram, i, p. 199 (Amer., ii, p. 73). February 2, Kálnoky to Széchényi. The last condition is not given in Reuss's despatch of February 1, printed in *G. F. O.*, iv, pp. 244–246.

[4] Another consideration in his favor, however, was the fact that, since December 15, the position of Italy as a free agent had been weakened by her denunciation of the commercial treaty of 1881 with France — the prelude to the disastrous tariff war between the two countries. The defeat of Dogali has been alleged as a cause of Robilant's change of attitude; but news of that disaster did not reach Rome until February 1, some days after his acceptance of the idea of separate treaties, which broke the deadlock.

a fairly satisfactory position. Salisbury told the Lords on January 27: "Our desire in reference to the condition of things in the South-East of Europe is, in the first place, to perform our duties as signatories of the Treaty of Berlin; and in the second place, we wish . . . to strengthen and to uphold the freedom of those Christian communities which, in proportion as they maintain their freedom and cohesion, will be the greatest security against any possible overflow of military power into that distracted part of Europe." Referring directly to Russia, his definition of policy was: "We do not desire to deny to Russia any legitimate object she may have in view; on the contrary, subject to the conditions which I have already stated, we shall be glad that her legitimate wishes should be fulfilled. But we feel, above all things, that the influence which she may claim in consequence of race, or faith, or history, must not be expanded into domination." [5] The Austrian press found this attitude weak and yielding.[6] Yet it reasserted England's position in principle without attaching any of Churchill's troublesome conditions to the practice.

As for the special accord with Italy, Robilant had begun his efforts to attain it as soon as Bismarck's suggestion came to him.[7] Salisbury had shown himself favorably impressed by the proposal, but entertained some doubts about its general effect and its practicability from a constitutional point of view.[8] In order to hasten matters, Bismarck himself took a hand by having a long talk with the British ambassador, on February 1, into which entered all the matters involved in this important transaction. Bismarck admitted to Sir Edward Malet the existence of "a sort of alliance" with Italy, the usefulness of which was impaired, he said, by Italy's inability to make use of sea transport in the event of a war involving a strong naval power. "But this could be remedied," he added, "with England's help, by an arrangement which would assure these two Powers the supremacy of the Mediterranean." When Sir Edward Malet objected that England

[5] Hansard, 3d series, cccx, coll. 36–37.  [6] *N. F. P.*, January 28.
[7] *G. F. O.*, iv, p. 297. January 31, report from Hatzfeldt, ambassador at London.
[8] *Ibid.*, iv, pp. 297–298. February 2, from the same.

could not enter into an accord directed specifically against France, Bismarck went on to threaten: "If England persists in withdrawing from all participation in European politics, we shall have no further reason to withhold our approval of French desires in Egypt or those of Russia in the Near East, however far they go." He indicated the scope which he intended the proposed agreement to attain by saying that Austria needed help besides that of Italy in maintaining her Balkan interests, and that these would be much more secure "if England stood back of Italy." As for Germany's rôle in this connection, he confined himself to saying that she would hold France in check, but maintained that this was no small service.[9]

When this conversation was reported to London, Lord Salisbury agreed that Bismarck had set forth a "desirable grouping of the Powers, including England." He also made haste to assure himself that Germany's continued support of his Egyptian policy would be one of the conditions of the new accord.[10]

The temptations offered by Bismarck coincided with a perverse phase in the conduct of France which went far to overcome England's reluctance to enter combinations against her. Incidents involving the Newfoundland fisheries, the New Hebrides, Egypt, Morocco, and Dongorita had followed upon each other in such rapid succession that, on February 5, Lord Salisbury wrote to Lyons at Paris: "The French are inexplicable. One would have thought that under existing circumstances it was not necessary to *make* enemies — that there were enough provided for France by nature just now. But she seems bent upon aggravating the patient beast of burden here by every insult and worry her ingenuity can devise. . . . It is very difficult to prevent oneself from wishing for another Franco-German war to put a stop to this incessant vexation."[11] Sinister words, coming at a time when Bismarck was actually expecting license for such a war from St. Petersburg! Yet the war scare was over before arrangements were completed between England and the Triple Alliance.

[9] G. F. O., iv, pp. 301–302. February 3, Bismarck to Hatzfeldt. Crispi, pp. 130–131 (*Memoirs*, ii, pp. 162–164).
[10] G. F. O., iv, p. 303. February 3, Hatzfeldt to the foreign office.
[11] Newton, ii, p. 386.

England's relations with that combination of Powers were established through Italy alone; but Bismarck was the moving spirit of the accord. It never took the form of a treaty of alliance, but was confined to an exchange of notes, establishing an entente cordiale of the sort British diplomacy has resorted to at times in order to get round its responsibilities to Parliament. In this case the notes could by no means be called identical; for the British Government ignored completely Italy's proposals for reciprocal support in Egypt and Tripoli and for mutual support of Mediterranean policies in general, and substituted 'desires' for definite engagements on the two other points. These were for coöperation in maintaining the status quo on "the shores of the Euxine, the Aegean, the Adriatic and the northern coast of Africa," and in preventing the "extension of the domination of any other Great Power over any portion of those coasts."[12] A German despatch to Vienna made much of the mention of the Black Sea in the notes, and stated: "We have pushed the conclusion of this . . . agreement so energetically, in order to provide a basis of defence on which Austria can rely in case of necessity."[13] And an English memorandum sent to Queen Victoria spoke of common action with Austria and Italy in restraint of Russia as one of the objects of the transaction.[14] The German despatch pointed out that all this went to show "how much advantage there is for Kálnoky in the alliance with Italy."

This accomplishment of Bismarck's diplomacy also made it easier for Italy to renounce the claim to Austria's support of her interests in the Mediterranean. With all obstacles out of the way and so many considerations raised in its favor, the renewal of the Triple Alliance was quickly consummated. It came about in complicated wise, requiring four new documents. The treaty of

---

[12] Pribram, i, p. 38 (Amer., i, pp. 96–97). February 12, Salisbury to Corti. The notification that England was committing herself to nothing definite was reiterated at the beginning and end of the document: "The character of that coöperation must be decided by them, when the occasion for it arises, according to the circumstances of the case. . . . It will be the earnest desire of H. M's. Government to give their best coöperation, as hereinbefore expressed . . ."

[13] G. F. O., iv, p. 316. February 16, Bismarck to Reuss.

[14] Ibid. February 23.

1882 was left as it stood. An additional act renewed it for another five-year term.[15] A separate agreement between Italy and Austria embodied the Near Eastern clause, its scope extended to cover "the regions of the Balkans." Any action by Austria or Italy tending to modify the status quo must take place only after an accord between the two providing compensation to the other for any advantages obtained "beyond the present status quo." [16] The separate agreement between Italy and Germany called for only the joint use of influence to maintain the status quo on the Ottoman coasts, leaving a free hand regarding agreements on the Egyptian question.[17] Germany further recognized the extension of the *casus foederis* with all its implications to the event of a war between Italy and France arising out of the latter's aggression in Morocco or Tripoli, and engaged to favor Italian claims to acquisitions as a result.[18] A final protocol, signed by all three parties on the same day (February 20) as the other documents, declared that the treaties, though separate, were to be considered parts of a general accord of spirit.

The heavy obligations assumed by Germany and forced upon Austria in this arrangement indicate the value Bismarck set upon retaining Italy in his system of alliances and coalitions. Her place had indeed become pivotal, affecting all aspects of his policy from the Rhine to the Dardanelles and from the Nile to the Danube. His intention to fulfil his promises is indicated by the opinion, later expressed to Crown Prince Rudolf of Hapsburg, that Italy must be bound to the Central Powers by gifts such as Nice, Corsica, Albania, and territories in North Africa.[19] This was, of course, loose speaking, but showed the direction of his thoughts.

The total result of the transactions of February was a strengthening of Bismarck's position in all respects; while the weight of the obligations was in fact greatly diminished through being

[15] Pribram, i, p. 43 (Amer., i, p. 104).
[16] *Ibid.*, i, pp. 44–45 (Amer., i, p. 108).
[17] *Ibid.*, i, p. 46 (Amer., i, pp. 110–113). Articles i and ii.
[18] *Ibid.*, i, pp. 46–47 (Amer., i, pp. 112–113). Articles iii and iv.
[19] *Ibid.*, i, p. 206 (Amer., ii, p. 80). Notes of an interview, March 17, 1887. Also in *Österreichische Rundschau*, January, 1921, p. 65.

shared by England. The application of the Triple Alliance to an immediate war with France was a closed possibility before the treaties were signed; but the usefulness of the Anglo-Italian understanding remained. It only required the adhesion of Austria to make it the foundation of a triple accord which would effectively block Russia's progress in the Near East and conserve all the interests of the Dual Monarchy without involving Germany except as a last resort. The Austrians were reluctant to enter an agreement embracing Italy's Mediterranean interests, and were very doubtful about coöperating against Russia with England on a basis admitting the latter's interests, which in some respects were more extensive than their own. Some attempt was made at a separate understanding on a new basis; but Salisbury insisted on Austria's adhesion to the agreement with Italy.[20] He admitted, however, that she could not be expected to take on equal interest in Mediterranean affairs.[21]

Bismarck strongly advised Kálnoky to enter the accord as it stood, granting England's terms in order to be sure of her help, which now promised to be sincere and substantial. He spoke of the failure of his past efforts at a policy of concessions to Russia with at least assumed regret, but let it be seen that he had abandoned them. He reiterated his previous declaration that no help could be expected from Germany beyond the checking of France. In offering this advice, he said, "I am guided only by the wish to see Austria strengthened even for contests *extra casum nostri foederis.*"[22] Austria did not follow his advice at once, but could not avoid doing so in the end. The treacherous intrigue against Russia was practically complete.

## II

With the Reichstag reduced to order and the army bill assured, with the Triple Alliance renewed and the attitude of England satisfactorily determined, Bismarck was free to revise his

[20] *G. F. O.*, iv, p. 320–321. February 28, March 5, Hatzfeldt to the foreign office.
[21] *Ibid.*, iv, p. 326. March 17, Hatzfeldt to Herbert Bismarck.
[22] *Ibid.*, iv, p. 324. March 11, Bismarck to Reuss.

policy in regard to Eastern Europe, reducing his apparent support of Russia to its lowest terms and allowing the anti-Russian combination to work out its results. As early as February 17, we find him instructing Radowitz, at Constantinople, to withdraw from the attitude of support to Russia so strongly assumed at the close of the preceding year. Her failure to respond to his recent advances (through Shuvalov), he said, was "proof that there is little or no willingness on the part of the Russian cabinet to repay the services we are able to render it in the East with even so much as security against Franco-Russian aggression." In view of this disappointment, the significant gravity of which is here evident, the German ambassador was, "in all questions of dispute between Russia and England, to avoid championing actively the views of Russia, . . . and to be even more careful not to oppose those of England." As some chance still remained of Russia's coming round, Radowitz was to confine himself for the time being to an attitude of "reserve and impartiality." [23]

Meanwhile, the war clouds in the West cleared themselves away after the German elections, yet not so completely as to leave Europe quite reassured. The tone of the German press in letting drop the recent theme of war was that it was not doing so for good. The utterances of Bismarck himself showed that he still had the thought of war with France on his mind. On March 2, he confided to the cabinet: "Our relations with France are as strained as ever; and we must look forward to an invasion of Alsace if Boulanger ever takes the helm of state." His feeling toward the Alsatians was significantly revealed in the remark, "If Alsace should be devastated, there would be no great harm done; for after its wretched showing in the elections, it deserves nothing better." With regard to Russia, he displayed a blustering confidence, apparently not damped by the recent setback. "We are on as good terms with Russia now as we ever were," was his comment. "The last press campaign was conducted by Jomini and Katkov, who are following a policy of their own." [24] And again, on March 7, he told his friend, the forester, Booth: "In

[23] *G. F. O.*, v, p. 119.   [24] Lucius von Ballhausen, p. 373.

France all depends upon what Boulanger does. . . . Only France threatens us: from Russia we have nothing to fear." [25]

This optimism with respect to Russia was not shared by the German military authorities, who since the beginning of the year had displayed an increasing distrust of their eastern neighbor. Toward the end of January, speaking with the Austrian ambassador, Moltke had seen fit to dwell upon the necessity of employing offensive strategy in a coming war with Russia.[26] Several considerations combined to turn the attention of the German high command in the direction of such a war. For about a year the Russians had been working out a scheme of reconcentration which shifted the centre of gravity of their active forces far to the west — a disposition deemed necessary to compensate for the superior railway facilities of Russia's neighbors.[27] In the light of political circumstances, these military measures took on a more and more alarming significance. The treaty of 1881 was nearing its expiration, and as yet no progress had been made toward its renewal. Russia had just administered a sharp rebuff to Germany's attempt to take advantage of its provisions. In so doing, she had taken the part of France in a manner that boded ill for the future. Decidedly, the German army could no longer keep its face turned only to the westward. A movement of troops to the eastern frontier quietly set in.[28] From this moment unquestionably dates the conviction that Germany's military resources were still inadequate and in need of further expansion, and even a shift of competent opinion round to the point of view that Russia, not

---

[25] John Booth, *Persönliche Erinnerungen an den Fürsten Bismarck* (edited by Poschinger, Hamburg, 1899), p. 69.

[26] Corti, pp. 293–294.

[27] Richard von Pfeil, *Neun Jahre in russischen Diensten* (Leipzig, 1907), pp. 182, 185.

[28] *Kölnische Zeitung*, December 20, 1887. "Der Ursprung der allgemeinen Erhöhung des Friedenstandes waren offenkundig die ungeheuren Rüstungen Frankreichs, durch welche Deutschland gezwungen wurde, die Truppentheile in den Reichslanden zu belassen, die in die östlichen Provinzen gehörten. Als Russland 1887 die Hauptmasse seiner Truppen nach den Westprovinzen verlegte und in der russischen Presse der Ton äusserster Feindseligkeit gegen Deutschland hervortrat, schob Deutschland zum ersten Male einige Bataillone und Schwadronen an die bis dahin militärisch fast entblösste Ostgränze."

France, was the chief military danger to the empire. The influence of this conviction upon German foreign policy, however, was slow in making itself felt, and did not become formidable until late in the year.

For a time, too, the military threat was accompanied by a real danger that the rapprochement between Russia and France would develop into a definite agreement. Flourens had exerted himself to make the most of his opportunity, probably dreaming even of an eventual defensive alliance. Following his usual preference for informal negotiations through secret agents, he first suggested the establishment of a channel of confidential intercourse with the Tsar. Alexander approved the suggestion when it was transmitted by Mohrenheim.[29] Viscount Melchior de Vogüé was designated for the mission; but on February 27, before he had started, Mohrenheim reported the receipt of a letter from Giers stating that the Tsar had decided against the proposition.[30] A counter-proposal followed for a special agreement concerning Bulgaria, to which France in turn demurred.[31]

Bismarck combated this drawing together on the part of his two neighbors by every means in his power. On the one hand, he adopted a conciliatory policy toward France, going apparently more than half way toward closing the breach opened by the late unpleasantness. He welcomed, even encouraged, the visit, in March, of the distinguished engineer, de Lesseps, on a tour obviously designed to promote good feeling between the two countries. His effusive greeting to the honored guest, in their in-

---

[29] Goriainov in *American Historical Review*, January, 1918, p. 332. The Tsar's marginal comment on the despatch was: "This might be very useful to us, in certain contingencies [*à un moment donné*], and we ought not to discourage them."

[30] Hansen, *Mohrenheim*, p. 36.

[31] *Preussische Jahrbücher*, April, 1887, p. 373. "Erst in diesem Monat (März) ist von Petersburg in Paris angefragt worden, was Frankreich thun würde, wenn Russland Bulgarien besetzte. Paris hat geantwortet: das könne man sogleich nicht sagen, man müsse erst sehen u. s. w." Newton, ii, p, 393. March 8, 1887, Lyons to Salisbury. "I hear on good authority that the Russians have been trying again, though without success, to come to a special understanding with the French Government." *G. F. O.*, iv, p. 328. March 17, Hatzfeldt to Bismarck. "Lord Salisbury erwähnte gestern abend auch noch die Demarchen, welche die russische Regierung kürzlich in der bulgarischen Frage in Paris gemacht hat."

terview of March 11, conveyed the impression that France was in no danger of war so long as she behaved herself, but also that a grave crisis had been passed which ought to serve as a warning for the future. "I am happy to see you," the Chancellor is reported to have said, "now that the dark clouds have been dispersed. No one wishes for peace more heartily than I. And yet people can believe that I am a warlike man! For a moment I did fear things would turn out badly and that I should have to gird on my weapons and take the road to the frontier with my people. For I must tell you that the greatness of my yearning to live in peace with France would be matched by my zeal for war if ever France attacks or threatens us." He closed the conversation with high praise of the good intentions and abilities of President Grévy and the French ambassador, Herbette.[32]

While Bismarck was thus lulling French susceptibilities, his design of hindering the Franco-Russian accord was marvellously favored by an event in Russia which came near being a repetition of the tragedy of six years before. This was the abortive attempt upon the Tsar's life, on March 1/13. There is a mysterious side to this event — its connection with the German secret police. The effort has even been made to fix the original responsibility for the plot upon Bismarck.[33] *Is fecit cui prodest*, wrote Katkov on the 16th. The charge in that form is too gross to be pressed seriously; but there is some reason to believe that the German government had a foreknowledge of the attempt, which it skilfully exploited to produce the maximum moral effect upon the Tsar without exposing him to actual danger. This foreknowledge was derived

[32] *Vossische Zeitung*, March 17, 1887. *Zur europäischen Politik*, v, pp. 180–181. March 18, the Belgian minister reported an account of the interview by de Lesseps which he had received from a sure source: "Je ne serais pas venu à Berlin, . . . moi, homme pacifique, si je n'avais pas été certain d'y trouver les mêmes dispositions. — J'ai dit à l'Empereur et au Prince de Bismarck: il y a eu un malentendu entre nous. On nous a attribué la pensée de rechercher des alliances; c'est faux. Nous voulons la paix. M. Grévy a encore sept années de présidence. C'est son septennal à lui. Il ne laissera pas dévier le gouvernement de la direction suivie jusqu'à présent. L'Empereur et le Chancelier ont parfaitement reçu ces assurances. Ils m'ont dit que l'Allemagne ne voulait pas la guerre. Puisque la France ne la voulait pas non plus, une longue paix s'assurait entre elles."

[33] Cyon, pp. 263–266. Two of Katkov's articles, on March 16 and 17, are quoted in support of the argument.

from the secret agents which the Prussian police maintained within the radical circles of Europe, especially in Switzerland, where many victims of the Socialist Law of 1878 had taken refuge. In the Reichstag debate on the renewal of this law in January, 1888, the fact was established that Police Director Krüger had written to one of these agents, Haupt: "The next attempt upon the Emperor's life will be organized at Geneva. Write to me: I await your reports concerning it."[34] The fact that this same Krüger, as chief of the secret police abroad, was connected with the foreign office, as well as the department of the interior, places his part in the affair upon a high plane of governmental policy.[35] Since the agents he controlled — described by Puttkamer, minister of the interior, as "no gentlemen" — served upon occasion as *agents provocateurs* in stirring up German Socialists to deeds discrediting their party, it was more than hinted that they had played a similar rôle in their connections with Russian Nihilists for reasons of higher policy.[36] The mon-

[34] *Stenographische Berichte*, session of 1887–88, p. 612. The sensational disclosures connected with the arrest by the Swiss authorities of the German agents, Schröder and Haupt, were first published by the *Agence Libre* of Paris toward the end of December, 1887. Deputies Singer and Bebel addressed a list of questions concerning the disclosures to Captain Fischer of the Zurich police, who replied, affirming that "die vollständige Richtigkeit sämmtlicher in dem zurückfolgenden Schriftstücke aufgestellten Behauptungen festgestellt ist." *Stenographische Berichte*, p. 534. The debate in the Reichstag lasted from the 27th to the 30th of January. The government attempted to deny none of the Socialists' allegations regarding its activities in Switzerland, except the one that its secret agents there had ever taken the positive rôle of *agents provocateurs*.

[35] *Ibid.*, p. 584. The *Handbuch des deutschen Reiches* was cited, giving his official designation as: "Königlich preussischer Polizeidirektor und ständiger Hilfsarbeiter im Auswärtigen Amt." On the last day of the debate, Bebel played up this circumstance to indict the entire policy of the government (p. 609): "Herr von Puttkamer wird mir vielleicht auch weiter bestätigen, dass der Herr Polizeidirektor Krüger genau die Intentionen des Herrn von Puttkamer und seines gegenwärtigen Chefs, des Fürsten Bismarck, kennt. Er bestreitet es nicht; ich nehme an, er ist mit meiner Ansicht einverstanden."

[36] *Ibid.*, p. 612. Bebel: "Ich sage, meine Herren, die russische Presse denunzirt die preussische Polizei, dass sie *agents provocateurs* anstellt, die solche Attentate planen, und dass, nachdem sie rechtzeitig die russische Regierung unterrichtet habe, das Attentat nicht zur Ausführung komme. Wie weit das wahr ist, weiss ich nicht; aber ich kann Ihnen das eine sagen: nach dem, was ich bisher auf diesem Gebiet erfahren habe, bin ich geneigt, alles zu glauben."

strous allegation has little to support it.[37] The most that can be maintained is that the German authorities delayed communicating their knowledge of developments to the Russians long enough to give the event a properly dramatic turn.[38] The reaction upon foreign policy was thereby greatly enhanced.

The effects in Russia did work out as desired, in spite of some contrary possibilities. A certain faction of the ruling class in Russia might be made all the more anxious to bring on a crisis in foreign affairs in order to distract the country from internal unrest; but Alexander III was too strong a character to be swayed by their agitation. His own conservative temperament and the political convictions of his foreign minister impelled him to cling with new firmness to the modern Holy Alliance. The drift toward France was definitely checked.

Flourens appreciated the change in the situation and altered the direction of his attempt to lead France out of her isolation. Abandoning the direct issue between France and Germany, he hit upon the idea of a sort of mediation between England and Russia in the Bulgarian question — a subtle method of approach to both. Once more he set to work through private, unofficial channels, employing Count de Chaudordy, who was on rather good terms with both the ambassador and the prime minister of England, and who had already been employed to sound the

[37] Madame Adam contributed, in the *Nouvelle Revue*, August 1, 1888, some revelations of her own concerning further evidence said to have been disclosed by the Swiss investigations. Her statements regarding the source and value of her information are highly unsatisfactory. She writes (p. 668): "Les lettres qui furent saisies sur les espions allemands Schmid et Friedmann établissent que Schmid devait inventer un attentat. Je traduis textuellement la phrase de la police allemande: '*Quelque chose de vraiment important et encore inconnu.*'"

[38] *Stenographische Berichte*, pp. 587–588. Puttkamer came very near giving the affair away when he triumphantly declared (p. 543): "Aber er [Singer] hat unter anderen Anführungen davon gesprochen, dass diese Agenten der preussischen Polizei mit russischen und polnischen Emigranten in Verbindung ständen. Allerdings, meine Herren; und was war der Erfolg? Die preussische Polizei ist in der Lage gewesen, der Polizei in Petersburg das bevorstehende Attentat . . ., und zwar rechtzeitig, mitzutheilen." By what could only have been a slip of the tongue, Puttkamer called it the attempt "gegen das Winterpalais": that attempt upon Alexander II failed only through the accident of the party being delayed in entering the room where the explosion took place.

former as to the terms of a reconciliation.³⁹ Chaudordy now resumed his attempt. Lord Lyons reports that he "spoke of Flourens's readiness to give to Russia on the Bulgarian question advice which you might suggest, and he mentioned various things which he thought M. Flourens might be ready to do to please England." The ambassador's own conclusions regarding these overtures were: "that the French are horribly afraid of our being led to join the Italo-Austro-German Alliance, and that they have been urged by Russia to exert themselves to prevent this. I do not conceive that the French expect to induce us to join them against the Germans and the German Alliance. What they want is to feel sure that we shall not join the others against France and Russia." ⁴⁰ Unfortunately for Flourens, such an effort came too late. Unknown apparently even to Lyons, the dreaded combination had already taken more or less definite shape. France remained isolated, then, and, despite Bismarck's recent assurances to de Lesseps, in very real danger. The visit of the famous engineer had, indeed, affected the situation little on either side.⁴¹

Within a week there came another visitor to Berlin, the Crown Prince Rudolf of Austria. He was armed with a virulent memorandum from the Archduke Albert, stigmatizing as a rank desertion and betrayal of Austria the recent revision of the war plans of the German general staff, which provided for a concentration of offensive measures against France. Another memorandum, drafted by Kálnoky, balanced these effusions by justifying Germany's preoccupation with the French menace and reiterating the opinions regarding the German alliance which the foreign minister had expressed in his speeches of the preceding November.⁴²

The crown prince's interview with Bismarck took place on the

³⁹ Newton, ii, p. 390. February 25, 1887, Lyons to Salisbury.
⁴⁰ *Ibid.*, p. 399. March 29, 1887, Lyons to Salisbury.
⁴¹ *Preussische Jahrbücher*, April, 1887, p. 375. "Herr v. Lesseps hat die Dinge in Berlin richtig gesehen; denn unter keinen Umständen wird Deutschland den Angriff auf Frankreich beginnen. . . . Allein Herr v. Lesseps hat in seinem eigenen Vaterland die Dinge nicht eben so richtig gesehen. Es mag wahr sein, dass dort niemand jetzt an einen Angriff denkt. Aber das genügt doch nicht, um eine politische Freundschaft zwischen Deutschland und Frankreich herzustellen."
⁴² Pribram, in *Österreichische Rundschau*, January, 1921, pp. 60–62.

17th of the month, and turned first upon the late crisis in relations with France. Bismarck began by denying the existence of any war party in Germany, but contradicted himself immediately afterward by a querulous denunciation of Moltke and Waldersee. "They want to force me into war," he complained, "while I want only peace. Such a causeless war would be criminal frivolity. We are no predatory state to plunge into war just because it suits a few such fire-eaters." He assured the crown prince that Germany would never attack anybody, and that no war could possibly occur unless France or Russia started one. His apprehensions on the score of a French attack appeared less acute than had of late been the case. He still maintained that the advent of Boulanger to control of the government would mean war, but he asserted that peace would be kept as long as *verjudete Geldmenschen* of the type of the existing ministry remained in power.[43]

The future war to which Bismarck most frequently referred was now the war on two fronts, with both France and Russia at once. His insistence upon the reality of this peril was doubtless calculated to influence Austria's decision about adhering to the Anglo-Italian accord; for he dwelt repeatedly on the importance of forming a special combination with Italy and England which would enable Austria to engage Russia successfully without any considerable German aid. He advised that all care should be taken to stave off this double conflict until Austria's auxiliaries were well involved. He repeated his well worn counsel that Austria should let Russia walk into the mousetrap of Constantinople and not fall upon her until the English were engaged. If Russia should refrain from the attempt to take advantage of a Franco-German war by advancing in the East, so much the better: France and she could then be dealt with separately in turn. If war with Russia should come, Austria must act courageously and quickly; for the advantage would be all on her side at the start. Germany would lend all the aid she could spare, but it would not be great unless the war were with Russia alone.[44]

[43] Pribram, p. 64. Crown Prince Rudolf's report of the conversation.
[44] *Ibid.*, pp. 64–66. Bismarck's account of the interview to the cabinet is given by

On the following day Bismarck had a talk with Mittnacht, who reports: "To my question whether war or peace, the Prince answered that he could only repeat what he had said yesterday to the Crown Prince of Austria, who had come to interrogate him: We shall not attack France. Quite apart from the advanced age and peace-loving disposition of the Emperor, it would be a frivolous enterprise to begin a war just because our prospects might be more favorable now than later on. Besides, the French are having difficulties with the powder for their new rifle and with their melinite, and they may be even weaker with the new armament than with the old."[45] From these declarations it appears that Bismarck had been giving serious thought to the arguments of the military party, and that the attitude of the Emperor had been instrumental in deterring him from adopting their views. The doubts he now expressed as to the validity of their contentions have rather the air of justifications after the fact for a decision he had been constrained to make on other grounds. That decision was still not necessarily final; but the possibility of going back upon it depended largely on the chance of making the responsibility for a new encounter fall more definitely upon France. The train of powder leading up to a new crisis was already being laid in the western provinces, but it was not to catch the spark for another month.

## III

The results of Bismarck's activity in promoting the understanding among the powers hostile to Russia were decisive for the development of Eastern affairs. His conversation with the Austrian crown prince had the desired effect of at last completing the triple accord against Russia's designs in Bulgaria. Austria found a solution of her difficulties similar to that which had made pos-

---

Lucius von Ballhausen (p. 378): "Der Erzherzog habe sehr bedauert, dass Bismarck so entschieden betont hat, der Orient ginge uns nichts an. Sie würden von Russland allein geschlagen, denn das habe einen so enormen Nachschub, während Österreichs Kräfte schnell erschöpft seien. Bismarck entgegnete: Hunderttausend Österreicher seien ebensoviel wert wie hunderttausend Russen und ihr Offizierkorps sei besser. Man müsse nur energisch vorgehen und nötigenfalls Russisch-Polen insurgieren."

[45] Mittnacht, ii, p. 51.

sible the conclusion of the new Triple Alliance. In her note of adhesion to the Anglo-Italian agreement, on March 24, she dissociated herself from the aspect of that agreement which had to do with the Mediterranean interests of the other two powers, confining her pledge of coöperation to the maintenance of the status quo in the Near East and the prevention of the aggrandizement there of any single power at the expense of others.[46] The combination was now complete, although its basic principles were not defined with all the clearness that might be desired. It served at least to hold Russia to a stalemate in Bulgaria, to block her designs without requiring Germany to abate her own ostensibly favorable attitude toward them. As a German political writer annoyingly remarked, "Russia dares not attempt what Germany has declared a hundred times she will not move a finger to prevent." [47]

All Russia's efforts to amend the situation in Bulgaria after the retirement of Kaulbars had come to nothing. The regency remained obdurate in its refusal to bow to Russia's will; and an attempt, carried on through the Sultan, to arrange a coalition government admitting pro-Russian elements broke down before the end of February.[48] Russia could see her way to no definite action. A deadlock set in, with no election of a prince in prospect, but with the Russian cause sinking lower with every day of delay and successful defiance. A coup d'état attempted by Russia's partisans at Silistria, on March 3, only cast further discredit upon their cause. Giers was reduced to declaring that the rising "had paralyzed all his efforts to find a solution, and that he did not think that for the present there was any other alternative for Russia than to wait and see the turn events would take ' les bras croisés.' " [49]

There was another alternative, that of armed intervention, but it was one against which Russia had already decided and one which she was less able than ever to attempt. It involved the

[46] Pribram, i, pp. 39–40 (Amer., i, p. 98). March 24, Károlyi to Salisbury.
[47] *Preussische Jahrbücher*, April, 1887, pp. 372–373.
[48] P. P., 1888, cix, Turkey no. 1, pp. 12, 37, 44, 69.
[49] Ibid., p. 82. April 20, 1887, Morier to Salisbury.

risk of a war in which she would have to face three Great Powers, not counting Germany, whose forces would more than offset those of her only possible ally, France. The situation was hopeless. Even if the support of England and Italy somehow failed Austria, there was still Germany to be reckoned with as an obstacle in the way of a Russian victory. The words of Dilke are significant: "In surveying once more the entire field, a fact that must strike the observer is that . . . there is one obvious consideration which makes against an attack by Russia against Austria. In simple language it may be expressed by the phrase, ' It is heads I win, and tails you lose,' for Austria against Russia, for however completely beaten the Austrian forces might be, Germany could not . . . allow Austria to be seriously dismembered. It is the knowledge possessed in Russia of this fact which, more than the speeches of Austrian and English and Italian members, has caused Prince Bismarck's advice to be up to the present time followed in the main at St. Petersburg." [50]

Bismarck did not conceal from Russia the fact that she would have to reckon with the German army if she threw in her lot with France. To the Grand Duke Vladimir, the third distinguished visitor with whom he conversed in the month of March, he declared that Germany would not be frightened by the prospect of having to fight France and Russia at once. "Germany," he said, "is perfectly capable of waging a war on two fronts. She can spare a million men for the defence of her eastern frontier." [51] The statement was intended to demonstrate to Russia the valuelessness of a French alliance, and it was not mere bravado. The thought of a war on two fronts had become definitely rooted in the minds of Germany's leaders, both political and military; and precautions against such a conflict were being taken. But Bismarck still had in view the possibility of avoiding the contingency by cajoling or threatening Russia into remaining quiet while he dealt with France. He even went so far as to revive the Shuvalov proposal for a special agreement making Germany's neutrality with respect to Russia's designs upon Turkey a quid pro quo for Russia's non-intervention in Germany's quarrel with France. In

[50] *Present Position*, pp. 50–51.   [51] Lucius von Ballhausen, p. 378.

view of the fact that a combination had just been created which assured the failure of any Russian projects in the Near East without need of action by Germany, this proposition had now become a sufficiently disloyal snare.

But worse was behind. If Russia would not simply grant Bismarck's interpretation of the *casus foederis*, she might be forced into a position which would allow her no opportunity to contest it. In the crisis of February she had refused his appeal, and since then she had carefully kept out of complications in Bulgaria which might call into question the designated quid pro quo. Before Germany came once more to grips with France, Russia's hand might be forced and a situation developed which would effectively distract her attention from events beyond the Rhine. The existence of the new anti-Russian entente made it possible to face with equanimity the risk of a general European war which such an adventure involved.

As a means of reviving Russia's interest in the Bulgarian question, Bismarck even attempted the expedient of stirring up Prince Alexander of Battenberg, despite assurances conveyed in a letter of January 30 from the Emperor William to Alexander III that Germany would use all her influence to prevent his return to Bulgaria.[52] The prince records that, on March 24, a private emissary of Bismarck, one Dr. Langenbuch, came to his retreat at Darmstadt seeking a personal audience. He was refused, but left word with Alexander's private secretary that he had come to invite the prince to return to Bulgaria.[53] Five days later came Freiherr von Biegeleben, who had represented Austria at Sofia during Alexander's reign, to paint in rosy colors the prospect of his speedy return to occupy, no longer a mere princely, but a royal throne. The prince steadily refused to be tempted into any action not formally sanctioned in advance by Germany and all her associates.[54] There followed a series of conferences at Vienna, in which Kálnoky, Stoilov for the Bulgarian regency, Langenbuch as the agent of Bismarck, and Alexander's private secretary, Menges, took part. Langenbuch urged the Bulgarians to recall Alexander,

---

[52] *G. F. O.*, v, p. 165.  [53] Corti, p. 295.
[54] *Ibid.*, pp. 295–298. From Alexander's memorandum.

trusting to the support of Germany and her allies. He even went so far as to assure Stoilov that Germany was prepared to admit the Balkan status quo as included in the *casus foederis* of her Austrian alliance, and to recognize Russian intervention in Bulgaria as *casus belli*.[55] His authorization for making such statements remains doubtful, since he carefully avoided assuming any official status throughout the affair. The whole intrigue was rendered ineffective by Alexander's persistent refusal to move unless backed by formal commitments.[56] These Bismarck would never give. The only result of the conferences was to demonstrate to all concerned that if they desired more activity in Bulgaria, they must look for another instrument than Alexander to bring it about. The substitute was suggested by Alexander himself, in the person of Ferdinand of Coburg, on whom the Bulgarians already had their eye.[57] On the Bulgarian side, Stoilov displayed an indifference as to personalities, but took careful note of the attitude of the Central Empires. "Kálnoky," he wrote, "seemed less Russian than formerly, and apparently contemplates a solution of our problem excluding consideration of Russia." [58] And behind Kálnoky stood Bismarck, ready to welcome a new turn of developments in the Bulgarian question.

All these underhand negotiations with Prince Alexander spring from an apparently extraordinary reversal of Bismarck's policy toward the former ruler of Bulgaria. Yet in reality, the incident is by no means the most obscure and suspicious of this troubled period in the Chancellor's career. He was simply playing an unscrupulous and well hidden game. Officially he had not compromised himself. Alexander was sure his personal animosity remained undiminished.[59] He left untouched the question of the

[55] Corti, p. 300. Communicated to Menges by Stoilov.
[56] *Ibid.*, pp. 298–301. Memorandum by Menges.
[57] See below, p. 206.     [58] Corti, p. 301.
[59] *Ibid.*, p. 298. See also Lucius von Ballhausen, p. 377. Under the date March 28, Lucius records the curious incident: "Ganz wütend war der Fürst auf die Frau Kronprinzess und die Prinzess Christian, welche den Kronprinzen von Österreich zwischen sich genommen hätten und ihm zugeredet, Österreich müsse den Battenberger nach Bulgarien zurückführen und ihn dort auch gegen Russlands Willen wieder zum Regenten einsetzen."

prince's marriage. A logical interpretation of his conduct was at once offered by Lord Salisbury, who was informed of the affair through the prince's correspondence with Queen Victoria. Bismarck, wrote the English minister to his sovereign, was aiming to involve Russia seriously in Bulgaria in order to have his hands free to deal with France.[60] Salisbury probably pushed his interpretation too far in assuming that Bismarck desired to provoke a general European war. Such a result of his policy would not be inevitable; while it could be attained more easily in other ways if he really desired it. Many considerations worked against it. New wedges has just been driven between Russia and France. A safe rampart had been built up against Russian aggression in the Balkans. The defence there would be solidified, so far as England's part in it was concerned, if the queen's protégé were once more a factor in the situation. If a general war did occur, the prospects of a favorable outcome for Germany were decidedly good. Yet the sacrifices and the ensuing complications were to be avoided if possible. All that was really necessary to the success of Bismarck's design was that Russia's interest in Bulgaria should be reawakened and the conviction pressed home that German support in the question was worth the sacrifice of France. The scheme was shattered by Prince Alexander's cautious firmness; and the second crisis of the year in relations with France was upon Bismarck before a new intrigue could be launched.

[60] Corti, pp. 294–295, 296, 301. Extracts and summaries from Salisbury's letters were attached by the queen to her letter of April 7 to Prince Alexander.

# CHAPTER VIII

## THE SCHNAEBELE INCIDENT

THE situation at the end of March, 1887, was one of calm, but with clouds lowering all round the political horizon. There was small hope of their disappearing completely as yet: the only doubt was as to whether those of East or West would roll up first. This doubt was resolved in the month of April, which saw the development of the second crisis of the year in the relations between France and Germany. The Schnaebele incident, which at this period brought the two countries so near to war, has important complications reaching both back and forward of the time, thickening the plot without making it much more intelligible. One of these threads leads back to the unsatisfactory local conditions in Alsace-Lorraine and Bismarck's attempts to influence them. Another leads to the recurring problem of his intentions toward France, which continued to be more than suspect. Still another leads to the League of the Three Emperors, with its promise of a free hand in the West, which was due to expire in June. An elusive but interesting clew leads forward to certain later disclosures concerning the relations of the Bismarcks with the police officer who plays the clumsy villain of the piece.

The earlier crisis of the year, accompanying the elections to the Reichstag, had had some of its most deplorable and unprofitable manifestations in the annexed provinces. Bismarck had urged on the administration there to acts provocative both of France and of the local population. While designed ostensibly to influence the elections, these measures entailed far more serious possible consequences, which were frankly faced. The preparations for them went even so far as discussion between the civil and military authorities concerning their respective rôles in the event of mobilization.[1] It is to be noted that these discussions did not cease with the passing of the acute phase of the crisis of early

---

[1] Hohenlohe, ii, pp. 406, 409 (Amer., ii, pp. 372, 374-375).

February. On the very day of the Reichstag elections, Bismarck was urging the prosecuting authorities of Alsace-Lorraine to greater activity against possible internal enemies in time of war.[2]

So far as influencing the elections was concerned, the efforts of the government only defeated themselves.[3] The old set of protesting deputies was solidly returned. The entire German bureaucracy, from Statthalter down, was furious at the outcome, and seethed with threats of stern reprisals upon its luckless charges.[4] Projects of all kinds were discussed, even to the partition of Alsace-Lorraine among Baden, Bavaria, and Prussia.[5] Bismarck was at first inclined to radical measures, but, finding the Emperor opposed, later repudiated them himself.[6] Only a severe programme of local repression was inaugurated, in the

---

[2] Hohenlohe, ii, p. 410 (Amer., ii, p. 376). February 21, Bismarck to Hohenlohe. "Eurer Durchlaucht darf ich daher zur hochgeneigten Erwägung stellen, ob es nicht angezeigt sei, angesichts der Gefahren, welche im Kriegsfalle der Mobilmachung und den Eisenbahnverbindungen durch inländische Feinde erwachsen können, dem Herrn Staatssekretär und der reichsländischen Staatsanwaltschaft wegen ihres passiven Verhaltens Vorhaltungen zu machen."

[3] Ibid., ii, p. 407 (Amer., ii, p. 373). February 11, Hohenlohe to Bismarck. "Ueberhaupt haben die Befürchtungen vor dem Kriege, die in Deutschland günstig auf die Wahlen wirken, hier den entgegengesetzten Effekt, da der Elsass-Lothringer meint, man könne nicht wissen, wie die Sache ausgehe, und da dürfe man sich nicht kompromittieren und tue am klügsten, die alten Abgeordneten zu wählen."

[4] Ibid., ii, p. 410 (Amer., ii, p. 376). February 22. "Die Wahlen sind, wie erwartet wurde, schlecht ausgefallen, und es wird hier unter den deutschen Beamten viel darüber gesprochen, was geschehen müsse, um dem durch diesen französischen Gesinnungsausdruck beleidigten deutschen Nationalgefühle Satisfaktion zu verschaffen. So meint einer, man solle den Landesausschuss aufheben, der andre, man solle den Elsass-Lothringern das Wahlrecht zum Reichstage nehmen."

[5] Ibid., ii, pp. 412–413 (Amer., ii, pp. 377–380). March 19.

[6] Ibid., ii, p. 414 (Amer., ii, p. 380). Mittnacht, ii, pp. 51–52. March 18, interview with Bismarck on this subject: "Der Kaiser der im vorigen Herbst im Elsass so gut empfangen worden, würde auch zu strengen Massregeln nur ungern entschliessen." Busch, iii, p. 167 (Amer., ii, p. 408; *Tagebuchblätter*, iii, p. 219). April 28, Bismarck told Busch: "To unite it to Prussia would strengthen by thirty votes the Opposition in the Lower House of the Prussian Diet, where things are now very tolerable. The Bavarians will not hear of it either, and still less the people in Baden, who are in absolute terror of such a change. If we were only living in the time of Charlemagne, we could remove the Alsatians to Posen, and place the inhabitants of the latter country between the Rhine and the Vosges, or form an uninhabited desert between ourselves and the French. As it is, however, we must try some other method."

form of passport requirements, censorship, police activity, and prosecutions for disloyalty.[7]

Among the last of these measures was a case, the Klein trial, involving one Schnaebele, an Alsatian who had emigrated to France and become a French police officer. By a somewhat questionable legal procedure, Schnaebele was indicted before the Imperial Court at Leipzig for high treason against the German Empire. Upon direct authorization from Bismarck, who informed the department of justice, on March 12, that "from a political standpoint, he saw no obstacle in the way," warrants were issued for his arrest whenever he should appear on German soil.[8] They failed of execution, since Schnaebele, warned of his danger, suspended the little trips in the interest of the League of Patriots and the French war office which had brought about his indictment. He was taken at last by a ruse. Invited to a conference over certain local matters by a German police official, he crossed the frontier on April 20 and was instantly seized by secret agents, who carried him off after a struggle in which it was even uncertain on which side of the line the arrest took place.

Whether or not the German authorities were acting under explicit instructions from higher quarters was never established. On the assumption that Bismarck himself was responsible, his French biographer, Welschinger, still speaks of the affair as "le guet-apens de Pagny-sur-Moselle inventé par lui pour effrayer et mater les Lorrains annexés."[9] The hypothesis is a plausible one, in view of the antecedents of the event; yet the complications involved are too serious to make it tenable as a leading motive.

All the circumstances of the case at once made it a matter of international significance. The original right of the German authorities to indict and arrest a French citizen on a charge of treason was at least questionable. Then, too, the arrested man was in the employ of the French government, wearing its uniform, and in performance of his duties at the time he was taken. The very question of whether or not the arrest was made on German

[7] Hohenlohe, ii, pp. 412–414 (Amer., ii, pp. 377–380).
[8] G. F. O., vi, p. 182, note.
[9] Henri Welschinger, *Bismarck* (2d ed., Paris, 1912), p. 211.

territory was in dispute. Finally, the capture had been brought about through a most dishonorable stratagem. Out of all these complications, the last became the decisive issue and proved the only one upon which the German government recognized that it must yield. Had the point not been quickly and clearly established, infinite and dangerous possibilities of diplomatic controversy lay ahead.

The incident took place, moreover, in an atmosphere still somewhat disturbed by another diplomatic flutter. Early in April had come the disclosure of a scandal in the French war office involving a German officer, one of those licensed international spies known as military attachés. Much unpleasantness resulted. The Berlin *Post* went so far as to write: "The French ask us to recall our military attaché. We may go further: we may recall our ambassador." It was reported in Paris, with some foundation, that the statement was actually taken from the mouth of Bismarck.[10] This affair had hardly blown over when Schnaebele's arrest took place.

There was at first little disposition anywhere to regard the new incident as likely to lead to serious consequences. Investigations were opened on both sides to determine the facts of the case; and it was supposed that communication of their results between the governments would soon lead to an orderly settlement. Yet there was cause for misgiving in Bismarck's telegram of the 22d to the German chargé d'affaires. Ignoring all the political and legal questions involved, the Chancellor simply said: "Schnaebele will be set at liberty immediately, if the investigation in progress establishes his innocence."[11] Bismarck saw in the situation no reason for moderating the tone of his public remarks about France. On the very day of this telegram, in a speech before the Prussian

---

[10] *Times*, April 12, 1887. Paris, April 11. "This was not bravado, for a Berlin letter states that Prince Bismarck was much irritated, that he expressed himself with his usual frankness before several Ambassadors, and that the *Post* had simply reflected his remarks." Hansen writes (*Mohrenheim*, p. 38) that Count Münster told one of Hansen's friends that Bismarck had telegraphed him: "Si on vous demande le changement de notre attaché, répondez que vous avez ordre de partir en même temps que lui."

[11] *G. F. O.*, vi, p. 183.

Landtag, he threw his customary allegation of incurable hostility in her face with all his usual studied brutality.[12] This disregard of French susceptibilities, indeed, only foreshadows a still greater ruthlessness of treatment after the affair had become much more critical, casting suspicion upon the honesty of his intention to bring it to a peaceful outcome.

As day after day went by, the tone at Berlin began to grow arrogant, and the contention to assert itself that the right was all on Germany's side, barring only a failure to take up the matter diplomatically instead of simply through the police.[13] Excuses were made on this score through the German chargé d'affaires at Paris, the government maintaining that it had been kept in ignorance of the action of the courts.[14] In this connection it may be noted that more than a month had elapsed since the issue of the warrant, during which time the matter would probably have given rise to a good deal of official correspondence. Further tele-

[12] *Reden*, xii, p. 404. The debate was on the reconciliation with Rome, to which a speaker objected on the ground that it could not be permanent. Bismarck replied; "Nach Ihrer Meinung müssten wir auch heute noch in Versailles stehen, weil es nicht möglich ist, mit einer so kriegerischen Nation, wie die französische, die uns in jedem Jahrhundert drei bis vier Mal angefallen hat, einen dauernden Frieden zu schliessen."

[13] *Times*, April 26. Berlin, April 25. "It is, perhaps, natural for French writers, who must feel convinced that M. Schnaebele was a spy and an anti-German intriguer, to soothe their mortification at his arrest by trying hard to believe that he was captured on the wrong side of the border, but they will soon be undeceived on this point, and this proved, the French Government will have nothing whatever to complain of. The most it can say will be to express a regret that a proper diplomatic communication on the subject of M. Schnaebele was not made direct from Berlin to Paris instead of the German Government taking the law into its own hands in a manner which, though rightful and effective, must be admitted to be a little brusque and uncustomary." (The correspondent, Mr. Charles Lowe, takes the German side pretty consistently in this crisis, faithfully reflecting the dominant public opinion as it was shaped by authoritative influence.)

[14] *Ibid.*, April 26. Paris, April 25. "A telegram from Prince Bismarck communicated yesterday to M. de Flourens by Count Leyden, the German Chargé d'Affaires in Paris, explained that if the course of diplomacy had not been followed from the outset it was because the High Court of Justice at Leipsic took the initiative in instituting proceedings and ordering the arrest of M. Schnaebele without informing the Imperial Chancellery at Berlin, which did not intervene in the affair until the matter was brought before it by the French Government." The telegram of April 24 printed in the German foreign office publication (vi, pp. 183–184) bears only upon the point of the government's lack of knowledge.

grams from Bismarck to Paris had asserted that the arrest was proved to have taken place on German soil, and that, even supposing a ruse to have been employed, this was less regrettable than the participation of a French official in conspiracies in the Reichsland.[15]

But the French government was able to bring forward evidence giving the affair an entirely special character. The letters from the German police commissioner, Gautsch, inviting Schnaebele to the fateful rendezvous were found, and photographic copies of them sent to Berlin. On the 25th, the French ambassador laid these, together with the other documents in the French case, before Count Herbert Bismarck.

Upon sight of them, the French ambassador reported, Count Bismarck was "visibly put out of countenance."[16] His admission that "it was a regrettable ruse" smacked more of disappointment than contrition. While he could not approve the proceeding, he said drily, he did not expect "chivalrous consideration" from subordinate police officers.[17] The French case, as stated by Flourens, was, briefly: "It is not Schnaebele who was called to the frontier by somebody or other; it is the police commissioner of Pagny who was summoned by the police commissioner of Ars on official business. That alone made the arrest illegal."[18] The argument was unanswerable, yet Herbert Bismarck merely replied that he would have to look further into the material. Although the Chancellor at once recognized the validity of the French argument, in a marginal note on Herbert's report, it was not until the fourth day following the interview that the unhappy Schnaebele was set at liberty. During the interval, the strain on international relations increased rather than diminished.

By the 26th, the delay was already beginning to get on the nerves of the French. "So far as one can judge at present," wrote Lord Lyons to his government on that date, "the French are irritated beyond measure at the arrest at Pagny, but generally

[15] G. F. O., vi, p. 184, note.
[16] Pagès (Senate Report), p. 232. See also Daudet, *Bismarck*, p. 124, and an article by Valfrey in *Figaro*, May 27, 1890.
[17] G. F. O., vi, p. 185. April 25, Herbert Bismarck's memorandum.
[18] Pagès (Senate Report), p. 232. April 25, telegram from Flourens to Herbette.

they still shrink from war. It will not, I conceive, be difficult for Bismarck to keep at peace with them, if he really wishes to do so. The danger is that they are persuaded that he is only looking out for a pretext, and that however much they may now give way, he will be bent upon humiliating them till they *must* resent and resist."[19] If this was Bismarck's design — and much in his conduct certainly points that way — it had well founded prospects of a favorable result, and, in fact, came perilously near to success. General Boulanger had reacted to the crisis with all the rashness that the Germans could have expected of him. He advocated a military demonstration on an imposing scale, and even took measures in preparation for it on his own responsibility.[20] Some of his colleagues in the ministry, including Goblet himself, supported his proposals against the advice of Flourens to rest quietly on France's legal case; and the intervention of President Grévy was required to put a stop to the compromising programme.[21] Such measures would unquestionably have increased the gravity of the situation; they might well have led to the clash which Bismarck had been predicting for months.

With matters in this feverish state, the German government continued its exasperatingly deliberate and arrogant conduct of the case. On the 28th, the ministry of justice, in disregard of the evidence submitted by France, issued a report giving only the baldest statement of events, admitting no fault, charging no mis-

[19] Newton, ii, pp. 400–401. April 26, Lyons to Salisbury. *Times*, April 28. Paris, April 27. "Most of this morning's newspapers again refer to the Schnaebele incident, and several of them ask whether Prince Bismarck, by delaying the negotiations for the settlement of the question, does not hope to push the French to the commission of some act of folly. The journals therefore unanimously declare that it is more necessary than ever for the public to remain calm."

[20] *G. F. O.*, vi, p. 186. April 27, report of the German military attaché at Paris.

[21] Pagès (pp. 233–234) relates that, when Herbette returned to Paris on May 1, Goblet greeted him with the exclamation, "L'incident est clos, soit! Mais il eût été peut-être préférable d'en finir par la guerre avec toutes ces querelles d'Allemands!" Pagès adds: "Pour éviter la piège, l'habileté du Ministre des Affaires étrangères et de son représentant à Berlin n'aurait peut-être pas suffi, si la haute autorité du Président Grévy n'était pas venue à leur aide." See also Freycinet, p. 371. "Au général qui se jetait à la traverse et se campait fièrement, il lança un jour cette apostrophe: 'On dirait que vous voulez amener la guerre!'"

take to anyone.[22] Next day, Herbette received the German government's final pronouncement upon the matter.

In the stiffest possible terms, Bismarck justified every action taken on the German side, except that of the agents who actually performed the arrest, even denying any complicity between them and the official who had issued the invitation to the rendezvous. "The undersigned ventures to hope," he wrote, "that the documents communicated will convince the ambassador that the judicial order for the arrest of Schnaebele was well justified, and that it was executed entirely on German territory without any violation of French sovereignty. Nevertheless, the undersigned thought it his duty to beg the Emperor, his most gracious master, to command the liberation of Schnaebele. He was guided in so doing by the doctrine of international law that the crossing of a frontier, when done on the strength of official agreement between the functionaries of neighboring states, must always be looked upon as carrying with it the tacit assurance of a safe-conduct. It is not credible that the German official, Gautsch, invited Schnaebele to a conference with the object of facilitating his arrest. . . . Thus, while fully acknowledging the right of the German tribunals and officials to act as they did, he has submitted all the facts of the case to His Imperial Majesty the Emperor, and His Imperial Majesty has been graciously pleased to decide that in consideration of the reasons of international law in favor of the unconditional security of international negotiations, the aforesaid Schnaebele shall be set at liberty, notwithstanding his arrest on German territory and the evidence there is of his guilt." [23]

The entire note breathes the very opposite of regrets and conciliation. Its haughty language clearly proclaims the writer's vindictive disappointment at a lost opportunity. It might have

[22] The report, printed in the *Norddeutsche Allgemeine Zeitung*, read in part: "In Folge des Geständnisses Klein's ertheilte der Untersuchungsrichter dem ihm beigegebenen Criminal-Commissar v. Tausch den Auftrag, auf den des Landesverrathes beschuldigten französischen Polizei-Commissar Schnaebele zu fahnden und ihn, im Falle er das deutsche Gebiet betreten sollte, zu verhaften und vorzuführen. In Ausführung dieses Auftrages ist Schnaebele am 20 d. M. verhaftet worden."

[23] *G. F. O.*, vi, pp. 187–189; *Staatsarchiv*, 1888, pp. 228–230. Translation from the *Times*, May 2.

been only the opportunity of striking a blow at the irritating opposition in Alsace-Lorraine; but necessarily such a blow would have carried further and have been keenly felt by France. In the actual case, France was officially, as well as sentimentally, most deeply concerned. Bismarck's insistence upon his case was in no way diminished by the fact. Every point on the German side was unconditionally maintained by him; only the preservation of some wretched letters had cut the ground from under an excellent opportunity of dispute, in which arguments might easily have led to blows without any one's being able to say clearly who started the fight. Many contemporaries sagely remarked upon France's good fortune in being able to produce the decisive letters.[24] Had they not been forthcoming, it would have been very difficult to avoid the choice between national humiliation and war. As it was, the French government simply made a brief reply, formally taking exception to some of the secretary's statements, and gladly let the whole affair blow over.[25] The final decision to release Schnaebele — carried out only on the 29th — was, as the official note admitted, made by the Emperor himself. He was far from pleased at so much having been made of the affair, and long retained a grudge against Count Herbert Bismarck as somehow to blame for it.[26]

If Bismarck was seeking a quarrel with France, he must have realized that, in order to derive any benefit from Russia's promise of neutrality in the treaty of 1881, the responsibility must be cast in plausible fashion upon the other side. The crisis of February had shown him at least that much. Several circumstances point to the conclusion that he was trying to provoke France into giving

---

[24] Daudet (*Bismarck*, p. 128) writes that Schnaebele testified to a rigorous search by the agents who arrested him, one of whom he heard cry in disappointment, "*Er hat sie nicht!*"

[25] *Times*, May 3. Paris, May 2.

[26] *Times*, October 3, 1887. Paris, October 2. "On the occurrence of the Schnaebele affair the Emperor of Germany, having had the papers relating to the case brought to him, wrote on the back, ' Give the French their rights, their whole rights, and nothing but their rights, and do not put me at my age in a position to have to make excuses.'" Hohenlohe, ii, p. 426 (Amer., ii, p. 390). October 9, 1887. "Heute früh bei Wilmowski, der mir von der gereizten Stimmung des Kaisers gegen Herbert Bismarck in der Affäre Schnäbele sprach."

him this advantage before the treaty of 1881 expired. But when the French government presented an irrefutable argument and stood calmly upon it through a mortal week of anxiety, there was no question of holding out for more. Germany's case was less good than it had been in February, when Russia had refused her support. The disappointment expressed in Bismarck's note to Herbette on April 28 was made all the more keen by the consideration that this was probably the last chance to profit by that treaty. The Russians, far from hastening to renew the engagement ahead of time, as they had done in 1884, were giving no sign of willingness to renew it at all.[27] The Panslavist party was carrying its campaign into the very cabinet of the Emperor, where Katkov's voice was increasingly heard in denunciation of the policies of Giers. That minister's tenure of office seemed actually in danger; and if he went, in all probability the German alliance would go also.[28]

In connection with this struggle at the Russian court is to be noted a well timed step on Bismarck's part. At the very inception of the Schnaebele crisis, he had made an audacious move calculated to disarm the anti-German agitation in Russia. On April 20, the *Norddeutsche Allgemeine Zeitung* published the first account of the secret negotiations between Russia and Austria at Reichstadt in 1876. The effect of this disclosure was to show that Russia was, in the last analysis, herself responsible for her misfortunes, for which it was quite unfair that Germany should be blamed.[29] The irrepressible Katkov was not silenced by this

[27] *G. F. O.*, v, p. 222. On April 14, Bülow sent a very doubtful report from St. Petersburg.

[28] Cyon, pp. 268, 272–275. Lucius von Ballhausen, p. 382. On April 10, Bismarck read to the cabinet a report from Russia on the situation: "Katkoff habe über Giers gesiegt, welcher als von Deutschland gewonnen angefochten werde. Genug — unser Verhältnis zu Russland erschien nach diesem Bericht äusserst trübe, und Bismarck teilt diese Empfindung und wünscht nicht, sie uns vorzuenthalten. Boulanger und Obrutscheff konspirieren gegen uns, das ist klar, und so sieht Bismarck die Lage an."

[29] The most significant passage from the article ran: "Die Unterstützung der Orientpolitik Oesterreichs datirt keineswegs vom Berliner Traktat und ist auch nicht von Deutschland, sondern vom Fürsten Gortschakow ausgegangen. Ueber Jahr und Tag vor dem Zusammentritt des Berliner Kongresses hat Fürst Gortschakow der Orientpolitik Oesterreichs diejenigen Zugeständnisse gemacht, welche

hit, but he did find himself thrown momentarily upon the defensive in his campaign.[30] The disconcerting of this powerful adversary and his party would have worked greatly to Bismarck's advantage if the crisis in his relations with France had developed as for a time it threatened to do. But when the controversy over Schnaebele collapsed, the advantage was lost. Russia was not called upon to define her attitude toward Germany in a new war. And the Reichstadt matter soon dropped back into its proper place among the factors which had determined Russo-German relations from the beginning. Bismarck's sudden counter-offensive against the Panslavists at this moment, however, falls in with other indications that there was more behind the Schnaebele crisis than can be definitely proved.

The indications of a desire to turn a strained situation into an actual conflict are, indeed, plentiful enough; but it is much more difficult to establish the responsibility for bringing about the crisis. Certainly it seems stretching a point to suppose any causal connection between the policies of the imperial chancery and the actions of the police official who created the incident by his execution of the warrant of a Leipzig court. But the courts were acting under the special inspiration of the Chancellor in these prosecutions for treason. Presumably he did not lose touch with what they were doing. The affair of the attempt upon the Tsar's life reveals the existence of a decidedly seamy side to Germany's foreign policy, in its relations with the secret police. Moreover, a curious thread leads from the Schnaebele case to the Leckert-Lützow trial of December, 1896, in which the political police, and the Bismarcks behind them, came under fire for disloyalty to the existing government. Among the officials accused of disloyal activities was Commissioner von Tausch, who had framed the ill-starred plot of Pagny-sur-Moselle.

This leading character in the plot had received very little notice in the current discussions of the affair — so little that, in the ver-

der ' Dniewnik Warschawski ' nunmehr der ' unaufrichtigen Politik ' der deutschen Regierung zuschreibt."

[30] Cyon, pp. 292–297. It is to be noted that Katkov was not unacquainted with what had taken place at Reichstadt. He had pilloried the government for its policy in that affair in his newspaper on January 2, 1883. Remmer, p. 83.

sions sent abroad of the report of the ministry of justice, the name was altered to ' Gautsch,' that of the commissioner who had written the letters to Schnaebele.[31] In a letter dated April 30 to the editor of the *Temps*, Gautsch protested against the confusion of names and stoutly maintained that he had acted with no intention of betraying Schnaebele into a snare.[32] The same contention was made by Bismarck in his note of April 28. Granting that Gautsch may have been only an unconscious tool of the real author of the stratagem, the connections of Tausch with superior agencies in the German political system still remain to be traced.

It may be of some significance for the relations of von Tausch with his superiors that his career was not noticeably blighted by the indiscretion of 1887. Three years afterward he is found occupying the post at Berlin where he later displayed the obnoxious activity which dragged his name before the public. Busybodies were not wanting then to pry into his past in the search for a *Hintermann* behind his exploits: they had to look no further than Friedrichsruh.[33] Eventually they hit upon his part in the Schnaebele incident. The Bismarcks, father and son, were rendered highly uncomfortable by the whole scandal, but showed themselves particularly sensitive about the affair of 1887.

The father chose the *Hamburger Nachrichten* as the vehicle for his denials of any connection with the commissioner in that affair. "It is not improbable," runs an article of January 16, 1897, "that the name of Herr von Tausch was hardly known in

[31] *Times*, April 29, May 1, 1887.

[32] "Monsieur — Dans l'article que vous publiez dans le numéro du 30 avril, article concernant la communication faite au ministère des affaires étrangères de Berlin par le ministère de la justice de l'empire, il est dit; ' A la suite de ces aveux, le juge d'instruction chargea M. Gautsch, qui avait été mis à sa disposition.' Veuillez, je vous prie, consulter les journaux allemands et rectifier. Ce n'est pas M. Gautsch, mais M. von Tausch, qui avait été mis à sa disposition. M. von Tausch est également commissaire de police, mais ce n'est pas moi. Je n'avais du reste, jusqu'au 20 avril, aucune connaissance que M. Schnoebele devait être arrêté."

[33] *Times*, December 12, 1896. Berlin, December 11. "In very many of the episodes related Herr von Tausch would seem to have allowed his strong Bismarckian sympathies to carry him beyond his purely official duties, and the marked preference shown by him and his under-studies for the *régime* previous to 1890 in contradistinction to the *neuer Kurs* has afforded his biographers several opportunities to point a moral and adorn the tale."

the foreign office at the time of the Schnaebele incident. He was merely a police officer, more zealous in his functions than learned in international law; otherwise he would never have resorted to the illegal project of an official rendezvous as a trap for Schnaebele, when the latter could have been arrested as a voluntary visitor in Metz." [34] The alibi rather overreaches itself. It was precisely because Schnaebele had ceased to be a 'voluntary visitor' in Metz that Tausch had had recourse to his stratagem.[35] The *Strassburger Post*, which had pointed this out at the time, had also affirmed explicitly that, in falling back upon plots, Tausch was acting under orders from above to take Schnaebele, no matter how, and that the whole machinery of the ambuscade was under his direction. The inference would be that Tausch was personally responsible only for bungling the details of the plot.

Count Herbert took up the defence of the family in the Reichstag, where the case gave rise to an interpellation, and went even further than the ex-Chancellor in his professions of innocence. His statement runs: "This police commissioner, whose name has been so frequently mentioned here today, came to Berlin for the first time in the winter of 1890. Prince Bismarck never saw him in his life; and I have no personal acquaintance with him either. All the time I was in office I never heard his name mentioned except once, in connection with an unskilfully managed affair in the *Reichsland*, of which I will say no more at this time." [36] Yet Count Herbert had been somehow especially blamed by the old Emperor for his share in the affair. Deputy Bebel contributed to the debate the comment: "Gentlemen, as I said yesterday, the Tausch system is in reality the Bismarck system. If one wishes to give this system a specific name, it can only be that of Bismarck." [37]

The revelations of 1896–97 are far from clearing up the events of 1887; but they do indicate a closer connection of the Bismarcks with the affair than appeared evident at the time. The proceed-

[34] Johannes Penzler, *Fürst Bismarck nach seiner Entlassung* (Leipzig, 1897–98, 7 vols.), vii, p. 214.
[35] *M. A. Z.*, April 24, 1887. Strassburg, April 22.
[36] *Stenographische Berichte*, session of 1895–97, vi, p. 4493.
[37] *Ibid.*, p. 4512.

ings against Schnaebele, down to his actual arrest, must have had their sanction, in full knowledge of the infinite possibilities of international difficulties which that act would open up. Only the choice of means by the local agent proved unfortunate. When proof of the character of the plot was produced, Count Bismarck betrayed surprise and chagrin; yet the agent never suffered for his clumsiness. The Chancellor had let it be seen that he yielded solely on this issue among all those that were raised — and he further displayed extreme irritation at being obliged to yield at all. The settlement was deliberately delayed in the face of a growing agitation in France which affected even the ministry. But counsels of moderation prevailed. The French government took its stand firmly upon an irrefutable case and could not be pricked into assuming a shade of responsibility for a conflict. Failing to throw this responsibility upon France, Bismarck knew from previous experience that he could not count upon Russia's neutrality if the conflict came. Germany simply had to back down: Schnaebele was set free. After his liberation this second crisis of 1887 passed quietly away.

# CHAPTER IX

## THE REINSURANCE TREATY

### I

IN the Franco-German crises both of February and April the League of the Three Emperors had disappointed Bismarck greatly. The free hand against France apparently assured by the treaty of 1881 had been denied him by Russia, with decisive effect upon his policies. Yet Bismarck earnestly desired the renewal of the treaty, which had less than two months to run after the closing of the Schnaebele incident. At another time the situation might be less unfavorable for invoking the pledge with regard to France — the French might take a more rash initiative, or the Russians might be in a better humor toward Germany. Bismarck realized how distasteful was the Bulgarian solution he was obliging Russia to accept; but he might hope that relations would improve again, once she had resigned herself to the new situation. Moreover, the treaty of alliance was a useful means of influencing Russia's policy in the East. And, finally, it was his guarantee against the Franco-Russian alliance and many other unpleasant possibilities. Whatever may be said, or even proved, regarding the insincerity of Bismarck's friendship for Russia, no doubt can be cast upon the reality of his determination to keep open the wire to Petersburg.'[1] He was prepared even to sacrifice many formal advantages in order to retain the essence of the agreement with Russia.

[1] *Gedanken und Erinnerungen*, American edition, iii, p. 110. In a declaration read to the cabinet on March 17, 1890, Bismarck stated: "Notwithstanding my confidence in the Triple Alliance, I have never lost sight of the possibility that it might at some time be dissolved; for in Italy the monarchy is not very firmly established; the engagement between Italy and Austria might be endangered by the Irredenta; in Austria only the trustworthiness of the present Emperor excludes a change during his lifetime; and it is never safe to count upon the attitude of Hungary. On this account I have constantly endeavored never quite to break down the bridge between us and Russia."

For a time the very principle of the alliance hung trembling in the balance. The conflict of policies in Russia was still undecided in the early days of May, although the Katkov party was gradually losing ground before the clever and unscrupulous tactics of Giers and his friends.[2] The pro-French faction had made some headway in the financial field; and on May 5 was signed an agreement between the ministry of finance and the firm of Rothschild for the conversion by Paris banks of a block of Russian credit obligations.[3] The operation was carried out in the following month.[4] It proved the beginning of the shift of Russia's financial orientation away from Berlin and toward Paris, which advocates of the Franco-Russian alliance desired. Yet the obstacles in the way of that alliance were still too serious to be easily overcome. Chief among these was the mental attitude of Alexander III. The Russian autocrat was sincerely attached to the cause of upholding the conservative principle in Europe and to the conception of the 'Emperors' Peace.' His prospective ally, on the other hand, seemed quite as deeply committed to the opposite tendencies of radicalism and 'jingoism.' The instability of the French government was reëmphasized by the rumors, already current at the beginning of May, of another ministerial crisis.

A means of saving the policy of the German alliance was found by recurring to the proposal of a separate agreement, excluding Austria, made by Shuvalov in January. Giers had been unfavorable to this proposal, but, on April 24, he told the German chargé

[2] Cyon, chapters x and xi. There is a long tale in chapter xi concerning the publication in Paris of reports alleging interference in the French ministerial crisis by Katkov and Cyon and referring to a letter supposedly written by Katkov to Floquet. All this scandal, said to have been concocted by the German embassy, is given as the cause of Katkov's disgrace by his own sovereign, to whom Mohrenheim repeated it as fact. The whole account of the plot is too involved and too obviously colored by self-glorification to constitute any definite evidence against Bismarck. Doubtless the German Chancellor favored all moves of the Giers party against Katkov; but there is small occasion to drag him into this obscure intrigue.

[3] Ibid., p. 298. A. E. Horn, A History of Banking in the Russian Empire, in A History of Banking in All the Leading Nations, ii (New York, 1896), p. 404. The transaction was a relatively small one, involving only the bond issues of the Joint-Stock Land Credit Company of St. Petersburg, which had been taken over by the government in 1885 on a basis of conversion from 5% to $4\frac{1}{2}$% interest.

[4] Cyon, pp. 333-334.

d'affaires that, finding the Tsar unalterably opposed to a renewal of the League of the Three Emperors, he had obtained his consent to the new combination.[5] The submission of a draft to the German government, however, was delayed for more than a fortnight.

During this time, Bismarck used all the means at his command to convince the Tsar of the value of Germany's friendship. He made the most of Boulanger's indiscretions in the recent crisis, which, if they had failed to bring on a war, still served to discredit France in Alexander's eyes.[6] "In the interest of the Prussian dynasty and of peaceful relations with Russia," he secured a formal prohibition against the marriage of the Princess Victoria with Alexander of Battenberg, in the shape of a document addressed by the Emperor to the Crown Prince and countersigned by the Chancellor as a matter of ministerial record.[7] In an interview with General Kaulbars, early in May, he used all his arts to produce an impression of real friendliness to Russia and of sincerity in his offers to support her advance in the Balkans — provided it were carried out in accordance with a liberal partition agreement with Austria.[8] Just how much Bismarck meant by such propositions was always doubtful, and had become especially so since the transactions of February with Italy and England; but he was obliged to advocate something of the sort in his character of 'honest broker.' He carefully pointed out that if some peaceful

[5] *G. F. O.*, v, p. 224.
[6] Lucius von Ballhausen, p. 385. In discussing this aspect of the Schnaebele incident on May 4, Bismarck observed: "Im übrigen sei die französische Regierung im höchsten Mass kompromittiert, und er werde dafür sorgen, dass der Fall weiter fruktifiziert werde."
[7] *Ibid.*, pp. 385–386.
[8] Schiemann, in the *Beilage zur Allgemeinen Zeitung* (Munich) for February 18, 1905, publishes a letter from a friend to whom Kaulbars recounted the conversation. "Bismarck fragte, warum Russland gar keine Anstalten zur Lösung der bulgarischen Frage treffe. 'Wir würden jeden Vorschlag acceptieren und auch Oesterreich dazu bewegen.' . . . Fürst Bismarck plädierte übrigens auch jetzt noch für eine friedliche Aufteilung der Balkanhalbinsel zwischen Oesterreich und Russland, etwa in der Weise, dass Salonichi noch an Oesterreich fiele, oder sonst bei einer beliebigen Linie. Er sagte, er habe sowohl auf der einen als auf der anderen Seite angeklopft, aber kein Entgegenkommen gefunden. 'Mir scheint es,' sagte er, 'weil beide Teile mehr wollen, als sie bekommen sollen. Bei Ihnen schielt man nach den slawischen Provinzen Oesterreichs, und Oesterreich möchte auch gern Konstantinopel haben.'"

solution were not found, Germany would stand in the way of a Russian victory over Austria in war.⁹ As a personal touch to the interview, Bismarck condemned Kálnoky's "tactless and blundering" declarations against Kaulbars in parliament. His auditor was by no means won over by all this reasoning. Kaulbars felt, and expressed his feeling, that there were other factors in the situation, not to be dismissed by Bismarck's mere word; and he came away with the impression that the Chancellor really wanted to engage Russia in Bulgaria in order to gain his coveted free hand against France.¹⁰ This conception of Bismarck's policy had been current in Russia since the crisis of February. Although correct up to a certain point, the theory still needed qualifying by the conditions that an outcome based on a Russo-Austrian agreement should mean no permanent gain to Russia, and that an intervention without Austria's consent should take place only if the proper combination was in existence to insure Russia's defeat in a war.

At last, on the 11th of May, Paul Shuvalov came to Bismarck with the Russian proposals for a separate treaty. The essential article proved a great shock to the Chancellor. He had approved the project of January, which, in exchange for Russia's unqualified pledge of benevolent neutrality in a Franco-German war, had stipulated only Germany's approval of the closure of the Straits. As Giers had remarked, this last was a very remote eventuality.¹¹ The new draft provided for a nearer one. Its first article was simply a mutual pledge of benevolent neutrality in the event of

⁹ Schiemann. "Bismarck schien für die Idee einer Teilung ohne Schwertstreich sehr eingenommen. 'Wenn Sie den Sultan stürzen, werden wir *sehr weinen*, denn wir stehen mit ihm in den besten Beziehungen, er ist uns wirklich ein guter Freund, aber wir werden für ihn nicht die geringste Waffe brauchen. Ein Krieg zwischen Russland und Oesterreich würde uns sehr unbequem sein, sagte Bismarck. Oesterreichs Existenz ist uns durchaus notwendig. Sobald also russische Truppen vor Wien oder Brünn erscheinen, würden wir gegen Russland eingreifen.'"

¹⁰ *Ibid.* "Kaulbars erwiderte, dass doch Russland schon genug getan habe und sich als Grossmacht nicht dem aussetzen könne, dass seinem Vorschlag entgegengearbeitet würde oder dass er durchfalle. . . . Kaulbars gewann aber dabei den Eindruck, dass Bismarck es sehr gern sähe, wenn Russland sich in Bulgarien festrennen und engagieren würde, um seinerseits gegen Frankreich freie Hand zu behalten."

¹¹ *G. F. O.*, v, p. 226. April 30, Schweinitz to Bismarck.

war between either party and a third Great Power.[12] This meant that Germany must pay for her free hand against France by granting Russia an equally free hand against Austria. Bismarck at once objected that such a pledge would conflict with his obligations to Austria-Hungary. To demonstrate the reality of his objection, he read to Shuvalov the "text itself" of the secret treaty of 1879. The existence of this agreement, he stated, obliged him to limit his pledge of neutrality in a war between Russia and Austria to the case that Austria should be the aggressor. Shuvalov's reply betrayed a certain lack of confidence in Bismarck's judgment as to the facts of aggression. He declared that the nature of the conflict of interests between Russia and Austria in the Balkans rendered the question of aggression extremely complicated, and that the clause had been purposely framed as it was, in order to avoid the necessity of interpretation.[13] The difference of opinions on this point was so serious that a week of negotiations was required to find a solution.

It must be noted here that, in communicating the treaty of 1879 to the Russian ambassador, Bismarck was violating his engagement with Austria to hold it secret. He had written to Vienna, on May 8, concerning the advisability of publishing this document, but had as yet received no reply.[14] In his later accounts of the interview with Shuvalov, he admitted only having described the terms of the treaty.[15] In order to protect himself, he then asked Austria's permission to supply Russia with a copy of the text, and was much annoyed by the Emperor Francis

[12] *G. F. O.*, v, p. 230.

[13] Красный Архив, i, 1922. "Русско-Германские Отношения." A collection of documents, including Shuvalov's reports of his conversations with Bismarck, May 11–18. These reports, which are the ones used by Goriainov in writing his article published in the *American Historical Review*, January, 1918, were all transmitted together to the Tsar after Shuvalov's return from Berlin. They contain no evidence of communication between Shuvalov and his government during the course of the negotiations. It is noteworthy that no documents on this first period of the negotiations appear in the German foreign office publication, while on the later phase, which it covers fully, no material is available from Russian sources. For the conversation of May 11, see Красный Архив, i, pp. 92–105, and Goriainov, p. 335.

[14] *G. F. O.*, v, pp. 271–272.

[15] *Ibid.*, v, pp. 275, 278. May 15, 23, Bismarck to Reuss.

Joseph's insistence that the clause defining its duration should be withheld. Although this clause had already been communicated to Shuvalov it was omitted from the version of the text finally handed him on June 13.[16] Throughout these negotiations with Austria, Bismarck gave the impression that he was working for a renewal of the League of the Three Emperors, although Giers had already informed the Austrian government that Russia had decided to let that agreement drop.[17]

On May 13 and 14, Shuvalov and Bismarck had two more conversations in which they strove vainly to find a way satisfactory to Russia of getting around the treaty of 1879. Bismarck went very far in assuring the Russian ambassador that this treaty was not a 'blanket' guaranty of Austria. "She knows very well," he said, "that she would have no right to count on our support in case of aggression from her side. It is not our intention to guarantee her territorial integrity at all costs." This misleading declaration did not convince Shuvalov, who replied that Austria still had it in her power to undertake "all sorts of activities in the Balkan Peninsula which would lead to serious clashes not bearing formally the character of aggression, which we should have to endure with folded arms for fear that both Germany and her ally would fall upon us."[18]

On the 17th, Shuvalov gave the negotiation a new turn. "Having in mind," he writes, "the absolute necessity of adding to the reservations proposed by the prince . . . the reservation which His Majesty means to attach to the case of a war between France and Germany," he proposed the further qualification "and saving also, for Russia, the case of an attack on France by Germany." From the first, the Russian ambassador, in discussing the neutrality clause, had spoken only of its application in the event of a French attack, taking note of Bismarck's repeated declarations that Germany would never be the aggressor; but certainly no such limitation was to be inferred from the original draft. Its inclusion as a mental reservation was hardly straight dealing. Now

[16] *G. F. O.*, v, p. 281. June 13, Bismarck to Schweinitz.
[17] *Ibid.*, v, p. 233. May 11, Schweinitz to Bismarck.
[18] Красный Архив, i, pp. 106–115.

that it was expressed in words, Bismarck protested vehemently against admitting it into the treaty. Failing to demolish the condition, he replied with a proposal of his own to make the neutrality clause apply only to wars of defence against any third Power. Shuvalov in turn objected firmly to such tying of Russia's hands with respect to Turkey, England, or other possible enemies. In the face of a stubborn refusal to argue the point, Bismarck gave way, and, on the 18th, dictated a neutrality clause unconditional except as to wars with Austria or France, but limited in these cases to wars of defence.[19] Shuvalov returned to St. Petersburg to obtain a decision on the new text.

The full revelation of the terms of the Austro-German treaty must have been a severe shock to the Tsar; but he did not swerve from his resolve to pursue the negotiations. The trend of political developments in France was making her less attractive as an ally every day. The ministerial crisis there was revolving feverishly round the question of whether Boulanger should be included in the new cabinet or not. To retain him would increase the discredit of the government in the eyes of the world; to drop him might well raise up a danger to the government itself. The situation was especially fraught with danger because of the fact that peaceful relations with Germany appeared still far from secure.[20] The new cabinet was at length constituted by Rouvier on May 30 without Boulanger; but, as shrewd politicians had apprehended, the general's popularity only increased, and, with it, the peril he represented to the internal and external peace of the country. Under these circumstances a Franco-Russian alliance was out of the question.[21] The German alliance became all the more desirable by contrast.

[19] Красный Архив, i, pp. 116–127. Goriainov, in the *American Historical Review*, January, 1918, pp. 336–338.

[20] Newton, ii, p. 402. May 13, 1887, Lyons to Salisbury. "I have not heard of any new incident between France and Germany, but the suspicion and susceptibility with which the two nations, and indeed the two Governments, regard each other, are certainly not diminishing."

[21] *Zur europäischen Politik*, v, p. 199. June 9, 1887, Errembault de Dudzeele: "J'ai causé . . ., Prince, avec des personnes ayant des attaches avec le gouvernement et je les ai trouvées dans l'idée que si la France n'a pas perdu les sympathies de la Russie elle a du moins ébranlé dans ces derniers temps sa confiance par de trop

In the situation as it was now developing, one of the determining factors was again Bismarck's policy with respect to Bulgaria. Besides the draft of the Russo-German treaty, Shuvalov had brought with him to Berlin a proposal for replacing the Bulgarian council of regency by a single regent, whose mission should be to restore normal conditions in the country preparatory to the election of a prince. Bismarck was asked to exert in favor of this plan "the influence which the cabinet of Berlin possesses both with the Great Powers and at Constantinople." [22] This proposal was most embarassing to the Chancellor, in view of the existence of the triple combination against Russia which he had recently helped to form. That he did not wish to detract from the purpose and effectiveness of this accord is indicated in a despatch of May 15 to Vienna, in which he made the curious statement: "If the Russians were certain that Austria, Italy, and England were firmly united against their plans and had good prospects of winning over Turkey, I believe they would be inclined to seek their own security and avert their isolation by prolonging the League of the Three Emperors." [23] Yet so strong was Bismarck's desire to bring the negotiations with Russia to a successful conclusion, that he promised Shuvalov he would commission his son Count Herbert to try to persuade Salisbury "to be more accommodating in his attitude toward the subject of the provisional regent." Shuvalov acclaimed this promise as a significant departure from Bismarck's policy of leaving the initiative in Bulgarian matters entirely to Russia.[24] However limited this championship of Russia's interests was meant to be, Herbert Bismarck was actually instructed to urge the British government to make some conces-

fréquents revirements politiques. Ne se sentant pas sûr avec elle du lendemain, on est naturellement obligé d'imposer silence aux sympathies et d'observer une prudente réserve. Bon gré, malgré, on doit conserver la plus grande courtoisie vis-à-vis de Berlin pour ne pas s'aventurer dans quelque situation risquée où la Russie pourrait se trouver inopinément isolée. D'autre part, l'Empereur Alexandre III veut sincèrement le maintien de la paix et comme tout nouveau pas de la Russie vers la France, compromettrait cette paix en alarmant et irritant l'Allemagne, le gouvernement russe s'abstient de donner une forme concrète aux tendances actuelles de rapprochement des nations russes et francaises."

[22] *G. F. O.*, v, p. 171.    [23] *Ibid.*, v, p. 234.
[24] Красный Архив, i, pp. 120–121. Report of May 17.

sions. The argument advanced was that they would be repaid by Russian concessions in Afghanistan, and that the new proposal regarding Bulgaria would create a situation no more abnormal than the existing one. Salisbury replied that he would support a proposition to send in Aleko Pasha, former governor general of Eastern Rumelia, as regent.[25]

These efforts in Russia's behalf, however, did not reconcile her to the effects of the disclosure of the Austro-German treaty upon the new project of alliance. Paul Shuvalov himself expressed grave misgivings as to Germany's loyalty. Admitting the original reasons for the conclusion of the treaty of 1879, he said he still failed to understand its prolongation after the revival of the League of the Three Emperors. He thought Russia's interests in the Balkans required more specific support than a general guaranty against Austrian attack, and suggested an additional article extending the *casus foederis* to a war arising out of Austria's interference with Russia's rights under the arrangements of the congress of Berlin. He also thought Germany should be called upon to show her good will by taking the lead in putting through the latest proposal regarding Bulgaria.[26]

Shuvalov reappeared at Berlin, on June 12, with the draft of an annex to the proposed treaty which Bismarck rightly considered a remarkable piece of diplomatic fatuity. It provided, for one thing, that Germany should notify Austria that their *casus foederis* could in no case extend to a conflict brought about by interference with Russia's action in Bulgaria or Rumelia or at Constantinople.[27] That the stark reality of Germany's guaranty of Austria could be effectively altered by such a pettifogging gloss upon her pledge of neutrality in the event of an Austrian attack on Russia was indeed a futile assumption. Bismarck replied:

[25] *G. F. O.*, v, pp. 176–177. May 21, Bismarck to Count Herbert; May 24, Hatzfeldt to the foreign office.

[26] *Ibid.*, v, pp. 241–242. June 6, Schweinitz to Bismarck.

[27] *Ibid.*, v, p. 250. "Mais, en cas d'empiètement, l'Allemagne préviendrait le Cabinet de Vienne qu'il agirait à ses risques et périls et constaterait que toute entrave à l'action de la Russie soit en Bulgarie soit en Roumélie soit à Constantinople ne pourrait jamais aboutir à un 'casus foederis' entre l'Allemagne et l'Autriche-Hongrie."

"The question of what constitutes an aggressive war cannot be defined in a treaty . . . . Least of all . . . can words of such vague and elastic scope as 'empiètements' and 'entraves' serve as guides for determination of the future." [28] This whole section of the annex was finally omitted.

Another section provided that "Germany will aid Russia to reëstablish in Bulgaria a regular and legal government." [29] This condition was supplemented by a despatch repeating the proposal for a new regency as the first step toward this consummation, and suggesting General Ernroth, former minister of war in Bulgaria, for the post. For the accomplishment of this design, Bismarck was again asked, in somewhat stronger terms than before, to "associate himself energetically with our efforts at Constantinople" and to "make his influence felt upon the European cabinets." [30] The Chancellor made consistent answers to both propositions. In a marginal note on the despatch, which was handed back to Shuvalov, he wrote: "As soon as *there is* a *Russian* proposal to support, we will bring to bear in its behalf whatever influence we may have with the Powers or the Porte — naming Ernroth at the start. It is for Russia to speak first; we could not take the initiative, but our support will not be lacking." [31] As for the pledge of aid in the annex to the treaty, he insisted that it be qualified by the phrase, "as in the past." [32]

Disappointed at Bismarck's refusal of active coöperation, the Russian government refrained from going on with the project of a change of regents in Bulgaria. How well justified Russia was in abandoning this project is indicated in the negotiations to which it gave rise at Vienna, where the German ambassador was instructed to give notice of what his government had undertaken to do and to urge the Austrians to common action. The ambassador wrote, in his report of a conversation with Kálnoky, who had expressed doubts about all aspects of the proposition: "I held this to be a fortunate opportunity to do the Emperor of Russia a favor which would cost Austria nothing at all. If the Bulgarians

---

[28] *G. F. O.*, v, p. 248. June 12, Bismarck to Schweinitz.
[29] *Ibid.*, v, p. 249.   [30] *Ibid.*, v, p. 178.   [31] *Ibid.*, v, p. 179.
[32] *Ibid.*, v, p. 247. June 12, Bismarck to Schweinitz.

will have none of the general, the matter stands just as before." [33] "Richtig," was Bismarck's marginal comment.

Notwithstanding the disappointment over Bulgaria, the Russian government went through with the new treaty of alliance, accepting Bismarck's revisions without demur. It was signed on June 18, the very day the League of the Three Emperors expired. The first article was left as redrafted in May.

In addition to the engagements of the treaty of 1881 in support of the closure of the Straits, Germany pledged herself to benevolent neutrality and diplomatic support in case Russia should be obliged to undertake their defence. The two allies bound themselves to permit no changes in the territorial status quo of the Balkan Peninsula; while Germany recognized Russia's "preponderant and decisive influence in Bulgaria," agreed to aid her "as in the past" to reëstablish a regular and legal government there, and promised not to consent to the restoration of the Prince of Battenberg.[34]

On the surface it appeared that Russia had made a great gain over the terms of 1881. Germany was restrained from supporting Austria in an aggressive war and from herself undertaking any aggression against France. She had apparently underwritten Russia's policy in Bulgaria and even very much beyond. Giers pointed to two facts — that the Germans had shortened the duration of the treaty from the proposed five years to three, and that the signature was left by the Chancellor to Herbert Bismarck — as indicating how much Russia had got the best of it. The Tsar commented upon his minister's triumphant conclusions by the single word, "Perhaps." [35]

In accordance with Russia's wish the treaty was kept strictly secret. Bismarck merely informed the Austrian government that, despite all his efforts and the communication of the Austro-German treaty, Russia had declined to renew the League of the Three Emperors. His intention was, however, he wrote, "to conduct the relations among the three empires just as if the treaty

[33] *G. F. O.*, v, p. 185. June 17, Reuss to Bismarck.
[34] Goriainov, in the *American Historical Review*, January, 1918, pp. 338–339. Pribram, i, pp. 306 *et seq.* (Amer., i, pp. 274 *et seq.*). *G. F. O.*, v, pp. 253–255.
[35] Goriainov, p. 338.

had been renewed." [36] The Emperor William breathed no word of the new agreement to Francis Joseph when the two met at Gastein on August 6, although the latter expressed his regret at the dropping of the treaty of 1881; and Bismarck assured Shuvalov, "I shall do the same when I see Kálnoky." [37] Apparently he kept his word. An assertion in the *Hamburger Nachrichten* implying that Germany's partners in the Triple Alliance were informed of his action goes almost undoubtedly beyond the facts.[38] Kálnoky's biographers agree in stating that he was not told about the treaty, though Molden asserts that he more than suspected its existence.[39]

But to maintain that the Austrian government was informed of the treaty is one thing: to maintain that it had no reason to complain of the new agreement and its application is another. The latter contention forms the burden of Bismarck's defence of his loyalty in the newspaper articles of 1896 which first revealed the treaty's existence. He had put it forward in a letter to the Emperor William, on July 28, 1887, saying that, if Austria knew of the treaty, "the Emperor . . . would have confidence enough in Your Majesty to know that we shall use the influence the treaty gives us over Russian policy in the interest of peace, and never to the damage of Austria." [40] Upon all that he needed to know Kálnoky was kept informed; and he regulated his policy accordingly. He knew that he could count upon no direct German sup-

[36] *G. F. O.*, v, p. 264. July 20, Bismarck to Reuss.   [37] Goriainov, p. 338.
[38] *Hamburger Nachrichten*, November 1, 1896. "Denselben war die Rückversicherung mit Russland nicht unbekannt und schwerlich unerwünscht." Hofmann, ii, p. 378.
[39] Friedjung, *Biographisches Jahrbuch*, iii, p. 367 (*Aufsätze*, pp. 341–342). Berthold Molden, "Kálnoky," in *Allgemeine Deutsche Biographie*, li, pp. 16–17. "K. war, wie gesagt, von dem Rückversicherungsvertrage nicht unterrichtet; es lag jedoch nahe für ihn, die Möglichkeit einer solchen Vereinbarung in Betracht zu ziehen . . . Bei seinem Besuche in Friedrichsruh im September 1887 fühlte er sich in seiner Vermuthung, dass zwischen Deutschland und Russland ein besonderes Verhältniss bestehe, bestärkt, denn es fiel ihm auf, dass Bismarck, der sonst immer offen mit ihm gesprochen hatte, eine gewisse Reserve bewahrte, wenn die Rede auf Russland kam." Caprivi and Holstein were sure the treaty had not been communicated to Austria and Italy. See Hohenlohe, ii, p. 484 (Amer., ii, p. 442); and Harden, *Köpfe* (9th ed., Berlin, 1910), p. 100.
[40] *G. F. O.*, v, pp. 266–267.

port in any adventures, but he knew also that another combination had been built up to stand by him and that there was always Germany's guaranty of Austria's existence as a great power to fall back on. Germany had not changed her position as holder of the balance between Russia and Austria — apparently the 'honest broker,' yet repeatedly 'fixing' the transactions in favor of one client at the expense of the other.[41] Austria had indeed lost nothing by the signature of the new treaty: German policy had swerved not an inch farther than before in Russia's favor. The alliance of 1879 had lost none of its force.

The assertion put forward in 1896 that the contracting parties hardly considered the possibility of a Russo-Austrian war, but were mainly concerned with the British threat to Russia, is borne out neither by the documents nor by the circumstances of the moment.[42] Bismarck might have been willing enough to pull this particular kind of wool over Russia's eyes; but the opportunity was not especially favorable. The Afghan boundary dispute was nearer settlement than ever; while England's opposition to Russia's Bulgarian policy did not loom nearly so large as Austria's. The issue in the Balkans, with which the treaty chiefly dealt, was fundamentally between Russia and Austria.

Germany's attitude toward the rivalry of these two remained unchanged. Bismarck was cordial as ever to his Russian ally, inviting her to go ahead, but himself holding back. In Bulgaria the deadlock over the election of a prince continued. The Russian

[41] Hofmann, i, pp. 115–116. Hofmann in the *Neue Freie Presse*: "Endlich hat es nur im österreichischen Interesse gelegen, wenn Deutschland auf Grund seiner guten Beziehungen zu Russland, und als gleichzeitiger Verbündeter Österreichs in der Lage blieb, als 'ehrlicher Makler' zwischen Russland und Österreich zu vermitteln."

[42] *Hamburger Nachrichten*, November 7, 1896. "Ein anderer als ein englischer Angriff auf Russland wird den Contrahenden wohl kaum vorgeschwebt haben und namentlich keiner von Seiten Oesterreichs." Penzler, vii, p. 144. See also Reventlow, pp. 20–21. Oncken (pp. 54–55) offers an inversion of this theory: "So paradox es klingt, der Rückversicherungsvertrag ist nicht nur ein Versuch, den Draht nach Petersburg wieder anzuknüpfen: er gehört zugleich in die Reihe der Anläufe, mit indirekten Mitteln auf die Verstärkung des Dreibundes durch England hinzuwirken." While superficially plausible, this statement is contradicted by the fact that the English were first informed of the treaty by the Russians. Eckardstein, ii, p. 154 (Salisbury's statement to Eckardstein).

cause might have been improved by the presentation of a strong candidate; but even its most sincere advocates balked at such a figure as the Prince of Mingrelia, who could never be more than a tool of the Tsar's bureaucracy. Russia seemed to confine her efforts to opposition politics, awaiting some move on the part of the regency which might justify a new appeal to Europe for stronger measures.

Bismarck was content to let the affair take its course. He knew how matters stood, and that the final outcome would be to Russia's disadvantage without his being obliged to show his own hand. The comment of Delbrück in 1896, when the terms of the Reinsurance Treaty were still incompletely known, well describes the effect of that agreement upon the situation at the time when it was signed. "Had the sense of the Russo-German treaty," he writes, "been to hold Germany to neutrality in the event of Austria's taking the aggressive, the Russians would have put through their programme in Bulgaria by force. But the subsequent events show clearly how far such disloyalty to Austria was from Bismarck's thoughts. The justifiable foreboding that Germany's interpretation of the treaty would be that he who provokes to war is the aggressor restrained Russia from direct provocation of Austria despite the treaty's existence. The consequence was that Bulgaria remained independent, and finally chose a new prince without Russia's permission." [43]

## II

The Tsar's "perhaps," in reply to his minister's rosy prophecies of advantages to accrue from the new treaty with Germany, was very soon justified by events. Yet Russia was far from guiltless of responsibility for their course. The diplomatic question most pressingly demanding attention in the early summer of 1887 was one in which Russia had little direct interest, but in which she proceeded to take a very active part. This was the matter of ratification of the Anglo-Turkish convention of May 22 regarding the evacuation of Egypt. Queen Victoria had ratified

[43] *Preussische Jahrbücher*, December, 1896, p. 625.

it without delay; but the Sultan dawdled over it for weeks. The reason for his hesitation lay in the pressure to which he was subjected by France. In spite of the French Chamber's repeated condemnation of a strong policy regarding Egypt, no French government was able to keep its hands off the question. Desirable as it was that England should give a definite undertaking to evacuate Egypt, an even more important consideration seemed to be that the glory of obtaining it should go to France. The Rouvier government, therefore, combated England's separate negotiations with Turkey as earnestly as its predecessors had done, and probably for much the same reasons.[44]

In this dispute Russia took the French side, as she had done in November, 1886, observing in it apparently an opportunity to render an inexpensive favor to France, while at the same time repaying England for her opposition in the Bulgarian question. Her act was probably intended mainly as a strategic move for position. Relations with England were not especially strained at the moment: in fact, the Afghanistan boundary convention was signed on July 10, while the suspense in Constantinople was at its height. But as long as the Bulgarian question remained open, Russia felt it to be as well that the Egyptian question should be kept open too. So Russia cheerfully helped France to damage her own prospects of recovering lost opportunities. A circumstance which the Russian government overlooked was the fact that this supposed setback to England reacted, not only upon France, but upon Germany as well. Support to England in this matter had been in a measure a reward for her adhesion to the Triple Alliance.

[44] Newton, ii, pp. 377-378. The attitude of Freycinet was defined by Lord Lyons in a despatch of November 23, 1886: "Freycinet's aim seems to be to improve his own position in the Chambers and in the country by obtaining our withdrawal from Egypt, and of course the object cannot be attained unless he can make it appear that the withdrawal is his doing. Hence his strong desire that we should negotiate with him and his dislike to our negotiating with Turkey or any other Power." Salisbury, in a letter to Lyons on February 19, 1887 (*ibid.*, p. 389) made the following comment on the Goblet government's policy: "Our negotiations are dragging on with little prospect of success. We are willing to fix a distant date for our leaving, if we receive a treaty power to go back whenever internal or external security are threatened. The tone in which both France and Turkey have received this proposal may be best expressed by the colloquial phrase ' Damn their impudence!' "

The ambassadors of the allies had helped Sir Henry Drummond Wolff to negotiate his convention, and now stood for its ratification.[45] Bismarck could not fail to resent Russia's opposing it, especially since she was doing so in concert with the outlaw, France.[46] It was highly annoying that the precious Egyptian question, which had served Bismarck so long as a hold upon both England and France, should at last have turned upon him and furnished an occasion for a Franco-Russian rapprochement.

His annoyance was emphasized by the existing situation in the West. Although no hostility between France and Germany was just then in evidence, relations had not improved; and the prospect of war stood always not far distant.[47] Of course, under the new terms of the Russo-German alliance, that war would have to come about through French aggression — at least in appearance. Such things could be managed; and, while Bismarck was not at the moment actively picking a quarrel, he still gave the impression of desiring nothing better.[48] The time could not have

[45] Wolff, ii, pp. 313, 317, 319.

[46] *Zur europäischen Politik*, v, p. 200. July 9, Count de Jonghe d'Ardoye (Vienna): "La question de la ratification par la Porte de la Convention Anglo-Turque reste toujours indécise. Le Sultan hésite entre les exigences opposées de la France et de la Russie, d'une part, de l'Angleterre, de l'Allemagne, de l'Autriche et de l'Italie, de l'autre. . . . le fait le plus important, et le plus sérieux de la convention, c'est qu'elle fait sortir la France de son isolement et qu'elle a fait constater avec ostentation l'union politique intime Franco-russe, restée jusqu'à ces derniers temps à l'état d'aspirations réciproques, plus ou moins platoniques . . ."

[47] See *G. F. O.*, vi, pp. 192–203. Herbert Bismarck's memoranda of conversations with Herbette and despatches to Münster. The treason trials at Leipzig were continuing, and kept the German papers filled with reports of the extent of French espionage in Alsace-Lorraine. Early in July a second French citizen, Köchlin, was convicted, but pardoned immediately by the Emperor without any diplomatic intervention.

[48] Newton, ii, pp. 405–406. July 12, Lyons to Salisbury. "Baron Alphonse de Rothschild came to see me this afternoon, and told me that the last accounts he had received from Berlin caused him to feel more than usual alarm as to the feelings of Prince Bismarck and of the Germans in general towards France. They did not indeed imply that Germany was actually contemplating any immediate declaration of war, but they did show that in Germany war with France was regarded as a contingency that could not be long postponed, and of which the postponement was not desirable for German interests. The Germans did not seem to be prepared to incur the opprobrium of Europe by attacking France without having the appearance of a good reason for doing so, but they did seem to be looking out impatiently for a

been more favorable for one, so far as the attitude of England was concerned. The injudicious forwardness of the French, not only at Constantinople, but in Somaliland, the New Hebrides, Newfoundland, and West Africa as well, was driving the British government to distraction. "Our relations with France," wrote Salisbury on July 20, "are not pleasant at present. There are five or six different places where we are at odds. . . . Can you wonder that there is, to my eyes, a silver lining even to the great black cloud of a Franco-German War?"[49] With the British prime minister taking such a tone, the moment could not have been more inopportune in Bismarck's view for Russia to be giving aid and comfort to France.

Yet she persisted in doing so; and, thanks largely to her action, the Egyptian convention failed of acceptance by the Sultan.[50] The victory was to Russia rather than to France, but it was a hollow one for both. France had deliberately ruined her only chance of seeing the English out of Egypt; Russia had needlessly given Bismarck new cause for antagonism. On July 22, the Belgian minister at Berlin wrote: "The Chancellor cannot conceal his chagrin at the setback he has received at Constantinople through the check which the Russo-French accord has just inflicted upon England. This accord, if it persists and becomes firmly established, may have more important results than the Sultan's refusal to ratify the Anglo-Turkish convention."[51] Reprisals upon Russia were already under way in the form of an attack in the financial field.[52]

plausible pretext for a rupture; far from being sorry, they would be very glad if France would furnish them with such a pretext."

[49] Newton, ii, p. 409.

[50] *N. F. P.*, July 20. "Nicht Frankreich hat einen diplomatischen Sieg über England in Konstantinopel davon getragen, sondern Russland. . . . Abdul Hamid hatte die Feder schon in der Hand, um die von der Königin Victoria bereits unterzeichnete Convention ebenfalls zu ratificiren; da tauchte Arm in Arm mit dem französischen Botschafter Montebello Herr v. Nelidow vor ihm auf und vor seinem erschreckten Auge wurde die gleichzeitige Besetzung Syriens durch Frankreich und Armeniens durch Russland an die Wand gemalt. Das war zu viel für seine Widerstandsfähigkeit. . . ."

[51] *Zur europäischen Politik*, v, p. 202.

[52] *N. F. P.*, July 20. "Die diplomatische Niederlage Englands ist um so empfindlicher, als unwidersprochenermassen seitens der drei Centralmächte . . . der

The new Russo-German treaty had thus been in existence hardly more than a month when Bismarck was expressing a fear that his "judgment of the curability of the evil had been false, and that our efforts to win Russia over to recognition and acceptance of our friendly approaches are hopeless."[53] He added that only the hope of their success had hitherto kept him from yielding to the demands of the country for higher duties on Russian grain. This 'demand,' chiefly observable in the press controlled by the agrarian interests, did notably increase thereafter, until eventually it was taken up by the government.

But this was not all. The German public gradually became aware of an increasingly vehement newspaper campaign directed against the standing of Russian bonds as investments. Russia was pictured in these articles as facing ruin and dragging German credit toward the abyss into which she was about to fall. The campaign was carefully kept on the very periphery of official inspiration. Only two or three journals known to be at all in touch with the government took part. The *Kreuzzeitung* and *Politische Nachrichten* led the chorus, with the *Post, Vossische Zeitung*, and *Nationalzeitung* occasionally joining in. The Belgian minister was driven to remark: "The persistency and energy of this hostility have given it a political scope. So far, it is true, the *Norddeutsche Allgemeine Zeitung* has not taken part in the campaign. Its abstention proves only that the Chancellor is reserving the power to disavow the other papers if it suits him to do so. It is quite certain that their articles would not have been published . . . if they did not serve the Chancellor's purposes."[54] A despatch of July 14 to the German ambassador at St. Petersburg, while denying that the press campaign was 'inspired,' admitted that "the whole polemic and the fall of Russian bonds . . . is not unwelcome

---

Abschluss der Convention bei dem Sultan befürwortet wurde. Herr v. Radowitz . . . hat noch am letzten Freitag, knapp vor der Abreise Sir Drummond Wolff's, sich für die Ratification bei dem Grossherrn eingesetzt. . . . Der Kampf, der in Deutschland gegen die russischen Werthe begonnen worden, ist vielleicht der Gegencoup gegen das Zusammenwirken Russlands mit Frankreich in Konstantinopel; jedenfalls besteht ein Zusammenhang zwischen der Niederlage Englands am Goldenen Horn und der Stimmung, welche in Berlin gegen Russland herrscht."

[53] B. M. M., p. 254.   [54] *Zur europäischen Politik*, v, p. 201. July 22, 1887.

to us." [55] The government itself did not quite succeed in keeping its hands clear of the affair. The pronouncements of German courts against the investment of trust funds in Russian bonds lacked little of being official acts.[56]

The German bankers kept aloof from the campaign, which obviously contained a certain element of danger to themselves. Their own holdings of Russian paper were too heavy for them to risk a 'bear' movement, and they apparently did their best to check it. They conferred with the Russian ambassador on the subject, accepted his reassuring statements, and by their own efforts held up the quoted prices of the bonds.[57] Yet privately bonds were being thrown constantly upon the market by suspicious investors at the rate of tens of millions of marks a week.

Many reasons were publicly alleged for this covert offensive against Russia's national credit. Chief among these was the assertion that Germany was only replying to Russia's economic measures earlier in the year, directed against German landholding in Poland and against the importation of German manufactured goods.[58] However, "the acts giving rise to serious causes of complaint against St. Petersburg" — to quote the Belgian minister again — "date back several months, and they have not previously affected the extremely considerate policy which the Chancellor has followed in all questions involving Russian interests. The aggression against Russia's credit is recent and unexpected. There must be other explanations than that of reprisal. . . . The Chancellor wishes to make it felt at Petersburg that

[55] *G. F. O.*, v, p. 332.

[56] Cyon writes (p. 336): "Une circulaire confidentielle du gouvernement allemand ordonna aux fonctionnaires de vendre à bref délai leurs fonds russes; même injonction fut adressée aux tribunaux dépositaires de valeurs russes appartenant à des mineurs." *M. A. Z.*, July 30. Berlin, July 28. "Deutsche Amtsgerichte den Vormündern empfehlen, die in russischen Papieren angelegten Mündelgelder durch andere Papiere zu ersetzen."

[57] *M. A. Z.*, July 22. Berlin, July 21.

[58] See *G. F. O.*, v, p. 333. July 17, memorandum by Rantzau. The much berated ukaz restricting the holding of land by foreigners in the western provinces had hitherto received little notice. Some measure of this sort had been expected since the expulsion of Russian subjects from Germany's eastern provinces in the previous year. Although dated March 26, 1887, the ukaz was not published until May 24, while the negotiations for the Reinsurance Treaty were in progress.

Russian credit is at Germany's mercy . . . at a time when Russia is showing signs of sacrificing her time-honored German relationship to an entente with France." [59] The Rothschild conversion agreement and the defeat of the Anglo-Turkish convention are much more likely causes for this campaign than the Russian tariffs and land laws. The campaign itself stands out as marking a change in Bismarck's policy toward Russia — the substitution of browbeating for conciliation.

The logic of such a course is apparent enough. Russia, like France, should be taught her place and made to feel her dependence upon the good will of Germany by experience of her ill will. She should be made to pay for her assumption of a free hand in February, when Germany had wanted her pledge of neutrality in a French war, for her hard bargaining in the negotiations for the Reinsurance Treaty, and for her recent coquettings with France. It was a course not unattended by dangers; but Bismarck seemed determined to take the risk. The moment was favorable so far as the possibility of a further Franco-Russian rapprochement was concerned; for France, shaken by Boulangist demonstrations of increasing violence, must more and more inspire distrust and aversion in the Tsar. Besides, the browbeating need not be quite so direct and brutal as in the case of France. In large part, it might be even less outright than the newspaper campaign against Russia's credit. Bismarck might keep his hand concealed to the extent of continuing to pose as friend and conciliator while others did his bullying for him. Opportunity for such a course of action was soon offered by the developments in the Bulgarian question.

[59] *Zur europäischen Politik*, v, p. 202. July 22, 1887.

# CHAPTER X

## FERDINAND OF COBURG

### I

THE Tsar's doubts concerning the advantage to Russia of the Reinsurance Treaty had been supplemented by Bismarck's reply to Shuvalov's request for help in the Eastern Question — "La parole est à la Russie." It was a safe statement to make, with a combination of Austria, England, and Italy ready to offer a united opposition to any Russian proposals regarding Bulgaria. Its application was further emphasized when the anti-Russian elements in Bulgaria and in Europe at large turned to the offensive.

This new development in the Bulgarian question came about over the election of a prince. So long as the factor of a personal sovereign remained absent from the Bulgarian combination, it would continue unstable and subject to unexpected alterations. At the same time, the possibility of giving Bulgaria a suitable prince by legal means was as remote as that of legitimizing the existing *de facto* regime. So long as Russia persisted in regarding as absolutely illegal the Stambulov dictatorship and the Sobranie of united Bulgaria on which it rested, she would never recognize a prince elected by such agencies. And the treaty of Berlin required unanimous approval of such an election by the signatory powers before the prince could legally assume his position. So far, however, Russia had failed to shake the stability of the Bulgarian provisional government; and its replacement by a real sovereign authority, through its own act, would render Russia's discomfiture final and complete. The combination against her had only to hold firm, and Bulgaria was lost to her for good.

The Bulgarian regency proceeded to take full advantage of this state of affairs. Through its special agent, Stoilov, it was pushing intrigues at Vienna that went even as far as a project for a declaration of independence. Despite the failure of recent conferences, some hope remained of procuring the return of Alexander of Battenberg. On June 24, a definite offer was made to him by telegraph: he refused it, again urging the election of Ferdinand of Coburg if some one must be had at once.[1]

The suggestion was not unfavorably received; indeed, the candidacy involved had been under consideration for some time. When the Bulgarian deputation started on its canvass of the European courts in the preceding December, the young lieutenant of Hungarian Honveds, Prince Ferdinand of Saxe-Coburg-Kohary, had put himself forward in a manner flattering to Bulgarian aspirations.[2] His candidacy received the approval of the Austrian Emperor.[3] The prince came of a sufficiently exalted and well connected German family, while through his mother, the Princess Clémentine of Orleans, his family ties reached to still greater heights of royalty and wealth. There were influences in his favor which might even move the Russian sovereign to toleration of his enterprise. For the moment, Russia's only comment on his proposed candidacy was the reiterated assertion that the whole course of proceedings involved was illegal.[4] Ferdinand's name had been filed away for future reference.

With Alexander out of consideration, Ferdinand appeared decidedly the best hope of the Bulgarian nationalists and their friends at Vienna. The change was not made willingly; for the new candidate lacked Alexander's great asset, the cordial backing of England. But Alexander would not take the chances which the situation demanded. With the connivance of the Austrians, therefore, the preparation of Ferdinand's candidacy was begun.[5] The

[1] Corti, p. 307.
[2] P. P., 1888, cix, Turkey no. 1, p. 3. December 15, 1886, O'Conor to Iddesleigh. "In a conversation with Sir Frank Lascelles to-day the [Bulgarian] Minister for Foreign Affairs said that the deputation had been received at Vienna by Prince Ferdinand of Coburg, and that his Highness had shown that he was a fervent advocate of Bulgarian independence, and not an unwilling candidate for the vacant Throne."
[3] Ibid., p. 3. December 16, Malet to Iddesleigh.
[4] G. B., 1889, Bulgaria, p. 58. December 18, Nigra to Robilant.
[5] Late in December, 1887, the Kölnische Zeitung published a series of articles entitled, "Bulgarien und die orleanistischen Intrigue," which were later collected and

young prince proved eager as ever, but proceeded to arrange his campaign in his own way. Willing as he was to become the hero of the Bulgarian nationalists, Ferdinand did not wish to incur any dangers that could be avoided. He would vastly prefer conciliating to defying the Tsar, and accordingly began at once to bring his family influences into play at St. Petersburg.[6] This was probably the course which the Austrian government preferred he should follow, in view of his lack of English support. But at the same time Ferdinand engaged in an intrigue with Stambulov of the most questionable character. Its outcome was the declaration of the Bulgarian semi-official journal, *Svobada*, on July 3, that "the government of the Regency will present to the Deputies . . . the candidate to the princely throne, a candidate who has been found, and who is prepared to come to Bulgaria."[7] These words indicated that the prince had given some undertaking in advance to disregard the conditions of the treaty of Berlin if his title to the throne could not be legally established.

In spite of his readiness to follow the lead of his advisers, Ferdinand remained a second choice down to the last moment. A final offer of the crown to Alexander, on July 6, was rejected.[8]

reprinted at Berlin as the "Geheimgeschichte der Kandidatur des Fürsten Ferdinand." Although designed to establish a theory exculpating Germany and Austria, the narrative contains many extraordinary indiscretions which fit amazingly well into the exactly contrary version of the affair. In this particular connection it states that Stambulov "sandte Dr. Stoilow nach Wien, um durch ihn die Verbindung zwischen dem Prinzen und dem Wiener Auswärtigen Amte herzustellen und veranlasste dann, dass auch in Bulgarien für den Prinzen gewählt wurde." Robolsky, *Fürst Bismarck unter drei Kaisern* (Leipzig, 1888), pp. 117-119. See also Friedjung, *Das Zeitalter des Imperialismus*, i (Berlin, 1919), p. 102.

[6] The "Geheimgeschichte" continues: "Während Prinz Ferdinand in Wien durch Vermittelung Stoilows seine Verbindungen mit der Regentschaft unterhielt, war er seinerseits nicht unthätig . . . Er setzte seine Familienbeziehungen in Bewegung, um sich dem russischen Kaiser genehm zu machen und ihn seiner Ergebenheit zu versichern; er trug sich der russischen Politik als Vermittler und Versöhner zwischen Bulgarien und Russland an; er erklärt sich zu allem bereit, was man in dieser Richtung von ihm verlangen werde." Robolsky, p. 119. A Havas despatch from Sofia on December 27, intended as an authoritative contravention of this account, states: "The prince was not acting a part in seeking to conciliate the Russians; on the contrary, he honestly sought this result, and Europe should give him credit for doing so." *M. A. Z.*, December 30.

[7] Charles de Maurel, *Le prince de Bismarck démasqué* (Paris, 1889), p. 12.
[8] Corti, p. 308.

Next day the election of the alternative candidate was put through without a hitch under the skilful direction of Stambulov. In his replies to the telegrams of notification from the regents and the Sobranie, Ferdinand evinced an intention to abide by legal forms, in that he conditioned his assumption of the proffered crown upon the phrase, "as soon as my election shall be approved by the Sublime Porte and recognized by the Powers." [9] However, the important thing was to see what he would do if this condition were not realized; and the prospects for its fulfilment were, in reality, hopeless.

The comments of the Powers upon the event were generally umpromising for Ferdinand's success. All the governments withheld any formal pronouncements until the Sultan should declare his attitude, but at the same time they more or less revealed their private views. Austria's position was the most encouraging, as was to be expected. Kálnoky admitted no objection to the prince personally, and announced clearly that Austria's approval would follow promptly upon a favorable move by the Sultan.[10] The British government assumed an attitude of reserve tending toward disapproval, but obviously subject to the influence of other Powers in its later development.[11] The moment was unfavorable for securing any decisive expression of opinion from Italy, as that country was then engaged in a protracted ministerial crisis, dur-

[9] *P. P.*, 1888, cix, Turkey no. 1, p. 102.

[10] *Ibid.*, p. 104. July 10, Paget to Salisbury. Kálnoky "said he should rejoice if, by the election of a Prince, the present provisional state of things in Bulgaria were to be brought to a satisfactory termination, that there was no political objection to the Prince, who had been freely chosen by the Bulgarians, and if his election should be confirmed by the Porte no difficulties would be made by Austria in assenting to him." *G. B.*, 1887, Bulgaria, p. 121. July 11, Nigra to the ministry. "Dal linguaggio tenuto da Sua Eccelenzia il conte Kàlnoky . . . risulterebbe che se la Turchia conferma quell' elezione, il governo austro-ungarico le darà la sua approvazione per parte sua, senza far dipendere questa approvazione da quella di altre potenze."

[11] *P. P.*, 1888, cix, Turkey no. i, p. 105. July 11, Salisbury to Paget. "In reply to your request for instructions, I have informed your Excellency to-day, by telegraph, that Her Majesty's Government doubt whether the election of Prince Ferdinand of Saxe-Coburg will promote a satisfactory solution of the Bulgarian question, and that they do not wish to assume any responsibility with respect to it. They would wish you therefore to maintain an attitude of reserve, though not one of hostility to the selection."

ing which she could play only a negative rôle.[12] As for Russia, no new definition of her attitude was deemed necessary.[13] Here was the immovable stumblingblock in the way of Ferdinand's recognition.

The policy of Germany promised to be guided by loyalty to her engagements in the Reinsurance Treaty and by the regard which Bismarck always professed for Russia's special position in Bulgaria. Only she made it clear from the beginning that, as the Chancellor had already indicated to Shuvalov, the initiative would be left strictly to Russia. It further appeared from the pronouncements of the foreign office at Berlin that Germany's line of action would not be essentially changed by her specific commitments to Russia regarding Bulgaria. Bismarck's instructions of July 8, from Friedrichsruh, were that Schweinitz should announce at St. Petersburg: "The Chancellor will request His Majesty to model our attitude toward the election exactly after Russia's, and, until Russia has taken her position, to refrain on our part from any declaration."[14] "As in the past," proved indeed the deciding phrase of the Bulgarian clauses in the Reinsurance Treaty. Germany's repudiation of responsibility in the affair was

[12] *G. B.*, 1889, p. 118. This negative attitude was expressed by acting minister Malvano in a despatch of July 13 to Blanc: "Avvenuta l'elezione del principe di Coburgo, non abbiamo creduto di affrettarci ad enunciare la nostra opinione. Ci parve conveniente di astenerci dal pregiudicare, con premature dichiarazioni, una questione, rispetto alla quale una considerazione elementare di reciproco riguardo . . . suggeriva che si lasciasse anzitutto la parola alle potenze aventi nel problema che si agita in Bulgaria un interesse più diretto ed immediato."

[13] *P. P.*, 1888, cix, Turkey no. 1, p. 113. July 13, Morier to Salisbury. "As regards Russia's own attitude, he [Giers] observed that it remained unchanged. She has never admitted the legality of the Sobranje, and could as little admit the legality of its acts. She would continue to wait and see what course matters would take."

[14] *G. F. O.*, v, p. 187. *G. B.*, 1889, p. 122. July 10, Launay to the ministry. "Dés le 8 juillet, je télégraphiais quelle serait l'attitude de l'Allemagne. Elle cède la parole au cabinet de St. Pétersbourg. Quand on la pressentira, elle répondra donc qu'il faut d'abord s'entendre avec la Russie. Le mot d'ordre donné au département des affaires étrangères est celui de répéter que l'Allemagne, désintéressée dans la question bulgare, persévère dans la ligne de conduite qu'elle s'est tracée dès le début de la crise, ainsi que cela résultait nettement déjá des déclarations du chancelier du [?au] Reichstag." The accuracy of this report, showing how closely in touch the Italian ambassador was with the foreign office, is significant for the later development of Italian policy.

emphasized by a speedy denial of the assumption, put forward by the *Coburger Zeitung*, that the Emperor's consent would be required for Ferdinand's acceptance.[15]

There seemed at first every reason to believe that Ferdinand's candidacy would be, as it was later described in Berlin, "stillborn."[16] Yet the prince himself seemed to be of another mind. He received the formal notice of his election confidently, assuring the deputation which brought it that they might "count upon me and upon my devotion to your country — devotion of which I hope to give proof when I judge the moment has arrived."[17] His reply received the approval of the Austrian government.[18] Kálnoky was aware of the prince's intention not to regard too strictly the formalities of the treaty of Berlin.[19] He believed, however, that several factors still stood in the way of any hasty action. There had been as yet no formal decision upon the case by the Porte or by any of the Powers; and Ferdinand had not received his final answer from St. Petersburg.[20]

So long as Russia's attitude remained in doubt, the impatient Bulgarians were kept waiting for the fulfilment of Ferdinand's secret promises.[21] By the 20th of July, the prince and his mother

[15] *Norddeutsche Allgemeine Zeitung*, July 14. "Dagegen ist aus der Reichsverfassung nicht erfindlich noch erklärlich, dass der Deutsche Kaiser mit der Angelegenheit zu thun hätte. Nach dem Berliner Vertrag hat der Kaiser bei der Gutheissung der Wahl eines Fürsten von Bulgarien mitzuwirken, aber nur als Mitunterzeichner."

[16] *Journal des Débats*, Berlin, July 20.

[17] G. B., 1889, p. 129.

[18] *Ibid.*, p. 166. August 19, a summary of recent events by Count Nigra.

[19] P. P., 1888, cix, Turkey no. 1, p. 104. July 10, Paget to Salisbury. Kálnoky admitted that the prince "intimated . . . that should he be strongly pressed by the Bulgarians to come earlier to Sophia, and should his election have been accepted by the Porte and the majority of the Powers, he would not think it necessary to await the assent of all of them."

[20] M. A. Z., July 19. Pest, July 17. "Der Actionsplan des neuen Fürsten ist somit festgestellt: er geht nicht nach Bulgarien (vorläufig), sondern in eigener Person oder vertreten durch Verwandte seines Hauses an den Hof des russischen Zaren, um den Versuch zu machen, den abgerissenen Faden der Unterhandlungen zwischen der bulgarischen Regentschaft und dem Zaren wieder aufzunehmen." Also, July 21 (Vienna, July 19).

[21] *Ibid.*, July 21. Vienna, July 19. "Prinz Ferdinand soll den Herren erwidert haben, sie sollen sich mindestens 14 Tage gedulden, dann werde er seine Entscheidung fällen."

seem to have come to the point of resorting to secret agents and bribery at the Russian court to gain their ends; but they were still hopeful.[22] As time went on, however, this hope declined. Their agent at St. Petersburg shook their illusions by demands for more money. The prospect of winning over the Tsar had to be abandoned. Ferdinand was left to make his choice between a bold decision and the loss of his popularity with the Bulgarians. It was soon rumored at Vienna that the bolder course had been adopted.[23] At last, on the night of August 9, Ferdinand took his departure for Bulgaria, in disregard of all treaties and of the opinion of Russia. Curiously enough, he moved just in time to forestall a revival of the Ernroth regency proposal, which had been suggested anew by Russia on August 6, and which Bismarck had, as before, promised to support.[24]

Ferdinand's action was made to appear a consequence of pressure from the Bulgarian regency, which had been bombarding him for some days with special missions; but doubts were properly expressed as to whether the canny Prince of Coburg would have yielded without some assurances of success in addition to their pleas.[25] Whence could such assurances have been obtained? The family intrigues at St. Petersburg had proved fruitless. The government with which Ferdinand was most closely in touch, that of Vienna, does not seem to have approved this particular move. Kálnoky's action in attempting to dissuade the prince, in conveying to him the protests of the Porte and the foreign ambassadors, and in forcing him and his companions to resign their Austro-Hungarian military titles, does not appear to have been taken in bad faith.[26] It is highly probable that the desire of the Austrian

[22] *Times*, December 21, 1887. Vienna, December 20. Lavino tells the story of the employment of a secret agent who made the most sanguine representations: "It is certain that his reports for a long time induced Prince Ferdinand to believe that the dispositions of the Czar towards him were being altered for the better."

[23] *M. A. Z.*, July 30. Vienna, July 28.

[24] *G. F. O.*, v, pp. 189–190. Telegrams exchanged between the foreign office and Bismarck, who was at Varzin.

[25] *Ibid.*, August 12. Pest, August 11.

[26] *G. B.*, 1889, p. 167. August 19, Nigra's summary of events. "Il principe . . si risolse di partire e partì per la Bulgaria il 9 agosto corrente. Non valsero a trattenerlo nè le osservazioni fattegli in via privata da alcuni miei colleghi e da me, nè

government was to keep Ferdinand at Vienna as prince-elect of Bulgaria, thereby holding the key to the situation in its hands during the further progress of the affair.[27] His departure was in the nature of a distasteful surprise, although the government took no effective steps to prevent it.

An inkling as to what lay behind his action is given by the 'inside story' of Ferdinand's adventure printed by the *Kölnische Zeitung* in December. According to that indiscreet narrative, Ferdinand continued, after his arrival in Bulgaria, to vaunt the influence of his family connections upon the policy of the European courts toward him; but he made one assertion still more significant. "As regards the attitude of Germany, he told his ministers, it should not be taken too seriously, giving them to understand that there was no cause for alarm in this quarter, since he was fully informed of Germany's real policy in the Bulgarian question."[28]

This clew leads directly up to the 'false Bulgarian documents,' which must be introduced here, although full discussion of them is reserved for a later chapter. The first two of these documents, purporting to establish Bismarck's complicity in Ferdinand's ad-

le insistenti dissuasioni della Sublime Porta, portate a di lui notizia dal conte Kàlnoky, nè i consigli di questo ministro, avvalorati della stessa autorità dell'Imperatore Francesco Giuseppe."

[27] Daudet, *Ferdinand I*ᵉʳ (Paris, 1919), p. 100. ' Un rapport diplomatique daté de Vienne,' July 29, 1887. "L'Autriche avait pris en main la candidature de Ferdinand, et maintenant elle lui donne beaucoup de soucis. On se plaint de . . . son manque de docilité aux conseils. . . . Ce que le Cabinet de Vienne aurait voulu obtenir de lui, c'est qu'il continuât à être l'élu du Sobranié et que, fidèle à sa déclaration d'Ebenthal, il attendît à Vienne l'issue des négociations engagées par la Porte . . ., et en attendant, le trône de Bulgarie ne serait ni renversé, ni occupé par un autre. C'est là le conseil donné par le Ballplatz au prince Ferdinand."

[28] Robolsky, *Fürst Bismarck unter drei Kaisern*, p. 121. The passage cannot be used without at least considering the interpretation placed by the *Kölnische Zeitung* upon its facts. This is, that Ferdinand was inspired from the beginning by the aim of creating a European complication and precipitating a great war by which the House of Orleans might hope to profit; and that he, therefore, sought deliberately to sow dissension between Germany and Russia. The hypothesis, which makes Ferdinand himself the creator of a fable of German support, appears too improbable on the face of it to be taken seriously; but it will be dealt with in connection with the exposure of the documents in the case. All that can be said in advance is that Ferdinand's conduct is far more liable to the interpretation of having been really encouraged by Germany.

venture — and later denounced as forgeries — date from the period of Ferdinand's journey to Bulgaria. The first is a letter alleged to have been written by him to the Countess Marie of Flanders, the sister-in-law of Leopold II of Belgium and a rather remote relation of his own. It is dated August 27. The second is an undated and unsigned piece, described in the letter as written by the German ambassador at Vienna. Admission must be made at the start that, while the essential genuineness of the 'Bulgarian documents' may be maintained, they became public through such obscure, indirect, and even suspect channels, that their textual accuracy and complete authenticity is very questionable.

The letter of August 27 seems, in the main, genuine. In it the prince outlines his position, which he describes as in direct antagonism to Russia and doubtful even at Vienna.[29] But he affirms that he has assurances from another quarter. "I would not have accepted definitely," runs the letter, "and especially, I would not have gone so readily to Sofia, if I had not received very satisfactory communications from Berlin as to my situation." The writer admits a proper realization of the risks attending his rôle as a "pawn in Prince Bismarck's game," but believes the chances are in favor of his advancement rather than his sacrifice. He goes on to ask the Countess to intercede for him with her brother-in-law at Brussels and with her own brother, King Charles of Rumania, asking them to use their influence in his favor at St. Petersburg and Vienna. So much rings true enough; but the passage introducing the enclosure as proof of German support is of doubtful veracity, to say the least. The document is referred to as unsigned, but "authentic and written entirely in the hand of the German ambassador at Vienna."[30]

[29] "De Vienne, les sentiments ne sont guère plus encourageants et je sais, de source certaine . . . que l'on y a fait prier S. M. le roi des Belges d'intervenir auprès de moi, pour me déterminer à ne pas accepter le pouvoir bulgare!" From the text published by the *Reichsanzeiger*, December 31, 1887. The statement seems so incredible at first sight, in view of Austria's general attitude, that it has been cited as a proof of the letter's falsity. Cyon, p. 364. Taken in connection with the view advanced above of Austria's policy at the moment (p. 212, note 27), however, it lends additional plausibility to it.

[30] For some reason, this phrase is placed in special quotation marks in the rendi-

The enclosure, the most striking document of the whole series, takes the form of a personal note from the German ambassador, Prince Reuss, to Prince Ferdinand. This would indeed be an unusual sort of diplomatic document; and the chances are strongly against its authenticity. A possible supposition is that a memorandum of a conversation has been worked over by some one into this direct form to add pungency to the disclosure — either by Ferdinand for his own purposes, or by the secret agents who later conveyed the documents to Flourens. In a letter written by Prince Reuss for transmission to St. Petersburg, when these documents were under discussion, he admitted having granted a private interview to Ferdinand, in which he told him he could not count on the approval of Germany any more than on that of the other Great Powers. The writer adds: "I most decisively rejected the suggestion . . . that I should give him any advice." [31] All this coincides rather remarkably with the first part of the document in question.

The note as it stands informs Ferdinand that, since Germany's public action is determined by binding treaties, she can give him no advice, but must leave him to act upon his own responsibility. "However," it continues, "it does not follow that the German government may not, for reasons of general policy, encourage semi-officially, through such legitimate means of action as it possesses in Bulgaria, the enterprise of occupying the Bulgarian throne in the interest of European peace and German policy. It is evident that, if Your Highness goes to Bulgaria with this idea seriously in mind, the moment will come when, however hostile the attitude of Germany may now appear toward Your Highness's enterprise, the sentiments which the government of Berlin entertains in secret toward the success of your monarchical endeavor in Bulgaria will come to light with all the efficacy that attends the open and decided action of a powerful Empire." [32] This communi-

tion of the document in Maurel, *Le prince de Bismarck démasqué* (p. 147), although none such appear in the texts published in the newspapers in December. This fact assumes a strange significance in a book coming from the secret agents who handled the documents.

[31] *G. F. O.*, v, p. 339. November 24, 1887, Reuss to Bismarck.
[32] *Reichsanzeiger*, December 31, 1887.

cation, in the form attributed to it, is almost certainly not authentic; but its substance is not thereby completely invalidated. Ferdinand's confidence in the strength of his position, and the policy of Germany as it later developed, indicate that the wily prince was relying upon some such assurances as these when he set forth upon his adventure.

## II

In allowing Ferdinand to hope for support from Germany, Bismarck had, of course, no idea of taking any direct action to fulfil his promises, any more than he had of actively supporting Russia's opposition to the new Prince of Bulgaria. Ferdinand had moved; Bismarck stood aside, politely repeating, "La parole est à la Russie." But if Russia opened her mouth to pronounce that word, a trusty combination of three Great Powers stood ready to seize her by the throat before Germany could hear it. Bismarck's position seemed safe. Russia must finally come to his feet, realizing that her attempts to disturb the order of things he stood for was hopeless.

For a time, it is true, he had had occasion to doubt the reliability of one element in his combination, Italy; but these doubts had been cleared up before Ferdinand started on his trip to Sofia. The political convulsions which had seized Italy even before the Triple Alliance was signed were practically over by the end of July. The prospect of a radical government had at first filled Bismarck with horror.[33] The stop-gap regime of Depretis had inspired no confidence in him. When assured that it would live up to Italy's treaties, he had remarked pettishly: "Treaties are scraps of paper: everything depends upon the manner of their execution. While in themselves excellent weapons, in unskilful hands they may work more harm than good."[34] Then Depretis died, on July 29, bringing the arch-Radical, Crispi, to the fore. Bismarck knew Crispi of old, and, whatever aversion he may have

[33] Chiala, p. 497. Count Herbert Bismarck told Launay in March that "les bras tombaient à son père, en voyant qu'un remaniement du cabinet se faisait au profit de la gauche avancée."
[34] Ibid., p. 498.

felt for the hoary conspirator's revolutionary past, he had no cause to complain of his views on foreign politics, which were more nationalistic and aggressive than those of any reactionary monarchist. Indeed, Crispi more than met Bismarck's expectations of Italy by adopting an attitude of opposition to Russia even more vigorous than that maintained by Austria.[35]

Under Crispi's energetic direction Italian policy emerged from its indecision and quickly assumed sharp outline. On August 8, the eve of Ferdinand's bold leap, Crispi, then minister *ad interim*, issued a circular despatch defining the new course. Ferdinand, he wrote, "by the very fact of his election, represents in our eyes, unless the contrary be proved, the expression of the will of the Bulgarian people," and, therefore, a "principle of solution," if properly supported by the Powers. "So we must desire," he continues, "that the Powers now displaying a community of aims and pacific intentions should contribute, as we are disposed to do, a willing moral support."[36] This ardor in the cause was as agreeable to Italy's allies as it was unexpected, although they could only respond to it with caution.[37]

Germany, in fact, was ostensibly taking a directly opposite course, calculated to produce a favorable impression upon Russia. While all the Powers were obliged to withhold diplomatic recognition from Ferdinand, the German government deemed it necessary to go even further, instructing its consul general at Sofia to regard him "in the light of an entirely private person, and . . . not even . . . as a member of a reigning German dynasty."[38] The very exaggeration of brutality indicates that there was something to cover up. However, no exception was taken privately to the more lenient attitude assumed by Germany's allies. Count Berchem, in charge at the foreign office, assured the Italian ambassador, on the same day as the despatch of Crispi's circular, "that his government understands very well, so far as it is con-

---

[35] See Friedjung, *Biographisches Jahrbuch*, iii, p. 366 (*Aufsätze*, p. 339).

[36] *G. B.*, 1889, p. 137.

[37] See *La politica estera italiana* (Bitonto, 1916), p. 398.

[38] *P. P.*, 1888, cix, Turkey no. 1, p. 122. August 9, 1887, Scott (Berlin) to Salisbury.

cerned, that our position is different from its own and that we may properly seek, on the basis of Your Excellency's project of instructions, to place ourselves in line with Austria-Hungary and, especially, with England, which countries have interests in the Balkans not shared by Germany." [39]

At this very time, Bismarck was conducting a strange and delicate negotiation with England arising out of certain cryptic questions put to the German ambassador by Salisbury on August 2.[40] As nearly as could be made out, the prime minister was driving at the possibility of an Anglo-Russian understanding. Bismarck's reply was that he would have no objection to such an understanding, provided Austria were included. He also suggested taking in Italy and making the acceptance of Ernroth as Bulgarian regent the basis of the accord with Russia.[41] In marginal notes on subsequent despatches, he admitted having gone into all this discussion only because he feared Salisbury's suggestion of an Anglo-Russian understanding might be used by him as a means of pressure on Germany if she showed herself too much disturbed by it. He also wrote: "we desire *primo loco* the maintenance of the Anglo-Austro-Italian understanding." [42] The relation between all these statements and the course of policy struck out by Crispi is important for the further development of events. That Ferdinand's adventurous move cut into the midst of this negotiation is perhaps also not without significance.

In regard to that event, the two other associates in Bismarck's combination took up positions between those of Italy and Germany. England was rather the more cautious, reserving definite pronouncements until the Continental Powers should be heard from, but declining to go so far in accord with Russia as to admit the original invalidity of Ferdinand's election.[43] Kálnoky, although displeased that Ferdinand had taken matters into his own hands, could not now desert him, and could not do less than the

---

[39] *G. B.*, 1889, p. 138. August 8, Launay to Crispi.
[40] *G. F. O.*, iv, pp. 335–337. August 3, Hatzfeldt to Bismarck.
[41] *Ibid.*, iv, pp. 338–342. August 8, Bismarck to Hatzfeldt.   [42] *Ibid.*, iv, p. 343.
[43] *P. P.*, 1888, cix, Turkey no. 1, p. 123. August 12, Salisbury to Morier.

English partner in coming to his defence.[44] But Crispi desired more than this, and continued to press for the formation of a quadruple accord designed frankly to support Ferdinand.[45] To such an accord Germany would certainly never become a party; yet Bismarck recognized the desirability of obtaining from England a more definite adhesion to his plans than that contained in the somewhat vague entente of February. He did not discourage Crispi's efforts, but sought to turn them in the direction of a triple, rather than a quadruple, combination.

While privately encouraging the opposition to Russia, the German government was louder than ever in its professions of Platonic support. A Russian circular note of protest against Ferdinand's action met a hearty response at Berlin. Shuvalov was assured "that the Imperial government shares the views expressed in this circular and that the German representatives at all capitals would receive orders to speak accordingly, especially as concerns the invalidity of the Prince of Coburg's election, the illegality of his assumption of the Bulgarian throne, and the manifest infraction of the Treaty of Berlin." Any expectation of concrete results from these assurances, however, was damped by the familiar caution that "the Cabinet of Berlin limits itself to pronouncing a judgment in general terms, since the Russian government itself puts forward no concrete and practical proposition for remedying the state of affairs." The Italian ambassador, in reporting this reply to his government, did not hesitate to add, possibly under inspiration: "It seems to me that, under these circumstances, we ought to try to reach an understanding with Austria, and especially with England, for a common course of action. This attitude, even if it did not accord in all respects with that of Germany, would none the less be perfectly understood here."[46] Crispi could have had no doubt that Germany's official

[44] P. P., 1888, cix, Turkey no. 1, p. 128. August 12, Paget to Salisbury. Kálnoky's reply to Russia's protest was much the same as Salisbury's.

[45] G. B., 1889, p. 145. August 13, Crispi to Launay and Corti. "Io ritengo che sia nell'interesse delle tre potenze alleate e dell'Inghilterra di risolvere definitivamente e al più presto questa questione bulgara che costituisce una minaccia permanente per la pace europea."

[46] Ibid., pp. 160–161. August 14, Launay to Crispi.

utterances in this case meant nothing; for, on August 16, he advised the king: "We believe we ought to give him [Ferdinand] all the help possible, without, of course, in any way conflicting with the agreement of principles that exists between Austria, England, and ourselves, especially as this agreement is looked upon with favor by Germany." [47]

This advice was offered on the very day that the bombardment directed against the rash prince by the German semiofficial newspapers culminated in a heavy broadside from the *Norddeutsche Allgemeine Zeitung*, condemning all his recent actions as violations of the treaty of Berlin in language which the Russians could hardly improve upon. The Russians for the most part, in fact, applauded this outburst; but it received less attention in quarters where Bismarck was known more intimately.[48] An utterance of the *Kölnische Zeitung* next day put German official opinion somewhat more in doubt by stating: "Germany has no reason to be enthusiastic over the adventure of Coburg. But from the humane standpoint it is to be desired that the sorely tried principality may at last find rest from its Russian liberator, yet tormentor, and be left to itself. If no one help the country, it must in despair seek to help itself." Again, on the 18th, the *Norddeutsche Allgemeine Zeitung* thundered to inspire Russian confidence, albeit with a slight backfire of irony. "The Great Powers," it asserted, "will not hesitate to accept Russia's view of the question fully and unconditionally. This is especially indicated by England's attitude. . . . The final settlement of the question of a Bulgarian Prince does not, therefore, appear to afford real grounds for disquiet."

The Great Powers most closely associated with Germany paid so little heed to these thunderings that they went quietly ahead with their plans for support of Ferdinand under the energetic

[47] Crispi, p. 148 (*Memoirs*, ii, p. 180).

[48] *Journal des Débats*. Vienna, August 17. "On n'attache pas ici une grande importance à l'article fulminant de la *Gazette de l'Allemagne du Nord* au sujet du prince Ferdinand. L'Allemagne se considérant comme la gardienne du traité de Berlin proteste contre sa violation, et les derniers entretiens du comte Schouvaloff avec M. de Bismarck ont eu pour résultat un langage plus vif à l'égard du prince; mais les conséquences ne vont pas au delà."

impulsion of Crispi.[49] Bismarck had let them see how little sincerity lay behind his bluster.[50]

Under such circumstances any projects of Russia for dealing with the situation had scant prospect of success. The reception accorded her protests, and those of the Porte as well, revealed a hostile attitude on the part of three Great Powers to anything she might propose. It has been asserted that only this prompt arraying of the forces of opposition deterred Russia from a resort to arms against the Stambulov government.[51] The existence of a combination of powers in restraint of her policies undoubtedly discouraged Russia; but, with the peaceable Giers now firmly in control, it is little likely that measures of violence were even seriously considered.[52] Both the English and Italian ambassa-

---

[49] Crispi, pp. 149-150. *G. B.*, 1889, p. 155. (The *Green Book* version appears to have been cut.) August 18, Crispi to Blanc. "Riguardo al modo di considerare questa elezione . . . io l'autorizzo a porsi d'accordo coi suoi colleghi d'Austria-Ungheria ed Inghilterra per esprimere l'opinione che nella avvenuta elezione noi dobbiamo ravvisare, fino a prova contraria ed equivalente, una valida testimonianza della volontà del popolo bulgaro."

[50] *La politica estera italiana*, pp. 379-380. "Ora Bismarck aveva tutto l'interesse di mantenere in questa illusione la Russia per conservarla lontana dalla Francia, e per questo egli aveva dovuto domandare ai Governi di Vienna e di Roma libera azione nella forma, pur dichiarandosi solidale con essi nella loro resistenza alla Russia." This is doubtless an exaggerated statement of the case. Nevertheless, it is somewhat remarkable that the German foreign office publication contains no documents pertaining to relations with Italy at this time.

[51] Crispi, p. 150. August 24, circular despatch. "In presenza dell'eventualità ravvisata possibile dell'occupazione russa di Varna e di Erzerum, qualora la Turchia non intervenisse attivamente in Bulgaria, il gabinetto italiano si dichiara contraria ad ogni violenza e ad ogni violazione del trattato di Berlino." Friedjung, *Imperialismus*, i, p. 102. "Zar Alexander verzehrte sich in Ingrimm und erwog mit seinen Ratgebern, ob er in Bulgarien nicht mit den Waffen durchgreifen sollte. Indessen schreckte er vor diesem Entschlüsse zurück. . . . Er sah sich einer überlegenen Koalition gegenüber."

[52] Baddeley, pp. 316-317. "*5th September.* Hardinge and Dumba between them told me what follows: De Giers, coming straight from the Emperor declares that his Imperial Majesty won't hear of Russian interference in Bulgaria. He has only one policy — letting them stew in their own juice, knowing very well that it would be the ruin of Russia if she incurred hostilities with the probable coalition against her. De Giers was never so strong as at present; he has it all his own way." Shuvalov, in a conversation with Berchem, on August 18, hinted at the possibility of armed intervention, but very vaguely and only in the event of Turkey's failing to support the Ernroth proposal.

dors at St. Petersburg, writes Sir Robert Morier, "were ' put out ' at the persistent way in which we heard on all sides that it was beyond doubt that Giers had threatened an occupation of Varna or Erzeroum when we *knew* this was not true." [53]

The fact seems to be that the Russians had never frankly faced the question as to what means of coercion would be employed against the Bulgarians if they resisted the imposition of General Ernroth upon them as regent. Regarding the men in control of Bulgaria at the time as mere adventurers with no real hold on the country, the Russian government probably felt that only a push from legal authority was needed to send them toppling. It looked no further than united action by the Powers and the Porte. This lack of any effective provision for enforcement was what had rendered Bismarck's support of the scheme so lighthearted. Moreover, almost certain as it was of breaking down in the end, its only possible chance of success lay in the absolutely firm unity of action on which the Russians relied. In the way of getting the plan accepted by the other Powers stood the anti-Russian accord of February which Bismarck had sponsored. The only possibility of bending the resolution of that combination depended, in turn, upon decisive action by Bismarck at the start. Such action the Chancellor consistently declined to take. His final word on the subject, when Shuvalov again expressed hope of his support for the proposal, on August 18, was still: "after Russia has *made* it." [54] This attitude left the other Powers free to reject the proposal, as they were certain to do. On the very day Shuvalov was pressing it at Berlin, Hatzfeldt telegraphed from London that Salisbury had decided to drop his suggestion of an accord with Russia and to recur to his previous policy.[55] On the same day, also, the Austrian ambassador announced that Kálnoky was no more favorably disposed toward the Ernroth proposal itself than toward the idea of putting it into force by the use of Russian troops.[56] Count Berchem, who received this declaration, had no

[53] Edwards, p. 246. November, 1887, Morier to White. See also *G. B.*, 1889, p. 167. August 19, Nigra's summary of events.
[54] *G. F. O.*, v, p. 192. Marginal note on Count Berchem's report.
[55] *Ibid.*, iv, pp. 344–345.
[56] *Ibid.*, v, pp. 192–193. August 19, report by Berchem.

better argument to urge against it than the dubious one of the military advantage for Austria of a Russian advance in the Balkans.

The Russians were still encouraged by the German government, however, to go forward with the proposal, and the Turks were urged to take it up.[57] But the Turkish government showed its usual aversion to any positive steps. Although named first in the treaty of Berlin among the Powers whose sanctions were necessary to a Bulgarian election, Turkey had declined to pronounce for or against Ferdinand, but instead had referred to the Powers for their opinions. The nature of these was not calculated to clear up Turkey's indecision. Kálnoky's reply, in particular, only served further to confuse the situation. He advised the Turks "to abstain above all things from the employment of coercive measures, which in the present frame of mind of the Bulgarians might very possibly drive them to some desperate measure, such as the proclamation of their independence, accompanied by the promotion of risings in Macedonia . . .; and to abstain also from entering into any arrangements with any one of the European Powers separately, but to communicate freely with all."[58] Crispi was even striving to win Turkey over to the anti-Russian coalition.[59] A state of affairs ensued in which neither the Porte nor the Powers moved, each side conditioning its action upon the initiative of the other.

Meanwhile, the opposition to Russia was growing more and more compact.[60] That the Ernroth mission would never be approved was a foregone conclusion. "Following the example of

[57] *G. F. O.*, v, p. 190. August 15, memorandum by Berchem.

[58] *P. P.*, 1888, cix, Turkey no. 1, pp. 135-136. August 20, Paget to Salisbury.

[59] *G. B.*, 1889, p. 164. August 19, Crispi to Blanc. Crispi tells of taking the matter up with the Turkish Ambassador. "Ho soggiunto che, se si potesse formare tra il gruppo delle potenze centrali un accordo per la soluzione di tale questione, io non dubitavo punto che l'adesione della Turchia sarebbe già acquista per tale accordo."

[60] *P. P.*, 1888, cix, Turkey no. 1, p. 141. August 23, Paget to Salisbury. "Count Kálnoky expressed his satisfaction at seeing how entirely your Lordship's views coincided with his own, and his gratification at the cordial manner in which the Ambassadors of the three Powers, Austria, England, and Italy, were acting together for the attainment of a peaceful solution of the present crisis."

Austria-Hungary," wrote Crispi on August 20, "we must refuse to accept a regency entrusted to a Russian general. This arrangement would be simply prolonging and intensifying an endless state of provisional expedients. We entertain no partialities, but to us Prince Ferdinand represents the beginning of an adjustment. On this point London and Vienna entirely agree with us." [61] The old fire-eater even wished to proceed at once to the negotiation of military conventions providing for armed resistance to Russian aggression, but was met by a *non possumus* from Salisbury.[62]

Bismarck was careful to keep Germany from getting involved directly in the affair. On August 23, he drafted for Reuss at Vienna a despatch framed in the same sort of language as he had used during the previous autumn, even to reasserting that the line of demarcation was the basis of Germany's policy toward the Austro-Russian conflict of interests.[63] This despatch, which can hardly have been meant to do more than impose caution upon Kálnoky, rings very hollow after the transactions of February.

A better insight into Germany's real policy is given by Herbert Bismarck's account of a conversation with Lord Salisbury on the very day that Bismarck was writing this despatch. When Salisbury remarked that his recent idea of a reconciliation with Russia had been inspired by the fear that, in the event of an Austro-Russian war, Germany's assistance to her ally would be rendered of no account by a probable French attack, Count Bismarck assured him that Germany did not lack forces for a war on two fronts. Herbert also applied himself to confirming the English

[61] Crispi, p. 150 (*Memoirs*, ii, p. 183). August 20, Crispi to Nigra. The English reply is given in the blue book just cited, "Turkey no. 1, 1888," p. 137. August 25, Salisbury to Morier. "I agreed with M. de Staal that the appointment of a single Regent for Bulgaria and Eastern Roumelia would be the best temporary arrangement, but I said that Her Majesty's Government were not likely to be able to agree to the selection of either a Russian or a Turk for that post."

[62] Crispi, p. 153 (*Memoirs*, ii, pp. 186–187). August 29, Crispi to Catalani: August 31, Catalani to Crispi. "Lord Salisbury . . . mi ha detto che presentandosene l'occasione sarebbe fiero della cooperazione dell' esercito italiano e che poteva giungere il momento in cui essa fosse necessaria. Ma S. S. ha soggiunto che sino a quando il pericolo di guerra non era imminente, la costituzione . . . lo ponevano nella impossibilità di stipulare un atto di tal genere."

[63] G. F. O., v, p. 194.

minister's decision against the idea by casting aspersions upon Russia's good faith and by calling attention to Italy as a factor in the anti-Russian league. The turning point of the interview was Herbert's suggestion "that an agreement of limited scope might be made between the triple group and the Sultan, somewhat like the *pactum de contrahendo* which exists between Italy and Spain with Austria and ourselves in the background. Italy could be pushed to the front, thereby flattering her self-esteem through such a recognition of her importance." [64] This suggestion, indeed, appears to be the key to the whole development of the Bulgarian problem.

Herbert Bismarck's further hints at the possibility of calling a congress on the Bulgarian question in London, on the basis of a German mediation between England and Russia, indicate that the Chancellor was seriously considering at this time a repetition of the manoeuvres connected with the congress of Berlin. The development of this idea is probably related to the project then current of a visit of the Tsar Alexander to the German capital — an event from which important consequences might well be expected to ensue. Expectations of this visit, however, were suddenly brought to disappointment.

[64] *G. F. O.*, iv, p. 347. August 24, report by Herbert Bismarck.

# CHAPTER XI

## BISMARCK AND ALEXANDER III

### I

AT the beginning of September, 1887, an interview between the Tsar and the German Emperor was generally regarded as an event certain to take place in the near future. Alexander III was enjoying at the time a respite from Nihilist perils at the castle of Fredensborg in Denmark. William I was preparing to attend the army manoeuvres in East Prussia. Arrangements were being made to accommodate both courts at Stettin. The initiative in arranging this meeting seems certainly to have come from Berlin in the form of hints transmitted through Shuvalov.[1] For the rest, it was a sufficiently natural visit to expect, in view of the advanced age of the German Emperor, which made it possible that any interview might be the last. Then, just as all seemed comfortably arranged, the situation was suddenly obscured; and presently the German newspapers were energetically denying that there had ever been any thought of such a meeting.

This abrupt collapse of what seemed a settled project was the result of a revelation to the Tsar of Germany's real policy in the Bulgarian question. That policy had long been characterized as treacherous by the Panslavist press and had even become suspect in official eyes. Now documentary proof of Bismarck's duplicity was placed in the hands of the Tsar through some unknown subterranean agencies. The first link in the chain of transmission

[1] *N. F. P.*, September 9, 1887. "Die Behauptung dass dieselbe [die Kaiser-Zusammenkunft] von Berlin aus angeregt, von Petersburg abgelehnt worden sei, taucht heute an verschiedenen Orten auf." Maurel (pp. 160–163) and the *Nouvelle Revue* (September 1, 1888) maintain that, in addition to the hints conveyed to Shuvalov by Count Herbert Bismarck, there was a direct letter of invitation from the Emperor to the Tsar. The affirmation is based mainly upon a statement in an alleged secret report of Bismarck to Frederick III, printed in the *Nouvelle Revue* for August 1, 1888. The invitation was denied by the *Journal de St. Pétersbourg* on September 16.

of these papers reached from Brussels to Paris. At the Belgian capital it rested upon George Nieter, an official connected with the foreign office. At the Paris end stood Foucault de Mondion, a spy in the French service, who also had good connections in Belgian governmental circles, due to a former residence as tutor in the family of the minister of foreign affairs.[2]

It was in the Belgian foreign office that Nieter is said to have picked up the trail of Ferdinand's correspondence with the Countess of Flanders. According to the conspirators' own version in the book *Le prince de Bismarck démasqué*, a report came in from

[2] Wilhelm Müller, *Fürst Bismarck* (Stuttgart, 1898), p. 257. "Ueber die Person der Fälscher und diejenigen Personen, welche die gefälschten Schreiben als echte dem Zaren in Kopenhagen vorgelegt haben, ist erst nach einigen Jahren so viel in die Oeffentlichkeit gedrungen, dass wir wissen, der belgische Sektionschef Nieter habe in Verbindung mit dem französischen Spion Mondion jene Briefe ve·fertigt." These personalities were revealed in the course of a campaign waged against the Belgian government by the *Nouvelle Revue* in the years 1888 and 1889. The theft of certain despatches of admitted authenticity from the ministry of the interior, published in the *Revue* for July 15, 1889, was traced to Nieter; while Mondion was brought into prominence at the same time by the Boulanger trial in Paris. Both belonged to the 'secret document ring' then dominating the editorial policy of Madame Adam and the *Nouvelle Revue*. They enter into the compound personality of 'Charles de Maurel,' the name signed to *Le prince de Bismarck démasqué* and a couple of articles in the *Revue*. Their connection with the affair of the Bulgarian documents is indisputable. The following passages concerning their exposure may be quoted. *N. F. P.*, November 14, 1889 (Brussels, November 13). "Der Inspector der schönen Künste, Georg Nieter, der früher dem clericalen Cabinet als Vertrauensperson grosse Dienste geleistet hatte und vielfach in Anspruch genommen wurde, ist durch Ministerial-Rescript für sechs Monate mit Einstellung des Gehalts suspendirt worden. Man bringt diese Massregel mit der geheimnissvolle Geschichte der aus dem Ministerial-Archiv verschwundenen officiellen Actenstücke in Verbindung, die in der Nouvelle Revue von Madame Adam und Mondion in bekannter Weise ausgenützt wurden." *Annales parlementaires de Belgique*, Chambre des représentants, session of 1889–90, p. 535. The Prince de Chimay, minister of foreign affairs, stated, regarding Nieter's connection with his department: "M. Nieter, très initié aux choses de la presse, avait pour mission de dépouiller, de traduire les journaux et de m'indiquer les articles intéressants pour mes collègues et pour moi; il ne comptait pas parmi le personnel de l'administration et ne recevait pas de traitement." The *Gaulois* of Paris published, on August 10, an interview with Foucault de Mondion, in which he declared: "It was I who procured the incontrovertible proofs of Germany's duplicity toward Russia, which others contrived to convey to the Tsar." Further information concerning his past is given by *M. A. Z.*, September 3, 1889 (Brussels, September 1): "Mondion wohnte einige Zeit in Mons und wurde Hauslehrer bei den Kindern des Fürsten von Chimay, des gegenwärtigen Ministers des Aeussern."

the Belgian consul general at Sofia, in which he wrote of the confidence existing in Bulgarian official circles of a coming change in the attitude of Germany, and in which he stated that he was transmitting a letter from the prince to the Countess of Flanders, intrusted to him through secret channels.[3] By necessarily unscrupulous means, according to the conspirators' story, a copy was obtained of the letter, together with an enclosure.[4] These appear throughout the later transactions in the form of doubtless very corrupt and 'doctored' versions in French, passing as translations from German originals. Some wonder was still later expressed as to why translations should have been thought necessary in conveying the documents to the Tsar. The simple explanation is that he was not their first destination.

Obtained through Nieter, the documents appear to have been handled at Paris by de Mondion, who laid them before Flourens for whatever use he could make of them.[5] It was Flourens who undertook the bold course of transmitting them to the Tsar.[6]

[3] Maurel, pp. 142–143. The report is quoted in full. It is given without date, but purports to have been written shortly before Belgium broke relations with the provisional government as the result of a dispute over certain contracts for railway material. The authenticity of the despatch was specifically denied by the *Moniteur Belge* on August 3, 1889, with the remark that it deals with events subsequent to the consul's departure from Sofia. An examination of the text reveals nothing that might not have been written on or about August 15; while the breach of relations occurred on the 17th. In a despatch of January 30, 1890, Schweinitz related: "Herr von Giers erwiderte, er sei schon lange der festen Überzeugung gewesen, dass Mondion die Fälschung begangen habe, und zwar unter Mitwirkung des damaligen Consuls in Sofia namens Cartuyvels." G. F. O., v, pp. 349–350.

[4] Maurel, pp. 144–145.

[5] Cyon, pp. 360–363. Daudet, *Alliance*, p. 218. "C'est dans ces circonstances qu'une communication assez bizarre est faite à M. Flourens par un personnage dépourvue de tout caractère officiel, mais qu'on sait initié aux secrets des chancelleries diplomatiques et très habile à les pénétrer. Chargé par le général Boulanger de diverses missions secrètes en Allemagne et en Belgique, il apporte à M. Flourens, en lui proposant de les vendre, divers documents manuscrits, qu'il dit être des originaux relatifs aux affaires bulgares."

[6] Cyon, p. 361. Daudet, *Alliance*, pp. 224–225. "En les examinant, il a conçu tout un plan. Il les fera passer sous les yeux du Tsar. Il est convaincu que tels qu'ils sont, et réunis à d'autres qu'il possède déjà, ils auront pour effet de briser le lien qui attache encore la Russie à l'Allemagne." No more is heard of the other documents which Flourens is said to have added to the dossier: they may have been French

The link connecting Paris and Copenhagen is somewhat more difficult to reconstruct, but is of less importance as affecting the genuineness of the papers. It seems to have included, at the Paris end, the semiofficial agent of the Russian embassy, Julius Hansen, through whom Flourens transacted much business by preference.[7] Whether or not the ambassador himself was involved is uncertain.[8] Both the Princess Waldemar, wife of the Tsar's brother-in-law, and Prince Obolenski, of the imperial suite, have been spoken of as the final agencies of transmission: perhaps both were implicated.[9] At any rate, the papers were placed before the Tsar

consular reports from Bulgaria, which France was more or less in the habit of communicating to Russia since the latter's withdrawal of her agents from the country. Hansen, *Mohrenheim*, p. 27.

[7] Hansen, in his books, says nothing of his part in this affair. In his *Mohrenheim* (p. 71) he makes the extremely doubtful statement that Bismarck accused him and the ambassador of having forged the papers, and that the Tsar refuted the accusation. Eckardstein writes (i, p. 137): "Dass aber Jules Hansen in diese Affäre verwickelt war, ist unzweifelhaft sicher. Dahingestellt möge bleiben, ob die Briefe echt oder ob sie gefälscht waren, fest steht jedenfalls, dass Jules Hansen sie mit Hilfe der Prinzessin Waldemar von Dänemark in die Hände Alexanders III. gespielt hat. Letzteres bestätigte mir auch Blowitz auf bestimmteste." Münster confirmed the supposition further; while Hansen, when complimented on his achievement, flushed, stammered, and hurried away. Crispi's information from Vienna, under date of December 18, 1887 (p. 215) also implicates Hansen. Giers admitted to Schweinitz, on December 23, that the papers had been forwarded by "ein sehr geschickter Agent, welchen ich nicht opfern kann; er ist getauscht worden." *G. F. O.*, v, p. 348.

[8] *M. A. Z.*, December 7, 1887. Berlin, December 5. "Allgemein wird geglaubt, dass Baron Mohrenheim . . . in die angeblichen orleanistischen Ränke verwickelt ist. . . . Der bekannte dänische Zeitungsschreiber Julius Hansen . . . soll ebenfalls thätigen Antheil an der Sache genommen haben."

[9] Eckardstein refers to the former; Daudet, to the latter (*Alliance*, p. 225). Baddeley (p. 408) gives the following statements from a conversation with Peter Shuvalov: " ' The forged documents came from two sides. De Giers received them in St. Petersburg, but before he had time to send them to the Emperor, then at Copenhagen, he received news of them from him, thence.' *Baron von Bär*: ' They are said to have come from Princess Waldemar at a picnic when the Tsar and she stayed behind the rest for some time.' *Schouvaloff*: ' It may be so; what is certain is that they came from France, and not from the Orleanists, as stated in the German press, but from the French Government itself.' " Baddeley adds the note: "It is supposed that M. Flourens sent them to Princess Waldemar through the wife of the Russian minister at Copenhagen, a daughter of Mr. Berdan — the American whose rifle had been adopted for the Russian army — and sister to Mrs. Marion Crawford." See also *G. F. O.*, v, pp. 340, 346, for Giers's admission that copies of the papers had also been sent to him.

about the 1st of September, just as he was preparing for the trip to Stettin. The trip was at once called off.[10]

The failure of the project for an interview did not come as a complete surprise to the German government. Bismarck seems to have had an inkling of what was going on at Copenhagen and to have prepared the way for a retreat. On September 2, while the meeting was still publicly regarded as a foreordained event, the *Kölnische Zeitung* published an article to the effect that it would probably be without influence upon the situation in any case, since confidence on both sides had been too far destroyed for restoration. The caution was added that, "Under these circumstances, German statecraft must take care not to allow the rivalry with France for Russia's favor to develop into a crawling contest (*Wettkriechen*). It must, above all, in its endeavors to conciliate Russia, not lose sight of the interests of Austria." Furthermore, the campaign against Russian credit, which had lately fallen off in intensity, received at the same moment a new impetus from the semiofficial confirmation of a rumor that the government was planning a tax on foreign securities. On the morrow the expected interview was being disposed of by reports that the Emperor would not attend the manoeuvres after all, because of a fall he had recently sustained — a slight accident, pronounced not at all serious at the moment, and which did not finally prevent his journey to East Prussia. To such expedients had the government in its chagrin been reduced.

A curious newspaper discussion of Germany's policy followed. Those two most trusty of inspired organs, the *Kölnische Zeitung* and the *Norddeutsche Allgemeine Zeitung*, tossed arguments endlessly back and forth in an apparent polemic as to the proper course for the government now to follow. In reality, these articles served to bring home to Russia how little she had to expect from the German alliance and how far the responsibility for its fruitlessness rested upon herself. On September 5, *Norddeutsche* replied to *Kölnische's* article of the 2d by stating that "German policy is

[10] Hohenlohe, ii, p. 436 (Amer., ii, p. 399). Berlin, May 25, a conversation with the Crown Prince. "Alles sei bereit gewesen, die Jacht im Hafen geheizt, als der Kaiser die Aktenstücke auf seinem Schreibtisch gefunden habe. Das habe ihn geärgert und deshalb sei die Entrevue in Stettin unterblieben."

engaged in no rivalry with France for Russia's favor, but is keeping quite independently to the road marked out for it by the interests of the German Empire and by the existing treaties." The same article prepared the ground for a contention by which German semiofficial opinion later set great store — that Ferdinand's whole enterprise was inspired by the desire to stir up troubled waters in which the Orleanist princes might fish for a French crown.[11] When *Kölnische* ventured to lament the collapse of the projected Stettin interview as a blow to all hopes for a better understanding with Russia, *Norddeutsche* declaimed against creating the impression that Germany cared anything about such an understanding.[12] Yet below the surface at Berlin persisted the conviction that Germany's Chancellor cared a great deal, and that he would strive diligently to clear away this new cloud of suspicion that had arisen between him and Russia.[13]

Nevertheless, Bismarck persisted in his refusal to take the initiative in behalf of the Ernroth proposal. When the Turkish government besought his good offices in its favor, his reply was that he would recommend it "as soon as it is made, and on condition that it has simultaneously the authentic and open support of Russia" — in order to make its real origin evident from the first.[14] This declaration amounted to exactly the same thing as those he had previously made to the Russian government. The Turks declined to follow up a proposal with no more prospect of

[11] "Nur wenn man den Prinzen Ferdinand als Träger einer ausschliesslich orleanistischen Politik auffasst vermag man sein Unternehmen unter einen logischen Gesichtspunkt zu bringen. Die Interessen des Hauses Orléans sind derartige, das dauernder Friede in Europa sie nicht fördern wird."

[12] *Norddeutsche Allgemeine Zeitung*, September 9. "Die ' Köln. Ztg.' spricht ihr Bedauern über das Ausbleiben einer Kaiserzusammenkunft in Stettin aus, und knüpft heiran die Bemerkung, ' dass nur ein unzweideutiges russisches Entgegenkommen jenen dunklen Schatten, der uns die Russenfreundlichkeit nach wie vor verleidet, zu befreien vermag.' . . . Es überrascht uns, dass ein mit so viel politischer Einsicht redigirtes Blatt wie die ' Köln. Ztg.,' sich darüber täuschen kann, dass gerade ihr dringendes Bedürfnis nach ' russischem Entgegenkommen ' den Eindruck hervorrufen muss, als ob Deutschland eines solches bedürftig sei."

[13] *M. A. Z.*, September 13. "Der Reichskanzler scheint unter allen Umständen entschlossen zu sein, die Klärung der Verhältnisse, die bei den persönlichen Eigenschaften des Zaren immer unberechenbarer werden, herbeizuführen."

[14] *G. F. O.*, v, p. 200. September 3, Bismarck to Kiderlen.

success than this answer gave. Moreover, they found it hard to reconcile Bismarck's apparent support of the Russian plan with the advice he was now giving them to come to an understanding with the anti-Russian entente. The German explanation that advice in favor of a general accord, providing security in the event of war, was not incompatible with approval of a particular proposal in the interest of peace, is a refinement of logic that hardly meets the demands of the case.[15]

This question of the Ernroth proposal was ventilated in the course of the press controversy in Germany. The *Norddeutsche Allgemeine Zeitung* now publicly proclaimed: "Germany has not only herself agreed to the mission of General Ernroth, but she is also prepared to recommend that the other Powers give their consent to this scheme, when the cabinets especially interested, namely, the Porte and Russia, have made an official proposition to that effect."

Disregarding this grudging olive branch held out to Russia by its opponent in the debate, the *Kölnische Zeitung* went on with the development of its former theme. The loss of German friendship, it maintained, was due entirely to Russia's 'see-saw policy,' endeavoring to draw Germany into bidding against France for her favors. The attempt had been frustrated by Germany's withdrawal behind the strict terms of her treaty obligations, indifferent to the effect her action would have upon Russian opinion. "We expect no gratitude from the Russians," ran the article of September 12; "and their hostility we do not fear." Germany, it continued, owed nothing to the reigning Tsar: "The Russo-German account is balanced; and the word, 'gratitude,' may be stricken from the vocabulary of foreign policy of both states." A still later article, entitled "Without friendship and without enmity," made it clear that the most Russia could expect from Germany in the Eastern Question was to be left alone with her difficulties.[16]

[15] *G. F. O.*, iv, p. 349. September 4, Derenthall to Reuss.
[16] *Kölnische Zeitung*, September 18. "Wir Deutsche lassen den Russen in Bulgarien freie Bahn, aber seit wir jede Hoffnung aufgeben mussten, Russland zu versöhnen, kann es nicht unsere Aufgabe sein, die Widerstandskräfte, welche in Europa gegen die russischen Pläne regen, diplomatisch zu beugen."

Naturally, this unwonted sharpness of tone toward Russia came as an agreeable surprise to the Danubian monarchy, and was received with especial relief by the Hungarians.[17] The *Norddeutsche Allgemeine Zeitung* even reprinted one audacious article from Pest, affirming that the declaration in favor of Ernroth's mission was only a manoeuvre not to be taken seriously.[18]

While Bismarck's newspapers were lecturing Russia on the sins by which she had forfeited Germany's friendship, the Chancellor himself undertook to demonstrate the value of the support she had sacrificed — and incidentally to prove how little regard he really had for the upstart Bulgarian government. A newspaper libel against the German consul at Rushchuk set the whole force of the empire in motion; and satisfaction was sought directly of the suzerain power, ignoring the pretensions of the local government to responsible authority. A demand was addressed to the Sultan for reparation of the injury and for permission to send three cruisers to blockade Bulgarian ports. The unreasonableness of directing such measures of force against an authority at the same time treated as not legally responsible may be passed over on the assumption that the whole procedure was mere 'bluff.' Germany contented herself, after all, with the action taken by the Bulgarian authorities on their own initiative when the protest reached them by roundabout ways.[19]

Besides impressing upon Russia the fact that Germany held

---

[17] *M. A. Z.*, September 14. Pest, September 12. "Wir brauchen nicht hinzufügen, wie befriedigt die öffentliche Meinung hier von jener Auslassung, des deutschen officiösen Organs ist; denn die bisherige Haltung Deutschlands in der bulgarischen Frage hatte manche Bedenken wachgerufen, den Werth der deutschen Allianz für Oesterreich-Ungarn betreffend."

[18] *Norddeutsche Allgemeine Zeitung*, September 13: article from *Egyetertés*. "Das Ziel der deutschen Politik war und bleibt die Isolirung Frankreichs, um zu verhüten, dass diese Macht sich mit einer anderen Macht, insbesondere mit Russland, verbinden könne. Wenn Deutschland durch dieses Bestreben in der Frage der Mission Erenrot auf die Seite Russlands geführt wurde, so sehen wir darin keine besondere Ursache zur Unruhe, denn es ist das schliesslich nur eine vorübergehende Stellungnahme und kann in keinem Falle dahin führen, dass die Geltendmachung unserer wesentlichen Interessen von Seiten Deutschlands auf ernste Hindernisse stösst."

[19] *G. B.*, 1889, pp. 182–183. September 14, Stranski (Bulgarian minister of foreign affairs) to Baron Thielmann (German consul general).

the Bulgarian government in as low esteem as she herself did, this action produced a curious effect as an example. Its complete success at first aroused hope that Russia too might get results by a similar display of energy. However, Russia's impulse to yield to the temptation was short-lived. A reluctance reasserted itself against turning Russian arms upon the people those arms had set free.[20] The Russian government went back to its hopeless task of finding a way out of the morass by diplomatic means.

## II

While Russia floundered in her diplomatic bog, her exultant enemies devoted themselves to building up their own position more solidly. The Austrian government's instructions of August 29 to its ambassador at Constantinople were sent to the other two governments for approval and support. In this document, it was stated that if, in disregard of Austria's advice, the Sultan should send a Russian commissioner into Bulgaria with the backing of Turkish troops, "we must reserve the question of our attitude toward the consequences of such a decision."[21] This was all too mild a course of conduct for the Italian government, which pressed for more active and positive measures.[22] Its ardor was held safely enough in check, but the community of interest in support of Ferdinand was indicated by the fact that in the course of the month of September, the Italian, Austrian, and English consuls at Sofia all held private unofficial interviews with Ferdinand, which helped consolidate locally the triumph of the anti-Russian elements.[23]

Germany extended her full approval to this solidarity among the three Powers. In an interview with Kálnoky on September 16, Bismarck accepted, although with a formal protest, the Austrian minister's declaration that he intended to stand by his previous policy with regard to Bulgaria.[24] This interview was followed im-

[20] *M. A. Z.*, October 2; St. Petersburg, September 26. Вѣстникъ Европы, September, 1887, p. 403.
[21] *G. F. O.*, v, pp. 198–199.
[22] *Ibid.*, v, p. 202; iv, p. 350. September 6, 13, Reuss to Bismarck.
[23] *G. B.*, 1889, pp. 178–179, 192. September 9, 27, Gerbaix de Sonnaz to Crispi.
[24] Friedjung, *Biographisches Jahrbuch*, iii, p. 367 (*Aufsätze*, p. 340).

mediately by an invitation to the still more ardent opponent of Russia, Crispi.[25]

Bismarck also continued his support of the project of rendering the triple entente more solid and definite — a task to which Crispi had long been energetically applying himself. On September 24, Herbert Bismarck wrote to Reuss that, while the German government had no interest in the Balkan question, it was glad to observe the solidarity prevailing among the interested Powers. He added: "It would, without doubt, be to England's interest to establish still closer relations with Austria and Italy and to yield to the importunities of Crispi." [26] The English government would not allow itself to be hurried into action; but the general trend of developments was certainly most unpromising for a solution of the Bulgarian problem which would satisfy Russia.

Attempts at such a solution were, nevertheless, still under way. Russia continued her efforts to induce Turkey to take the initiative in bringing forward the ' definite proposals ' which Bismarck demanded before passing an opinion upon anything. At last the Sultan was brought to present a positive programme which was first submitted to Russia for approval. He proposed that Russia and Turkey both send commissioners into the principality to act together under joint sanction and responsibility. Their task should be the holding of new elections for a Sobranie to which Russia should submit a list of acceptable candidates for the throne. An international commission was suggested as a possible alternative to the joint commission, if it should prove unacceptable to the other Powers.[27] Germany's diplomatic representatives conveyed advance notice of these proposals to the other parties most interested, sounding out their opinions without disclosing Bismarck's.[28] The attitude of the other governments was

[25] Crispi, pp. 170–171 (*Memoirs*, ii, p. 208).
[26] *G. F. O.*, iv, p. 351.
[27] *N. F. P.*, September 28. *G. B.*, 1889, p. 189.
[28] *G. B.*, 1889, p. 189. September 27, Crispi to Blanc. "Nel darmi notizia di quanto precede, il conte di Solms non ha aggiunto parola circa l'opinione del suo governo a tale riguardo. E neppure ha mostrato desiderio di conoscere la nostra. . . . io Le dica, rimane pur sempre la stessa."

not difficult to predict. Still, in the acceptance of these terms lay Russia's only chance of effectively reopening the negotiation. They would have to be taken seriously. Germany's support was pledged; and France could undoubtedly be counted upon to favor them. No better opportunity of influencing Bulgarian affairs was likely to offer itself.

One factor deserving note in the situation was the rather surprising weight France carried in the international scales at this moment. The Rouvier ministry seemed in a fair way to belie the evil omens under which it had begun its existence. Undaunted by the clamor of Boulangist demonstrations, it strove persistently to raise the country's diplomatic and military prestige. The experimental mobilization of an army corps attracted the serious attention of Europe. France was still isolated, but was making some progress toward diminishing the hostility that surrounded her. Relations with Italy were stubbornly difficult, it is true. The Italians had passed, in July, a new and stringent tariff, which was held in readiness to go into effect as soon as the denounced treaty of 1881 should expire. Yet the possibility of negotiating a new commercial treaty was still open. While nursing this possibility of a reconciliation with Italy, France was also bidding against her Latin neighbor for the favor of England, and with some prospect of success. Flourens, who had remained in office under the new government, continued patiently his efforts to reach an understanding over the Canal and the New Hebrides and was on the point of concluding one.[29]

The negotiation for this agreement was pushed forward with energy, Chaudordy being sent to take the matter up directly with Lord Salisbury, who was then at Dieppe. Flourens even dreamed of giving it a still wider scope, comprising not only the great outstanding issue between France and England, the Egyptian ques-

[29] *M. A. Z.*, September 8. Paris, September 5. "Die französischen Minister weder geneigt sind, noch in der Lage sich befinden, das politische Wohlwollen Italiens um den Preis handelspolitischer Zugeständnisse oder Opfer zu erkaufen . . . seitdem es den HH. Flourens und Waddington gelingt die Annäherung an England zu bewerkstelligen und das Eivernehmen mit dem Londoner Cabinet vorzubereiten, indem sie die wechselseitige Verständigung bezüglich der Hebriden und der Neutralität des Suezcanals vervollständigen." See also Chaudordy, *La France en 1889* (Paris, 1889) pp. 229–232.

tion, but also the main diplomatic difficulty of all Europe, the Bulgarian question.[30] In undertaking this enterprise, he kept in touch with the Russian embassy, still through the semiofficial intermediary, Hansen. The entire position of France seemed very much stronger than in the early summer.

Bismarck, moreover, was treating her with a new consideration. The delicate situation into which his policy had led him obliged him to move with caution. An angry Tsar and a strong, well behaved France formed an obviously threatening conjuncture of circumstances. Two new frontier incidents at this period were cleared up with a remarkable smoothness that contrasted sharply with Germany's belligerent attitude in the spring. The less serious of the two, but brought prominently into public notice by the celebrated name involved, was the arrest, on September 19, of the son of Schnaebele for having posted an impudent placard in a commune of annexed Lorraine. Of graver character was the killing of a French hunter by a German forest guard in the Vosges, on the 24th. Both incidents were settled quietly by the end of the month. Although the German authorities contested the proofs offered that the killing had taken place in the French commune of Vexaincourt, the government offered, through its ambassador, on September 30, an expression of regret, an indemnity to the slain man's family, and a promise to prosecute the soldier who had shot him. These advances were accepted as satisfactory.[31] On the same day young Schnaebele was released.

This consideration for France, this hushing up of affairs that might well have been developed into pretexts of conflict, coincides with the apparent severing of all Germany's ties with Russia. In addition to the polemics on foreign policy begun after the abandonment of the Stettin interview, the German newspapers were persistently circulating a rumor, started by the *Kölnische Zeitung* on September 10, to the effect that the Russo-Austro-German alliance, commonly referred to as the treaty of Skierne-

[30] Hansen, *Mohrenheim*, p. 52. September 11, Flourens to Hansen. "Il faudrait qu'il [Chaudordy] obtînt de lord Salisbury deux choses: 1° Qu'il ne retarde pas davantage la signature de la convention de Suez. . . . 2° Qu'il vienne me voir à Paris avant son retour à Londres pour causer de la Bulgarie et de l'Egypte."
[31] Albin, pp. 116 *et seq. M. A. Z.* and *N. F. P., passim.*

wice, had expired in the spring and had not been renewed. Nothing was whispered of the new Reinsurance Treaty. Elaborate demonstrations were now being made to convince Europe that another system of alliances had definitely replaced the old.[32] Crispi's visit to Friedrichsruh, on October 2, following closely on Kálnoky's, completed the evidence in the case.

According to Crispi's own account of this visit, Bismarck began their conversation by extolling the Triple Alliance as the bulwark of peace against disturbers like France and Russia.[33] But he also declared that he did not fear war and was even ready to face both enemies at once if necessary.[34] This was a statement he had made six months before to the Grand Duke Vladimir. He also recurred to the suggestion he had made to Archduke Rudolf concerning the possibility of using the Poles against Russia.[35] On the whole, however, he considered the chances to be against a war in the near future.[36]

In approaching the Bulgarian question, the Chancellor left the initiative in all statements of policy to Crispi, as he had done with Kálnoky before. On his own part, he repeated his familiar declarations of indifference and detachment, but added that he trusted the allies to handle matters in that quarter.[37] Crispi was

[32] *Times*, October 3. Berlin, October 2. "The 'Drei Kaiser Bündniss' has come to an end — according to a semi-official statement it expired this spring — and the Austro-German-Italian alliance has taken its place as the firm bulwark of European peace."

[33] Crispi, p. 174 (*Memoirs*, ii, p. 212). Memorandum of conversation. "Egli vuole la pace; e constata con dispiacere come a turbarla esistano due sole Potenze, la Russia e la Francia. Egli però non ne teme. La triplice alleanza è una potente garanzia alla conservazione della pace."

[34] *Ibid.* "Ripete ch'egli vuole la pace; ma che, se la deplora, non teme la guerra. . . . Collocandone un milione alle frontiere del sud ed un milione a quelle del nord, la Germania non temerà l'offesa. Al resto penseranno gli alleati."

[35] *Ibid.* (*Memoirs*, ii, p. 213). "La Polonia è una debolezza e l'Austria in Polonia è simpatica. Per poco che si aiutino ad insorgere, i polacchi potranno essere emancipati e costituire uno Stato da potersi dare ad un arciduca austriaco."

[36] *Ibid.* "Alessandro III non è partigiano della guerra. E quando pure volesse farla, non gli converrebbe andare in Bulgaria. Là, a poco distanza, è la Transylvania, e l'Austria avrebbe facile via per piombare sopra i russi."

[37] *Ibid.*, p. 175 (*Memoirs*, ii, p. 213). "Al principe di Bismarck poco importa che i russi vadano a Costantinopoli. La Russia con quella conquista sarebbe più debole. A lui poco importa la soluzione della quistione bulgara . . ."

shocked by his casual reference to the possibility of Russia's occupying Constantinople. "We could not allow Russia to get to Constantinople," was his passionate reply; "Russia at Constantinople would be mistress of the Mediterranean." Bismarck welcomed his ardor with cool reassurances. He admitted that he "entirely approved of this group of three Powers, and that he hoped it would become still more closely united and make its authority felt." He further added: "Germany will always be with Italy wherever the interests of peace are at stake. Should a breach of the peace occur in the East, Germany would stand with her allies, acting as their rearguard." He also advised Crispi to work in close harmony with Austria in this matter, and suggested a special treaty to govern their common action.[38]

His auditor drank in all these heartening words eagerly, then turned to matters directly affecting Italy's relations with Germany. The *casus foederis* between them was a war with France, which Crispi said he hoped was improbable, but for which provision should be made by a military convention — such conventions being his particular hobby. Bismarck agreed as to the advisability of such a step, but said he must first refer it to the Emperor and the chief of the general staff.[39] Here ends the chapter on France in the Crispi memorandum as published. The report of further conversation on this interesting topic comes from a most untrustworthy source, but is borne out by some external evidence. According to an account of the interview published in the *Nouvelle Revue* in the following summer, Bismarck followed up Crispi's remarks on the probability of war with France by assuring him that the spoils of such a conflict would go chiefly to Italy.[40] But another party to profit, willingly or unwillingly, by

[38] Crispi, pp. 175–177 (*Memoirs*, ii, pp. 214–216). See also G. F. O., iv, pp. 361–362, for a partial account given by Crispi to the Austrian ambassador, with Bismarck's marginal notes on the same.

[39] Crispi, pp. 177–178 (*Memoirs*, ii, p. 217).

[40] *Nouvelle Revue*, July 1, 1888, p. 7. "Un secret d'état," signed 'Comte Paul Vasili.' "D'après M. Crispi lui-même, M. de Bismarck s'était surtout attaché à lui démontrer que l'Allemagne n'avait aucune ambition d'annexion nouvelle, et que, en cas de victoire de l'Allemagne, les compensations territoriales n'auraient de raison d'être que pour ses alliés; c'est à dire: ' Pour ceux qui croient comme lui que la disparition de la France comme grande puissance est le gage de longues

France's defeat, he said, would be Belgium. In this connection the Chancellor mentioned arrangements then being concluded with King Leopold II.[41] Plenty of rumors of these transactions appear later; moreover, it is to be noted that, about the middle of September, Count Herbert Bismarck spent some time at Ostend, where he found not only the Italian diplomat, Marquis Maffei, but King Leopold himself as well, enjoying the pleasures of the seaside.[42] The conjuncture of circumstances was little noted at the time, but assumes importance in perspective.

Significant developments were expected from the conferences at Friedrichsruh.[43] These developments took shape rapidly enough. A draft fathered by Baron Calice, Austrian ambassador at Constantinople, was brought from Vienna to Rome by the Italian ambassador, on October 6. It comprised a programme of eight points as the basis of a triple entente, including England. The points were: "1. The maintenance of peace. — 2. The status quo as founded upon treaties. Exclusion of compensations. — 3. Local autonomy. — 4. The independence of Turkey and of the

années de paix pour l'Europe." It may be recalled here that Bismarck had outlined a policy of *pourboires* for Italy to the Austrian Crown Prince as early as March, after the renewal of the Triple Alliance. See p. 155, *supra*.

[41] 'Vasili,' pp. 7–8. The words reported as "à peu près textuellement les paroles prononcées par le chancelier," if not authentic, are at least interesting enough to bear reproduction. "La Belgique ne peut nous rendre qu'un service, *qu'elle le veuille ou non*: c'est de laisser passer par son territoire une armée allemande. Du reste cette question sera définitivement réglée avec le roi Léopold, et de ce côté toutes nos dispositions sont prises et résolues. La Belgique doit être associée aux projets de notre avenir, et si elle doit subir une transformation de territoire, elle la subira d'accord avec nous sous certaines conditions déterminées qui ne dépendront que de nous. A mon avis, je verrais avec plaisir le rétablissement de la Flandre française et même un peu plus au profit de la Belgique, sans parler de ce qu'on pourrait faire au sud. C'est encore la seule solution qui permettrait à l'Allemagne de se compléter géographiquement par les ports de la Hollande, et ce serait sans doute la seule combinaison que l'Angleterre serait le mieux disposée à accepter."

[42] Maurel, p. 207. *Times*, September 14. Herbert arrived at Ostend on the 13th.

[43] *M. A. Z.*, October 8. Berlin, October 6. "Man nimmt nun . . . als gewiss an, dass eine noch grössere Uebereinstimmung als seither mit dem italienischen Cabinet in Betreff der Behandlung der Orient-Angelegenheiten und in besonderem Bezug auf die bulgarische Frage herbeigeführt worden sei, in welcher ersteres wenig oder nicht geneigt war, Russland irgendwelche Concessionen, wenn auch nur von theoretischer Bedeutung, zu machen; ebenso hinsichtlich des politischen Verhältnisses zu Frankreich."

Straits, etc., of any preponderating foreign influence. — 5. The Porte not to be allowed to cede its rights over Bulgaria to another Power. — 6. Association with Turkey for guaranteeing the above. — 7. In case of resistance on the part of Turkey or illegal pretensions on the part of Russia, the three Powers to concert together their measures of support. — 8. In case of connivance or passivity on the part of Turkey, the three Powers to agree upon the occupation of certain points for the purpose of maintaining the balance of power." [44]

Another month was to pass before the accord on the basis of these points was actually completed, but action in the spirit of them continued at Constantinople. There was already practically no further hope of success for Russia's efforts, but her final discomfiture was greatly facilitated by her own unskilful handling of the situation.

The Turkish proposals of September had probably had little sincerity behind them.[45] Nevertheless, they did constitute a commitment upon which Russia should have seized without delay. Instead of hastening the submission of these proposals to the Powers, however, the Russian government made the mistake of first trying to modify them by private negotiation. It suggested that the Russian commissioner be placed above the Turkish, with powers amplified and prolonged, and that the preliminary list of princely candidates be dispensed with.[46] The result of this delay was fatal, especially in view of the attitude of Germany. The Sultan took time to survey the situation before making his counter-reply.[47] Finally he announced that he would discuss the

[44] Crispi, pp. 182–183 (*Memoirs*, ii, pp. 223–224). The draft was not presented to Crispi by the Austrian ambassador until the 15th. See *G. F. O.*, iv, p. 391. See also the same, p. 354, for the slightly more expanded text finally used.

[45] *M. A. Z.*, October 7. Sophia, October 1. "In hiesigen politischen Kreisen glaubt man, dass die neueste Note der hohen Pforte nur den Zweck hat, ' die Zeit verstreichen zu lassen.' Diese Zeit sollten aber auch die Bulgaren auszunützen trachten."

[46] *L'Univers*, October 6. Varna, October 5, Havas despatch.

[47] *N. F. P.*, October 19. Constantinople, October 15, *Correspondance de l'Est* despatch. "Die Pforte erblickte . . . in der Tripel-Allianz eine moralische Ermunterung des Fürsten Ferdinand. Der Sultan wolle Zeit gewinnen, bis Deutschland, England, Italien, und Oesterreich ihre Anschauungen in klarer Weise ausgesprochen

question no further, since Russia had chosen, not only to shoulder off upon him all the odious initiative, including that of shutting out Eastern Rumelia from the new Sobranie, but to quibble over everything he proposed.[48]

The game was definitely lost. Even the German newspapers now impressed that fact upon Russia's consciousness. The *Kölnische Zeitung*, on October 7, cynically remarked: "Germany still leaves Russia a free hand in Bulgaria, subject to her reckoning with England, Austria, and Italy. Unfortunately, St. Petersburg will hardly be satisfied with that." Semiofficial organs abandoned their harshness toward Bulgaria and intimated that Ferdinand's tenure of his throne might not be so fleeting after all.[49] The change predicted by the first of the 'Bulgarian documents' seemed to be coming over German policy.

## III

The Tsar, still at Copenhagen, felt the change in Germany's conduct and resented it hotly. New proofs of it were constantly coming in. Toward the end of September, a second letter from Ferdinand to the Countess of Flanders reached his hands, acknowledging a reply to the first and indicating that the hoped for alteration in Germany's attitude was under way. It was dated September 16, after the Stettin fiasco and before the Kálnoky and Crispi interviews. "I may tell you," says the writer, "that in spite of the open political war Germany is carrying on against me at present, every four or five days some one of the German agents established here gets word to us that we must wait, that for im-

haben würden. . . . In dieser Beziehung sei es auch höchst bezeichnend, dass Abdul Hamid die von Herrn Nelidow nachgesuchte Audienz immer wieder vertagte."

[48] *N. F. P.*, October 17. Constantinople, October 16, Reuter despatch.

[49] *Ibid.*, October 18. "Es ist eine interessante Thatsache, dass namentlich seit Crispis Besuch die Berliner Officiösen nicht mehr so schonungslos wie früher über den Bulgaren und den Prinzen Ferdinand aburtheilen." *Post*, October 16. "Der grosse europäische Conflict, den die Panslawisten erwarten, erscheint, seitdem der Besuch des Hrn. Crispi die Entschlossenheit der Tripelallianz den *status quo* zu wahren, vor Augen gelegt hat, einigermassen in die Ferne gerückt. . . . Je länger der grosse Conflict ausbleibt, desto mehr wird das Regiment des Prinzen von Coburg in Bulgarien sich befestigen."

portant reasons Germany's foreign policy must be what it appears, but that it may be modified unexpectedly in the most favorable sense." [50]

The communication of this document did not fail of its effect upon Alexander. Reports of his state of mind reached the European capitals from Copenhagen. "He gave way to violent fits of temper," runs one of these. "He remained silent when Prince Bismarck was referred to. He showed his dissatisfaction with the attitude of Germany, and when the Stettin question was spoken of he made the following remark in presence of five or six persons: — 'Well, I, too, will not be made to go to Canossa.'" [51]

At this juncture occurred a minor incident, probably unconnected with developments in the Tsar's household, but significant as showing which way the wind blew. Grand Duke Nicholas Mikhailovich was just arriving in France on the steamer *Uruguay*. On the evening of October 4, as the ship came off Dunkirk, the young man, whose head had been turned by the champagne of the farewell dinner and by the flow of talk around him, made an extremely indiscreet speech on the friendship of Russia for France and their brotherhood in arms in the coming struggle with Germany. His words were, of course, not taken down at the time, but they lost nothing by transmission through the French newspapers.[52] Although the Russian embassy at Paris pronounced these reports fantastic, they were, nevertheless, probably correct enough in substance. The grand duke was speedily recalled from France and given a severe reprimand by the Tsar — not so much

---

[50] *Reichsanzeiger*, December 31, 1887. Maurel, p. 223.

[51] *Times*, October 7. Paris, October 6.

[52] As reported by *Figaro* on October 7, the speech ran: "France is working at preparation for the *revanche*, and she does well in so doing. But she shows good sense in not letting herself be roused by the continual provocations of her neighbor. She should continue her preparations calmly. . . . Russia also is not idle. Our entire House, be it known, loves France. All the endeavors of the Tsar are directed toward diminishing the German influence, which at one time was great among our officials. Soon our government will consist only of men who love France. Until then France should refrain from becoming aroused; for at the present moment it would be difficult to obtain our effective alliance in the event of war. But in a short time all obstacles will disappear; and in case of war, I would be the first to enter the ranks of the French army, which I heartily admire. Be sure that my example will be followed by many Russians."

on account of his language as because of his transgression of the rule that the Emperor should do all the talking in public for the family.[53] The affair created quite a stir in Europe. German opinion, scouting all disavowals, pointed to the speech as confirmation of Russia's surrender to Panslavism, but proudly maintained Germany's indifference to the outcome.[54]

This incident came as the climax to a series of Francophile demonstrations in the Russian press, accompanying a tour of the country by Paul Déroulède, chief of the League of Patriots. The most striking incident of the Frenchman's triumphal progress had been his reception by General Baranov, governor of Nizhni Novgorod. These matters had already given rise to diplomatic protests, which Giers answered by deploring what had taken place, but maintaining that he could do nothing about it in the absence of the Tsar.[55] Now, on October 9, the Chancellor dictated a lengthy despatch for Schweinitz asserting that his faith in Russia's peaceable intentions had been sadly shaken. He would be driven, he wrote, to meet the threat of a Franco-Russian alliance "by other coalitions." He would also be obliged, he continued, "to seek the good will of other Powers by alterations in our policy and to encourage these other Powers in their anti-Russian tendencies. We shall be obliged to alter in this sense our former policy in Constantinople and in Bulgaria."[56] In view of the stage negotiations among the other Powers had already reached, under Bismarck's impulsion, it is hard to see how he could go much further in the direction of building up combinations against Russia without entering them himself. He could and did, however, display new activity in their behalf. The threat was followed by a warning — by this time familiar — that Russian advocates of a French alliance were seriously mistaken in fancying that Germany could not give a good account of herself in a war on two fronts.

[53] Pfeil, p. 205. As told to Pfeil by the Grand Duke Sergius.

[54] *M. A. Z.*, October 12. Berlin, October 9. "Die russischen Grossfürsten können thun oder lassen, was sie wollen; auf die russisch-deutschen Beziehungen können sie keinen Einfluss mehr ausüben. Dieselben sind aber schon auf dem Gefrierpunkt und es kann sich nur darum handeln, ob der Kaiser Alexander den Augenblick für gekommen hält, seinen Ansichten auch öffentlich Ausdruck zu geben."

[55] *G. F. O.*, v, pp. 293–303.      [56] *Ibid.*, v, p. 304.

The moment seemed a not unlikely one for the eventualities foreshadowed in the Grand Duke's speech at last to take definite shape. But, with the talent so often displayed for ruining their own cause, the French interfered with the course of developments. Mid-October was the time chosen by them for revealing the scandals in the war office, centring first round the name of Caffarel but soon to involve much more highly connected persons. The impression made by these disclosures upon the Tsar was deplorable. Widespread as was the similar corruption in his own administration and hopeless as he found the struggle against it, his upright nature never lost its aversion to this as to all other forms of dishonor. He found it particularly hard to pardon in a country already possessing so many other characteristics distasteful to him.[57]

This reaction against France, however, did not take place at once. On the one hand, France continued to strengthen her diplomatic position. Flourens carried his lengthy negotiations with England to a successful conclusion on October 24. The troublesome questions of the New Hebrides and the Suez Canal seemed disposed of in a fashion creditable to France and promising for the future of her international relations.[58] The French government received a well earned meed of applause from all its neighbors, even from Germany.[59] The Tsar could not, therefore, find it wholly and hopelessly corrupt, although he was disposed to treat it with more caution than formerly. The diplomacy of Flourens had even opened up the prospect of a real rapprochement be-

---

[57] *M. A. Z.*, October 25. St. Petersburg, October 19. "Ueber die französische Scandalaffaire Caffarel sind unsere Blätter sehr verstimmt, weil ihrem Traum von einem Bündnis mit Frankreich dadurch ein empfindlicher Schlag versetzt worden ist und die Chancen für ein Zustandekommen desselben jetzt geringer geworden sind als je. Gerade in solchen Dingen, wie sie durch diesen Scandal in Paris blossgelegt worden, ist der Kaiser äusserst peinlich; er vergisst Unehrenhaftigkeiten nie, so dass die Abneigung, sich in irgendein politisches Verhältnis mit dem radicalen und in solcher Weise blossgestellten Frankreich einzulassen, noch mehr gewachsen ist."

[58] Chaudordy, pp. 229–232.

[59] *Kölnische Zeitung*, October 25. "Am wenigsten hat irgend eine dritte europäische Macht, etwa Deutschland, Anlass, das Einvernehmen der beiden Mächte ungern zu sehen. Alle Welt wünscht die Frage des Suezcanals geordnet zu wissen."

tween England and Russia through French mediation.⁶⁰ He gave to the Russians accounts, undoubtedly much too highly colored, of his progress toward success.⁶¹ Decidedly, the coöperation of France was not yet lightly to be discarded.

On the other hand, new fuel was heaped in timely wise upon the flames of the Tsar's anger against the Germans. A third instalment of Ferdinand's correspondence with the Countess of Flanders reached him about the end of October. It took the form this time of a summary of a letter supposedly written about October 21. In it, "The prince announces that he has received new assurances from Prince Bismarck since the Kálnoky and Crispi interviews. Only, he says, the latest advances are much more formal. The German communication, instead of coming, like the others, through the German ambassador at Vienna, arrived directly from Berlin. It states clearly that, in the Kálnoky and Crispi interviews, 'the Bulgarian situation was thoroughly examined, and that the Central Powers are unquestionably most favorably disposed toward a permanent settlement under these conditions.'"⁶²

But documents of doubtful origin no longer constituted the whole of Alexander's collection of proofs of Bismarck's perfidy. Reports had been coming in from Russian agents in various quarters which bore out in a general way the precise allegations contained in the Ferdinand letters.⁶³ Indications to this effect were

⁶⁰ Hansen, *Mohrenheim*, p. 56.
⁶¹ *Ibid.*, pp. 55–56. October 28, Flourens to Mohrenheim. "Je dois dire que j'ai trouvé chez lord Salisbury, avec un sincère désir de clore l'ère des contestations, soit avec la Russie, soit avec nous, une saine appréciation des périls que pourrait faire courir à la paix et à l'indépendance des peuples une coalition permanente de puissances de création récente et, par suite, agitées d'un besoin inassouvi d'extension."
⁶² *Reichsanzeiger*, December 31, 1887. Maurel, pp. 272–273. Late in December the *Agence Libre* published the terms of an alleged secret note sent to Sofia at this time setting forth the conditions arrived at in the Friedrichsruh conferences for the continued existence of Bulgaria. They are given as: "1. The acceptance of the moral and actual protectorate of the Powers of the Triple Alliance; 2. Bulgaria not to alter its political situation, since this is to be converted into a definite one; 3. The maintenance of internal order and, at least a temporary and apparent, submissiveness to the Sublime Porte." This very doubtful document adds nothing in particular to the case.
⁶³ *N. F. P.*, December 12. According to an article in the *Standard* reprinted by the *Kölnische Zeitung*.

not difficult to discover. There was the new tone taken by Turkey since Bismarck's recent interviews, which pointed clearly enough to a change in front on his part.[64] Moreover, the way of the new Bulgarian government had been surprisingly smoothed in various directions. On September 26, a convention with Serbia settled certain points regarding work on the Eastern Railway to Constantinople, a matter of importance for the extension of Austria's influence in the Balkan Peninsula. On November 3, an accord was reached with the administration of the Ottoman debt for assumption of the tribute of Eastern Rumelia. The formal abolition at this time of the customs line between Eastern Rumelia and Bulgaria was viewed as a recognition of the union by the Sultan.[65] The Italian ambassador later reports action in common with "mei tre colleghi favorevoli" in securing ratification of this arrangement at Constantinople.[66] The hand of Germany in these developments was not hard to see.[67] In fact, no pains were taken to conceal it. On October 19, Giers complained to the German chargé d'affaires that he already felt "everywhere, but especially at Constantinople, our attitude had changed." All he got by way of reply was the statement that this change was a consequence of Russia's attitude toward Germany.[68]

It appears, indeed, that for a time the Tsar himself contemplated the possibility of a general war as the outcome of the situation which had developed, and that he attempted to marshal

[64] *Zur europäischen Politik*, v, p. 205. November 7, Errembault de Dudzeele: "De Turquie . . . une lettre que j'ai lue, parle de la situation très embrouillée ainsi que de la résolution de la Porte de ne rien faire dans la question bulgare et de la comédie qu'elle joue simplement vis-à-vis de la Russie depuis surtout que l'Allemagne ne lui conseille plus l'accord avec cette puissance. Cette lettre signale aussi un rapprochement du Sultan avec l'Autriche."

[65] *G. B.*, 1889, pp. 202–203. December 2, Sonnaz to Crispi.

[66] *Ibid.*, p. 201. December 2, Blanc to Crispi.

[67] Maurel (pp. 289–290) prints at this point a letter purporting to be from Ferdinand to King Leopold of Belgium, requesting officers of instruction for the Bulgarian army, in which he writes: "Notre situation extérieure s'est subitement changée par la modification seule de l'attitude de l'Allemagne qui seconde en ce moment nos efforts avec vivacité, après ne nous avoir donné que des conseils indirects. On nous fait entrevoir la reconnaissance de la Bulgarie dans un avenir même peu éloigné."

[68] *G. F. O.*, vi, p. 117.

his forces for it, regardless of his personal feelings toward the allies designated by circumstances. On France he could count with sufficient certainty; and her help promised to be a factor of respectable importance. The powers of the Triple Alliance would, of course, stand solidly together against him. But the attitude of England appeared undetermined. The extent of her adhesion to the hostile group was not known, while she seemed to be getting on fairly good terms with France. Impressed by the sense of coming danger and enraged by the evidence of Germany's bad faith, Alexander nerved himself to hasten the roundabout negotiations for an understanding with England which had been initiated by Flourens. He took the startling course of a direct appeal to the British prime minister to declare his position.

The Russian government had already informed the British of the existence of the Reinsurance Treaty, possibly in order to influence the negotiations over Afghanistan in July. The story of the Tsar's approach to England in October was later told to a German diplomat by Salisbury himself in these words: "As for the Reinsurance Treaty, I, personally, never attributed any too great significance to it. In spite of this secret treaty, the outbreak of war between Germany and Russia, involving France, more than once hung by a silken thread during the eighties — for example, in the summer and autumn of 1887. Alexander III, who was then making a stay of some months at Copenhagen, conveyed to me secretly, through a highly-placed personage, the inquiry as to what price England would set upon her benevolent neutrality toward Russia and France in the event of a war between them and Germany. Since we in England at that time held most strictly to the doctrine of the free hand, I returned a dilatory answer." [69]

As matters stood between Germany and Russia in late October, surely nothing could have seemed more unlikely than that the deferred interview of the Emperors would after all take place. Alexander certainly meant to keep away: his plans called for a return from Denmark to Russia by sea, as he had come. Yet minor circumstances brought him to change his course. The im-

---

[69] Eckardstein, ii, p. 154. The "doctrine of the free hand" is a poor euphemism for England's commitment to the anti-Russian side.

perial children were stricken by measles; and the voyage had to be deferred until the Russian ports began to freeze over. The Tsar's yacht was sent back before Cronstadt should become ice-bound, leaving the party no choice but a return, in part at least, by rail. Deliberately to select the roundabout way through Sweden and Finland, or to pass through Germany without stopping at Berlin, would have constituted an obvious slight which Alexander could not bring himself to inflict upon his aged great-uncle. Finally, on November 4, Shuvalov announced that the Tsar would spend a day in the German capital.[70]

Rumors that such would be the outcome had been in circulation long beforehand, but had been scouted as stock exchange gossip designed to strengthen the quotations on Russian bonds. While adhering to this view, the *Post* had been careful to point out that, if the unexpected should happen, the event might be of far reaching significance: "It will either restore the old friendship between Germany and Russia — which would necessarily have the immediate consequence of an about-face on the part of the Russian press — or deepen the wounds long since inflicted upon this friendship."[71] The *Kölnische Zeitung* displayed complete scepticism regarding the first of these possibilities. After recounting all the indications of increasing enmity on the part of Russia, its article concluded: "All these phenomena possess a significance which allows far seeing politicians to cherish no illusions and alongside which the occurrence or non-occurrence of an imperial visit counts for little."[72] The fact remained that the Tsar was coming and that his visit would be an historic event. Its political significance, however, was diminished by the news that it would be attended by no conference of ministers. Giers's suggestion that he should come to Berlin was vetoed by Alexander, who was reported to be resolved not even to receive Bismarck himself.[73]

[70] *G. F. O.*, v, p. 318.

[71] Quoted by Robolsky, *Fürst Bismarck unter drei Kaisern*, p. 114.

[72] *Kölnische Zeitung*, November 1.

[73] *Times*, November 11. St. Petersburg, November 10. Lucius von Ballhausen, p. 404.

As the time for the visit drew near, matters took a turn calculated to shake that resolve. Nothing happened to lessen the Tsar's indignation — rather the contrary — but several developments contributed to darken the view of his future course. Everything went badly. Salisbury evaded his inquiries in a suspicious manner. The troubles in France assumed a more and more serious aspect, until the obscure scandal of a few awards of decorations seemed to set the republic rocking to its foundations. France sacrificed the fruits of her diplomatic success with England by recklessly playing on the assumption that the Canal treaty was a step toward ousting the British from Egypt.[74] This conduct not only cost her most of the good will she had lately acquired, but helped to drive England further into her conspiracy with the Triple Alliance. Salisbury continued for a time, however, to allow Flourens to hope for a complete success, even in the matter of Egypt.[75] On the 12th of November, he admitted that there were still two opinions in the cabinet in regard to going into any combination that the French might believe was hostile to them.[76]

Salisbury himself was favorably disposed toward the project of the new triple entente, but progress toward its completion was not very rapid. The Austrian draft was not communicated to the British government until late in October. There had first been a delay caused by Crispi's attempt to insert a clause providing for the event of the breaking up of Turkey, which Kálnoky refused to consider.[77] Then Kálnoky declined to approach Salisbury until he had Bismarck's approval of the programme.[78] The Chancellor replied that he "had no objections to the eight points," that he

[74] *Journal des Débats*, October 25. "In truth, we can see in it only a first step toward a solution of the Egyptian question. For many years England has not ceased to avow her desire to evacuate Egypt. One of the obstacles, and not the least serious, has been the fear that after her withdrawal the Suez Canal might fall into the hands of some other Power. This obstacle is now removed; and we venture to hope that the others will not be insurmountable."

[75] Hansen, *Mohrenheim*, p. 57.

[76] G. F. O., iv, p. 368. November 12, Hatzfeldt to Bismarck.

[77] *Ibid.*, iv, pp. 361–363. October 15, Bruck to Kálnoky. October 20, Kálnoky to Bruck.

[78] *Ibid.*, iv, p. 353. October 20, memorandum by Herbert Bismarck.

would sound the British ambassador in regard to the project, and that Hatzfeldt would be instructed to support it at London.[79] After the points had been transmitted through Sir Edward Malet, Salisbury found the cabinet divided on the question, and put off a decision until the German ambassador had returned from his leave.[80]

When Salisbury began the serious discussion with Hatzfeldt, he raised a number of new and far reaching considerations. He asked for certain modifications in the agreement itself, of which the most important was its extension to cover Asia Minor. But his chief concern was in regard to Germany's relations with the proposed combination of Powers. He did not ask active support, but only her moral approval of the compact and an assurance that German policy would never go counter to it. He was anxious, however, to get this assurance in some written form, and suggested an addition to the Austro-German treaty of alliance. This treaty he wished, in any case, to see, in order to compare it with the commitments he was asked to make. The definite assurances required from Germany, Lord Salisbury stated, were wanted as a safeguard against the coming to the throne of Prince William, "whose strong pro-Russian sympathies were well known."[81]

As an earnest of his favorable intentions, Bismarck took steps to have the text of the Austro-German treaty communicated as soon as possible. It was handed to Sir Edward Malet on the 13th — that is to say, all the clauses except the one regarding its duration, which had also been finally withheld from the Russians.[82] But the written assurance concerning Germany's attitude toward the new triple entente was a more serious matter. Bismarck had at once rejected the idea of an addition to the Austro-German treaty, and he was several days longer making up his mind to comply with the request at all. Finally, on the 18th, the day of the Tsar's visit to Berlin, the Chancellor telegraphed

[79] *G. F. O.*, iv, pp. 356–357. October 21, memorandum by Count Rantzau.
[80] *Ibid.*, iv, p. 365. November 7, Malet to Herbert Bismarck.
[81] *Ibid.*, iv, pp. 367–374. November 10, 11, Hatzfeldt to the foreign office.
[82] *Ibid.*, iv, p. 375. November 13, memorandum by Herbert Bismarck.

Hatzfeldt to inform Salisbury: "I intend, within the next few days, to express myself directly to him concerning the situation in a private letter." [83] Whether this telegram was sent before or after the famous interview between the Chancellor and the Tsar is, unhappily, not certain; but in either case it indicates how little influence this meeting had upon Bismarck's general policy.

In all these developments there was but cold comfort for Alexander. He must have approached Berlin with the feeling that the outlook could not be blacker and that nothing said or done there could change his prospects for the worse. Bismarck and his associates, meanwhile, did all in their power to deepen that impression.

## IV

Before the Tsar could reach his Canossa, he was made to pass through valleys of humiliation in which the conviction of helplessness was driven deep into his heart. A group of speeches, within the space of a fortnight, by the chief ministers of Italy, Austria-Hungary, and England reëmphasized the solidity of the opposition to Russia's Near-Eastern policy. A severe blow at Russia's financial standing in Berlin showed how little regard for her good will prevailed there on the eve of her sovereign's arrival.

The hostile ministers spoke in the order of their relative activity in the cause. Crispi's utterance came on October 25, following a great banquet at Turin. He was expected to disclose there something of the recent transactions at Friedrichsruh, and he did not wholly disappoint his audience. His first care was to reassure France that he and Bismarck had plotted nothing against her.[84] Then in dramatic fashion he challenged all suspicion of his motives. "It is said that we conspired at Friedrichsruh," he flung out. "Suppose we did: for me, hardened conspirator that I am, that word has no terrors. Yes, if you will, we did conspire, but it

[83] *G. F. O.*, iv, p. 376, note.

[84] Crispi, p. 184 (*Memoirs*, ii, pp. 225–226). "Il mio recente viaggio in Germania inquietò la pubblica opinione in Francia. Fortunatamente però non alterò la fiducia di quel governo, il quale conosce la lealtà delle mie intenzioni, e sa che nulla io vorrò ordire contro il popolo vicino, a cui l'Italia è legata per analogia di razza e tradizioni di civiltà."

was for peace." And he repeated Bismarck's closing words: "We have rendered Europe a great service." [85]

Behind his flowers of rhetoric, however, appeared a certain fixed intent, at least in regard to the Eastern Question. The policy he outlined in general terms — maintenance of the rights of peoples, while respecting existing treaties as far as possible — covered neatly the situation as it stood in Bulgaria.[86] The passage was favorably commented upon in Austria-Hungary, where the words were soon reëchoed in more precise form by the Emperor's greeting to the Delegations.[87]

Two speeches by Count Kálnoky followed, on the 5th and the 8th of November, in reply to addresses from the Delegations complimenting him highly on his past success in promoting the interests of the monarchy. He modestly admitted as a significant achievement, "that the danger of foreign intervention had been dispelled, we hope, forever, and the Bulgarians assured their freedom of internal development." While disavowing responsibility for Ferdinand's candidacy and conduct, and acknowledging the impossibility of legal recognition, he asserted openly that Austria would treat the existing regime in Bulgaria as a de facto government. He gave full credit to Italy for her part in his success, and to Germany for bringing the two together.[88] His second

[85] Crispi, p. 185 (*Memoirs*, ii, pp. 227–228).

[86] *Ibid.*, pp. 185–186 (*Memoirs*, ii, p. 228).

[87] *N. F. P.*, October 27. "Dass Crispi nach seiner Unterredung mit Bismarck unverrückt auf dem früheren Standpunkt steht, gewährt einen Einblick in die Wandlung, welche die deutsche Liebe für Russland erfahren." October 29, speech from the Throne: "Die bulgarische Frage ist zu Meinem Bedauern noch nicht zu ihrem Abschlusse gelangt, doch gebe Ich mich gerne der Hoffnung hin, dass dieselbe auch fernerhin ihren localen Character bewahren und schliesslich in einer Weise gelöst werden wird, welche die zulässigen Wünsche der Bulgaren mit den europäischen Verträgen und Interessen in Einklang bringt." *Geschichtskalender*, 1888, p. 251.

[88] *Geschichtskalender*, 1887, p. 254. Speech of November 5 to the Hungarian Delegation. "He believes that Austria-Hungary and Germany have made very fruitful propaganda with the policy of peace which they have followed for years, and that the adhesion of Italy . . . and the identity of our aims with those of the Italian government, permitting a well grounded hope of support from that quarter in our peaceful policy in the Orient, should be reckoned one of the most encouraging factors in the present situation."

speech, that to the Austrians, revealed England's place at their side.[89]

Certain of his expressions are of interest as indicating the intentions of the allies toward Russia at this moment, when the Tsar's visit to Berlin still hung in the balance. He declared he had not given up the hope "that Russia will once more associate herself more closely than at the present moment with the peaceable and conservative tendencies of the Central Powers." For his part, he would never abandon the hope of an understanding, which he described as "not only consonant with the monarchy's interests, but almost a fundamental condition for the establishment of a lasting peace in Europe." [90] His basis of accord was simple: let Bulgaria alone. No elaborate compromises and compensations found place here. The desired accord was treated as already in existence when the minister stated, on the 8th, that "all the cabinets, the Russian included . . . are agreed upon one point — that the Bulgarian question shall not become the occasion of a European war." [91] Such an accord could only be founded upon Russia's renunciation of all claims to a special interest in Bulgaria, since her adversaries would be content with no less and were prepared to resist the assertion of the smallest of such claims. Russia had not yet gone quite that far, though she was rapidly on the way.

Several newspapers pointed out the bearing of Kálnoky's utterances upon the coming event at Berlin, as defining its significance and indicating its probable outcome. A reconciliation between Germany and Russia could now mean only a general reconciliation with the allies as a group, which Kálnoky had expressed the hope of seeing brought about. After all that had passed, "a Russian approach cannot concern Germany alone, but must affect the Central Powers in general." [92]

[89] *N. F. P.*, November 9. Speech of November 8 to the Austrian Delegation. "Auch in England bewegt sich fast die gesammte öffentliche Meinung in dieser Richtung, so dass ich hoffen darf, dass bei der Durchführung unseres Programms uns die so gewichtige Unterstützung dieser Macht deren politische Ziele und Interessen im Osten mit den unseren und jenen Italiens identisch sind, nicht fehlen wird." [90] *Ibid.*, November 6. [91] *Ibid.*, November 9.
[92] *M. A. Z.*, November 10. Vienna, November 7. *Kölnische Zeitung*, Novem-

The last speech of the group was delivered by Lord Salisbury at the Lord Mayor's banquet, on November 9. His treatment of foreign policy was, for the most part, intended to reassure the nation in the midst of current alarms.[93] But he also described certain aims in language much the same as that used by Crispi; then he expressed his agreement with both ministers who had spoken before him. "We have read recently," he stated, "the speeches of two distinguished men — the Foreign Ministers of Austria and Italy — two States with whom our sympathies are deeply bound up, and whose interests are in many respects closely coincident with our own. We have read their speeches — speeches which have given encouragement to the world to hope for the maintenance of peace, and we believe that they both aim at the objects which I have defined as the objects of English policy. They have expressed, not without justice, not without ground, a hope that they will have the sympathy of England on their side; and the sympathy of England I believe they will have with them, and all the influence she can command will be cast on the side of the nations whose efforts are directed to the maintenance of freedom, of legality, and of peace."

The accord against Russia showed itself complete and unbroken: every mesh of Bismarck's net held fast. Russia had practically ceased to struggle; but the trapper may have reckoned that a blow on the head would quiet his game still more thoroughly.

ber 8: "Wenn Russland sich der conservativen Politik der Mittelmächte nähern will, wollen wir nicht prüfen ob dies gutem Willen oder der erkannten eisernen Nothwendigkeit entspringt. Wir werden jede Lösung der Orient-Frage gutheissen, welche gleichermassen Oesterreich und Russland befriedigt. Deutschland wird keiner Verständigung Russlands mit Oesterreich in den Weg treten, dabei aber überzeugt bleiben,dass Russlands Politik gegen Deutschland um kein Haar ehrlicher werden als seither."

[93] *Times*, November 10. "Speaking . . . of the general prospects of the world in respect to peace, I am aware that a certain uneasiness exists, yet I know nothing within the compass of diplomatic knowledge that could give to uneasiness ground. As long as great nations maintain enormous and increasing armies, and spend still greater sums every year in sharpening the weapons which, if the necessity should arise, they may use against each other, as long as that competition of armaments continues it is idle to hope that tranquillity can prevail over the world. But . . . I do not believe that there is any justification for the uneasiness to which I have referred." The confidence is touching, after the approaches recently made to him by the Tsar.

Bismarck's last blow to Russia before the Tsar reached Berlin fell on November 10. It took the form of an order to the Reichsbank to accept no more Russian paper as security for loans. It gave the not unexpected official turn to the campaign against Russia's credit, which had been actively resumed after a short lull while the Stettin interview stood in prospect. A month before the action, Herbert Bismarck had addressed a memorandum to his father, reminding him that "Your Highness has given instructions that the newspaper campaign against Russian bonds should be continued," and, likewise, the orders affecting the investment of trust funds by public authorities. What Count Herbert had further recommended was an order against the discounting of any foreign bonds by the Reichsbank.[94] The material effects of such a measure would have been largely confined to Russian paper, which was by far the most plentiful in the country. The special designation of Russia could have been for moral effect alone. It was still not a fatal stroke; for private bankers continued to deal in Russian securities. Indeed, the whole campaign was managed in a fashion conducive to a gradual unloading of Russian obligations without injuring German investors by a serious break in the market.

Public opinion in Europe was at a loss to account for this measure, timed as it was between the announcement of Alexander's visit and the visit itself. A not unnatural supposition was that "Bismarck's intention has been either to hinder the Czar from going to Berlin or else to make it plainly known to the world that His Majesty's visit has no political significance."[95] The Chancellor's knowledge of the Tsar's state of mind and its causes might well have prompted him to avoid an encounter that promised to be extremely embarrassing; but the motives behind his action lay actually deeper still.

The reasons officially alleged for the measure were economic, based largely upon the theory of reprisal for similar acts on the part of Russia. A long article in the *Kölnische Zeitung*, on November 14, explained the order as simply one stroke — neither the first nor to be the last — in a battle begun some time ago, and on

[94] G. F. O., v, pp. 333–334.  [95] *Times*, November 12. Vienna, November 11.

which the Tsar's visit could have no bearing.[96] The "Economist" of the *Neue Freie Presse* took issue with all economic and financial interpretations of the order, maintaining that the effects aimed at were purely moral and political. This had been the interpretation placed upon the earlier press campaign by the Belgian minister at Berlin. Now the Vienna journalist wrote: "Prince Bismarck aims to conduct Russia into the paths of his own peaceful policy; he aims to bring home to the powerful Tsar the consciousness that the Russian monarchy is dependent economically upon Germany; he aims to wound the state economically in order to dominate it politically." [97] Lavino from Vienna even ventured to circulate the report in the *Times* that Bismarck would set definite conditions upon the ending of the financial strife — not only the curbing of Russia's tendencies toward France, but the dismissal of her minister of finance, Vyshnegradski, as well.[98] The report was not denied in Germany until after the interview.[99]

In the same batch of correspondence with this report Lavino included certain observations on the diplomatic possibilities of

[96] "Unsere Industrie ist der Eingang über die russische Gränze nahezu verschlossen, neuerdings sind Zölle eingeführt worden, die nur als eine feindselige politische Kundgebung aufgefasst werden konnten. Den deutschen Staatsangehörigen ist der Erwerb von Grundeigenthum, die Anlegung von Fabriken in den russischen Gränzprovinzen untersagt. Der Ankauf von Wechseln in deutscher Sprache ist von der russischen Reichsbank abgelehnt worden. Wenn Deutschland gegen solche wirthschaftliche Feindseligkeiten wie sie seit Jahr und Tag von seiten Russlands sich häufen, Gegenmassregeln ergreift, so ist es damit vollkommen in seinem Recht, weil in der Nothwehr. Eine solche Gegenmassregel ist die Ablehnung der Lombardirung russischer Werthe durch die deutsche Reichsbank. Sie ist aber auch ein Glied in der Kette der Bestrebungen, den deutschen Markt von den russischen Werthpapieren möglichst zu befreien, was, von aller Politik abgesehen, volkswirthschaftlich geboten erscheint. . . . Es ist auch in jüngster Zeit, sehr ernstlich die Frage erörtert worden, ob man nicht besondere Zölle gegen russisches Getreide . . . einführen solle, und die Acten dürfen auch über diesen Vorschlag noch schwerlich geschlossen sein."

[97] *N. F. P.*, November 11. In a memorandum of October 24, 1894, recommending withdrawal of the order, Caprivi describes it as having had "a political as well as a financial motive." *G. F. O.*, v, p. 336. On Herbert Bismarck's report, November 1, of Count Shuvalov's remark, "Vous savez, on se fâche sérieusement dès que l'on touche aux poches," the Chancellor made the marginal note: "nicht nur dann, sondern auch,- wenn man mit franz[ösisch-]russ[ischem] Angriff *bedroht* wird." *Ibid.*, v, p. 312.

[98] *Times*, November 16. Vienna, November 15.

[99] *Ibid.*, November 21. Berlin, November 20.

the case. An accord between Russia and the Triple Alliance he pronounced out of the question, disregarding Kálnoky's recent utterances, on the ground that the Alliance formed a closed corporation. "Nevertheless," he added, "it may be that the Czar . . . will be able to conclude a secret treaty of peace with the German Government; and such a treaty, if faithfully observed by Russia, could not fail to have a beneficial effect as regards European peace by leaving France completely isolated."[100] This particular correspondent contributes notably toward building up the universal misconception as to the date of the Reinsurance Treaty — which had already been in existence five months before he penned his lines forecasting it.

Despite Bismarck's brutal stroke at Russia's credit, the Tsar did not draw back this time from his intended visit. His own situation was already too desperate to be greatly affected by another measure more or less on Germany's part. Bismarck displayed a coyness, not wholly affected, about his own share in the coming event. The *Norddeutsche Allgemeine Zeitung*, on November 13, took pains to point out that his presence in Berlin at the time was only "auf Befehl des Kaisers," implying that he would much prefer to keep away and leave the visit restricted to its character of family courtesy. The venerable Emperor did, indeed, display an uncommon interest in the proceedings, and a special desire to make them as productive as possible of results.[101] The harsh and indifferent tone still employed by the semiofficial press in treating the subject was far from prevailing at the Court.

[100] *Times*, November 16. Vienna, November 15.

[101] *M. A. Z.*, November 20. Berlin, November 17. "Während in der Presse der unmittelbar bevorstehende Besuch des Kaisers von Russland mit möglichster Kühle behandelt wird, herrscht in Hofkreisen eine fast fieberhafte Spannung. Der Kaiser selbst betreibt die Vorbereitung für den Empfang seines Grossneffen mit grossem Eifer. Darüber, dass der russische Minister des Auswärtigen, Hr. v. Giers, der Zusammenkunft nicht beiwohnt, versuchen einige Blätter sich mit der Erwägung zu trösten, dass Kaiser Alexander thatsächlich die russische auswärtige Politik selbst mache, so dass eine Besprechung desselben mit dem Reichskanzler völlig genügen würde. . . . Es ist allerdings ein sehr merkwürdiges Zusammentreffen, dass der Besuch des Kaisers von Russland in Berlin mit einer Krisis . . . in Frankreich zusammentrifft."

## V

The Tsar arrived in Berlin on November 18 and spent only the day there. His visit with the Emperor William attracted little attention, yet was of great political significance. At the Emperor's request, Bismarck had supplied him with a memorandum of topics to be taken up with the Tsar. These fell into five numbered groups. The first comprised Germany's complaints against Russia's tariff policy and the conduct of the Russian press. The second had to do with the connection between foreign policy and internal party politics, pointing out the fact that the parties hostile to Germany were also hostile to the monarchical principle everywhere. "Is it the business of a Russian Emperor," was the query William I was to put, "to encourage republican France and to prepare for its [the democratic party's] progress toward Eastern Europe?" The third group of considerations was concerned with the folly and futility of a Russian war against Germany, and included statements of German military strength. The fourth group dwelt in detail upon the political consequences of a general war — the revival of Poland by the Central Powers, a military dictatorship in France, a set of republics replacing the Hapsburg empire in the event of its defeat. And all these consequences depended, according to the memorandum, upon Russia's encouragement of France. The last group of topics outlined by Bismarck touched on the Eastern Question. The statement that Russia's attitude toward Germany had brought about a change in the latter's policy was again put forward, as it had been in the instructions to Schweinitz a month previously. The former state of affairs — meaning Germany's professed support of Russian interests — could only be restored on a condition of reciprocity, under which "Russia would give proof of her good will where, in turn, it would be most useful to us, for example, at Paris, in calming the warlike spirit there." Bismarck's concluding sentence is probably more prophetic than he himself realized: "In sum, the eventual war in prospect would have less the character of a conflict between governments than of a struggle of the red flag against the elements of order and conservatism." [102]

[102] *G. F. O.*, v, pp. 320–323.

A conversation in which all these points were brought out could not have failed to make a profound impression upon the mind of the Tsar. Nevertheless, the main interest of the day centred on the interview between Alexander and Bismarck, which took place after all, in spite of the apparent unwillingness on both sides. Whether still acting under imperial command or not, the Chancellor took the initiative in seeking the encounter. The request was embodied in a note transmitted beforehand to Shuvalov.[103] After Bismarck had paid a formal call at the Russian embassy, the Tsar sent him word that he would be received.

The conversation that ensued was strictly tête-à-tête, and has been reported only in indirect accounts. It lasted for more than an hour, and covered all the points at issue between Germany and Russia, probably in much the same way, on Bismarck's side, as in his memorandum for the Emperor. The Tsar, on his side, had two principal grievances. The less important, the affair of the recent measures against Russia's credit, was dismissed by Bismarck as a matter of general financial policy.[104] The main subject of discussion was Germany's policy in the Bulgarian question. One of the most straightforward newspaper accounts of the interview runs: "It is rumored that the Tsar at this interview made objection to German policy, more especially in the Bulgarian question, as being directed against Russia, this being clear from the mass of correspondence on the subject lying at the Russian foreign office. To this Prince Bismarck is said to have replied that Germany had always considered Bulgaria as lying within the sphere of Russia's interests and had acted accordingly where strictly German inter-

---

[103] *G. F. O.*, v, p. 323.

[104] In volume v of *Zur europäischen Politik*, there occurs at this point a large gap in the reports of the Belgian minister at Berlin. In Maurel are printed several despatches covering the period, described as emanating from 'un des membres les plus distingués du corps diplomatique,' which tally fairly well in the matter of style with the papers of Count van der Straten Ponthoz, whose reports Nieter at Brussels may well have seen. The despatch of November 21 (p. 300) gives an account of the interview said to have been circulated by Count Herbert Bismarck, Holstein, and their friends, according to which, "L'Empereur de Russie aurait commencé par reprocher à l'Allemagne la mesure prise contre les fonds russes; le prince de Bismarck se serait expliqué à ce sujet et aurait annoncé que ces mesures seraient générales et applicables à tous les pays étrangers."

ests were not concerned. Moreover, the Chancellor is said to have expressed a wish to see the correspondence which maintained a contrary view." [105]

Alexander replied by producing copies of the famous 'Bulgarian documents,' together with the despatches of Russian diplomatic agents confirming their allegations against Germany's conduct in regard to Bulgaria.[106] Bismarck was doubtless prepared for something of the sort and had his defence ready, although, according to one account, he appears to have been startled by the nature and volume of the evidence placed before him.[107] His defence was that the documents attributed to Ferdinand and Prince Reuss were simply forgeries, and that the recent change in the instructions to the German ambassador at Constantinople had been brought about by Russia's demonstrations of hostility toward Germany.[108] Bismarck himself afterwards told the Prussian cabinet that, in further refutation of Alexander's charges that he had favored Ferdinand's adventure in Bulgaria, "He had shown him, on the faith of a letter from the Duke of Coburg, that he had done the contrary, and had expressed the strongest opposition to seeing any German prince go there." [109] But Bismarck was never con-

---

[105] *Nationalzeitung*, November 22.

[106] Maurel, pp. 300–301. Despatch of November 21. "Après s'être plaint d'un changement imprévu et complet dans la politique allemande en Bulgarie, et le prince de Bismarck protestant avec force contre cette affirmation, disant que si l'Allemagne a des intérêts directs en Bulgarie qu'elle ne voudrait pour aucune considération ne pas soutenir, elle croit que la Russie doit avoir la plus grande part d'influence en ce pays, le Czar mit sous les yeux du prince de Bismarck cinq rapports confidentiels et secrets sur les menées soi-disant d'agents allemands en Bulgarie, puis une copie de documents qui avaient été échangés entre le prince de Bismarck et le prince Ferdinand." See also *Kölnische Zeitung*, November 23.

[107] Maurel, p. 303. Despatch of November 22. General Albedyll is said to have passed on the story told him by the Tsar's aide, General Cherevin, "que le chancelier avait été extrêmement interloqué des pièces et des faits que le Czar lui avait exhibés. Interloqué complètement, ' comme un homme pris à la jambe par un piège,' — expression du Czar racontant l'affaire à Tchérévine,—il avait assez promptement repris son aplomb et avait répliqué avec force qu'il était tout saisi de l'impudence de ses ennemis: qu'il désirait connaître le source, qu'elle devait être française, qu'il pouvait prouver au Czar en lui montrant les pièces diplomatiques, vraies, relatives à la Bulgarie, addressées surtout à Vienne, qu'on avait abusé du Czar."

[108] *G. F. O.*, v, p. 203.     [109] Lucius von Ballhausen, pp. 404–405.

tent to maintain the defensive in a controversy. In debate, as in warfare, he understood the advantage of attack. He passed quickly from his justification of Germany's policy to a denunciation of those responsible for the charges brought against him and of the conduct of the Tsar's own subjects toward his country.

Taking up first the intrigue by which Alexander had been deceived, the Chancellor alleged that it was of Orleanist origin, the work of a European war party, adherents of which might have to be hunted out in Germany itself by the public prosecutor. So runs, at any rate, the account of the well informed *Kölnische Zeitung*, which continues in the same vein: "In the course of the interview, it was further brought out that a small but influential group in court circles here is partly responsible for arousing in the Tsar's mind the groundless belief that the Emperor William is not in full accord with his Chancellor's policy." [110]

Turning then to Russia, Bismarck complained of the massing of troops on her western frontiers as a cause of public alarm and ill feeling: the Tsar replied that nothing had really taken place beyond certain readjustments of a routine character, with no ulterior motives that he was aware of.[111] It was now Alexander who had to do the explaining and defending. He acquitted himself of the task with rather bad grace, but in all frankness and anxiety to do the right thing. Bismarck told his cabinet that he had pressed the attack by continuing: "The attitude of the Russian press and of the generals has made it hard for Germany to remain friendly. He would have to speak quite frankly (whereupon, the Tsar 'avec un rire jaune' interjected, 'allez — allez'); Germany would be showing a lack of respect for the Russian power, if she did not look about her in every possible direction for allies against Russia's hostile attitude. The treaty with Italy was of old standing and had not been modified by Crispi's visit. If the

[110] *Kölnische Zeitung*, November 23. According to Lucius von Ballhausen (p. 406), this article and the ensuing one of the 25th (see note 120, *infra*) were directly 'inspired' by Bismarck.

[111] *N. F. P.*, November 29. "Jetzt wird erzählt, der Czar habe die Beschwerde des Fürsten Bismarck über die Truppenvorschiebungen an die russische Westgrenze mit dem Bemerken erwidert, es könnten dabei nur gewöhnliche dienstliche Rücksichten im Spiele sein; von anderen Motiven wisse er nichts." See also Corti, p. 310.

world could only learn that the Russian Emperor had told *him* he would not attack Germany, peace would be assured." Perceiving the implication of this last remark, "the Tsar repudiated the very idea of an alliance with France *et avec cet animal*, Boulanger, but he began abusing the Austrians." [112]

Here the conversation touched upon the broader aspect of the whole state of affairs, the fact that the strained relations between Germany and Russia were not simply the result of misunderstandings between themselves, but involved Germany's quarrel with France and Russia's with Austria. Bismarck hastened to impress upon Alexander's mind the further fact that these two elements in the situation stood on a totally different footing. He might ask and receive assurances that Russia would not enter into an alliance with France, but he could give no corresponding assurances on Germany's part with respect to Austria, for the very good reason that, in the latter case, the alliance already existed. In a circular telegram to the German ambassadors, on the 19th of the month, the Chancellor states: "The Emperor Alexander was already aware, from our official communications, that we are bound by a treaty to assist Austria against a Russian attack: the fact was brought out anew in our conversation yesterday." [113] This reminder amounted to a clear notification to the Tsar that, whatever treaties might be signed between Germany and Russia alone, Austria must always be taken into account in their relations with each other. It followed with equal clearness that no reconciliation between these two could be complete without including at least the elements of a reconciliation between Russia and Austria.

This seems to have been all that was said on the most fundamental aspect of the situation. It left matters on both sides about as they had stood before. Russia had not given up her case against Austria: Germany had not renounced her guaranty of Austria against any untoward consequences of her opposition to Russia. Nevertheless, assurances were exchanged which somewhat eased the existing strain. "The Tsar," Bismarck related to the cabi-

[112] Lucius von Ballhausen, p. 405.
[113] *G. F. O.*, v, p. 324. Crispi, p. 211 (*Memoirs*, ii, p. 262).

net, "promised him to take measures, on his return, to bring the press to order." The circular telegram referred to above states specifically that Alexander had also expressed "his resolution to enter into no aggressive coalition and never to attack Germany." The telegram goes on to say that the Tsar was informed "that from the future of Bulgaria no cause would ever arise for Germany to depart from her neutrality, and that our attitude in regard to the Bulgarian question will be regulated, in the future as in the past, by the terms of the treaty of Berlin."

Shortly afterward, the newspapers were printing what purported to be a circular despatch from the Russian foreign office, which summarized the main points of the interview as follows: "(1) After a careful review of the situation, Prince Bismarck and the Czar agreed that there was no present reason for a breach between the two Empires. (2) A declaration was made on the part of Prince Bismarck that in Bulgarian affairs he meant to observe the most perfect neutrality. (3) It was agreed that all misunderstandings between the two Empires were traceable to the intemperate language of their respective Presses, which would thenceforth be restrained by official dissuasion and interference." [114]

Supposing this to have been the sole result of the interview, Bismarck had yet spent an extremely profitable hour with the Tsar, and, between hard work and good fortune, had profited handsomely by the imperial visit. He had cleared himself of the charges brought against him and shifted the responsibility for recent misunderstandings from his own shoulders. The Tsar had made promises, which he would keep, even though he might wonder afterward how they had been obtained from him and suspect that the means had not been entirely honorable. A recently published story has it that he had begun to doubt before his visitor was out of sight, and that he remarked to Shuvalov as the two mounted the stairs: "I didn't believe a word Bismarck said; he is too clever for me." [115]

Yet at the court banquet that evening, Alexander showed only

[114] *Times*, December 8. Berlin, December 7.
[115] Eckardstein, i, p. 136. As told by Count Thiessenhausen, who was present.

the utmost good will.[116] He "pointedly drank to the health of Prince Bismarck, sending round his personal attendant to the Chancellor, who sat a good way off, to announce his intention of doing so. In return for this compliment the Chancellor rose, and with a profound bow emptied his glass 'to His Russian Majesty.'"[117] To all appearances, a new era of Russo-German friendship had set in.

As the Tsar's train drew out of Berlin, however, an atmosphere of mutual suspicion once more settled down over both parties to the understanding. Alexander's sense of having been duped became stronger.[118] Bismarck, on his side, began to question the Tsar's ability to resist the pernicious influences under which he was placing himself anew.[119] In his circular telegram next day, he wrote: "We must wait and see if His Majesty's good intentions have any moderating effect on the attitude of the Russian press, officials, and ambassadors — especially, of the one at Paris." No signs of an improvement in relations were discernible in the usual

[116] Maurel, p. 299. A despatch dated November 19 describes the attitudes of the principal personages at the banquet. — "Une attitude respectueuse du Czar pour l'empereur Guillaume . . .; froideur visible et caractérisée de l'empereur pour le comte Herbert de Bismarck à qui, dit-on, le Czar attribue une grosse part de responsabilité dans la récente affaire des fonds russes . . . Amabilités démonstratives pour le prince de Bismarck, qui plus que jamais avait l'air de les attendre et de les recevoir comme un dû."

[117] *Times*, November 21. Berlin, November 20. According to Lucius von Ballhausen (p. 405) the sending round of an attendant was made necessary by an error in the seating arrangement which put Bismarck in the thirteenth place to the Tsar's left. He was so angered at the slight, which he never forgot, that he came near leaving the hall before the banquet began.

[118] Maurel, pp. 301–304. Despatch of November 21. "L'irritation du Czar est restée très grande: il a quitté Berlin, convaincu que le prince de Bismarck s'était joué de lui et que cette action occulte se produit en Bulgarie d'accord avec le prince Ferdinand, et forme un des côtés de la nouvelle alliance austro-italo-allemande." Despatch of November 22. Cherevin has related "que le Czar était persuadé au fond que M. de Bismarck l'avait joué et qu'il lui mentait."

[119] *Zur europäischen Politik*, v, p. 209. December 9, Count van der Straten Ponthoz: "Dans l'audience qu'il lui a donnée le 18 novembre le Czar avait inspiré au Prince de Bismarck la plus entière certitude qu'il voulait la paix. Mais cette confiance qu'il donnait à Berlin aux assurances pacifiques du Czar, le Chancelier n'était pas convaincu que le Czar la justifierait encore lorsque rentré à Pétersbourg, il se retrouverait circonvenu par les panslavistes et les autres instigateurs de la guerre." Twice in Bismarck's telegram on the interview he makes the point that all the results must remain in doubt until after the Tsar's return.

indices of opinion. The *Kölnische Zeitung*, on November 25, dwelt upon the uncertainties that still lay ahead, following the Tsar's return to St. Petersburg. It brought out the fact that fundamental causes of differences had not been regulated — chief among these, Russia's continued hostility to Austria, Germany's inseparable ally. The conclusion was that, nevertheless, Germany would accept Russia's advances in good faith and recur to her thankless task of straightening out the entanglements in relations between Russia and Austria.[120]

The interview seemed by all indications to have brought forth no immediate results.[121] In fact, it had none, but formed only one step in the readjustment of Russo-German relations. The Tsar had promised; now let him perform. His defiance had been broken; his complete subjection must follow. If more pressure were needed, it would be applied; but no leniency was to be expected.

[120] "Man darf wohl annehmen, dass der Zar Berlin mit der Ueberzeugung verlassen hat, dass Leute, welche vorgaben, ihm zu dienen, es gewagt haben, ihn gründlich hinters Licht zu führen. Ob diese Ueberzeugung, mit welcher der Zar in Russland vorerst ziemlich vereinsamt stehen wird, stark genug sein wird, um sich inmitten einer feindlichen Welt zu behaupten, ob der Zar die Macht hat, derselben praktische Folge zu geben, seine Beamten zur Ordnung zu rufen, seine diplomatischen Agenten an Wahrheitsliebe zu gewöhnen, die russische Presse zu zügeln, das kann nur die Erfahrung lehren. . . . Wir möchten das Ergebniss des Zarenbesuches in Berlin, welches vielleicht auch der wankenden französischen Republik und ihrem Präsidenten mittelbar zu gute kommt, nicht unterschätzen, aber wir haben mit Russland zu üble Erfahrungen gemacht, als dass wir Lust haben könnten, dasselbe zu überschätzen. Auch nach Beseitigung des Unraths, welchen elende Ränkeschmiede zwischen Russland und Deutschland aufgehäuft haben, bleibt der Verstimmungsstoff, der seinen Grund in thatsächlichen Verhältnissen hat, noch schlimm genug. Wir brauchen nur das Wort Oesterreich auszusprechen, um eine Welt von Gegensätzen vor uns aufsteigen zu sehen; denn Russland grollt Oesterreich, Deutschland aber wird trotz aller Lockungen an dem Bündniss mit Oesterreich und Italien festhalten. . . . Wir jede Annäherung Russlands an den friedenverbürgenden Dreibund mit Freuden begrüssen würden, obgleich diese Annäherung die Aufgabe der deutschen Politik den Verbündeten gegenüber schwieriger und verwickelter machen würde und die jetzige Lage wenigstens den Vorzug der Klarheit und Einfachheit besitzt."

[121] *Times*, November 22. St. Petersburg, November 20. "The reiterated opinion of the German Press that no great political importance or change attaches to the Imperial interview is willingly repeated by the Russian newspapers . . ." Vienna, November 21. "The meeting between the two Emperors at Berlin has excited very little interest in Vienna. . . ."

# CHAPTER XII

## THE TRIPLE ENTENTE OF DECEMBER

### I

BACK in his retreat at Varzin, the more Bismarck thought over the interview with the Tsar, the lower fell his confidence in its results. To a guest who remarked upon his troubled mien and the failure of his accustomed appetite for meat and drink, he briefly replied: "Die Tagen in Berlin waren sehr sauer."[1] He was evidently determined not to relax his pressure upon Russia, and yet feared that he could not continue it with impunity. He felt sure that Russia would not of her own motion make the existing situation a cause of war; but there was no telling what she might do if pressed too far. The success of his whole combination depended upon England's fidelity to the Austro-Italian partnership; and, this secure, much would still depend upon England's activity in the common cause. "The Russians will not start a war there," he told his friend, Booth, on November 21, in speaking of the reports of troop movements on the Austrian border — "I answer for that. . . . The possibility of war depends upon something quite different — upon the attitude England takes toward Russia; whether she takes the part of a charging bull, or that of an asthmatic fatted ox. If the latter, our alliance with Italy will be of small assistance to us, since she would have to use up half her army in defence of her coasts against France. The combined German, Austrian, and Italian fleets are not yet a match for the French. But if England plays the charging bull, not only will the French fleet be neutralized, but even Turkey will then join against Russia."[2] Not from Russia, then, did the peril of war come: it lay in Bismarck's own combinations. Russia must surrender unconditionally, and she would do so peaceably only before an overwhelming show of force. And the force of the opposition

[1] Booth, p. 73.   [2] *Ibid.*, p. 72.

would be overwhelming in proportion as England's part in it was active and obvious.

Yet Bismarck persisted in following out his plan. His fears concerning the unreliability of England gave way before his fears as to the future of his relations with Russia unless a reckoning were definitely reached of a nature to prevent the recurrence of the existing situation. And the reckoning must be as Austria desired it. In connection with the conflict of doubts going on in his mind, he remarked: "While England's unreliability is the result of too many leaders, in Russia the single leadership of the Tsar is unreliable."[3] It was in this frame of mind that he composed the letter, defining Germany's policy, which Salisbury had asked to have before entering into the new agreement with Italy and Austria.

This letter, which was finally sent off on November 22, was drafted and revised with extraordinary care, as befitted its importance.[4] Bismarck took as his text Salisbury's remark to Hatzfeldt about the supposed pro-Russian sympathies of Prince William. He did not contest the English opinions as to the prince's sentiments; but he did maintain that these afforded no just grounds of apprehension as to his future policy as a ruler. No German sovereign, he asserted, would find it possible to frame his policy simply according to his personal feelings. The character of the German military system would forbid his entering upon a war not indorsed by the entire nation and justified by clearly evident aims of national interest.

Leaving Salisbury to infer that a war against England would never find the requisite popular approval, Bismarck went on to apply to the existing situation the principles he had laid down. He excluded the entire Eastern Question from the domain of pos-

[3] Booth, p. 72.
[4] *G. F. O.*, iv, p. 376, note. The text of the letter is given on pp. 329–333, *infra*. Holstein wrote in 1901: "Prince Bismarck's taking such an unusual step at the height of his power — I never remember his writing directly like this to any other foreign Prime Minister — shows the importance he attached to Lord Salisbury's reply." *Daily Telegraph*, May 13, 1912. Vienna, May 8. In connection with this statement, it must be noted that there had been an exchange of personal letters, on a matter of much less importance, between these two statesmen, in July, 1885, in which Salisbury wrote first. See *G. F. O.*, iv, pp. 132–134.

sible occasions of a popular war, concluding by implication that Germany could, therefore, not be expected to join the coalition he was urging England to enter. But he also assured Salisbury that Germany did acknowledge interests beyond the defence of her own frontiers against actual attack, for which she would be prepared to go to war. The most immediate of these would be the protection of Austria's integrity and her standing as a Great Power. Yet menaced as Germany was by a combined attack from an incorrigibly aggressive France and a Russia pushed into war by Panslavism and internal conflicts, she was bound to strive by diplomatic means to escape the hard necessity of taking up arms in defence of her Austrian neighbor. Bismarck was careful to point out that Germany's reluctance to take the risk of war would be greatly diminished by assurance of support from the other Powers similarly interested in maintaining the European status quo. "If the alliance of the friendly Powers threatened by *the same* warlike nations should fail us," he wrote, "our situation in a war on two frontiers would not be hopeless; but a war against both France and Russia, even if it turned out as glorious a military exploit for us as the Seven Years' War, would still be so great a calamity for the country that we should endeavor to avert it by a friendly arrangement with Russia — if it had to be waged *without* an ally."

This statement represents Bismarck's nearest approach to a proposal for an Anglo-German alliance in this letter. Serious misgivings restrained him from going further. Nothing had happened to alter his settled opinion that an English alliance was at best an uncertain speculation. His friend, Salisbury, was indeed in power; but the enemies of his policy, Gladstone and Churchill, were still active in political life, and might upset his calculations at any moment. At the outset he had made it clear to Lord Salisbury that, if an anti-English policy on Germany's part was not to be feared, neither was a pro-English policy to be hoped for. To dispel Salisbury's apprehensions on the score of Prince William's future conduct, Bismarck had written: "Such a thing would not be possible in Germany — nor, for that matter, could the contrary case arise. His Imperial Highness the Crown Prince would be no more willing or able, as Emperor, to mould his policy according to English influences, than Prince William, in his place, to conduct a policy dictated from St. Petersburg." [5]

The sentence apparently leading up to the offer of an alliance, then, was followed only by the cautious statement: "But so long as we have the assurance of not being left in the lurch by the Powers whose interests are identical with ours, no German Emperor can depart from the policy of protecting the independence of those friendly Powers which are satisfied like ourselves with the existing order in Europe and ready to act without hesitation or weakness, should their independence be threatened." Returning to the question at issue, the formation of an accord against Russia, Bismarck wrote: "We shall keep out of war with Russia so long as is compatible with our honor and safety, and so long as the independence of Austria-Hungary, whose existence as a Great Power is a primary necessity for us, is not called into question. We desire that the friendly Powers having interests in the East which we do not share should make themselves strong enough to hold Russia's sword in its scabbard or to make head against her if circumstances should lead to a breach. So long as no German interest were at stake, we should remain neutral; but there is not the remotest possibility that a German Emperor would ever give armed *support* to Russia in striking down or enfeebling one of the Powers on whose support we count for preventing a Russian war or helping us to face one. Holding this point of view, our policy will *always* compel Germany to take her place in the line of battle, if the independence of Austria-Hungary should be endangered by a Russian attack, or if England or Italy should be in peril of invasion by French armies."

[5] With regard to the crown prince's attitude, Bismarck had made some significant observations in July, 1887, to Lucius von Ballhausen (pp. 395-396): "Für die englische Politik sei die Meinung, der Kronprinz werde einst eine russenfeindliche und innerlich liberale Politik machen, von einer unschätzbaren Bedeutung, und darum erhielt man diese Meinung aufrecht. . . . Übrigens irre man sich in dieser Beurteilung des Kronprinzen. Der Kronprinz habe ihm noch jetzt vor seiner Abreise nach England in Gegenwart der Kronprinzess erklärt, er wünsche ihn als leitenden Minister zu behalten im Falle eines Thronwechsels. Bismarck hat darauf geantwortet; Das könne nur sein, wenn er eine deutsche und nicht eine fremde (englische) Politik machen wolle."

These declarations were not much to offer; but Bismarck would commit himself to nothing more. "For my own part," he concluded, "I must repeat my conviction that the principles of policy imposed upon Germany now and for the future are so absolutely fixed that the warmest sympathies for a foreign power or political party could never lead a German Emperor or government to depart from them." All that Bismarck actually proposed in his letter, therefore, was the formation of an accord for a special purpose between England and Germany's two allies. All that he specifically promised was that Germany would protect her friends against incurring any vital injury through the pursuit of their proper interests.[6]

Yet it is hard to believe that the German Chancellor would have taken so extraordinary a step without more far reaching possibilities in view. He had threatened the Russians with counter-coalitions if the project of a Franco-Russian alliance continued to develop. Despite all Bismarck's misgivings as to an English alliance, despite all his reserve in defining Germany's position and policy, the suspicion lingers that he had more in his mind than he ventured to put down on paper. If he saw the remotest possibility ahead that the progress of events might make an alliance desirable, he was the man to take his soundings in advance. This view of the case is borne out by the fact that, little more than a year later, he made a definite bid for a defensive treaty against France.[7] He had made one statement that might very well be taken as a hint. That he had immediately sheered off from the subject and taken refuge in a series of elaborately qualified definitions of policy, may have been calculated only to induce England to take the initiative.

[6] The interpretation of this letter has been the subject of considerable controversy. Eckardstein maintains (iii, p. 22) that it was intended as the first step in negotiations for an alliance. Rachfahl, after asserting that its sole purpose was to hasten the special agreement between England, Austria, and Italy (*Weltwirtschaftliches Archiv*, July 1, 1920), recanted to the extent of admitting that Bismarck may have intended incidentally to sound England regarding an alliance (*ibid.*, October, 1921). Hans Rothfels, in *Preussische Jahrbücher*, March, 1922 (pp. 283–284, note), insists that Rachfahl's first interpretation is the correct one. The editors of the German foreign office publication (iv, p. 376, note) take the same stand.

[7] *G. F. O.*, iv, pp. 400–403. January 11, 1889, Bismarck to Hatzfeldt.

If Bismarck was relying on Salisbury to read between the lines of his epistle, his confidence was not misplaced. Salisbury later told Eckardstein, following upon his account of the Tsar's previous approach: "But I likewise returned an evasive answer to Bismarck when he wrote me a long personal letter suggesting that England form an alliance with Germany and Austria, for the maintenance of world peace."[8] In this answer, given under date of November 30, the British prime minister only expressed his thanks for the confidence reposed in him, and concurred with Bismarck in testifying to "the sympathy and the close coincidence of interest existing between the two nations."[9]

Although Lord Salisbury avoided all reference to the subject of the alliance at which he may have felt Bismarck was really aiming, he gave ample satisfaction on the score of the accord with Italy and Austria, with which Bismarck's letter had been mainly concerned. The value of that accord, he stated, depended wholly upon Austria's intention to execute her engagements actively and without restraint. His apprehension was that, when the critical moment came, she would shrink from the war with Russia which the agreement might entail, and would accept compensation for letting Russia have her way. The hint was implied that the accord, ostensibly in defence of Turkey, might even serve Austria to extort more compensation at Turkey's expense. Whether she took one course or the other would depend in turn upon her confidence in Germany's ultimate support. "When therefore," he continued, "we were asked to join in an understanding upon the eight bases which were given to Sir Edward Malet, it became on consideration very evident that the one vital question to us was one which was not even alluded to in these eight bases — namely the probable attitude of Germany. If Austria could count on German support in such a struggle, it would be possible for her to carry out fully the policy indicated in the eight bases to which England was asked to adhere. In any other case, England by giving this adhesion might be committing herself to a policy pre-

[8] Eckardstein, ii, p. 154.
[9] For the text, see Appendix, *infra*, pp. 333-335. The first publication of both letters (in German translations) was in Hammann's *Zur Vorgeschichte des Weltkrieges* (Berlin, 1919).

doomed to failure." These misgivings had only been accentuated by the news that Prince William's accession to the throne might come about sooner than had been expected.

After registering all these shrewd hits at Bismarck's own apparent policy, Lord Salisbury professed satisfaction with the real policy he found behind it. He assured Bismarck: "Your Serene Highness has removed my apprehensions by the great frankness with which you have exposed the true situation to me. You have in the first place allowed me to see the Treaty between Austria and Germany which established that under no circumstances could the existence of Austria be imperilled by resistance to illegal Russian enterprises. In the second place you have conveyed to Sir Edward Malet, on the part of the Emperor, his moral approbation of any agreement which may be come to by Austria, Italy, and England on the three bases submitted to us: and in the third place you have convincingly explained to me that the course of Germany must be dictated by the considerations of national interest felt by the nation at large, and not by the personal prepossessions of the reigning Sovereign."

Satisfied with Germany's attitude toward the projected understanding, Salisbury stated that England was now prepared to enter it and to observe it loyally. He concluded: "The Grouping of States which has been the work of the last year, will be an effective barrier against any possible aggression of Russia; and the construction of it will not be among the least services, which Your Serene Highness has rendered to the cause of European peace." The extent of Bismarck's share in bringing about this combination in restraint of Russian policy is thus amply emphasized in Salisbury's letter. Rumors of the agreement were already being triumphantly circulated by German newspapers in advance of its actual formation.[10]

[10] *Kölnische Zeitung*, November 28. "After the renewal of the Central European Alliance last spring it was stated on good authority that this alliance had been entered into with the approval of England and for the restoration of the equilibrium in the Mediterranean. Since that time negotiations are said to have taken place providing for certain eventualities, in which the coöperation of the English fleet in concert with those of the Powers desiring peace was secured, without, however, any formal treaty being entered into. One of the practical results of these negotiations, it is said, is the protection of and inviolability of Turkish territory."

While Bismarck was engaged in these secret negotiations for imposing new bonds upon Russia's liberty of action, Germany was presenting officially a most forbidding front to her eastern neighbor. On November 24, the Emperor's opening address was read to the Reichstag and found to contain as many hits at Russia as if the recent interviews had never taken place. A new tariff on Russian grain was announced — this only a fortnight after the blow at Russian securities. But the most serious announcement from the point of view of foreign policy was that of a law extending the liability to service in the Landsturm. This proposal, as the minister of war later pointed out, stands in direct connection with a passage further on in the speech, dealing with foreign relations. "The un-Christian tendency toward aggression against neighboring peoples," it runs, "is foreign to the German character. The Constitution and military establishment of the Empire are not designed to disturb the peace of our neighbors by wanton attacks. But for the repelling of such attacks and for the defence of our independence, we are strong; and we want, with God's help, to become so strong that we may face any danger calmly." [11] The reference was unmistakable and indicated small confidence in the Tsar's recent assurances. The *Post* concluded its remarks upon the speech by a reference to the concentration of Russian troops near the frontier and by a warlike note of the sort for which it was becoming notorious: "The sun of a Russo-Austrian war stands in the morning sky." [12]

The zeal for expanding Germany's military strength and for arranging new alliances and accords surely did not indicate belief in a peaceful future. And there are indications at the same moment that Bismarck was making his bids for new partnerships, not only to England, but to certain second-rate Powers as well. Be it recalled that treaties already existed attaching Serbia and Rumania to the Triple Alliance as auxiliaries to its policy in the Near East. Indeed, the existing government of Bulgaria was practically a partner in the system. These humble associates were grouped round Austria for the restraint of Russian policy. The new agree-

[11] *Stenographische Berichte*, session of 1887–88, p. 2.
[12] *Post*, November 24.

ment in course of negotiation with England was designed to associate her more closely with this group. The agreement of February had brought England chiefly into contact with Italy over common interests in the Mediterranean. To this accordance Spain had become attached by an agreement with Italy in May, to which Austria and Germany had acceded.[13] Spain promised, among other things, to enter into no engagements with France prejudicial to any of the allies, and to coöperate with Italy in the affairs of North Africa. Thus there existed another group of associates centring round Italy and concerned with her rivalry with France. As the Eastern group incidentally served to strengthen Germany's hands against Russia, so the Mediterranean group gave her partners encircling France.

The new manner of approach to England indicates a desire to form a third group of associates connected directly with Germany. Designated by nature as candidates for this group were the two states lying between Germany and France and England. As early as November 24, it was rumored that the German government was making representations at Brussels and the Hague regarding the advisability of establishing closer relations between the two and with the Triple Alliance.[14] Austria and Italy were later reported to have lent their support to the step.[15] These representations of late November were probably neither the first nor the last of their kind. They do not appear to have been immediately successful; but a current of opinion was started in Belgian official circles in favor of the theory that the treaty of London, already proved worthless in any case by the develop-

---

[13] Pribram, i, pp. 48 et seq. (Amer., i, pp. 116 et seq.). Lucius von Ballhausen (p. 373) records, under date of March 2, 1887, an observation of Bismarck concerning Spain's relation to his system of alliances and accords: "Auch Spanien wolle mitgehen, habe aber wenig Entgegenkommen gefunden."

[14] *N. F. P.*, November 25. Brussels, November 24. "In diplomatischen Kreisen will man wissen, dass von Berlin hier und im Haag ein gewisser Druck ausgeübt werde, um zwischen Holland und Belgien ein militärisches Einverständniss anzubauen, das bei gewissen Eventualitäten den genannten Staaten ermöglichen würde, sich der Friedens-Liga anzuschliessen. Da aber Belgiens Neutralität keinen offenen Pact dieser Art gestattet, so müsste wenigstens officiell von einer derartigen Convention abgesehen werden." See also Plehn, p. 300.

[15] *Ibid.*, November 28. Brussels, November 28.

ments of February, did not really restrict Belgium's liberty to enter upon purely defensive agreements such as that proposed.[16]

The British negotiations found a speedier conclusion. The agreement, which embraced all the eight points proposed in October, together with an engagement to reveal them to Turkey only by common consent, was completed in the form of identic notes signed by Salisbury and Károlyi, the Austrian ambassador at London, on December 12.[17] Salisbury declared himself "charged by H. M<sup>y's</sup> Government to communicate to the Austro-Hungarian Government their entire adhesion to the nine points recited in the identic note of the two powers." This was much more binding than the previous indefinite agreement with Italy. The Italian note of adhesion to this agreement is dated December 16.[18]

The opposition to Russia was thus rendered solid and secure. Her setback had been converted into definite defeat, which it only remained for her to acknowledge. Germany, as Bismarck had planned, was still not directly involved; but his assurances to the members of the anti-Russian group left no doubt of his support of their policy.

For some time longer Russia continued to display a not unnatural reluctance to accept the decision as final. Doubts were current in St. Petersburg as to whether Bismarck's denial of the 'Bulgarian documents,' even if borne out, had any vital connection with his general policy toward Russia.[19] These documents

[16] *M. A. Z.*, December 3. Brussels, December 1. "Ob nun thatsächlich derartige Verhandlungen stattgefunden haben oder nicht, das *eine* steht fest, dass anlässlich der Erörterung der Frage, ob Belgien überhaupt allianzfähig ist, die Stellung des Königreichs im europäischen Staatencomplex fast von der gesammten Presse ganz falsch beurtheilt worden ist. . . . Unsere massgebenden Kreise fassen die belgische Neutralität durchaus nicht in dem Sinne auf, dass dem Königreich dadurch jedes selbständige Vorgehen versagt, seine Selbständigkeit also beeinträchtigt würde. . . . Dagegen ist es Belgien sehr wohl erlaubt, solche Bündnisse einzugehen, welche seine eigene Selbsterhaltung betreffen und keinen Angriff gegen irgendeine Nation in sich schliessen. Wäre die Tripelallianz eine Offensivallianz, so würde Belgien gegen die Londoner Conferenz handeln, wenn es sich derselben anschliessen wollte. Das deutsch-österreichisch-italienische Bündniss ist aber ausschliesslich Defensivallianz, und nichts hindert Belgien einer Friedensliga beizutreten, deren erhöhte Stärke seine eigene Neutralität schützt."

[17] Pribram, i, 52 *et seq.* (Amer., i, pp. 124–130).
[18] *Ibid.*, i, pp. 55–56 (Amer., i, pp. 130–133).
[19] *Times*, November 26. Vienna, November 25 (an estimate of the situation

were forwarded to Berlin for critical examination, arriving about November 23, at the same time as the arrival of Prince Reuss from Vienna.[20] The German official story could not have taken long to concoct; yet publication of the results of the investigation was delayed for weeks.

Although the Tsar appears to have been not quite fully convinced of Bismarck's sincerity, he gave Germany the benefit of the doubt and expressed himself as satisfied with the results of his visit.[21] He was even credited with saying: "The Bulgarians, who are hostile to Russia, would be wrong to rely on the encouragement of the Emperor of Germany," which did not quite answer for Bismarck.[22] The editors of Russian newspapers were officially warned to moderate their tone toward Germany.[23] The injunction was badly received and not particularly well observed; yet it indicates the loyalty of Alexander's intentions and his willingness to meet Germany half way. Unfortunately, that was no longer enough. The time had gone by for anything short of unconditional surrender all along the line.

## II

Russia's surrender to the new triple entente followed within a week after its completion. This outcome did not, however, prevent Europe from being shaken by a new 'war scare,' inspired partly by Russia herself; more largely by the military cliques in

---

based on German and Russian newspaper comment). "It may have been hinted to the Czar that, although Prince Bismarck pronounced certain letters to be forgeries, those letters were written by somebody intimately acquainted with the Chancellor's opinions." *Ibid.*, November 28. St. Petersburg, November 26. "Things have gone too far for anything except most crushing evidence to instil into Russian minds the belief of Prince Bismarck's political sincerity towards this country."

[20] *Nationalzeitung*, November 27. *Pester Lloyd*, November 29. Maurel, p. 3. Baddeley, p. 385.

[21] *G. F. O.*, v, p. 326. November 23, Bülow to Bismarck. *Times*, November 29. Vienna, November 28. According to the St. Petersburg correspondence of *Politische Correspondenz*.

[22] *Times*, November 29. Paris, November 28. According to a letter from St. Petersburg.

[23] *Ibid.* St. Petersburg, November 27. See also *G. F. O.*, v, pp. 328-329. December 2, Bülow to Bismarck.

Berlin and Vienna, as well as in St. Petersburg; but, to a considerable degree also, by Bismarck's toleration, and even employment, of this militaristic agitation for his own purposes. One thing that must not be lost sight of in the development of this crisis is the fact that there was a new military bill before the Reichstag; and that public opinion had to be kept at a properly warlike pitch, in order to insure its passage. But behind this consideration lay those which impelled the government to present the bill.

For one thing, attention had been turned back in some degree toward France, now rapidly recovering her lost prestige. Her recent scandals dropped from sight after the resignation of President Grévy and the election, on December 3, of Sadi-Carnot as his successor. The new president was highly regarded everywhere and could begin his administration with a clean slate. Germans discovered one disquieting element in the situation, however — the fact that his victory was a defeat for Jules Ferry. His speech of acceptance, affirming that he would strive to uphold France's standing abroad, was unfavorably commented upon; since Germany's dearest wish was to see that standing depressed to the lowest possible point.[24] The violent revival of anti-Ferryism, culminating in an attempt, on December 10, to assassinate the ex-minister, was an unwelcome development. The Tirard ministry, formed on the 12th, although regarded as provisional, had elements of great strength, and displayed its intention of keeping up a bold front by preparing a new tariff schedule in anticipation of the coming economic struggle with Italy. Germany's western horizon was becoming decidedly troubled again.

But it was toward the East that alarmists chiefly directed the gaze of their countrymen. There was more behind their clamor than mere lust for a new parliamentary success. The Russian concentrations, referred to by the *Post* in its "sun of a Russo-Austrian war" article, were not a matter of recent discovery, but a development that had been worrying German and Austrian military authorities for at least a year. Although the new plan

---

[24] *Politische Nachrichten*, December 5. "Noch deutlicher und nach deutschen Begriffen auch erwünschter hätte der neue Präsident sich ausgedrückt, wenn er an Stelle des Wortes ' Würde ' das Wort ' Friede ' gebracht hätte."

represented no immediate designs on Russia's part, it was regarded by some competent observers as a menace to the future of the Central Empires. There were even those who advocated taking the bull by the horns and disposing of the menace before it assumed more definite shape. In the opinion of the holders of such views, not only was the Landsturm law a real and pressing necessity, but an immediate war was preferable to a deferred one.

In the early days of November, the military authorities of both the Central Empires began making a great stir over the transfer of a cavalry division from the interior of Russia to the neighborhood of Lublin.[25] Presently, the Austrian military attaché was reporting a warlike spirit at St. Petersburg, directed mainly against Austria.[26] His opinion of the situation was confirmed by reports of harsh language against Austria used even by the usually fair-spoken Giers. When the German chargé d'affaires attempted to assure him that the Austrians had no intention of attacking Russia, he burst out: "Let them come on! We ask nothing better."[27] Although Bismarck had made light of the alleged military danger, he finally became alarmed and plunged into a correspondence with Vienna that came near leading him much further than he really meant to go.

The inference Bismarck drew from the reports was "that the Russians are doing their utmost to provoke Austria to an attack upon Russia. Since becoming acquainted with the terms of the Austro-German treaty, they perceive that it is to the interest of their relations with us not to make the attack themselves, but to wait for Austria to do so."[28] He thought he discerned a situation in Russia with respect to Austria similar to his own with respect to France; and he feared that it might develop as the latter had more than once been on the point of doing. The prospect was especially uncomfortable for him in view of his treaties with both parties to the threatened conflict. He could not allow Austria to be beaten, but in attempting to save her he would be much embarrassed by the existence of his treaty with Russia.

---

[25] *G. F. O.*, vi, pp. 3–6.  [26] *Ibid.*, vi, pp. 6–7. Report of November 16.
[27] *Ibid.*, vi, p. 8. November 18, Bülow to Bismarck.
[28] *Ibid.*, vi, p. 12. November 24, memorandum by Count Rantzau.

To relieve himself of the necessity of taking her part in a war in behalf of her Balkan interests, he had built up the entente with Italy and England; but that entente, in its new form, had not yet been completed by the end of November. He saw, therefore, two immediate necessities before him: to hasten the conclusion of the entente, and to restrain Austria from taking any aggressive action without its backing. Toward fulfilling the first need he had gone very nearly as far as possible in writing his letter to Salisbury. In fulfilment of the second, he directed that the Austrian government should be put on its guard against Russia's design.

Unhappily, he felt called upon also to introduce another element into his communication to Austria. This was a suggestion that she should make military preparations for coping with the Russian menace.[29] Bismarck could not fail to realize that, however carefully this counsel might be worded, it would open the door to the whole argument of 'preventive war' — that the best way of meeting the Russian threat was to attack Russia before she was ready. Although at no period of his career did Bismarck express so often and so decisively his abhorrence of this doctrine, he at no time allowed a freer rein to the activities of its adherents. There was, of course, an immediate reason for this conduct in the fact that Austria was very much behind her ally in the matter of preparedness and needed stirring up. But the character of the arguments invoked by Bismarck is such as to warrant the suspicion that other motives were not absent from his calculations.

His communication produced various effects at Vienna. Kálnoky did not dispute the existence of a hostile feeling at St. Petersburg, but he maintained that the recent movements of troops were of no great importance and called for no countermeasures, which would, indeed, only irritate Russia still more.[30] Bismarck's marginal notes on this report evince great impatience with Austria's unwillingness to make the financial sacrifices involved. The Emperor Francis Joseph, however, raised some awkward questions. He spoke of the possibility of a state of

[29] *G. F. O.*, vi, p. 13. November 30, Herbert Bismarck to Reuss.
[30] *Ibid.*, vi, pp. 1–17. December 1, Reuss to Bismarck.

affairs arising in which "Austria might find herself at war with Russia without our *casus foederis* being clearly involved." He referred to wars arising not only out of "purely military considerations," but also out of the triple understanding then in progress of formation, in which Germany was taking, "if not an open, at any rate a very important part."[31] Bismarck's comment on these considerations was that nothing could bring the *casus foederis* into operation but an attack on Austria, and that he had "striven to provide allies for Austria in cases not covered by the *foedus*." As for Germany's attitude toward the triple entente, he remarked: "the question cannot be answered *now* without encouraging Austria to bring on a war at *our* expense." On a later report he made the note: "If Austria is still anxious, with Rumania, Bulgaria, Italy, the Porte, England, and Serbia on her side, she must have a bad conscience."[32] He accepted, however, the Emperor's request for an exchange of views between the military authorities on the measures to be taken in the event of common action.

To Bismarck's great annoyance, the policy of inaction and reliance upon Germany prevailed at Vienna. The controversy got into the newspapers, the *Fremden-Blatt* standing for military measures, and the *Neue Freie Presse*, for the political course.[33] A

[31] *G. F. O.*, vi, pp. 19-22. December 6, Reuss to Bismarck.
[32] *Ibid.*, vi, p. 24.
[33] *Fremden-Blatt*, December 6. "Es könnte jeder aufrichtige Friedensfreund nur auf das tiefste bedauern, wenn weitergehende russische Truppenansammlungen eine ernste Bedrohung unserer Grenze befürchten liessen und uns zwingen würden, die Frage aufzuwerfen, ob die unabweisbare Sorge für die Sicherheit der Monarchie nicht auch die entsprechenden Vorkehrungen unsererseits erheischt, um gegenüber den ganz unprovocirten bedrohlichen Vorbereitungen des Nachbars nicht zurückzubleiben." *N. F. P.*, December 7. "Es ist längst kein Geheimniss mehr, dass die oberste Leitung der Armee die grosse Anhäufung russischer Truppen an der österreichischen Grenze mit dem äussersten Misstrauen verfolgt. . . . Wir hegen die Hoffnung, dass die Regierung sich nicht allein von den Eingebungen der militärischen, sondern auch von der Stimme der politischen Vorsicht leiten lassen werde. . . . Will Russland, gestützt auf die Sympathien Frankreichs, einen Weltbrand entfachen, der zehn Millionen Menschen zu den Waffen ruft? Will es sich allein den vereinten Kräften Deutschlands und Oesterreichs gegenüberstellen? Diese Annahme wäre wahnwitzig, und ebenso können, ja dürfen wir auch nicht daran glauben, dass es irgend eine Frage im Orient gibt, für deren Lösung Oesterreich an die Macht appelliren würde, wenn es nicht weiss, dass sofort auch die deutschen Säbel aus der Scheide fliegen."

staff council at the Hofburg, on December 8, decided against the former.

So great was the German Chancellor's irritation that he brought the most extreme arguments of the military party into the discussion. He had received, on November 30, a memorandum from Moltke painting the Russian military preparations in the darkest colors and concluding: "According to the above, there can be no doubt that Russia is arming for immediate war and is preparing the forward push of her armies by a general progressive ... mobilization." The whole tendency of the memorandum was to advocate anticipating the attack by attacking first. Although Bismarck expressed disagreement with the field marshal's conclusions, he forwarded this document to Vienna, on December 9. The accompanying instructions to Prince Reuss stated that it would show "that Austria should not lose precious time in taking the measures which her own general staff regard as *necessary* for the protection of the exposed Austrian territories."[34]

In a later despatch, the Chancellor explained: "My intention was only to warm the Austrian army command at the fire of ours." He would never agree to a "prophylactic attack" on Russia, he continued, and was "far from advising Austria to undertake one, *so long* as she is not absolutely sure of *England's* coöperation." This theme he elaborated significantly, saying frankly: "In anticipation of the case that the latter [an attack on Russia] should appear to be required by Austria's Balkan policy, we have successfully endeavored to bring Austria into closer relations with Italy and England. If Count Kálnoky finds these relations so firm and reliable that Austria is sure of having both these Powers, and the Porte as well, on her side, not only diplomatically, but *actively*, I myself, were I Austrian minister, would perhaps venture on an appeal to armed force." His usual argument that Germany would, in any case, be occupied with France, he now pushed to the point of saying: "If the Russian war is brought about by an Austrian attack on Russia, our course, in my opinion, would not be to take part in it, but to attack *France* immediately, conditioning our attitude toward the Russian war on our success in

[34] *G. F. O.*, vi, pp. 24–25, note.

the French." Such a notification might, as the editor of the document hastens to explain, show the Austrians how little help they had to expect from Germany. Bismarck might add and underscore the sentence: "We must not on any account encourage Austria in aggressive action against Russia, but only in strengthening herself for defence."[35] The total impression given by the despatch is one of the strongest encouragement to war, so long as Germany is left out of the calculation of forces for the campaign against Russia.

The effect of such language and of the license allowed to the military party was what might have been expected. The German military attaché in Vienna, Major von Deines, went so far in inciting the Austrians to immediate activity as to call down a sharp rebuke.[36] The Austrian staff put forward far reaching proposals for the disposal of German troops in the event of war. Count Waldersee discussed the general question of a Russian war with the Austrian ambassador.[37] The 'fire' of the German general staff threatened to spread into a general conflagration. Bismarck was, indeed, playing with fire in raising the military question in the way he had done, yet he had not hesitated to blow the flame.

The stirring up of public opinion in Germany favored the passage of the military bills then coming under consideration. General Bronsart von Schellendorff startled the Reichstag, on December 5, by a passage in his speech on a bill for compensations to the families of reservists called to the colors in time of war. When the Left shouted that a possible substitute governing ordinary periods of duty as well was more pressing, he replied vehemently: "Yes, gentlemen, if you will have it so, one may say it is more pressing, in that we are for the moment in a state of peace and not yet of war. But quite possibly war will be upon us before the next spring manoeuvres; and I must maintain that a law fixing these matters for the event of a war which may be upon us any day is the more pressing consideration."[38] The views thus

---

[35] *G. F. O.*, vi, pp. 25–28. December 15, Bismarck to Reuss.
[36] *Ibid.*, vi, pp. 28–29.
[37] *Ibid.*, vi, pp. 57–58, note.
[38] *Stenographische Berichte*, 1887–88, p. 114.

prevailing in high places were not long in communicating themselves to the public. The newspapers were filled with reports of huge movements of troops beyond the border and demands that something be done to counteract them — particularly by Austria.

## III

Russia had been preparing to give way as to Bulgaria since early in December. Her only desire by this time was to get rid of Prince Ferdinand: anything else seemed preferable to the existing state of affairs. On December 7, the Austrian military attaché at Berlin reported that Shuvalov had said to him: "It will be enough if you only declare him [Ferdinand] a usurper who has illegally mounted the throne: peace will then be assured for ten or twenty years. The Bulgarian question must be settled by an understanding with the Powers. Russia does not by any means insist on a Russian candidate. You name one — say, Paul of Mecklenburg; yes, even the Battenberger." [39] This suggestion apparently met with no response.

One final effort was made with Bismarck on the basis of an alleged promise given the Tsar that the German ambassador at Constantinople would be instructed to resume his support of the Russian influence there. On December 14, Shuvalov presented to Herbert Bismarck a letter from Giers putting forward the suggestion: "The Chancellor knows our proposals with regard to the settlement of the Bulgarian question. If, in his practical judgment, he has any helpful observations to offer, we are ready to listen to them. As far as we are concerned, the main thing is to get the Porte to declare Prince Ferdinand a usurper and to send him packing." As soon as the desired instructions had been sent to Constantinople, concluded Giers, he would make more definite propositions. Shuvalov added the pithy remark that "*support alone is not of much avail; something can be accomplished only if strong pressure* is brought to bear on the Sultan by Germany." [40]

[39] Corti, pp. 311–312. December 7, report of Lieutenant-Colonel von Steininger.
[40] *Kölnische Zeitung*, December 17. "Man wird wohl nicht fehlgriffen, wenn man annimmt, dass die heutige militärische Berathung, welche Kaiser Wilhelm mit dem Prinzen Wilhelm, dem Feldmarschall Grafen Moltke, dem Generalquartiermeister

Once more, Shuvalov received the well worn reply: "la parole est à la Russie." Bismarck denied having made the promise referred to, and refused to alter his course with respect to the situation at Constantinople until he had more definite proof of a change of heart toward Germany in Russia. Following this rebuff, the Russians renounced the idea of exerting any positive influence upon the course of events in Bulgaria.

Shortly afterward, General Bronsart von Schellendorff sounded another warlike note in introducing the Landsturm law in the Reichstag. This law increased the obligation to military service by seven classes of reservists and implied an increase of the army's war strength by nearly one-half its previous numbers. The minister recalled the Emperor's words on the foreign situation, demanding that Germany be made strong enough to face any danger. He added: "The only danger which threatens us lies in the possibility of an attack brought about by the rising tides of passion among our neighbors. We do not desire a war, but we must prepare ourselves to sustain it with honor. We are strong..., but on looking about us, we see that we are not strong enough." [41]

Next day the German Emperor called a military conference to discuss the Russian situation.[42] The question of Russia's activity had just been brought up afresh through the publication in the *Russki Invalid* of a long inspired article, citing statistics to prove that the regrouping of Russia's forces still left her far behind Germany and Austria and in no position to start an aggressive war. Round this article centred a whole new controversy, in turn provoking new alarms. The German council of war renewed the appeal to Austria for some definite military demonstration against

Grafen Waldersee, dem Kriegsminister und dem General v. Albedyll gehabt hat, wesentlich bedingt worden ist durch die Mittheilungen, welche der ' Russische Invalide ' über die Verhältnisse Deutschlands, Oesterreichs und Russlands zu einander veröffentlicht hat."

[41] *Stenographische Berichte*, 1887–88, p. 288. Speech of December 16.

[42] Lucius von Ballhausen, p. 409. December 18, 1887. "Der Grossherzog von Baden sprach . . . über die äussere Lage sehr ernst. Es werde in den nächsten Tagen eine Manifestation erfolgen Russland gegenüber, auf Grund eines Kriegsrats, welcher am 17. stattgefunden habe. Die Österreicher hätten zu wenig Selbstvertrauen und verlangten in allem Direktiven von hier."

the alleged Russian threat.[43] Under this pressure a second council was called at Vienna on the 18th, this time with the ministers of finance in attendance. Certain measures of defence for Galicia were decided upon, but of so minor a character that the ministers undertook to supply the few millions required without calling a special session of the Delegations.[44] This was the limit to which the Austrian government would allow itself to be pushed in this direction.

On the same day, Russia announced her surrender to the triple entente on the Bulgarian question. It was plain enough to her by this time that she could no longer stand out against the forces opposing her. This was one of the objects attained by the recent agitation of the subject of military forces. Lavino at Vienna probably made a correct estimate of the situation when he wrote to the *Times*, on December 19: "But this one fact must not be lost sight of, that the arrangement now to be settled between Russia and her two neighbors will admit of no quibble on Russia's part. Germany and Austria-Hungary mean to treat as being the stronger parties in any possible conflict. The essential point for them is to demonstrate that Russia can henceforth no longer play the part of arbiter of peace in Europe; that it is not open to her to make suspicious alliances with France; that she cannot march into Bulgaria at her pleasure; that she has not the permission to bully Turkey, and to coerce that Power into allowing the passage of Russian warships through the Dardanelles, under fallacious pretexts; and finally, that her attitude towards Germany and Austria-Hungary henceforth must not be that of a stronger and domineering, but of a weaker and subservient State."[45] Giers told Sir Robert Morier, on his departure for the holidays, that Russia would never do anything rash for the sake of the Bulgarians. "You may go to England," were his words, "with your mind perfectly at ease. They may do anything and everything they please, from cutting each other's throats to declaring themselves an Empire. We shall not move a finger to prevent them. We wash our hands of the whole concern."[46]

[43] *M. A. Z.*, December 22. Aus Oesterreich, December 20. *N. F. P.*, December 20.   [44] *G. F. O.*, v, pp. 203–205.   [45] *Times*, December 20.
[46] *P. P.*, 1888, cix, Turkey no. 1, p. 169. December 17, Morier to Salisbury.

Russia's capitulation to the forces Bismarck had marshalled against her was made directly to Austria. On December 18, the Russian ambassador came to Kálnoky and, according to the latter's account, "declared to me formally, in the name of the Russian government and with the approval of the Emperor, that Russia has not the slightest intention of going to war; still less of attacking Austria-Hungary." As for Bulgaria, he asserted: "No one thinks of shedding a single drop of blood for Bulgaria: a peaceful solution will be found for that question." Kálnoky took note of these declarations and undertook to give reciprocal assurances on the part of his own government and sovereign. On the 22d, he exchanged with Lobanov formal confirmation of the statements made on both sides.[47]

The undertaking thus given by the Russian government was virtually an unconditional surrender of its pretensions in the Bulgarian question. The understanding that this issue should not become a cause of armed conflict was really one-sided, since the active rôle in any further tampering with that question would necessarily fall to Russia. Austria and her allies were satisfied with the existing state of affairs and had no changes to advocate. Only Russia had any desire to turn the course of events. All her efforts to bring about a change had been checked by a hostile combination, which would continue to stand in her way in the future. Now Russia had renounced all appeal from the decisions of her opponents and limited her freedom of action to measures which would not provoke their active hostility. She was bound to accept their view of the case and to act only in harmony with them. Gone was all chance of making her ideas of right and legality prevail in Bulgaria — gone because Germany had failed to support them and backed her opponents instead. All the favorable clauses of the Reinsurance Treaty were renounced in Russia's capitulation to Austria.

Russia did not at once abandon the hope that affairs in Bulgaria would ultimately take a better turn; only she abandoned all attempts to influence them by direct action. It had long been evident to cooler heads in the empire that a policy based on such

[47] *G. F. O.*, vi, pp. 34–36. Kálnoky's memorandum.

action was not only doubtful and dangerous, but injurious in the long run to Russia's prestige in the Balkans. Granting that Stambulov and his followers were as unrepresentative of Bulgaria's real sentiments as had been maintained, Russia's policy, far from embarrassing them, had only rallied public opinion in their favor. If they were really unpopular with the mass of Bulgarians, surely the quickest way to be rid of them would be to leave them alone to face out the issue with their own fellow countrymen.[48]

To this standpoint of conservative 'Western' opinion official Russia had now adhered. Lobanov, who had concluded the new arrangement with Austria, expressed himself in this sense. "The Bulgarians will not be an occasion of war," he told a correspondent of *Le Figaro* at the end of January. "Russia is patient, because she knows her strength. Russia leaves everything to the common sense of the Bulgarians. The Bulgarians want a prince, but they do not want an out-and-out Austrian prince. Russia has no demands to impose. Every one knows what Russia has done and what she desires." While Russia could not cease to be interested in Bulgarian affairs, and while she continued in a general way to advocate a revision of the status quo, she abstained henceforward from anything like separate action toward that end. The resumption of the expected intimacy between the liberated people and its benefactor was left entirely to Bulgaria's initiative.[49]

The declarations made by Lobanov probably gave reasonable satisfaction to Bismarck. They would also, normally, have satisfied Kálnoky. Unfortunately, however, a highly abnormal state of affairs had been created by the exchange of views then in progress between the Austrian and German military authorities. This negotiation encouraged Kálnoky to hope for still larger results. When Lobanov, at the close of their second conversation, had asked him what would be the practical effect of their exchange of assurances upon the strained situation then existing, he merely replied that that depended still upon St. Petersburg. His

[48] Вѣстникъ Европы, December, 1887, pp. 830–831.
[49] Правительственный Вѣстникъ, February 11, 23, 1888. Жигаревъ, ii, p. 297.

reference to the concentrations of troops in Poland, of which he had formerly made little account, indicate that he had in mind requiring some military readjustments as proof of Russia's good will.

The prospect of inflicting so material a humiliation on Russia, attended as it was by grave danger of war, depended wholly upon the backing of Germany. The entente with England had no bearing upon the situation once Russia had renounced all positive designs on Bulgaria. The Austrian general staff had, indeed, made very serious requests upon Germany, amounting to a promise of help in an aggressive war. Beginning with the suggestion that Germany should keep a covering force on her eastern frontier even in case of a war not involving the *casus foederis*, the Austrians had extended their conditions to include a simultaneous declaration of war in a vaguely stated case of common action.[50]

Bismarck firmly declined to be led into such broad commitments. He did admit one contingency beyond the letter of the treaty of alliance, to wit: "Evident preparations for an attack upon Austria (Galicia), however, would furnish an occasion for us to make preparations (mobilization) to meet it, and so for our effective intervention in the Austro-Russian conflict." [51] He also reasserted his intention of attacking France if war should come in the East. "If, contrary to expectations, it should not come about of itself," he wrote, with reference to the French war, "we feel more or less obliged to bring it on without delay. We could not carry on a war in the East with *full forces* and *far* over the border, as long as we had behind our backs the entire military power of France unimpaired and ready for attack." [52]

The negotiations dragged on into the latter half of January, 1888. While hope remained of inducing the Chancellor to broaden and define his assurances with respect to the Russian threat to Galicia, the Austrians proved unwilling to bring the existing

[50] *G. F. O.*, vi, pp. 58–59, 65.

[51] *Ibid.*, vi, pp. 77–78. Marginal note incorporated by Herbert Bismarck in a despatch to Reuss, January 14, 1888.

[52] *Ibid.*, vi, p. 68. December 27, 1887, Bismarck to Reuss.

crisis to an end. In his first circular despatch of the new year, Kálnoky wrote to the diplomatic representatives of Austria-Hungary: "Sooner or later we shall be left with only one solution — the inevitable clash between the two Imperial Powers and Russia. The sword will decide whether Slavic Russia is to dominate the continent of Europe or not." [53] In a cabinet session on January 7, Bismarck insisted that all hopeful expressions be striken out of the coming speech from the throne.[54]

The Russians were vaguely aware that something was going on, and drew the darkest inferences from what little reached their ears. The suspicion became general that Germany was inciting Austria to war. Prince Lobanov shared in the anxiety.[55] The school of policy he represented, which favored the diversion of Russia's energies into Asiatic expansion, could make no headway in such an atmosphere. The effects of the understanding he had reached with Kálnoky remained, therefore, in abeyance, while rumors of war darkened the European sky. Nevertheless, the crisis was gradually dying away of its own accord. On January 19, after the failure of a last effort to obtain definite assurances of German military support outside the terms of the treaty, Kálnoky still spoke pessimistically to Reuss of the general outlook.[56] But he apparently pocketed his disappointment thereafter and prevailed upon the generals to do likewise. He had the Lobanov declarations to fall back on; and these came to influence relations between the two countries more and more from this time on.

The reaction of the Lobanov agreement upon the general course of Russian policy began to be evident. The influence of the future minister of foreign affairs upon his government was already being exerted toward the reorientation of Russia's national effort which was to be completed during his tenure of office. On January 20, the ministerial committee on railways approved projects for the lines from Tomsk to Krasnoiarsk and from Vladikavkaz

[53] Corti, p. 316.     [54] Lucius von Ballhausen, p. 416.
[55] *G. F. O.*, vi, pp. 37-38. December 29, Schweinitz to Bismarck (two despatches).
[56] *Ibid.*, vi, pp. 44-45. No important despatches are printed of a date later than this.

to Petrovsk.⁵⁷ If it be borne in mind that the lines connecting Austria's railway system with Salonica and Constantinople were just being completed at this time, a significant picture presents itself of the tendency in international developments.⁵⁸

Yet this shift of Russia's outlook from the Near East to Asia does not alone determine the future course of international politics. Had it done so, the policy imposed upon imperial Germany by Bismarck's conduct in these critical years might have been justified by complete success. Could Russia permanently abandon the Near East to the Central Powers? Could she have remained indifferent to the course of events in Europe, even if her vast Asiatic ambitions had not suffered the check of military defeat? At least, the retracing of her steps would have been far more difficult had there been no European ally to reach her a hand on the return. But the renunciation forced from Russia by Bismarck was followed by an inevitable drift toward the alliance with France.

The financial factor in this process of mutual attraction made itself felt at once. However completely Russia might dissociate herself from European politics, she could not escape from her need of a European banker. France was only too eager to assume this rôle, which Germany had declined to continue. And even after Russia had made her political surrender to the Central Empires, she encountered no relaxation in Germany's financial blockade. Her credit obligations, excluded by state banks, found no welcome among private institutions. Confidence in the future relations of the two countries had been badly shaken by the vehement press campaign, which had not slackened since the secret agreement. Soundings of the German money market brought only negative results.⁵⁹ So far were German investors

⁵⁷ *M. A. Z.*, January 26. St. Petersburg, January 21.

⁵⁸ Cyon asserts (pp. 338–339) that since the autumn of 1887, he had been acting as intermediary between the Russian ministry of finance and a group of French bankers who desired to buy out the Austrian and other interests in these lines for the benefit of Russia, and that their propositions were rebuffed at St. Petersburg. As the attitude of the Austrian interests toward this neat transaction is passed over, the matter was probably not so simple as Cyon would give one to understand.

⁵⁹ *M. A. Z.*, January 27. Berlin, January 25. "Der 'Kreuzztg.' wird aus Russland bestätigt, dass sich die europäischen Geldmärkte den finanziellen Wünschen

from taking up any more Russian loans that the unloading of their existing holdings went on unchecked. It was reported that, on February 1, Russian bonds to the value of seventy-two million rubles passed the Belgian frontier on their way to Paris.

Germans saw nothing ominous for the future in this turn of affairs — quite the contrary. The newspapers had maintained, since the first attacks on Russian credit, that the greater became France's financial stake in Russia, the less would be the likelihood of her urging the debtor into precarious adventures.[60] It seems well nigh incredible that Bismarck should have shared this cheerful view of events; but he did nothing to change their course. He appeared determined to unbend to Russia in no respect.

The Russian government showed great reluctance to drift with the financial tide. In February, Giers was still putting off a project for the rehabilitation of Russia's credit by a French syndicate on the ground that to admit French influence to any extent in Russian affairs "would profoundly annoy Berlin and put our foreign relations in a very delicate situation." [61] Yet ultimately there was no choice. Russia could not even carry out her change of front away from Europe without the means of prosecuting her new enterprises in Asia. If those means were denied her by Germany, she must find them where she could.

So the shift in Russia's *politique des chemins de fer* was accompanied by a tendency in her *politique de la haute finance* of quite contrary implications. In the end the latter of the two influences proved the more decisive in shaping her general course. Nor were Russia's finances alone involved in the eddy of politico-economic forces which carried her loan market from Berlin to Paris. The absorption of Russian obligations by French investors was accompanied by a discarding of Italian bonds.[62] The exchange appeared advantageous, since the latter were quoted high and the

der russischen Regierung gegenüber ablehnend verhalten, und der ' Magdeb. Ztg.' wird von hier mitgetheilt, dass die Versuche St. Petersburger Agenten, hiesige Bankinstitute für eine neue russische Anleihe zu gewinnen, über Tasten und Fühlen nicht hinausgekommen sind."

[69] *M. A. Z.*, February 5. Berlin, February 2.
[61] Cyon, p. 342.
[62] Pierre Petit, *La dette publique de la Russie* (Poitiers, 1912), p. 85, note.

former low. It was, moreover, a skirmish in preparation for the economic battle now regarded as inevitable by both 'Latin sisters.' The commercial treaty of 1881 had received a new temporary lease of life only until March 1; and there was now small hope of its replacement by another. Strangulation tariffs were in readiness to be clapped on by both sides. A campaign against Italy's credit was decidedly in order. As Russia's market was being shifted from Berlin to Paris, then so was Italy's to be shifted from Paris to Berlin. This outcome was in accordance with Bismarck's policy of strengthening the Triple Alliance; but the Franco-Russian alliance was its sinister accompaniment.

Although official Russia still tried to stand out against the financial currents which were drawing the country toward France, certain diplomatic concessions indicated a desire to keep all obstacles out of the way of a rapprochement. The project of enrolling two Orleanist princes in a Russian crack regiment was cancelled by the Tsar.[63] The Russian ambassador at Paris received in his house the rising political personage, Floquet, who was slated for leadership of the coming new government, but reputed to be in the bad graces of Russia since his youthful escapade of crying "Vive la Pologne!" in the presence of Alexander II. The pressure of events was forcing Russia toward France despite all the reluctance of her reactionary government. The situation was largely of Bismarck's own creating.

## IV

One evidence of Russia's acceptance of her defeat over the Bulgarian question was the Tsar's consent to a step which amounted to a public admission that he had misjudged Germany's policy in that connection. Hitherto, Alexander had denied Bismarck's request to be allowed to publish the results of his inquiry into the 'Bulgarian documents.' The Chancellor was anxious to clear himself publicly: the Tsar, even when measurably convinced that he had been imposed upon, was reluctant to expose publicly his gullibility and the part played by his own courtiers in

[63] *Kölnische Zeitung*, January 25, St. Petersburg telegram.

deceiving him. Moreover, great pains had been necessary to convince Giers finally of the spuriousness of the papers, which, he was still saying at the beginning of December, "m'intriguent de plus en plus." [64] At last came Count Peter Shuvalov, brother of the ambassador at Berlin, on a special mission to the German government; and, on December 27, the *Kölnische Zeitung*, which had been all along the chief purveyor of inside knowledge on the subject, published a detailed summary of the documents. This was not their first revelation to the public. Already, on November 20, an obscure Parisian sheet, the *Agence Libre*, had printed the text of the alleged Reuss note. The *Kölnische Zeitung*, in acknowledging it as one of the documents, stated that the famous forgeries were more or less common property in Paris at the time.[65] They were doubtless circulated by de Mondion.

Simultaneously with the Russian diplomat's visit to Berlin, another political portent flashed across the sky. Lord Randolph Churchill took a trip to St. Petersburg. But the ex-chancellor no longer counted as more than a passing meteor in the firmament. All newspaper comment to the contrary notwithstanding, he had no official mandate for his mission.[66] He talked with the Tsar chiefly about questions directly affecting relations between their two countries.[67] On his way home through Germany he remarked

[64] *G. F. O.*, v, p. 342. December 2, Bülow to Bismarck.

[65] *Kölnische Zeitung*, December 1. "Prinz Reuss hat bei seiner kürzlichen Anwesenheit nach Kenntnissnahme des Briefes nicht nur erklärt, dass er nicht den Brief geschrieben, sondern noch weiter, dass er überhaupt keinen Brief je an den Prinzen Ferdinand von Coburg gerichtet habe. Hier ist inzwischen bekannt geworden, dass mehrere Pariser Kreise von dem Vorhandensein solcher gefälschter Briefe bereits seit Wochen Kenntniss hatten. Was die Veröffentlichung eines derselben jetzt von Paris aus bedeutet, ist zur Zeit noch nicht recht klar, vielleicht beabsichtigt man, damit die Spur des eigentlichen Fälschers zu verwischen."

[66] Churchill, ii, pp. 356–358.

[67] According to Winston Churchill's account (ii, pp. 359–366). Baddeley (p. 390) quotes from his diary as follows; "*January 15th*. Yesterday I saw both Peter and Paul [Shuvalov]. Peter said that Randolph Churchill was going about saying that England would never intervene against Russia in a quarrel between her and Austro-Germany; that a great change had come about in public opinion, and the majority would no longer allow it. There is a rumour that Lord Salisbury has signed a document by which he adheres to the League of Peace (*i. e.* the Austro-German alliance). Lord Randolph declares that, if so, he will go back to England and make such a row in Parliament as never was heard, etc." The promised 'row' was made by the fam-

upon Bismarck's evading him, although he lunched with Count Herbert at Berlin.[68] The situation, particularly with regard to Anglo-German relations, had developed to a point beyond the power of a Churchill out of office to produce any serious effect upon it. Russia's unconditional surrender to the Central Powers had taken place: perhaps England would later have cause enough to regret its reaction upon Asiatic politics.

On the last day of the year, the famous Bulgarian documents, about which all Europe had been talking for weeks, were finally given to the public. The French text of Ferdinand's letters and the Reuss note was printed in full in the official *Reichsanzeiger*, with a brief introduction admitting that they would indeed have been damning evidence if genuine. The letters were said to have been placed in Bismarck's hands "with the view of testing their contents and discovering their origin." No declaration whatever was made touching the latter point; but the statements concerning the contents are worth repeating. "The inquiries which were instituted," ran the official introduction, "resulted in showing that no correspondence of any kind ever took place between Her Royal Highness the Countess of Flanders and Prince Ferdinand of Coburg, and that a political communication of the kind imputed to the Ambassador, Prince Reuss, was never made by the latter. Moreover, the parts ascribed in the documents to other august personages have proved to be mere inventions, and altogether these documents have been devised and put together without any foundation in fact by some persons hitherto undiscovered, for the simple purposes of sowing distrust among the European Powers." [69]

For the sake of giving these documents their proper places in the narrative, they have been treated up to this point as essentially genuine, without going into a detailed discussion of the

ous questions of Labouchère, but led only to evasive replies from the government benches.

[68] Churchill, ii, pp. 368–369. To his mother he wrote: "I have not a doubt that the Chancellor kept away purposely. He is a *grincheux* old creature, and knows quite well that I will use all my influence, as I have done, to prevent Lord S. from being towed in his wake."

[69] *Reichsanzeiger*, December 31, 1887.

arguments for and against them. The pronouncements of the *Reichsanzeiger* appear to be simple statements of fact, which, as is said of the letters, are conclusive if accepted as correct. It is permissible, however, to question Bismarck's statements, even when as categorical as these, on the frank issue of truthfulness. He must not now go unchallenged. In examining his declarations here, some of the facts previously cited concerning the documents in question will have to be repeated.

In the first place, it is stated that no correspondence ever took place between the persons involved. There is, of course, no direct evidence to oppose to this direct assertion, in making which Bismarck had the support of both the parties concerned. It can only be pointed out that the band of informers which put the documents into circulation did possess facilities for learning of and procuring genuine evidence. Two years later it was ascertained that members of this band had procured genuine documents from the archives of the Belgian ministry of the interior: their opportunities in the foreign office were almost equally good.[70] Their story regarding the subsequent fate of the letters was that Bismarck, through King Leopold II, had obtained from the Countess not only her promise to disavow them, but the originals of the letters themselves, thus disposing of the *corpus delicti*.[71] In view of the relations apparently being established between the German government and the Belgian sovereign toward the close of the year, the allegation contains an element of probability.

Giers's first remark, when informed that Bismarck had obtained from the Countess of Flanders a written denial that she

[70] See above, Chapter XI, note 2. The authenticity of the documents published in this case was grudgingly admitted in the *Moniteur Belge* on August 3, 1889, in the words: "Quelques-uns seulement des documents attribués à M. le duc d'Ursel sont réels et ont été reproduits avec plus ou moins d'exactitude." A long controversy went on between the Duc d'Ursel and Madame Adam concerning the most compromising of these documents, leaving its genuineness still very much in doubt. *Nouvelle Revue*, August 1, 1889, pp. 585–589. The *Étoile Belge* announced, on July 25, that the originals of the documents had been actually stolen from the archives, a statement which was confirmed by the *Journal de Bruxelles*.

[71] Maurel, p. 358. A receipt is said to have been given for deposit in the secretariat of the household — "et nous le possédons . . .: elle atteste qu'à la date du 7 décembre 1887 la comtesse de Flandre avait reçu quatre lettres du prince Ferdinand de Cobourg, et que ces quatre lettres ont été remises au roi Léopold II."

had ever received any letters from Ferdinand, was that perhaps the good lady was only shielding him "par un excès de générosité." [72] As for Ferdinand's confirmation of this denial, in a letter to Reuss, on December 10, pronouncing also against the alleged communication from the German ambassador, one has only to ask what else he could have said.[73] Reuss's repudiation of the document attributed to him is undoubtedly honest.[74] He does, however, admit having had a private interview with Ferdinand; and he says that the style of the letters strongly resembles the Prince's fashion of expressing himself.

No further evidence bearing directly upon the statements of the *Reichsanzeiger* can be adduced. The only additional commentary of anything like official character is a communication on the subject sent to Crispi from Vienna on December 18. It contains no evidence not elsewhere produced, except a statement that the Countess of Flanders had never been in Ischl, where the first letter said she and Ferdinand had been thrown together.[75]

Another point made much of, but already discussed, was that the letters appeared as translations from the German into French, whereas the original language would have been more familiar to the Tsar. It has been pointed out that the conspirators were not dealing with Alexander, but with the French government, which itself set up the other links in the chain.

The denial of any real foundation for the documents is greatly weakened by the fact that no dishonest origin was ever established or even officially alleged. Unofficially, of course, Bismarck had put forth his alibi of an Orleanist intrigue long in advance. It was received with general scepticism. The representative of the accused family in France, M. Bôcher, addressed a categorical denial to the *Kölnische Zeitung*, chief sponsor for the Bismarckian version of the affair. "None of the Princes of Orleans," he solemnly affirmed, "none of those who have the honor to bear the name and to acknowledge Monseigneur the Count of Paris as head of their house, has taken any part directly or indirectly in the acts you have revealed"; and further — "those princes are and have al-

[72] *G. F. O.*, v, p. 341. December 2, Bülow to Bismarck.
[73] *Ibid.*, v, p. 345.     [74] *Ibid.*, v, pp. 338–340.     [75] Crispi, p. 215.

ways been totally unconcerned in the events of which the Balkan Peninsula has been the scene." [76]

The letter did not carry conviction in the quarter designed; but the tales of the *Kölnische Zeitung* were already scouted by almost every one outside Germany. An interesting theory was put forward at Pest. "That an Orleanist conspiracy should have been spoken of at Berlin," was its tenor, "is due to a desire to avoid recriminating against Russian dignitaries at the present moment. As a matter of fact, Russians are the chief parties affected by the recent disclosures."[77] Russians were indeed involved in the transmission of the documents; and beyond that point the Tsar had probably not been enlightened. He might well desire to hush up the scandal. Bismarck could have no motives for doing so, other than to please Alexander and encourage him in his confusion of mind.

Ultimately, the theory of a Russian origin for the intrigue took still sharper form. A report from Brussels singled out as forger of the documents the former Russian minister to Washington, Catacazy, then resident at Paris and a collaborator on Russia's Western European mouthpiece, the *Nord* of Brussels.[78] The hypothesis is marred by the fact that the *Nord* represented in general the Russian administrative point of view, on the whole favorable to the German alliance, which the documents had the effect of destroying. A curious utilization of this argument will be discussed later. The indications that the letters, whatever their authorship, actually came from Brussels are too strong to be rejected in favor of the theory of an origin at Paris.

The accounts of an Orleanist plot put forward by the *Kölnische Zeitung* had carried a clear implication that Ferdinand himself was involved as a principal factor in the intrigue for bringing on a European war.[79] In reply to assertions to this effect, Ferdinand conveyed to the German press, through a 'high official,' a denial that he had had anything to do with the documents, then not yet published to the world. His spokesman further stated that a full

---

[76] Maurel, p. 332.    [77] *Times*, November 26. Pest, November 25.
[78] *N. F. P.*, January 9, 1888. Brussels, January 7.
[79] See above, p. 212, note 28.

explanation of the prince's motives in his adventure had been placed in Bismarck's hands through the head of his family, Duke Ernest of Coburg.[80] The story was finally abandoned in favor of the theory that the prince was guiltless as well as Reuss.

The clew leading to Sofia was remarkably elaborated upon in the reports from St. Petersburg. Opinion there was impressed by the denials that the documents were genuine, yet was unable to accept the Orleanist theory and reluctant to trace the fraud to Russian sources. A variant of the *Kölnische Zeitung's* theory was therefore circulated, to the effect that not Ferdinand, but persons in his entourage were the authors of the plot.[81] Elaborating upon this suggestion, the next report ran that the scheme was of a business, rather than a political, character.[82] Finally, the authorship of the letters was attributed to "a certain foreign agent in Bulgaria who has been striving to raise a loan for the Principality, and thus to forward his financial and industrial enterprises."[83] Here was a feeble outcome indeed! Giers himself accused the Bulgarian nationalist leaders, and sought to incriminate the Austrians as well.[84]

Still another clew was offered to the public by the very *Kölnische Zeitung* which had taken the leading part in circulating the Orleanist stories. This one led, not directly to Sofia, but to Bucharest. It incriminated, in the first place, one Frédéric Damé, formerly an editor there, and, along with him, the Russian minister to Rumania and his predecessor, then stationed at Brussels.[85]

---

[80] *N. F. P.*, December 3. The interview in question was printed by the *Vossische Zeitung*. In Maurel (p. 319) is reproduced an alleged fourth letter from Ferdinand to the Countess of Flanders, dated December 4, and first published in the *Nouvelle Revue*, September 1, 15, 1888. Ignorance as to the documents involved is indicated by the passage: "Je ne puis ni expliquer ni comprendre comment les documents que l'on ne m'a encore signalés de Berlin que d'une manière assez générale, ont été communiqués à l'empereur de Russie." The writer adds that he will be obliged to maintain a "silence de mensonge" in the face of Bismarck's explanations. It is worth noting that, on December 2, Reuss sent the prince only the enclosure which had accompanied the first letter, merely describing the other documents in a general way. See his letter to Ferdinand in *G. F. O.*, v, p. 344.

[81] *Times*, December 10, 1887. St. Petersburg, December 8.

[82] *Ibid.*, December 15. St. Petersburg, December 13.

[83] *Ibid.*, January 5, 1888. St. Petersburg, January 3.   [84] *G. F. O.*, v, p. 341.

[85] *Times*, January 4. Berlin, January 3. *N. F. P.*, December 23, 1887.

These persons were accused of fabricating and finally publishing the Reuss note. Some such bypath as this in the intrigue may be granted, but whether or not the proper persons are here designated as agents cannot be determined.

In all this multiplication and confusion of accounts can be recognized a familiar Bismarckian stratagem for relieving the pressure of an embarrassing situation.[86] No really straight or plausible story was ever put out. The persons most certainly involved in the plot, Nieter and Foucault de Mondion, were never named. No one seemed able to penetrate clearly beyond Hansen and the Russian embassy at Paris. That was enough to confuse and alarm the Tsar, but should not have deterred Bismarck. A Belgian official and a French spy were nothing to him; yet he never ran them down, or, at least, never exposed them. The motive instantly suggests itself that he feared the exposure might lead further than he desired. Nieter and de Mondion have since been designated as the forgers of the papers. Their position and connections open up possibilities far more damaging to Bismarck.

It is to be noted that the Chancellor never expressed himself personally on the subject at all. The words of the *Reichsanzeiger* are the nearest to authoritative utterances that we have.[87] The accounts of the origin of the plot are, at most, semiofficial. Eckardstein gives a suggestive picture of the conduct of the Prince and his son in this connection. He writes: "As regards the origin of the so-called Bulgarian letters, one thing is certain — that Bismarck himself, whenever the affair was brought up in the most intimate family gatherings, maintained an icy silence or quickly

---

[86] The manoeuvre is best exemplified by reference to the "War-Scare of 1875," *American Historical Review*, January, 1919, pp. 221–223. A notable addition to the sources therein employed is contained in volume v of Buckle's *Life of Benjamin Disraeli*, pp. 420–425. The crown princess wrote, on June 5, to Queen Victoria, "He even named the Empress Eugénie!!" The profusion of accounts becomes so bewildering that one is tempted to give up all effort to get at the truth. So the *Neue Freie Presse* remarked, as early as December 23: "Es ist kaum mehr möglich, der Kölnische Zeitung auf den vielverschlungenen Pfaden zu folgen, auf denen sie nach den Urhebern der gefälschten Actenstücke sucht."

[87] Nothing emanating from him is included in the scanty array of documents on the subject in the German foreign office publication, with the exception of a few inconsequential marginal notes (v, p. 343).

sought to turn the conversation into other channels. Herbert Bismarck several times acted rather indiscreetly when the incident was spoken of. I remember how, one evening at Hupka's when someone remarked in his presence that the forging of the Bulgarian documents was an unheard-of scandal, he listened in silence, then gazed up at the ceiling and whistled. After he had gone out, Count Conrad Lüttichau remarked: 'Lucky that Schuvalov or little Knorring were not here this evening, or they would surely have drawn their own conclusions from Herbert Bismarck's behavior.' " [88]

One more possibility remains of accounting for such conduct. It was suggested by Madame Juliette Adam at the time the documents were published. In the *Nouvelle Revue* for January 15, 1888, she wrote: "It is ascertained . . . that the famous forged papers . . . are not the product of an Orleanist conspiracy, nor the proof of a Russian diplomat's Machiavellism, nor yet the fruit of a French Chauvinist's hate. My readers, if they credit my deductions, will conclude with me that, if a patent is to be taken out for the original inspiration of these letters, only Bismarck is entitled to it." [89] His conduct, she continues, strongly suggests that of an unfaithful wife securing immunity from all suspicion by throwing her husband once upon a false trail.

This idea was taken up and elaborated upon by Élie de Cyon, her colleague in the campaign for the Franco-Russian alliance. Cyon condemns without hesitation the documents published in the *Reichsanzeiger* and all the revelations of de Mondion and his band. Of course, they are false, he maintains — so palpably false that they were obviously constructed to be proved so.[90] As for the person of the forger, he seizes upon the Catacazy story put forth at the time. The fact that Catacazy was a partisan of the German alliance only serves his purpose the better; for the whole plot, in his view, was carried out under the direction of Bismarck.[91] The letters were concocted in a manner to make detection of their falseness easy — yet they had to convince momentarily a

---

[88] Eckardstein, i, p. 136.   [89] *Nouvelle Revue*, January 15, 1888, p. 412.
[90] Cyon, p. 364. Yet his own proofs are far from conclusive and contribute nothing to the case.   [91] *Ibid.*, pp. 359 *et seq.*

French minister, several Russian personages, and the Tsar himself. They were invented to give Bismarck a clean bill of health for his whole policy through their exposure — yet they came very near preventing his ever getting the necessary chance to explain them at all. Clearly, the principle of *is fecit cui prodest* is being overworked in this case even more flagrantly than in the case of the attempt upon the Tsar's life.

Cyon was probably influenced by jealousy of the part that others were playing in a cause he wished to claim as his own province. He was jealous, too, of the ascendancy which the 'document ring' later obtained over his associate, Madame Adam. She, in fact, went over completely to their side of the case. Beginning with the summer of 1888, their revelations filled the *Nouvelle Revue* for more than a year. Madame Adam gave them her unlimited confidence and pledged her own honor in support of their disclosures, the Bulgarian documents included.[92] She probably collaborated with them in writing the book, *Le prince de Bismarck démasqué*, published under the name of 'Charles de Maurel,' which gave their story of the intrigue, maintaining the genuineness of the documents. It was the stir caused by her articles on the Belgian situation that finally led to the unmasking of Nieter and de Mondion and the disclosure of the fact that documents had actually been stolen from the Belgian archives. Then, somehow, just as bigger developments than ever seemed on the way, the whole affair was mysteriously hushed up. The actors dropped out of sight; and Madame Adam abruptly broke off her connection with them. This whole episode has left almost no mark upon the historical treatment of the Bulgarian documents; yet it merits far more attention than it has received.

One historian of recent years, Debidour, has made use of the 'Maurel' book at its face value and accepted the documents as fully authentic.[93] This confidence would appear too naïve. Cer-

[92] *Nouvelle Revue*, August 15, 1888, p. i. "J'affirme sur l'honneur l'authenticité de ce document, comme j'affirme l'authenticité du *Secret d'État* publié dans la *Nouvelle Revue* par le comte Vasili, comme j'affirme encore l'authenticité des documents bulgares."

[93] *Histoire diplomatique de l'Europe depuis le Congrès de Berlin jusqu'à nos jours* (Paris, 1916–17, 2 vols.), i, p. 116.

tain reservations must at least be made — for example, as to the Reuss note. Even the acceptance of the letters as essentially genuine is going further than absolute proof can warrant. The present conclusions are by no means safe from reversal. But they have the backing of the probabilities of the case.

On thing may be set down as certain: the acceptance of the documents goes contrary to none of the established facts concerning Bismarck's policy. They fit into the development of the story with a nicety difficult to attribute to a mere outsider's interpretation of passing and future events. This fact has been noted by writers who had not the courage to affirm their authenticity.[94] The picture they give of Bismarck's policy toward Russia is all that the *Reichsanzeiger* admitted it to be, with the addition of fidelity to the truth.

Against the drawing of any such conclusions by contemporaries stood out one startling fact. Bismarck had dared to give the documents publicity without reserve. A falsehood so brazen was unthinkable: he must be telling the truth. No one knew better than the Chancellor the value of publicity, of the brutal frankness that so disconcerted the diplomacy of the old school. Unhappily, there slipped in among his frank truths an occasional plump falsehood — and who could tell them apart? At any rate, the publication seemed to strengthen the Tsar's conviction of Bismarck's innocence. Alexander was no man for halfway decisions and mental reservations. Along with the mysterious documents must go the diplomatic reports of confirmation. Bismarck should be taken at his own estimate. Of course, the realities of the situation were not altered thereby. His exoneration left Russia's defeat no less complete and actual. But that was simply her misfortune and the work of forces over which he had no control.

[94] Daudet, *Alliance*, pp. 225–226. This was also Madame Adam's first view of the case, expressed in the *Nouvelle Revue*, January 15, 1888.

# CHAPTER XIII

## THE FRUITS OF BISMARCK'S DIPLOMACY

### I

A REMARKABLE picture of the European situation as it stood at the close of the year 1887 was that presented by the leading article of the *Neue Freie Presse* on the first day of the new year. This situation was described as the result, not simply of the events of a single year, but as the outcome of the entire course of European politics since 1871. It was a situation calling into question the fate of the world order established by the treaties of Frankfort and Berlin, treaties both essentially the work of imperial Germany. The line of division determining the grouping of European powers falls, according to the article, between those satisfied and those dissatisfied with this world order. In relation to the outcome of this divergence of aims, the year 1887 is treated as not decisive, but prophetic.

"History designates years which one may call prophetic," the writer begins, and points out how the great catastrophes of history have cast their shadows before them. He continues: "Among these prophetic years will be reckoned the one at whose end we now stand. The peace of the world has been preserved, it is true; and life in the several countries is still going on as usual; but no one can be sure any longer that the peaceful day will be followed by an equally peaceful morrow. The pulse of the century grows feverish. The political and economic atmosphere has become dull and oppressive. What we are experiencing is comparable to the crackling in the walls of an unsound house which usually precedes a catastrophe.

"The present situation of Europe is based almost entirely upon the historical phenomenon brought about by the war of 1870 — upon the establishment of the German Empire. . . . Only, Germany could not have attained to such greatness without obliging other once proud Powers to descend in the scale; and these must resent the way in which their own policies are affected by the preponderance of the German Empire. France, after contributing two provinces to Germany's establishment, must naturally feel the difference between her past and present position all the more painfully for her isolation by German diplomacy. It is almost inevitable that her whole national policy should be dominated by the idea of regaining what has been lost. Russia saw her advance in the East brought to a halt by this same German power; for she encountered Germany's ally, Austria, and, instead of laying down a victor's law to Turkey, had to submit to the arbitration of Europe at Berlin, which set up a new legal order, by no means consistent with Russia's plans . . .

"It is noteworthy that the year began with the most serious apprehensions of imminent war and that it . . . closes with similar anxieties. . . . The only distinction is that, while at the beginning of the year the French Peril stood in the foreground, at its close the threat seems to come from Russia. But even this distinction is only apparent; for a glance at the European situation will show that both dangers spring from a common source. What is driving us toward a catastrophe is the endeavor to overthrow the European legal system which Germany has created, protected, and firmly imposed upon the recalcitrant."

Bismarck sought to provide against the dangerous reaction of his policy toward Russia upon her relations with France. He redoubled his efforts to strengthen and expand the system of the Triple Alliance. On February 1, he concluded the military convention with Italy which Crispi so ardently desired.[1] His representations at Brussels seemed to be producing more and more of an impression.[2] The rumors concerning them multiplied; and by the middle of February, the *Volkszeitung* of Cologne had it that an engagement had been entered into by Leopold II under cover

---

[1] Pribram, i, p. 123 (Amer., i, p. 11). See also *G. F. O.*, vi, chapter xli.

[2] *N. F. P.*, January 12. Brussels, January 12. "Dieselben Organe, welche vor einiger Zeit die Meldung, betreffend den auf Belgien und Holland ausgeübten Druck wegen Entwicklung ihrer militärischen Streitkräfte und wegen eventueller Verständigung mit der Tripel-Allianz, in Abrede stellten, zeigen sich jetzt voller Furcht und verlangen Aufklärungen, welche die Regierung nicht geben kann und nicht geben will."

of Article 68 of the Belgian constitution, allowing the sovereign to conclude treaties without informing Parliament for a certain length of time.[3] The categorical denial of this report by the Belgian minister of foreign affairs, on February 21, almost certainly goes beyond the truth in affirming that no advances were made, and probably evades it in maintaining that no engagements existed.[4] There are indications that Sweden was also approached in the effort to annex to the German system of alliances all the possible outlying states.[5]

While taking these precautions for the future, the Chancellor freely expressed his opinion that there was no danger of war for the present. As his comment upon the triumph of the diplomacy of the Central Powers, we have his words of January 18: "According to my inmost convictions there will be no war within the next three years."[6] This was a little more hopeful than the cur-

[3] *Annales parlementaires de Belgique*, Chambre des représentants, session of 1887–88, pp. 597–598. On February 21, 1888, this and other articles were made the subject of an interpellation by M. Neujean.

[4] *Ibid.*, p. 598. Reply of the Prince de Chimay. "Ma réponse est connue d'avance: la Belgique neutre n'a point cessé de respecter, comme elle l'a d'ailleurs toujours fait, les devoirs qui s'attachent à son état politique, et personne n'a tenté d'ébranler sa résolution de n'y point manquer. Elle n'a fait aucun traité, n'a pris aucun engagement qui ne soient connus de tous. Tout ce qu'ont dit certains journaux de prétendues propositions qui nous auraient été faites en ce sens est une pure fable qui n'a pas même de prétexte." This alleged treaty was one of the chief subjects involved in the campaign of publicity waged by the *Nouvelle Revue* in the following two years. The Belgian government does not emerge from that campaign altogether cleared of suspicion, although the Prince de Chimay made a still more vehement denial of the treaty's existence on February 5, 1890, *Annales*, 1889–90, p. 543. The only rejoinder of Madame Adam was: "Certaine de l'existence d'un traité, dangereux hier, sans valeur aujourd'hui, puisqu'il est officiellement renié devant une Chambre souveraine, je suis d'avis que mes collaborateurs et moi nous soyons bons princes et oublions les démentis, les horions reçus pour applaudir avec plus de droits que personne à la déclaration du gouvernement belge que la Belgique n'a pris aucune espèce d'engagement avec aucun de ses voisins." *Nouvelle Revue*, February 15, 1890, p. 852.

[5] *N. F. P.*, February 2. According to the Berlin correspondence of a London newspaper.

[6] Report circulated on the Berlin Bourse, on the 19th, by the Hamburg banking house of Lappenberg of a conversation at dinner on the foregoing day. *N. F. P.*, January 20. See also Lucius von Ballhausen, p. 417, for a similar utterance on the 17th.

rent opinion of a month before, but did not set a high value upon the recent reconciliation with Russia.

Somewhat later appeared a curious interview enlarging upon this idea. The Chancellor was soon to address the Reichstag on the Landsturm law, and expressed some perplexity as to the line of argument he should follow. "What can I say in the Reichstag?" he demanded of his auditor. "If I say that everything is peaceful and that there is no probability of war this year, then all the opposition will raise a hue and cry about the army budget and insist on its being not increased but diminished. If, on the other hand, I tell them that war is imminent, then Russia will be irritated, France will be irritated, and Austria will be beside herself with excitement. This, in fact, might precipitate the war, which I hope will not take place before 1892." He explained this startling precision of date: "It will take four or five years before any of the Great Powers will have attained their maximum fighting strength. Until this maximum is reached I do not see any imminent probability of war." Bismarck added: "Now let me tell you something else. I am absolutely certain that, in spite of all that is said to the contrary, the Czar does not want war. The Emperor William does not want war. Austria, with the exception of a few Hungarians, does not want war. France does not want war, and I myself simply detest war. I think that the year 1888 will expire without being made historical by a European war." But this would never do to tell the Reichstag. "I should simply impress upon them," he concluded, "the fact that Germany's national existence depends upon at least keeping abreast of our neighbors in military strength and readiness, and that war can only be averted as long as Germany continues fully prepared for it." [7]

So Bismarck, apparently, placed a certain confidence in Russia's recent assurances. He probably placed even more in the combination of forces by which those assurances had been extorted from her. That combination, strengthened and extended by his efforts, was his hope for the future. If it could not continue

[7] *New York Herald*, February 4. Berlin, February 3. Interview said to have been with the "representative of a foreign European nation."

to ward off the encounter, it at least gave promise of a favorable decision. There was even a chance of retarding the threatened resort to arms by appealing to the Tsar's regard for the conservative principle in government which was the chief bond between Russia and the Central Empires. Only there should be no more political concessions or compromises. Come what might, however, Germany must be prepared for the worst. Her military strength must be brought to its highest possible point, for the deterring of potential foes or for dealing with actual ones. And to carry public opinion with the government, no argument should be neglected.

Yet the Chancellor realized, too, that when he spoke, he addressed not only a German Parliament, but all Europe as well. He must convince both audiences of the reasonableness and justice of his cause. He must show that he was preparing for defence, and not for aggression. He must maintain that Germany meant peace; that her intentions, her policies, her alliances were all defensive in implication; and that all danger of disturbance of the peace came from forces beyond her control. To this end he had paved the way by his exposure of the slanderous intrigue of the 'Bulgarian documents.' Now another revelation came to supplement the effect of that stroke.

On February 3, the text of the Austro-German treaty of 1879 was published simultaneously at Berlin, Vienna, and Pest. The text was complete, except for Article III, concerning the duration of the agreement, which had been omitted from the versions communicated to Russia, England, and Italy. Article IV was therefore numbered III in the published version. It concerned the communication of the treaty to third parties, and contained a paragraph highly applicable to the recent crisis. "The two High Contracting Parties," it ran, "venture to hope . . . that the armaments of Russia will not in reality prove to be menacing to them, and have on that account no reason for making a communication at present; should, however, this hope, contrary to their expectations, prove to be erroneous, the two High Contracting Parties would consider it their loyal obligation to let the Emperor Alexander know, at least confidentially, that they must consider an attack on either of them as directed against both." [8]

In view of the excitement lately prevailing over Russian troop movements, all this had a highly significant air, appearing as a warning to the Tsar's government. The London *Times* pronounced the revelation "a slap in the face which Russian pride must resent." [9] Of course, few could suppose the treaty had been quite unknown to the Tsar before this date; but no one suspected its full communication to Shuvalov in May, nor the fact that the crisis of December had already been patched up. There was much speculation as to the motives for publication.

The official statement, taking almost identical form in both countries, announced that publication of the treaty had been agreed upon, "in order to put an end to the doubts raised as to its purely defensive intent." [10] The obvious application of this statement was to Russian opinion. Yet the *Times* declared success in that quarter hopeless; while a Russian periodical called the revelation an attempt to "enfoncer la porte ouverte." [11] A remarkably good hypothesis was put forward by the Berlin *Post*: "With this treaty in his hand, the German Chancellor will have no difficulty in convincing Europe that the policy of the Central Powers is one of peace." [12] The publication of this document was, indeed, an excellent prelude to the coming speech.

In fact, Bismarck had made no mention of Russia among the reasons alleged by him in seeking Austria's consent to publication. His first argument was the necessity of putting a curb upon the extravagant hypotheses concerning the treaty put forward by the Magyar chauvinists. He undoubtedly had in mind also the

[8] Pribram, i, pp. 8–9 (Amer., i, pp. 28–31). *G. F. O.*, v, pp. 288–289.

[9] *Times*, February 4. "It is impossible to doubt that the Czar has long before now been confidentially informed of the opposition he must count upon facing if he attacks either Germany or Austria. Hence the actual publication of the treaty does not greatly alter the situation as it must have been conceived by statesmen, however it may bring home the truth to the public in the various countries interested. Were there a public in our sense in Russia, the publication would hardly rank as a revelation, and the Russian people being what it is, there is room to doubt whether the revelation will have any effect upon the course of events."

[10] *Reichsanzeiger, Wiener Abendpost, Budapesti Közlöny*, February 3.

[11] Вѣстникъ Европы, March, 1888, p. 397. [12] *Post*, February 5.

Austro-Hungarian generals, who were still engaged, at the time he wrote, in their effort to extend the *casus foederis*. The second reason advanced was: "In the military debate in the Reichstag, I shall have to touch on political considerations and shall not be able to avoid speaking the truth about the scope of our alliance."[13] His third reason was indiscreet. It was "the impression which will be made by publication upon our own peoples" with a view to the eventuality that "we should be forced into a war under circumstances giving rise to doubts concerning its *defensive* character." If people were assured in advance, he wrote, that there could be no war but a defensive one, "they would the more readily comprehend that, under certain circumstances, the first shot fired does not necessarily designate the attacking party."[14] This dubious doctrine pleased the Austrians and served to mitigate their disappointment over the failure of the military negotiations.

Before Bismarck had a chance to dilate upon the policy behind this treaty, however, it was seized upon by Crispi to point a terrible moral. Like her allies, Italy had a heavy programme of military expenditures to put through. On February 4, Crispi berated his penny-pinching Parliament with the words: "The country must realize that the time for sacrifices is not past. The proposed reduction of taxes would be most untimely. The administration still requires many millions to develop our capacity for resistance. In view of the international situation, this is doubly essential. The publication of the treaty of alliance between Germany and Austria should be taken, not as a threat, but as a warning addressed to all who dream of disturbing the allies' work of peace."[15] Such was in brief the line of argument which Bismarck was to follow two days later in his great speech to the Reichstag.

The speech of February 6, 1888, is probably the most notable in Bismarck's career. Although he was so ill that only recourse to stimulants enabled him to speak at all, and he was obliged to

[13] *G. F. O.*, v, p. 282. January 14, memorandum by Count Rantzau. January 18, Bismarck to Reuss.
[14] *Ibid.*, v, pp. 284–285. January 22, memorandum by Count Rantzau.
[15] *N. F. P.*, February 5.

deliver most of his address while seated, he spoke with a power and appeal which brought him a popular triumph unsurpassed in even his brilliant experience. His majestic survey of German policy in the past, present, and future makes this speech a historical document of great value. Next to the *Gedanken und Erinnerungen*, it is the most important and comprehensive exposition of the Chancellor's views on foreign policy which he has handed down. The aspects of it chiefly considered here will be those bearing upon the events of the two or three preceding years.

Bismarck was careful to begin by saying that he undertook his exposition less for the sake of convincing the Reichstag of the need for the proposed law than for that of convincing Europe that its passage implied no threat to peace.[16] The events of the recent past were represented as having reached, on the whole, a satisfactory outcome. The interpretation of them was, naturally, calculated to give the impression of German policy which Bismarck wished to produce upon the world — regardless of the deep-lying facts of the case. Thus, in the frontier incidents of the previous year, the blame was laid entirely upon France; the credit for their peaceable settlement was given entirely to Germany.[17] In this quarter affairs were admitted to have taken a decided turn for the better.[18]

Relations with Russia were dwelt upon at much greater length than those with France, in accordance with the statement that they had lately been the chief source of anxieties. And here again, the blame was all laid upon the other side. The occasions of anxiety lay, said the Chancellor, "partly in the Russian press,

[16] *Reden*, xii, p. 441.

[17] *Ibid.*, p. 473. "Wir haben in den vielen kleinen Vorfällen, die die Neigung unserer Nachbarn, zu spioniren und zu bestechen, verursacht hat, immer eine sehr gefällige und freundliche Beilegung herbeigeführt, weil ich es für ruchlos halten würde, um solcher Lappalien willen einen grossen nationalen Krieg zu entzünden oder auch nur wahrscheinlich zu machen. Das sind Fälle, wo es heisst: Der Vernünftigere gibt nach."

[18] *Ibid.*, p. 442. "Ich glaube also constatiren zu können — und thue es gern, weil ich wünsche, die öffentliche Meinung nicht aufzuregen, sondern zu beruhigen —, dass die Aspecten nach Frankreich hin friedlicher, viel weniger explosiv aussehen als vor einem Jahr."

partly in the Russian military dispositions." [19] In both these respects, he acknowledged that the grounds for anxiety had diminished. "Against the utterances of the Russian press," he stated, "I have the direct testimony of the Emperor Alexander himself, given when I had the honor . . . of an audience with him a few months ago. I was then amply reassured that the Emperor of Russia entertains no hostility toward us and has no intention of attacking us." [20] Since all newspaper bluster must weigh "feather-light" beside such assurances, he continued: "The press gives me no occasion to estimate our relations with Russia as worse than a year ago."[21] So the crisis of the autumn was accounted for with no word of the essential issues involved.

The crisis of the winter had come about over questions of troop movements, although these had been of much older standing. Nothing was said as to the means by which the alarms of December had been quieted; but Bismarck now gave his hearers a reassuring version of Russia's policy. No explanations had been asked or offered, he said; but his personal opinion was "that the Russian cabinet is convinced — and with reason — that in the next European crisis, the weight of Russia's word in the counsels of Europe will vary directly as her strength on her European frontiers." [22] Immediate application of this motive was made to Russia's own interests: "I assume that a new Eastern crisis is expected, and that Russia's idea is to put behind her proposals the full weight of an army, not at Kazan, but grouped far to the westward." [23] This belated estimate of Russia's motives contains a startling admission as to the real centre of gravity in the Eastern Question. It indicates the extent to which Russia's chances of a favorable decision had been damaged by Lobanov's declaration. The crisis, in fact, was no longer ' expected,' but passed, and to Russia's disadvantage.

Having introduced the Eastern Question in this roundabout

---

[19] *Reden*, xii, p. 442.   [20] *Ibid.*, p. 443.

[21] *Ibid.*, p. 444. But he remarked later on (p. 477): "Jedes Land ist auf die Dauer doch für die Fenster, die seine Presse einschlägt, irgend ein Mal verantwortlich; die Rechnung wird an irgend einem Tage präsentirt in der Verstimmung des anderen Landes."

[22] *Ibid.*, p. 445.   [23] *Ibid.*, p. 446.

manner, Bismarck took up the thread of his familiar justification of Germany's policy in respect to it. He repeated that Germany was not directly interested, and maintained that her conduct had been upright and loyal throughout. In 1876, she had refused to make a choice between Austria and Russia. At the congress of Berlin her Chancellor had borne himself like a "fourth Russian plenipotentiary." His reward had been an astounding campaign of vilification, culminating in open threats as a result of his refusal to constrain Austria to accept Russia's views regarding the application of certain clauses of the treaty. Hence he had been forced into the defensive alliance with Austria.[24] The explanation is totally misleading. Bismarck's declaration of 1876 was, in fact, a guarantee to Austria against the consequences of opposing Russia's will. It forced Russia to pay Austria an unearned price for acquiescence in an attempt to improve the lot of Turkey's Christian subjects by the only effective means left after the concert of Europe had been brought to blank failure, largely through Austria's own obstructive tactics. At the congress of Berlin Bismarck had enforced payment of the price, while so manipulating the other factors in the situation that Russia came off with a bare modicum of her own expectations. Then he expressed surprise that Russia resented being cozened in the settlement of accounts! He was indeed forced into the treaty of 1879 — forced by the logic of events flowing from his own partisanship for Austria.

So much for the origin of the alliance. It was a confessed necessity — "if we had not already concluded it, we should have to conclude it today."[25] It was based upon mutual fundamental interests.[26] For the publication he gave no new reason, but denied any intention of threatening Russia. The full text, he said, had been communicated to the Russian cabinet long ago — even before the interview of November.[27]

In the face of all misunderstandings and all misconstructions of his policies, Bismarck evinced a readiness still to go on in the path of loyalty to his conception of Russia's rights. He admitted that the decisions of the congress of Berlin had implied a "prepon-

[24] *Reden*, xii, pp. 461–464.  [26] *Ibid.*, p. 466.
[25] *Ibid.*, p. 464.  [27] *Ibid.*, p. 464.

derating influence in Bulgaria" as Russia's natural prerogative.[28] Germany would continue to recognize such a claim, and would "support diplomatically any diplomatic step that Russia can devise to regain her influence in Bulgaria." [29] Only, the initiative must come from Russia. This generous pledge left everything as it stood; since a faithful band of bravoes stood ready to knock any Russian proposals on the head as fast as they appeared, leaving Germany occasion only for consolations.

The results of Germany's honorable dealing, said the Chancellor, had been discouraging, especially where Russia was involved. But he would engage in no 'crawling contest' with France for the prize of the Muscovite friendship. "The time for that has gone by," he proudly stated: "we no longer seek to curry favor, either with France or with Russia. . . . We have sought to restore the old trustful relationship, but we dangle after no one." [30]

All these developments, he declared, had left Germany in a delicate situation between France and Russia — unstable for the future, but not immediately perilous, thanks to the attitude of the Tsar. "My confidence carries me so far," he said, with reference to Alexander's assurances, "that I am convinced, even if we should be involved in a war with France, through some outburst not to be predicted in advance and not intended by the present French government, a Russian war would not necessarily follow. On the other hand, though, if we should be involved in war with Russia, a French war would be inevitable: no French government would be strong enough to prevent it, even if it had the will to do so." [31] Then, despite his restored confidence in the Tsar, despite the Lobanov agreement, which remained concealed, Bismarck went on to assume that there was reason still to expect trouble with Russia.

"The crisis most likely to develop," he said, was "the Eastern." His treatment of Germany's position in the face of its appearance was as familiar as his justification of past policy. She was not implicated "in the first line." She was not called upon to take

---

[28] *Reden*, xii, p. 474.
[29] *Ibid.*, p. 475.
[30] *Ibid.*, p. 474.
[31] *Ibid.*, pp. 444–445.

a position in advance of the powers directly concerned. "If Eastern crises appear, we shall wait, before taking any stand with relation to them, until the more directly interested Powers have taken theirs." [32] This was the attitude, it must be pointed out again, which rendered valueless Germany's pledges of support to Russia. One may go further still and recall the fact that Bismarck had not even left the more interested Powers to themselves, but had encouraged them to concert and make more effective their resistance to Russian policy. Such was his betrayal of the 'old trustful relationship,' the decline of which he deplored.

The Chancellor did not reveal the existence of the Anglo-Austro-Italian combination which formed the first line of defence for his equivocal policy, but he did speak of the close community of interests between Germany and her two partners in the Triple Alliance.[33] So Germany had reliable assurances against the danger of a war; she was not primarily involved in the dispute most likely to occasion one; she had outposts behind which to lurk and allies in the event of a clash. Yet the Chancellor must justify a proposal to augment her military forces by 700,000 men — the equivalent of a fourth ally.

"I do not anticipate any immediate disturbance of the peace," ran his argument, "and I ask that you treat the proposed law independently of such considerations and anxieties." [34] But he had stipulated beforehand: "The fact that I hold these for the moment unfounded is far from leading me to the conclusion that we need no increase in our armed forces — quite the contrary." And why? Because, after all is said and done, the war on two fronts looms in the future; and Germany must neglect no preparations to face it. His words were impressive and yet reassuring: "I hope our fellow citizens will take comfort in the thought that, if we should be attacked from two sides at once — which I do not

---

[32] *Reden*, xii, p. 447.

[33] *Ibid.*, pp. 464–465. "Sie sind eben — nicht nur der Vertrag, den wir mit Oesterreich geschlossen haben, sondern ähnliche Verträge, die zwischen uns und anderen Regierungen bestehen, namentlich Verabredungen, die wir mit Italien haben, — sie sind nur der Ausdruck der Gemeinschaft in den Bestrebungen und in den Gefahren, die die Mächte zu laufen haben."

[34] *Ibid.*, p. 476.

anticipate, though the events of the past forty years show that all sorts of coalitions are still possible — we could have a million good soldiers for the defence of each of our frontiers. And we can raise, besides, a half-million, or even a million, reservists in the interior to send forward where needed." [35] This picture of power and security should suffice to convince his hearers of the wisdom of voting as they were asked to do.

But Germany and the world at large must have no idea that this great force would ever be turned to the uses of aggression. The possibility that Germany should have any ends of expansion to achieve was not even considered. But Bismarck did feel called upon to dispel the suspicion that she might sometime undertake a 'preventive war.' Upon the fantastic assumption that her Chancellor should ever conceive such a project, he ventured to hope that the Diet would withhold its support; and he expressed confidence that the nation would not rise to the occasion.[36] All this was merely persiflage. Had Bismarck desired a 'preventive war,' he would have found German public opinion the least of his obstacles. On the several occasions when he had appeared to be preparing for a new war, national sentiment outran him if anything: it was the failure of his ostensible occasions to develop properly that averted the explosions.

Such empty considerations brought the speaker round to his dramatic peroration. He had painted a picture of Germany, strong in her own might and in the consciousness of following ever the path of honor — a Germany misunderstood and maligned, standing between jealous neighbors who constituted always a potential threat to peace. Firm in her own peaceful intentions, she would arm to meet that threat in the most dangerous shape it could take. So Bismarck came to the rhetorical flourish which will ring forever in the hearts of his countrymen: "We Germans fear God, but nothing else in the world!"

## II

Leaving rhetoric and misrepresentation aside, what was the situation of Germany as pictured by Bismarck in the great speech

---

[35] *Reden*, xii, p. 468.   [36] *Ibid.*, pp. 470–471.

of 1888? Certainly it was far different from the situation of three years before, when the German Empire had stood at the centre of a system of alliances and understandings embracing the whole continent of Europe. The year 1888 found that system crumbling to ruin, the friendship with France destroyed and the alliance with Russia undermined. In 1885 Germany was fearlessly challenging England's supremacy in distant colonial fields: in 1888 she was preoccupied with the defence of her own frontiers and dependent upon England's help for preserving the remains of her structure of alliances. In 1885 Germany's diplomacy brilliantly sufficed for the attainment of her most ambitious ends: three years later she was straining every nerve to keep up a military establishment that would enable her to remain mistress of her own destiny. Bismarck's sounding phrases are a confession of the breakdown of his policy. The problem of assuring Germany's future had got so far beyond the resources of his diplomacy that he had nothing left to recommend but reliance on her own brute force. Another formidable military bill hardly a year after the preceding one — such was the culmination of Bismarck's diplomacy in the eventful year 1887. And such was the international situation which Bismarck left as heritage to his successors; for it had changed but little when they took it over two years later.

The only dependable diplomatic resource he left to them was the Austrian alliance, which they correctly appraised as the most solid element in his international system. They overdid the espousing of Austrian interests, perhaps; but in showing solicitude for those interests, they were only following the example set by Bismarck since 1876. In Bethmann-Hollweg's account of Germany's action in the crisis of 1914, the urgency of Austria's peril is no doubt exaggerated; but the justification of Germany's support to her is based almost wholly on Bismarck's arguments.[37] From the day of its conclusion, the Austrian alliance had been the cornerstone of Bismarck's system; and he had taken care to promote Austrian interests as far as the limits of caution allowed. His successors overstepped those limits in the end; but it is

[37] Theobald von Bethmann-Hollweg, *Betrachtungen zum Weltkriege*, i (Berlin, 1919), pp. 127–133.

questionable if Bismarck himself could have kept within them indefinitely. His mask of duplicity had slipped so far aside in 1887 that Russia could never again have any real confidence in his professions as 'honest broker.' The League of the Three Emperors as a complement to the Austrian alliance had definitely ceased to exist.

Its other complement, the Triple Alliance, remained; but Bismarck had never set great store by the friendship of Italy. He rated Italy's material value to his system hardly above that of the Balkan satellites of Austria, and he realized fully the unreliability of her engagements. His suggestion to the Austrian crown prince that her loyalty be assured by generous *pourboires* at the expense of France did not imply any intention to plunge Germany wantonly into adventures for the sake of bolstering up a second-rate alliance. The enterprising Crispi found small encouragement in his later attempts to drag his allies into an aggressive policy for Italy's profit. Bismarck had, it is true, made extensive commitments on Germany's behalf in renewing the alliance, but he never meant to go out of his way to fulfil them. He had made them during a crisis, when there had appeared an especial need for assuring himself of Italy's rôle with regard to both France and the Eastern Question. In the latter connection, he had skilfully contrived to make Italy and England influence each other. He had drawn England into his system by way of an understanding with Italy, and at the same time induced her to share Germany's burden of satisfying Italy's claims of support for her own interests. Masterly as had been the accomplishment of February, 1887, however, it was a *tour de force* of momentary, rather than permanent, significance.

By his dealings with England, Bismarck appeared to have secured a new addition to his international system, making up for the defection of France and the weakening of the Russian connection. But it was a compensation far from satisfactory in his own mind. His lack of confidence in the straightforwardness and continuity of English foreign policy prevented his ever regarding England's friendship as a permanent asset. He had made no serious effort to attach England directly to Germany by any formal bond. He was fully conscious of the fact that, in dealing with her at all, he was only taking advantage of a temporarily favorable situation for temporary ends. His utilization of England was, in reality, inconsistent with even the slight remnant of his old political system, which he had no idea of altering fundamentally. Germany's own relations with Russia, which Bismarck still valued highly, despite the ill services he had rendered her, would necessarily suffer through Germany's intimacy with England. Moreover, the agreement between England and Germany's two allies, brought about in 1887, had practically fulfilled its purpose when Russia abandoned her designs on Bulgaria. Deprived of its immediate object, the bonds of the agreement must slacken, following Bismarck's own theory that England's support could be counted upon only where English interests were pressingly involved.

Pursuing the consequences of the settlement of 1888 still further, they could entail only an increasing alienation of England from the Central Empires. She had nothing to gain through the replacement of Russian influence in the Balkan Peninsula by the Austrian penetration which followed the opening of the railways to Salonica and Constantinople. She was still less gratified by the diversion of Russia's expansive forces into the Far East which accompanied the development of the Trans-Siberian line. And both these tendencies would necessarily have at least the moral approval of even Bismarck's Germany. The weakening of England's connection with Bismarck's international system, therefore, began with the moment the connection was established. It was essentially self-destructive. Its disappearance would inevitably undermine Italy's position in the Triple Alliance. Italy's connection with England was of more importance to her than that with the Central Empires: once England had broken away from them, the Triple Alliance was practically dissolved. So the new Triple Alliance and the Austro-Italian entente with England were legacies of doubtful value at the best.

The most perplexing of Bismarck's diplomatic legacies was the Reinsurance Treaty with Russia. His heirs cannot be greatly blamed for renouncing their title to it. His most bitter criticisms of their policy arose from this action; yet it is doubtful if even in his hands this bond of alliance would ever have proved more than a rope of sand. His regard for the Russian connection was beyond question sincere, but it was a regard which embraced only Germany's interest in maintaining it. He was perpetually cut off from a proper appreciation of Russia's interest by his overweening solicitude for the greatness of Austria. He wished to retain the friendship of Russia as a check upon Austria; yet he could not employ it indefinitely as a mask behind which to contrive the balking of all Russia's designs running counter to Austria's. Perhaps he was not consciously striving to injure Russia; but, supposing he believed himself to be acting for her own good, he could not expect her always to accept his definition of her reasonable and salutary expectations.

Even after Bismarck had brought about Russia's renunciation of Bulgaria, she continued favorable to prolonging the Reinsurance Treaty. But the terms she would have insisted upon are not known. The desire to keep in touch with Europe's strongest champion of conservative monarchical government, which must have been Russia's chief motive for wanting to continue the alliance, would exist almost as well without it. Moreover, as her return to the fold after the congress of Berlin had not prevented the Bulgarian crises, so the settlement of 1888 was no guaranty against such another revival of the Eastern Question as actually occurred in 1908. Would Bismarck have been any more successful than his heirs in hoodwinking Russia a third time? He might have avoided ' shining armor ' speeches as comments upon his exploit; but his actual policy would probably have been much like theirs, and would hardly have been less acutely resented by Russia. The Reinsurance Treaty would have influenced Germany's course no more than it had in 1887.

As a matter of fact, Bismarck was none too considerate of Russia's feelings in the aftermath of the settlement of 1888. He gave only the old formal support to her efforts to save her face by proceeding with the proposal for a general condemnation of Ferdinand's position as illegal. In vain Russia undertook to abstain from the slightest single-handed interference with the consequences: the opposition stood firm and unbroken. Only Turkey took the desired course, with no result whatever; and Russia had to acknowledge an unmitigated defeat.[38] But still more serious for the future than Bismarck's refusal to ease Russia's diplomatic defeat was his refusal to relax the financial blockade he had imposed in the course of his struggle with Alexander III. The German market remained closed to Russian loans, despite the fact that the Asiatic enterprises into which Russia had been diverted required financial aid on a larger scale than she had ever sought before. The consequence could only be the acceleration of Russia's drift toward France. The renewal of the Reinsurance Treaty in 1890 could have checked that tendency only if it had been accompanied by a radical change in German policy, such as Bismarck had shown no signs of bringing about. The results of his conduct were inevitable, whether they took shape immediately in the binding and loosing of formal diplomatic ties or not.[39] The diverting of Russia into the Far East, accompanied by a refusal of the means to develop her projects, brought on the Franco-Russian alliance. That alliance gave Russia a partner in the West to reach her a hand for the return to Europe when those projects were undone by a military defeat in the East.

France's action in these developments was no more dependent upon formal agreements than was Russia's. The Reinsurance Treaty alone could not keep Russia away from France: a treaty with Russia was not necessary to assure France's coöperation against Germany. It was less necessary than ever, after the events of 1887. Whatever progress Bismarck had previously made toward a reconciliation with France had been annulled by his conduct in that critical year. The blame for the revival of enmity between France and Germany rests even more clearly on his shoulders than does that for the estrangement between

[38] See Plehn, pp. 294–298.
[39] Pagès (Senate Report), p. 235. On February 15, 1888, Herbette wrote that Shuvalov had just told him: "En tout cas, la Russie ne renoncera pas à sa politique traditionnelle en Orient et elle conservera sa liberté d'action en Europe. Elle est heureuse des sympathies qu'elle rencontre en France et elle les paye de retour. Pour que les deux peuples soient unis, pas n'est besoin d'une alliance formelle. Le jour du danger chacun d'eux saura bien où trouver ses amis."

Germany and Russia. Great as was his disappointment at the fall of Ferry, he was not justified in regarding that event as a demonstration of incurable hostility. Ferry had perhaps gone too far in his manifestations of friendliness: the reaction against him did not mean an end of peaceful relations. Below the superficial indications of that reaction, succeeding French governments had striven honestly to carry on the tradition, older than the Ferry ministry, of moderation in their conduct toward Germany. They had even rebuffed advances from Russia. If a real change was at last brought about in French policy, it was due to Bismarck's deliberate provocations. The fall of Ferry had seemed to demonstrate to him a lack of appreciation of his benevolence: the crises of 1887 demonstrated very clearly to France a positive malevolence against which she would do well to provide. Looked at from the western side, then, the Franco-Russian alliance appears again as the fruit of Bismarck's diplomacy. It would have taken more than his mere continuance in office, more than a simple renewal of the Reinsurance Treaty, to prevent this eventual alliance of hatred and suspicion.

Many tributes have been paid to Bismarck's personality, to his impressive renown, to his unequalled grasp of affairs and sureness of touch, as the essential elements in his policy, impossible to transmit to any successor.[40] Such explanations of the failure of his successors needlessly obscure the shortcomings of the policy they inherited. Of the critical period in which Bismarck's diplomacy put its final touches on Germany's destiny, Robertson has written: "The years 1887 and 1888 were . . . the severest touchstones of a German statesman's statecraft. Bismarck's performance was, when we appreciate the complex difficulties, a consummate one. The master proved his mastery."[41] The eulogy bears almost an ironic interpretation when examined in the light of the situation in which Bismarck's statecraft had placed his country. His performance, ' consummate ' in duplicity

[40] Walter Platzhoff, *Bismarcks Bündnispolitik* (Bonn and Leipzig, 1920), p. 16. "Das Werk war ganz auf seinen Schöpfer zugeschnitten, es stand und fiel mit seiner Person. Vererbt konnte es nicht werden."

[41] *Bismarck*, p. 442.

and brutality, left the main problem of the period regulated by a one-sided settlement which only entailed new difficulties.[42] It left Germany between two potential foes about to join hands across her frontiers. It left her with but one dependable alliance amid a set of unstable combinations. It left her frankly dependent upon a vast military establishment as the main reliance for her future. Could the 'master' himself have found a safe way out of this situation? If Bismarck's successors were to fall below his level in resourcefulness, the outlook was dark indeed!

One may well doubt if his successors fell as far short of their example as their critics would make out. They allowed the Reinsurance Treaty to go by the board, it is true, and did not prevent the Franco-Russian alliance from coming into being. But these natural results of Bismarck's diplomacy brought on no immediate disaster. The Reinsurance Treaty, with its complicated neutrality clause and its hollow promises bearing on the Eastern Question, did not concern the essence of Russia's interest in the friendship of Germany. The young Emperor who had dared question Bismarck's judgment took up the problem of relations with Russia from the more promising side of dynastic ties and common interest in principles of government. He had made some headway before the death of Alexander III, despite the French alliance; and he found his task even easier with the new Tsar.[43]

[42] Rachfahl, in the *Weltwirtschaftliches Archiv*, July, 1920, p. 64. "Viel verschlungener, hinterhältiger und dämonischer war Bismarcks Politik in diesem schweren Jahre 1887, als offensichtlich selbst der Zar es ahnte . . . Wiederum hatte der Kanzler, wie vor einem Jahrzehnt, für Österreich gegen Russland optiert, aber nicht mehr offen, sondern verdeckt und versteckt, und er hatte das Spiel so glänzend gewonnen, dass es überhaupt nicht erst zum Kriege zu kommen brauchte. Aber sollte er wirklich geglaubt haben, der Zar würde es nicht merken, wer hinter der russischen Niederlage stehe, so dürfte er sich doch wohl getäuscht haben."

[43] *Letters from the Kaiser to the Czar*, ed. by I. D. Levine (New York, 1920), pp. 1–2, 7. Letter of November 8, 1894. "What our political ideals are we both know perfectly and I have nothing to add to our last conversation in Berlin. I only can repeat the expression of absolute trust in you and the assurance that I shall always cultivate the old relations of mutual friendship with your house in which I was reared by my Grandfather, and some examples of which I was so glad to be able to give to your dear Papa in these last six months of his reign, and which I am happy to hear were fully appreciated by him." Again, on February 7, 1895: — "In short,

For the rest, he recurred to the situation of 1888, and found in it the means of actually turning the Franco-Russian alliance to profit.

The subsequent performance merits at least being called ' consummate.' In encouraging Russia's diversion into the Far East, the new German government contrived that she should drag France after her. All three Powers were associated in the intervention of 1895 against Japan.[44] Russia was so far diverted from the affairs of the Balkan Peninsula that she confirmed her renunciation of 1888 by recognizing Ferdinand of Bulgaria, and concluded the agreement of 1897 with Austria, based frankly on the existing status quo. By 1902, ' Willy ' was writing to ' Nicky ' in his quaint English: "For as rulers of the two leading Powers of the two great Continental Combinations we are able to exchange our views on any general question touching their interests, and as soon as we have settled how to takle it, we are able to bring our Allies to adopt the same views, so that the two Alliances — i. e. 5 Powers — having decided that Peace is to be kept, the World must remain at peace, and will be able to enjoy its blessings." [45] Germany was again mistress of the Continent and in a position to defy England and rebuff her advances.[46] Could Bismarck have done more? One may even ask, could he have done as much? The very exuberance of imagination and fertility in political projects

everywhere the ' principe de la Monarchie ' is called upon to show itself strong. That is why I am so glad at the capital speech you made the other day to the deputations in response to some addresses for reform."

[44] *Letters*, pp. 9–10. Letter of April 16, 1895. "I thank you sincerely for the excellent way in which you initiated the combined action of Europe for the sake of its interests against Japan. . . . It shows to evidence how necessary it is that we should hold together, and also that there is existent a base of common interests upon which *all* European nations may work in *joint action* for the welfare of all as is shown by the adherence of France to us two. May the conviction that this can be done without touching a nation's honour, take root more and more firmly, then no doubt the fear of war in Europe will dissipate more and more."

[45] *Ibid.*, pp. 85–86. Letter of September 2, 1902.

[46] *Ibid.*, p. 53. Letter of August 18, 1898. "Since I communicated to you this June, England has still now and then reopened negotiations with us but has never quite uncovered its hand; they are trying hard, as far as I can make out, to find a continental army to fight for their interests! But I fancy they won't easily find one, at least not *mine*!"

and expedients which led William II to his downfall were probably lacking in the Iron Chancellor to develop the possibilities of the situation he himself had brought about. The successors had ' out-Bismarcked Bismarck.' [47]

It may be justly alleged that the new situation was unstable, and that, at the time the Emperor penned his triumphant words, his own diplomacy was declining from its zenith, dragging Germany toward the abyss. Though such be the case, the new diplomacy cannot be charged with proving false to the traditions of the old. We may recur to Delbrück's dictum, quoted in the opening chapter, that all the undertakings of the ' New Course ' had their roots in the old.[48] Without new personalities and new ideas animating these policies, they might even have led to a crash sooner than they did. If it be held that the crash was inevitable, its causes must be sought far back in the past, as they were by the Vienna journalist who predicted it at the close of 1887. They lay not only back of the change of government in 1890, but back of the Empire's foundation. They were inherent in the first Chancellor's entire work. Their consequences could be averted in the long run only by remodelling that work from its very foundations. Without calling Bismarck's early, fundamental achievements into question — which is beyond the scope of this study — it is not possible to indicate what better courses could have been followed. It is at least clear, however, that his

[47] Otto Hammann concludes his lengthy criticism of the policy of William II, in *Der missverstandne Bismarck*, by inveighing particularly against this conception of a Continental coalition. It was, he states, a "lebensunfähiges Gebilde," the crowning result of a misunderstanding of Bismarck's principles of policy. Yet we have seen Bismarck pursuing exactly such a course in 1884, and abandoning it only when the French drew back from further colonial adventures. If they could be induced to coöperate again with Germany in distant fields, there was no obvious reason why the conception should not appear as valid as ever. Hammann's thesis, that strict adherence to Bismarckian principles would have led to coöperation instead of rivalry between Germany and England, remains unproved. A survey of the foreign policy of the years 1885–88 shows that the "Irrungen und Wirrungen" of the New Course, which Hammann charges to the misunderstanding of Bismarck, were hardly less characteristic of his own conduct of German affairs.

[48] Platzhoff (p. 19) adds: "Der neue Kurs . . . verharrte grundsätzlich in den alten Bahnen, auch dann, als diese nicht mehr zum Ziele führen konnten."

diplomacy contained no priceless and unique key to imperial Germany's future, irrecoverable once wantonly thrown away. Rather, it may be maintained that Bismarck's diplomacy, at the zenith of his power, contained all the causes of his Empire's downfall.

# APPENDIX

# APPENDIX

## THE LETTERS EXCHANGED BETWEEN BISMARCK AND SALISBURY IN NOVEMBER, 1887

(a)

*Prince von Bismarck, Chancellor of the German Empire, to the Marquis of Salisbury, Prime Minister and Secretary of State for Foreign Affairs of the United Kingdom*

A secr. 14281 22 November 1887.
Berlin, le 22. novembre 1887.
Son Excellence
  Lord Salisbury
etc. etc. etc.
    Londres.

Monsieur le Marquis,
Dans les pourparlers qui ont eu lieu entre Votre Excellence et le Comte Hatzfeldt afin de préciser l'appréciation anglaise de l'entente austro-italienne par rapport aux intérêts communs que ces deux Puissances ont en Orient, j'ai puisé la conviction qu'un échange d'idées direct entre nous pourrait être utile aux intérêts de nos deux pays et contribuer à écarter de part et d'autre quelques uns des doutes qui peuvent subsister au sujet des buts politiques que nous poursuivons de part et d'autre.

Nos deux nations ont en effet tant d'intérêts communs, et il y a un si petit nombre de points sur lesquels des divergences de vues peuvent se produire, que nous sommes à même d'admettre dans nos ouvertures mutuelles plus de franchise que les habitudes de notre diplomatie ne comportent. La confiance que nous avons de part et d'autre dans la loyauté personnelle l'un de l'autre nous permet de donner une étendue plus vaste encore à cette franchise. Au sujet de la politique anglaise la publicité de votre régime parlementaire nous offre une source suffisante d'informations, tandis que la manière moins transparente dont les affaires se traitent chez nous peut devenir une cause d'erreurs difficiles à éviter, comme par exemple celle, que commet Votre Excellence en exprimant l'appréhension que le Prince Guillaume pourrait, lorsqu'il tiendrait un jour les rênes du Gouvernement, incliner systématiquement à une politique hostile à l'Angleterre. Pareille chose ne serait pas possible en Allemagne — ni le contraire non plus. De même que Son Altesse Impériale le Prince de la Couronne ne voudrait et ne pourrait un jour, étant Empereur, faire dépendre sa politique d'inspirations anglaises, de même aussi le Prince Guillaume, se trouvant à sa place, ne penserait pas à faire et serait dans l'impossibilité de faire sa politique en suivant les impulsions venant de St. Pétersbourg. Les deux Princes, lorsqu'ils seront appelés à régner, l'un et l'autre suivront exactement la même ligne de conduite en obéissant à leurs sentiments personnels aussi bien qu'à la force de la tradition monarchique; ils ne voudront et ne pourront s'inspirer d'autres intérêts que de ceux de l'Allemagne. Or, la route à suivre pour sauvegarder ces intérêts est tracée d'une manière tellement rigoureuse, qu'il est impossible de s'en écarter. Il ne serait pas raisonnable d'admettre, que le Gouvernement d'un pays de 50 millions d'habitants — considérant le degré de civilisation et la puissance de l'opinion publique existant en Allemagne — pourrait infliger à ce pays les souffrances qui accompagnent et suivent toute grande guerre, victorieuse ou non, sans fournir à la nation des raisons assez graves et assez claires pour convaincre l'opinion publique de la *nécessité* de la guerre. Avec une armée, telle que la nôtre, qui se recrute indifféremment dans toutes les classes de la population, qui représente la totalité des forces vives du pays et qui n'est que la nation en armes — avec une telle armée les guerres des siècles passés, résultant de sympathies, d'antipathies ou d'ambitions dynastiques, ne pourraient se faire. Depuis près d'un quart de siècle l'Allemagne forme annuellement 150,000 soldats, de manière à pouvoir disposer aujourd'hui de 3 à 4 millions d'hommes, âgés de 20 à 45 ans et rompus au service militaire. Pour toute cette multitude d'hommes nous possédons, non seulement les armes et les objets d'équipement nécessaires, mais même les officiers et sous-officiers pour les conduire au combat. Nos cadres sont complets — avantage dont en fait d'officiers et de sous-officiers aucune autre nation ne pourrait se vanter.

Ces millions d'hommes sans exception, accourent au drapeau et se placent sous les armes aussitôt qu'une guerre sérieuse menace l'indépendance nationale et l'intégrité de l'Empire. Mais ce grand appareil de guerre est trop formidable pour que, même dans notre pays, imbu du sentiment monarchique, il puisse être arbitrairement mis en branle par la simple volonté royale; il faudrait au contraire que les Princes et les Peuples de l'Empire soient unis dans la pensée, que la patrie, son indépendance et son unité récemment faite, se trouvent en danger, pour que ces grandes levées d'hommes puissent s'effectuer sans danger. Il s'en suit que notre force militaire est en première ligne un appareil défensif, destiné à n'entrer en action que lorsque la nation aura acquis la conviction, qu'il s'agit de repousser une agression. L'Allemagne a peu d'aptitude à faire d'autre guerre qu'une guerre défensive. — En appliquant ce qui précède à un cas spécial, il ressort de l'état des choses en Allemagne que le Gouvernement de l'Empire ne pourrait pas assumer devant la nation la responsabilité d'une guerre, dans laquelle d'autres intérêts que ceux de l'Allemagne se trouveraient en litige, comme par exemple ceux de l'Orient. — Le Sultan est notre ami et il a toutes nos sympathies; mais de là jusqu'à nous battre pour lui, il y a une distance que nous ne pourrons proposer au peuple allemand de franchir.

En faisant ces déclarations, je ne veux pas faire supposer, que rien qu'une attaque directe contre nos frontières serait capable de justifier un appel aux armes des forces allemandes. L'Empire allemand a trois grandes puissances pour voisins, et ses frontières sont ouvertes. Il ne doit donc pas perdre de vue la question des coalitions qui *pourraient* se former contre lui. Si nous supposons l'Autriche vaincue, affaiblie ou devenue ennemie, nous serions isolés sur le continent de l'Europe en présence de la Russie et de la France, et en face de la possibilité d'une coalition de ces deux puissances. Il est de notre intérêt d'empêcher même par les armes que pareil état de choses puisse s'établir. — L'existence de l'Autriche comme Grande Puissance forte et indépendante est une nécessité pour l'Allemagne à laquelle les sympathies personnelles du souverain ne peuvent rien changer. — L'Autriche, de même que l'Allemagne et l'Angleterre d'aujourd'hui, appartient au nombre des nations satisfaites, "saturées" au dire de feu le prince Metternich, et partant pacifiques et conservatrices. L'Autriche et l'Angleterre ont loyalement accepté le *status quo* de l'Empire allemand et n'ont aucun intérêt de le voir affaibli. La France et la Russie au contraire paraissent nous menacer; la France en restant fidèle aux traditions des siècles passés qui la montrent comme ennemie constante de ses voisins, et par suite du caractère national des Français; la Russie en prenant aujourd'hui vis-à-vis de l'Europe l'attitude inquiétante pour la paix européenne qui caractérisait la France sous les règnes de Louis XIV. et de Napoléon I. C'est d'un côté l'ambition des meneurs slaves à laquelle incombe la responsabilité de cet état de choses; d'un autre côté il faut chercher les causes de l'attitude provocante de la Russie et de ses armées, dans les questions de sa politique intérieure; les révolutionnaires russes espèrent qu'une guerre étrangère les débarrassera de la monarchie; les monarchistes au contraire attendent de cette même guerre la fin de la révolution. Il faut considérer aussi le besoin, d'occuper une armée oisive et nombreuse, de donner satisfaction à l'ambition de ses généraux, et de détourner vers la politique étrangère l'attention des libéraux qui demandent des changements de constitution. Vu cet état de choses nous devons considérer comme permanent le danger de voir notre paix troublée par la France et la Russie. Notre politique par conséquent tendra nécessairement à nous assurer les alliances qui s'offrent en vue de l'éventualité d'avoir à combattre simultanément nos deux puissants voisins: Si l'alliance des puissances amies menacées par *les mêmes* nations belliqueuses nous faisait défaut notre situation dans une guerre sur nos deux frontières ne serait pas désespérée; mais la guerre contre la France et la Russie coalisées, en supposant même que comme exploit militaire elle finirait aussi glorieusement pour nous que la guerre de sept ans, serait toujours une assez grande calamité pour le pays pour que nous tâcherions de l'éviter par un arrangement à l'amiable avec la Russie s'il fallait la faire *sans* allié. Mais tant que nous n'avons pas la certitude d'être délaissés par les puissances dont les intérêts sont identiques aux nôtres, aucun empereur de l'Allemagne ne pourra suivre une autre ligne politique, que celle de défendre l'indépéndance des puissances amies, satisfaites comme nous de l'état actuel de l'Europe et prêtes à agir sans hésitations et sans faiblesses quand leur indépendance serait menacée. Nous éviterons donc une guerre russe autant que cela sera compatible avec notre honneur et notre sécurité, et autant que l'indépendance de l'Autriche-Hongrie, dont l'existence comme Grande-Puissance est d'une nécessité de premier ordre pour nous, ne soit pas mise en question. Nour désirons que les puissances amies qui en Orient ont des intérêts à sauvegarder qui ne sont pas les nôtres, se rendent assez fortes par leur union et leurs forces pour retenir l'épée de la Russie au fourreau ou pour y tenir tête en cas que les circonstances ameneraient une rupture. Tant qu'aucun intérêt de l'Allemagne s'y trouverait engagé, nous resterions neutres; mais il est impossible d'admettre, que jamais Empereur allemand puisse prêter *l'appui* de ses armes à la Russie pour l'aider à terrasser ou à affaiblir une des Puissances sur l'appui desquelles nous comptons soit pour empêcher une guerre russe soit pour nous assister à y faire face. A ce point de vue la politique allemande sera *toujours* obligée à entrer en ligne de combat, si l'indépendance de l'Autriche-Hongrie était menacée par une agression russe, ou si l'Angleterre ou l'Italie risquaient d'être entamées par des armées françaises. La politique allemande procède ainsi sur une route forcément prescrite par la situation politique de l'Europe et dont ni les antipathies ni les sympathies d'un Monarque ou d'un Ministre dirigeant pourraient la faire dévier.

Je me flatte de l'espoir que Votre Excellence voudra reconnaître la justesse des raisonnements de cet exposé que je viens de faire. Quant à moi, je le répète, j'y reconnais d'une manière tellement absolue les principes de la politique que l'Allemagne est et sera forcée de suivre, que les sympathies les plus chaleureuses pour une Puissance étrangère ou pour un parti politique quelconque, ne pourraient cependant jamais offrir la possibilité à un Empereur allemand ou à Son Gouvernement de s'en écarter.

Je prie Votre Excellence d'agréer l'expression de mes sentiments très dévoués.

gez. v. Bismarck.

(*b*)

*The Marquis of Salisbury to Prince von Bismarck, in reply to the preceding*

*Private and most confidential*      London November 30th 1887

Sir

I have the honour to acknowledge the letter which Your Serene Highness has been good enough to write to me, under date of the 22nd of November. I am very thankful for the unreserved confidence by which that letter is inspired — a confidence which I cordially concur with Your Serene Highness in believing, is fully justified by the sympathy, and the close coincidence of interest existing between our two nations.

It is right on that account that I should explain briefly the considerations which led me to entertain the apprehensions which I expressed to Count Hatzfeldt. If the lamentable event of a war between France and Germany should take place, Russia, if she was well-advised, would not take any step hostile to Germany, but would at once, by occupying positions either in the Balkan peninsula or in Asia Minor, compel the Sultan to assent to proposals which would make her mistress of the Bosphorus and Dardanelles. She would only abstain from this step if threatened by a formidable resistance. Italy and England alone would not be sufficient to deter her: and it is very doubtful whether English public opinion would consent to go to war for Turkey with only Italy for an ally. All would depend, therefore, on the attitude of Austria. Unless she was certain of assistance from Germany, she might not feel strong enough to hazard a war with Russia, and a consequent invasion on her north eastern frontier where Italy and England could hardly help her. In that case she would sit still, and accept compensation in Turkish territory. She has favoured that policy in former years and even now it is reported, I know not with what truth, that the Emperor of Austria personally inclines to it. She could only take the opposite and bolder line, if she felt sure of the ultimate support of Germany.

When therefore we were asked to join in an understanding upon the eight bases which were given to Sir Edward Malet, it became on consideration very evident that the one vital question to us was one which was not even alluded to in these eight bases — namely the probable attitude of Germany. If Austria could count on German support in such a struggle, it would be possible for her to carry out fully the policy indicated in the eight bases to which England was asked to adhere. In any other case, England by giving this adhesion might be committing herself to a policy predoomed to failure. We then asked ourselves what ground we had for assuming that Germany, engaged in a severe struggle with France, might not take a neutral line, or even a line favourable to Russia. Just at this time came the news that the succession to the German throne of a Prince who was believed to be more favourable to Russia and more averse to England than the present Heir to that throne, was a contingency which might arrive at an earlier date than was expected.

Your Serene Highness has removed my apprehensions by the great frankness with which you have exposed the true situation to me. You have in the first place allowed me to see the Treaty between Austria and Germany which established that under no circumstances could the existence of Austria be imperilled by resistance to illegal Russian enterprises. In the second place you have conveyed to Sir Edward Malet, on the part of the Emperor, his moral approbation of any agreement which may be come to by Austria, Italy, and England on the three bases submitted to us: and in the third place you have convincingly explained to me that the course of Germany must be dictated by the considerations of national interest felt by the nation at large, and not by the personal prepossessions of the reigning Sovereign.

I believe that the understanding into which England and the other two Powers are now prepared to enter, will be in complete accordance with her declared policy and will be loyally observed by her. The Grouping of States which has been the work of the last year, will be an effective barrier against any possible aggression of Russia; and the construction of it will not be among the least services, which Your Serene Highness has rendered to the cause of European peace.

I have the honour to be
Your Serene Highness' obedient
humble servant
    (sd.) Salisbury
His Serene Highness
The Prince von Bismarck
        Berlin

# BIBLIOGRAPHY

# BIBLIOGRAPHY

A SIMPLY alphabetical arrangement of the bibliography was adopted, because no classification by sources and secondary works seemed feasible. For so recent a period, the available sources are few and inadequate; and much of the material must necessarily be derived from books and other publications which cannot properly be listed as sources without an undue strain on the term. The attempt to classify these according to their nature and value would lead to endless difficulties. Official publications are listed under the respective countries; while the importance of other works is indicated by critical and descriptive notes. Newspapers and periodicals of which extensive use has been made are treated in special notes at the end of the list. The choice of these was in part determined by the fact that almost all the research was done with the resources of the Library of Harvard University.

Albin, Pierre. *L'Allemagne et la France en Europe (1885–1894)*. Paris, 1913.
*Archives diplomatiques.* A periodical publication, edited from 1883 to 1900 by Louis Renault, containing selected diplomatic correspondence, speeches, and other public records of international events.
Baddeley, J. F. *Russia in the 'Eighties.'* London, 1921. The memoirs of the St. Petersburg correspondent of the London *Standard*. The writer was especially intimate with Count Peter Shuvalov, former ambassador to London and plenipotentiary at the congress of Berlin, who was still active in public life. Count Peter was the brother of Count Paul Shuvalov, ambassador at Berlin, and frequently acted as his unofficial colleague in especially important negotiations. He enjoyed to a large degree the confidence of Prince Bismarck, which he reciprocated by faith in the Chancellor's loyalty to Russia. His conversations with Baddeley throw some light on Russo-German relations.
Belgium. *Annales parlementaires de Belgique.*
Billot, Albert. *La France et l'Italie.* Paris, 1905. 2 vols.
Bismarck, Otto, Fürst von. *Gedanken und Erinnerungen.* Stuttgart, 1898–1921. 3 vols. English translation of the first 2 vols. under the title, *Bismarck, the Man and the Statesman*. London and New York, 1899, 2 vols. The English edition of the translation of the third volume is entitled *New Chapters of Bismarck's Autobiography* (London, 1921); the American edition, *The Kaiser vs. Bismarck* (New York, 1921). Bismarck's own memoirs must always constitute a fundamental source for the study of

his diplomacy. But the 'Erinnerungen' often require verification; while the 'Gedanken' form a political testament designed to influence the future rather than to explain the past. The exposition of motives, therefore, needs supplementing by all the indications which can be assembled of Bismarck's actual opinions contemporaneous with his acts.

—— *Die politischen Reden des Fürsten Bismarck.* Edited by Horst Kohl. Stuttgart and Berlin, 1892–1905. 14 vols.

——. "Neue Briefe: Fürst Bismarck an Kriegsminister v. Bronsart." A weekly series published in the *Deutsche Allgemeine Zeitung*, beginning April 2, 1922. The most important letter politically is that of December 24, 1887, which was published on April 16.

*Blue Books.* See Great Britain.

Blum, Hans. *Fürst Bismarck und seine Zeit.* Munich, 1894–99. 6 vols. and supplement.

Booth, John. *Persönliche Erinnerungen an den Fürsten Bismarck.* Edited by Heinrich von Poschinger. Hamburg, 1899.

Brauer, A. von; Marcks, Erich; Müller, Alexander von, editors. *Erinnerungen an Bismarck.* Stuttgart and Berlin, 1915. A collection of fragments and special studies, of which the one most cited is that of K. A. von Müller, "Beiträge zur äusseren Politik Bismarcks in den achtziger Jahren — nach zeitgenössischen Aufzeichnungen bearbeitet." The source of the brief remarks quoted in this article, which has long been a mystery, is revealed by the publication of documents from the German foreign office. Most of them reappear in that publication as Bismarck's marginal notes on despatches.

Busch, Moritz. *Bismarck, some Secret Pages of his History.* London, 1898. 3 vols. American edition, New York, 1898. 2 vols. German edition, entitled *Tagebuchblätter*, Leipzig, 1899, in 3 vols. As Bismarck's biographer, journalistic mouthpiece, and self-appointed literary assistant, Busch was the recipient of many important confidences, the records of which are published in this work. References are primarily to the English edition.

Cappelli, Raffaele. "La politica estera del conte di Robilant," in *Nuova Antologia*, November 1, 1897. Some contributions by Robilant's private secretary.

Chaudordy, J. B. A. D., Comte de. *La France en 1889.* Paris, 1889. This book sheds a little light on the negotiations with England in 1887, in which the writer acted as the unofficial agent of Flourens.

Chiala, Luigi. *Pagine di storia contemporanea.* Vol. iii, *La triplice e la duplice alleanza.* Turin, 1898. An expansion of the latter part of the work as first published in two volumes, in 1892. Next to Crispi's memoirs, it is the most authoritative work on Italian policy of the period.

Churchill, W. S. *Lord Randolph Churchill.* London and New York, 1906. 2 vols. The biography of a statesman whose influence on British policy most profoundly affected his country's relations with Bismarck's Germany.

Corti, E. C. *Alexander von Battenberg. Sein Kampf mit den Zaren und Bismarck.* Vienna, 1920. The importance of this book transcends its subject. It is based on the prince's own archives and those of the Austrian ministry of foreign affairs. Material is incorporated bearing upon many other aspects of the international situation besides the Bulgarian question, with which the book is directly concerned; and much light is thrown on Bismarck's conduct of policy. The value of the book is impaired by too close confinement to the documents and a lack of the background of general knowledge required for their proper appreciation.

Crispi, Francesco. *Politica estera. Memorie e documenti raccolti e ordinati da T. Palamenghi-Crispi.* Milan, 1912. Appeared in English translation as volume ii of *Memoirs* of Francesco Crispi (New York and London, 1912–14, 3 vols.). The book is properly neither memoirs nor biography. Most of the material is from the hand of Crispi, with occasional comments and connecting passages written by his nephew. It is the most important source for Italy's foreign policy during Crispi's own ministry, and especially valuable for his relations with Bismarck.

Cyon, Élie de. *Histoire de l'entente franco-russe.* Paris and Lausanne, 1895. A journalist's book, magnifying the author's importance and interpreting all events according to his fixed ideas. Cyon led the campaign in France for a Russian alliance and served as intermediary between Katkov and Madame Adam. He also played a certain part in the financial negotiations between the two countries. While too highly colored, biassed, and inaccurate to have much value where unsupported by other evidence, the book has to be taken seriously, especially since the partial confirmation of its disclosures concerning the renewal of the League of the Three Emperors, long scoffed at as incredible. Katkov's position as spokesman of a faction including some of the highest Russian officials made him a considerable, if not always trustworthy, source of information.

*Daily Telegraph,* May 13, 1912. Contains an important article under the date line, Vienna, May 8, on Anglo-German relations. Letters of Holstein are quoted, giving an account of Bismarck's approaches to England in 1878 and 1887.

Daudet, Ernest. *Histoire diplomatique de l'alliance franco-russe.* Paris, 1894. This early book displays all the characteristics of the author's numerous later historical writings. It has a foundation of real knowledge of the facts, obtained through personal contact with political personages and their friends. But it is marred by sensationalism, by the failure to discriminate between serious disclosures and gossip, and by a readiness to jump to conclusions. Despite its defects, it remains an authority on the subject.

———. *Bismarck.* Paris, 1916. A book of untrustworthy character, owing especially to its sensational profusion of dialogue, but with a nucleus of real value derived from the recitals and papers of Jules Herbette, who replaced Courcel as ambassador at Berlin in August, 1886. Although published as volume i of a series called *Les auteurs de la guerre actuelle,* the book might better be considered as the third of the series noted below.

———. *L aFrance et l'Allemagne après le Congrès de Berlin.* Vol. i, *La mission du comte de Saint-Vallier.* Paris, 1918. Vol. ii, *La mission du baron* de Courcel. Paris, 1919. These narratives of the missions of Herbette's two predecessors are written from similar materials and in rather better style. Like it, they throw valuable light on Bismarck's relations with France.

——. *Ferdinand I$^{er}$ tsar de Bulgarie.* Paris, 1917. Published in the series *Les complices des auteurs de la guerre,* and apparently written in 1916. It is referred to in the author's "Le suicide bulgare," in *Revue des deux Mondes,* October 1, November 1, December 1, 1916, which cover the same ground. No contribution of any great value is made, and no light is thrown on the perplexed affair of the 'Bulgarian documents.' The most solid material employed is that derived from French diplomatic sources, and has mostly been utilized to better purpose in the author's other books.

——. "L'avènement d'Alexandre III.," in *Revue des deux Mondes,* November 15, 1918. "Le règne d'Alexandre III," in the same, May 15, June 15, 1919.

Dawson, W. H. *The German Empire.* New York and London, 1919. 2 vols.

Debidour, Antonin. *Histoire diplomatique de l'Europe depuis le Congrès de Berlin jusqu'à nos jours.* Paris, 1916–17. 2 vols.

Delbrück, Hans. *Bismarcks Erbe.* Berlin, 1915.

——. "Kaiser und Kanzler," in *Preussische Jahrbücher,* April, 1920.

Dilke, Sir Charles. *The Present Position of European Politics.* London, 1887. A republication, with some revision, of the author's articles of the first months of the year in the *Fortnightly Review.* Dilke had lately been excluded by circumstances connected with his private life from a promising career in the diplomatic service. His grasp of affairs and continued contact with official circles qualified him to write authoritatively on international events and conditions. His survey of these displays remarkable insight and keenness of judgment.

Drandar, A. G. *Les événements politiques en Bulgarie, depuis 1876 jusqu'à nos jours.* Brussels, 1896.

Eckardstein, Hermann, Freiherr von. *Lebens-Erinnerungen und politische Denkwürdigkeiten.* Leipzig, 1919–21. 3 vols. The author began his diplomatic career under Bismarck and spent a great part of it a counsellor to the embassy at London. His work is one of the strongest supports for the theory that Germany's destiny called for an alliance with England, and that Bismarck realized and sought to meet the need. It is also the source of a number of important revelations.

[Eckardt, Julius von.] *Berlin, Wien, Rom.* Leipzig, 1892. A defence of the policies of the 'New Course' against the criticisms of Bismarck and his followers. For an able review from an outsider's standpoint, see G. Valbert, "Un publiciste allemand et son plaidoyer en faveur de la triple-alliance," in *Revue des deux Mondes,* June 1, 1892.

——. *Bismarcks Kampf gegen Caprivi. Erinnerungen von Julius von Eckardt.* Leipzig, 1920.

Edwards, H. S. *Sir William White.* London, 1902. A biography of the British ambassador at Constantinople during the period of the Bulgarian crises.

Egelhaaf, Gottlob. *Bismarck*. Stuttgart, 1911.

Fester, Richard. "Verantwortlichkeiten," in *Deutsche Rundschau*, August, October, 1920. Surveys incorporating much recently published material.

Fitzmaurice, Lord Edmond. *The Life of Granville George Leveson Gower, Second Earl Granville*. London and New York, 1905. 2 vols. The most important source for Bismarck's relations with England during Gladstone's administration.

Flourens, Émile. *Alexandre III, sa vie, son oeuvre*. Paris, 1894. As minister of foreign affairs in 1887, Flourens writes with some authority on France's relations with Russia in that period.

———. "The relations between France and Russia since 1871," in the *New Review*, August, 1889. Not an important contribution.

France. *Journal officiel de la République Française*.

———. Ministère des affaires étrangères. *Documents diplomatiques. Affaires de Roumélie et de Grèce, 1885–1886*. Cited as Y. B. (= *Yellow Book*).

Freycinet, Charles de. *Souvenirs 1878–1893*. Paris, 1913. A valuable record from the French side. The author was minister of foreign affairs in 1885 and 1886, and was president of the council in the latter year, when Boulanger began his career as minister of war.

Friedjung, Heinrich. "Graf Kálnoky," in Bettelheim's *Biographisches Jahrbuch*, vol. iii, 1909. Republished in the author's *Historische Aufsätze* (Stuttgart, 1919), with several slight changes which rather detract from the article's value. It is extremely compact, but bristles with facts not generally known before its publication.

———. *Das Zeitalter des Imperialismus*. Vol. i. Berlin, 1919. A book which falls short of the expectations justified by the author's attainments.

Friis, Aage. "Ophaevelsen af Pragfredens Artikel 5," in *Tilskueren*, February, 1921. A little study which throws important light on Bismarck's relations with Austria.

*Fürst Bismarck und Russlands Orientpolitik*, von einem dreibundfreundlichen Diplomaten. Berlin, 1892. A controversial pamphlet of no serious value.

Galli, H. *Les dessous diplomatiques. Dix ans de politique étrangère 1884–1893*. Paris (1894?). This book first appeared as a series of anonymous articles in *Le Figaro*, which were commonly attributed to Flourens. The writer, a journalist, states that Flourens read and approved them before publication, besides furnishing much of the material.

Geffcken, F. H. *Frankreich, Russland, und der Dreibund*. Berlin, 1893. Another controversial publication deriving its importance from the fact of the author's intimacy with Frederick III. It is bitterly critical of Bismarck. Geffcken also published anonymously "Die russisch-französische Allianz und der Dreibund in geschichtlicher Beleuchtung," in *Deutsche Revue*, November, 1892. The article is more comprehensive and incisive than the pamphlet, charging Bismarck with the responsibility for the situation which developed after his dismissal.

Germany. *Stenographische Berichte über die Verhandlungen des deutschen Reichstages.*

—. *Die grosse Politik der europäischen Kabinette 1871–1914.* Edited by Johannes Lepsius, Albrecht Mendelssohn Bartholdy, and Friedrich Thimme. Berlin, 1922. 6 vols. covering the period to 1890. This publication of documents from the archives of the German foreign office is now the primary source for the study of Bismarck's diplomacy. His marginal notes are included. It is by no means all-sufficient; as there are numerous gaps, for example, in the negotiations over the Reinsurance Treaty. Such defects may be attributed to the inadequacy of the archives, rather than to the intention of the editors, who profess to have concealed nothing deliberately.

[Golitsyn] Galizyn, Prince Nicolai Nicolajewitch. *Lettre au 'Figaro' sur les théories de Katkow.* St. Petersburg, 1887. Review under the title, "A Franco-Russian Alliance," in *Edinburgh Review,* January, 1888.

Gopčević, Spiridion. *Bulgarien und Ostrumelien.* Leipzig, 1886.

Goriainov, Serge. "The End of the Alliance of the Emperors," in the *American Historical Review,* January, 1918. A most important and authoritative article, based on the documents, written by the late archivist of the Russian ministry of foreign affairs.

——. " Разрывъ Росіи съ Булгаріей въ 1886 году," in Историческій Вѣстникъ, January, 1917.

Gorlof, Valentin de. *Origines et bases de l'alliance franco-russe.* Paris, 1913.

Great Britain. See Hansard.

— —. *Parliamentary Papers* [*Blue Books*].
1886. Vol. lxxv, p. 1 [c. 4162]. Turkey no. 1. *Correspondence Respecting the Affairs of Eastern Roumelia and Bulgaria.* Vol. lxxv, p. 455 [c. 4767]. Turkey no. 2. *Further Correspondence Respecting the Affairs of Eastern Roumelia and Bulgaria.*
1887. Vol. xci, p. 317 [c. 4933]. Turkey no. 1. Vol. xci, p. 627 [c. 4934]. Turkey no. 2. *Further Correspondence Respecting the Affairs of Bulgaria and Eastern Roumelia.*
1888. Vol. cix, p. 397 [c. 5370]. *Further Correspondence Respecting the Affairs of Bulgaria and Eastern Roumelia.*

*Green Books.* See Italy.

Hagen, Maximilian von. *Voraussetzungen und Veranlassungen für Bismarcks Eintritt in die Weltpolitik.* Berlin, 1914.

Hahn, Ludwig. *Fürst Bismarck.* Berlin, 1878–91. 5 vols. A compilation of chronological tables and extracts from speeches, letters, newspaper articles, etc. All are to be found elsewhere; and the texts are not altogether trustworthy.

Hammann, Otto. *Zur Vorgeschichte des Weltkrieges.* Berlin, 1919. An important and authoritative work. German translations of the letters exchanged between Bismarck and Salisbury in November, 1887, are printed in the appendix.

― ―. *Der Neue Kurs.* Berlin, 1918.

― ―. *Der missverstandne Bismarck.* Berlin, 1921.

Hansard. *The Parliamentary Debates.* London, 1803–91. 422 vols.

Hansen, Jens Julius. *L'alliance franco-russe.* 2d edition. Paris, 1897. The author had a small part in the negotiations as private counsellor to the Russian embassy at Paris.

― ―. *Ambassade à Paris du Baron de Mohrenheim.* Paris, 1907. A work of some value, though not thoroughly reliable. It contains some important letters.

Harden, Maximilian. *Köpfe.* 9th edition. Berlin, 1910–11. 2 vols. The sketch of Holstein is one of the few sources of information about that enigmatic personage.

Headlam, J. W. *Bismarck.* New York, 1899; 2d ed., 1902.

Herrfurth, Kurt. *Fürst Bismarck und die Kolonialpolitik.* Berlin, 1909. Published as volume viii of Penzler's *Einzeldarstellungen.*

Hertslet, Sir Edward. *The Map of Africa by Treaty.* 3d edition. London, 1909. 3 vols. and maps.

Hofmann, Hermann. *Fürst Bismarck 1890–1898.* Stuttgart, Berlin, Leipzig, 1913–14. 3 vols. Based mainly on articles in the *Hamburger Nachrichten* written or inspired by Bismarck. An incomplete set of the articles is printed, arranged in simple chronological order. This arrangement, together with the lack of a subject-index, makes the work less useful than the older one of Penzler.

Hohenlohe-Schillingsfürst, Chlodwig, Fürst zu. *Denkwürdigkeiten.* Edited by Friedrich Curtius. Stuttgart, 1906. 2 vols. English translation under the title *Memoirs.* New York and London, 1906, 2 vols. The value of this storehouse of information is less for the period under discussion than for the earlier years. In September, 1885, Hohenlohe was transferred from the embassy at Paris to the governorship of Alsace-Lorraine. He still makes occasional important contributions on international affairs; while his testimony in connection with the Schnaebele incident is of especial significance.

Horn, A. E. "A History of Banking in the Russian Empire," in vol. ii of *A History of Banking in All the Leading Nations.* New York, 1896.

Huhn, Arthur von. *The Struggle of the Bulgarians for National Independence.* Translation from the German. London, 1886.

Italy. Ministero degli affari esteri. *Documenti diplomatici presentati al parlamento.* Rumelia Orientale. Serie 1, 1885. Serie 2, 1886. Bulgaria. 1889. Cited as *G. B.* ( = *Green Books*).

[Katkov, Michael.] "Lettres de Michel Katkov au tsar Alexandre III," in *Correspondant,* April 10, 1918. A group of five letters written at the period when Katkov's influence over the Tsar was at its height. They contain no information of especial value, and are, on the whole, disillusioning as to the writer's grasp of affairs.

Kjellen, R. "Die Koalitionspolitik im Zeitalter 1871–1914," in *Schmoller's Jahrbuch*, xlv, 1, 1921.

— —. *Dreibund und Dreiverband*. Munich, 1921.

Klaeber, Hans. *Fürst Alexander I von Bulgarien*. Dresden, 1904.

Koch, Adolf. *Fürst Alexander von Bulgarien*. Darmstadt, 1887.

Kohl, Horst. *Bismarck-Regesten*. Leipzig, 1891–92. 2 vols.

— —, editor. *Bismarck Jahrbuch*. Berlin, 1894–99. 6 vols. In volume i (pp. 125–130) appears a significant piece entitled "Deutschland und Russland seit dem Berliner Congress. 1879." It appears to be a memorandum written by Bismarck after his return from Vienna in September, 1879.

Красный Архив. Vol. i, 1922. "Русско-Германские отношения." A collection of documents with an introduction by M. N. Pokrovski. The group "Беседы II. А. Шувалова с кн.Бисмарком в апреле-мае 1887 г." gives Shuvalov's reports of the first series of conversations on the Reinsurance Treaty. These are the documents used by Goriainov in writing his article "The End of the Alliance of the Emperors."

Larmeroux, Jean. *La politique extérieure de l'Autriche-Hongrie*. Paris, 1918. 2 vols.

Lowe, Charles. *Prince Bismarck*. London, 1887, 1892.

— —. *Alexander III of Russia*. New York, 1895.

Lucius von Ballhausen, Robert, Freiherr. *Bismarck-Erinnerungen*. Stuttgart and Berlin, 1920. This is a source of the highest value. As Prussian minister of agriculture, domains, and forests, the writer attended the cabinet sessions and took notes of all matters discussed. These are regrettably brief, but they constitute one of the fullest records we possess of the development of Bismarck's policy. Notes of other important conversations and incidents are also included.

Manasevich, Boris. *Fürst Bismarck und das deutsch-russische Verhältnis*. 2d edition. Leipzig, 1891.

Marcks, Erich. *Otto von Bismarck; ein Lebensbild*. Stuttgart and Berlin, 1919.

"The Marquis of Salisbury," in the *Quarterly Review*, October, 1902.

Mater, André. *L'alliance russe*. Paris, 1906.

Matter, Paul. *Bismarck et son temps*. Paris, 1905–08. 3 vols.

Maurel, Charles de (pseud.) *Le prince de Bismarck démasqué*. Paris, 1889. Singer (*Bismarck in der Literatur*, p. 122) says the real author is Foucault de Mondion, a French spy. There is reason to believe that Madame Adam of the *Nouvelle Revue* and George Nieter, an official of the Belgian government, also helped in its preparation. It is the book of the band of conspirators involved in the intrigue of the 'false Bulgarian documents,' and presents their side of the case, with several new documents thrown in for good measure. The most interesting of these are the despatches, said to be those of a diplomatic agent at Berlin, presumably the Belgian minister, dated in November, 1887. The despatches of this period, which is that of the Tsar's visit to Berlin, are significantly omitted in the Schwertfeger collection.

Mévil, André. *De la paix de Francfort à la Conférence d'Algésiras.* Paris, 1909.

———. "Bismarck et la Russie," in *Revue hebdomadaire*, May 11, 1907.

Mittnacht, Hermann, Freiherr von. *Erinnerungen an Bismarck.* Stuttgart and Berlin, 1904–05. 2 vols. The writer, as minister-president of Württemberg, records several conversations with Bismarck throwing light on foreign affairs.

Molden, Berthold. "Kálnoky," in *Allgemeine Deutsche Biographie*, Nachträge, lv, Leipzig, 1906. Supplements Friedjung's article in several important respects.

Müller, Wilhelm. *Fürst Bismarck.* Stuttgart, 1898.

Newton, T. W. L., Lord. *Lord Lyons.* London, 1913. 2 vols. An excellent biography of the British ambassador at Paris, including many of his letters.

Notovich, Nikolai. *L'empereur Alexandre III et son entourage.* Paris, 1895.

Oncken, Hermann. *Das alte und das neue Mitteleuropa.* Gotha, 1917.

Pagès, Georges. "L'hégémonie allemande. 1871–1904." Part 2 of a "Mémoire sur les responsabilités de la guerre," by Émile Bourgeois and Georges Pagès, printed as annex to the *Rapport de la Commission d'Enquête sur les faits de la guerre*, vol. i, Sénat, 1919, no. 704. Paris, 1919. This is the most important source on the French side. It is based on research in the archives of the ministry of foreign affairs, and includes a large amount of documentary material taken from them, mainly despatches to and from the ambassadors at Berlin. But the work is not thoroughly done, and the documentation is haphazard. The study can be taken as authoritative only where documents are directly quoted or referred to.

Pahncke, Robert, *Die Parallel-Erzählungen Bismarcks zu seinen Gedanken und Erinnerungen.* Halle, 1914. A useful undertaking, assembling material from a great variety of sources, but not carried out on a sufficiently large scale. It is particularly deficient for the latter years of Bismarck's administration.

*Parliamentary Papers.* See Great Britain.

Penzler, Johannes, editor. *Fürst Bismarck nach seiner Entlassung.* Leipzig, 1897–98. 7 vols. A record mainly of the press discussions in which Bismarck was involved after his retirement, one volume being devoted to each year. Most of the *Hamburger Nachrichten* articles are reproduced. The arrangement is topical, with excellent indexes for each volume and for the whole work.

Petit, Pierre. *La dette publique de la Russie.* Poitiers, 1912.

Pfeil, Richard, Graf von. *Neun Jahre in russischen Diensten.* Leipzig, 1907.

Pinon, René. *France et Allemagne 1870–1913.* Paris, 1913.

Platzhoff, Walter. *Bismarcks Bündnispolitik.* Bonn and Leipzig, 1920. An excellent brief survey.

Plehn, Hans. *Bismarcks auswärtige Politik nach der Reichsgründung.* Munich and Berlin, 1920. The most comprehensive treatment of the subject yet attempted. Unfortunately, much of the most important material now available had not appeared before the author's death. The point of view is purely orthodox Bismarckian.

*La politica estera italiana 1875–1916.* Un Italiano. Bitonto, 1916.

Poschinger, Heinrich von. *Also sprach Bismarck.* Vienna, 1910–11. 3 vols. A convenient collection of dicta from known sources.

Pribram, A. F. *Die politischen Geheimverträge Österreich-Ungarns.* Vol. i. Vienna and Leipzig, 1920. English translation, edited by A. C. Coolidge, *The Secret Treaties of Austria-Hungary,* 2 vols. published. Cambridge, U. S., 1920–21. This is a fundamental source for recent diplomatic history. It contains the texts of the secret treaties and agreements in which Austria was concerned, and a history, based on the Austrian archives, of the negotiations over the Triple Alliance and its various renewals.

———. "Zwei Gespräche des Fürsten Bismarck mit dem Kronprinzen Rudolf von Österreich," in *Österreichische Rundschau,* January, 1921.

Queillé, Eumène. *Les commencements de l'indépendance bulgare.* Paris, 1910.

Rachfahl, Felix. "Der Rückversicherungsvertrag, der 'Balkandreibund,' und das angebliche Bündnisangebot Bismarcks an England vom Jahre 1887," in *Weltwirtschaftliches Archiv,* July 1, 1920.

Rambaud, Alfred. *Jules Ferry.* Paris, 1903.

Raschdau, L. "Der deutsch-russische Rückversicherungsvertrag," in *Grenzboten,* April 12, 1918. This is an authoritative presentation of the German side of the negotiations, written by a survivor of Bismarck's diplomatic corps, and forms an important complement to Goriainov's article.

*Reden.* See Bismarck.

Remmer, Hermann. *Russland und die europäische Lage.* Leipzig, 1888.

Reventlow, Ernst, Graf zu. *Deutschlands auswärtige Politik.* 2d edition. Berlin, 1915.

Robertson, C. G. *Bismarck.* London and New York, 1918.

[Robolsky, Hermann.] *Bismarck und Russland.* Berlin, 1887.

———. *Fürst Bismarck unter drei Kaisern.* Leipzig, 1888.

———. *Die mitteleuropäische Friedensliga.* Leipzig, 1891. The writer is a Bismarckian pamphleteer, prolific and diffuse. Although said by Hammann to be 'bismarckofficiös,' his publications are of little value, and appear to be based chiefly on newspaper cuttings.

Rothfels, Hans. "Zur Geschichte des Rückversicherungsvertrages," in *Preussische Jahrbücher,* March, 1922.

*Russland und der Dreibund.* Berlin, 1888.

Sanger, C. D., and Norton, H. T. J. *England's Guarantee to Belgium and Luxemburg.* London, 1915.

Schaefer, C. A. "Bismarcks Ägypten- und Indienpolitik," in *Das Grössere Deutschland*, November 6, 1915.

Schefer, Christian. "Treize années de politique extérieure (1879-1892)," in *Correspondant*, September 10, 25, October 25, 1919.

— —. *D'une guerre à l'autre.* Paris, 1920.

Schiemann, Theodor. "Eine Unterredung zwischen dem Fürsten Bismarck und dem General Nikolai Wassiliewitsch Baron Kaulbars," in *Beilage zur Allgemeinen Zeitung* (Munich), February 18, 1905.

Schmitt, B. E. *England and Germany 1740-1914.* Princeton, 1916.

Scholz, Wilhelm von. *Erlebnisse und Gespräche mit Bismarck.* Stuttgart and Berlin, 1922.

Schulthess. *Europäische Geschichtskalender.* Useful for public speeches and newspaper articles.

Schwertfeger, Bernhard, general editor. *Zur europäischen Politik.* Volume v, *Revanche-Idee und Panslawismus*, Wilhelm Köhler, editor. Berlin, 1919. Based upon research in the Belgian archives during the occupation. Selected despatches from the Belgian ministers are printed, with a brief introduction. This is an important source, but deficient in many respects. The despatches of the minister to Berlin are lacking between the dates July 22 and December 9, 1887, a period during which his reports would have been of great value.

— —. *Der geistige Kampf um die Verletzung der belgischen Neutralität.* Berlin, 1919.

Simon, Edouard. *L'Allemagne et la Russie au XIX$^e$ siècle.* Paris, 1893.

Simpson, J. Y. "Russo-German Relations and the Saburoff Memoirs," in *Nineteenth Century*, December, 1917; January, 1918.

Singer, Arthur. *Geschichte des Dreibundes.* Leipzig, 1914.

Sosnosky, Theodor von. *Die Balkanpolitik Österreich-Ungarns seit 1866.* Stuttgart and Berlin, 1913-14. 2 vols.

*Das Staatsarchiv.* Edited by Hans Delbrück. A periodical publication containing diplomatic correspondence, newspaper articles, and other material bearing on international politics.

Stead, W. T. *Truth about Russia.* London, 1888.

Татищевъ, С. С. *Изъ прошлаго русской дипломатіи.* St. Petersburg, 1890.

Trubetzkoi, Prince Grigorii. *Russland als Grossmacht.* Translation. Stuttgart and Berlin, 1917.

*Videant consules ne quid respublica detrimenti capiat.* Cassel, c. 1890. A pamphlet of uncertain attribution, which created a great stir by its disclosure of the connection of the Crown Prince Frederick with the war party in 1887.

Ward, Sir A. W. *Germany 1815-1890.* Volume iii (1871-1890). Cambridge, 1918.

Welschinger, Henri. *Bismarck*. Paris, 1912.

Wertheimer, Eduard von. *Graf Julius Andrássy*. Stuttgart, 1910–13. 3 vols. This authoritative work has little to contribute for the period during which Andrássy was out of office.

Whitman, Sidney. *Personal Reminiscences of Prince Bismarck*. London, 1902; New York, 1903.

William Hohenzollern. "Memoirs of the Ex-Kaiser." Published serially in the *New York Times*, beginning September 24, 1922.

Wolff, Sir H. Drummond. *Rambling Recollections*. London, 1908. 2 vols. The author gives some interesting information connected with the negotiations conducted by him at Constantinople for two special conventions concerning Egypt.

*Yellow Book*. See France.

Жигаревъ, С. Русская политика въ восточномъ вопросѣ. Moscow, 1896. 2 vols.

*Zur europäischen Politik*. See Schwertfeger.

NEWSPAPERS. The only newspapers to which primary reference is made are the London *Times*, the *Neue Freie Presse* of Vienna, the *Allgemeine Zeitung* of Munich, and *L'Univers* of Paris. The *Times* is valuable, not only for its usually sound comments on British policy, but also for its excellent foreign correspondence. It was served in this period by three correspondents of more than ordinary distinction. William Lavino, in the course of a long residence at Vienna, had made a large circle of friends among all parties, taking care to identify himself with none. His reports are often too daring in their conjectures, but they always deserve attention, as his sources of information were respectable and his own judgment was well trained. Charles Lowe, who served the paper at Berlin, is the author of a life of Bismarck which ran through several editions. He was in good favor there, and his correspondence almost always reflects the same views as the German inspired press. The personality of Blowitz, the Paris correspondent, stands revealed in his vainglorious memoirs. He was an impressive figure in the world of journalism, with his wealth of experience and numerous acquaintanceships among the eminent men of his time. Almost all the current anecdotes of diplomatic circles found their way into his correspondence. The *Neue Freie Presse*, under the able direction of Moritz Benedict, represents an independent German-Austrian point of view. It is distrustful of all things Slavic, yet distrustful also of Germany and jealous of the Dual Monarchy's freedom of action. These considerations determine its attitude toward the policy of the government, which it criticizes frankly. The foreign correspondence of this journal is also very good. The *Allgemeine Zeitung*, for this period, is of no particular significance in itself; but its correspondence is reliable and especially rich in reproductions of important articles from other German newspapers. The Clerical organ, *L'Univers*, serves less well as a guide to the French press.

The articles of other newspapers to which reference is made have been gleaned from the columns of these four and from various other publications. This fact will account for any errors in text or date. To avoid complication of the footnotes, these indirect origins have been, for the most part, omitted. The most significant German organs are, of course, the *Norddeutsche Allgemeine Zeitung* and the *Kölnische Zeitung*, which derived their inspiration most directly from official sources. All the articles of note in these two may be taken as reflecting the government's point of view or conveying an impression which it wished to produce. A less consistent rôle is that played by the *Post*, of which the inspiration was sporadic and unauthoritative. Its chief function was that of spreading alarmist rumors which the government wished to be at liberty to disavow.

Direct quotations not obtainable in the original tongue are given in English. The versions of the *Times* are used for this purpose when such exist: in other cases, the practice generally followed in the footnotes is departed from, and a translation made from the secondary source.

PERIODICALS. The current discussions of political events in certain of the European periodicals form a contemporary record of some importance. They usually contain little in the way of new material, being mainly reviews of the facts which have become public in the course of the month or fortnight, interpreted according to the views of the writer. They are often valuable as summing up the tendencies in public opinion represented by particular groups of leaders. The light thrown upon German policy by the political correspondence of the *Preussische Jahrbücher* is considerable. Under the able editorship of Hans Delbrück, this periodical represented no official inspiration, but an independent, well weighed judgment of events and policies in a spirit sympathetic to the government. For Russia, Вѣстникъ Европы has been chiefly relied upon. It is broadly 'Western' in spirit, reflecting neither the pro-German tendencies of the Giers administration, nor the pro-French sentiments of Katkov and the Panslavists.

It stood for a European orientation of Russian policy, avoiding subservience to any particular Western power. It criticized keenly the government's policy in the Bulgarian question, without leaning to the other extreme of advocating an aggressive policy in alliance with France. Madame Adam's biweekly letters on foreign policy in the *Nouvelle Revue* offer a running commentary on events which is usually more lively than accurate. Violently nationalistic, hostile to Bismarck, and ardent in their advocacy of the Russian alliance, these reviews are too biassed to form a reliable record; but they display some keenness of observation and reflect an important tendency in French public opinion. The summaries by Charles de Mazade in the *Revue des deux Mondes*, on the other hand, are too colorless to be of any particular value.

# INDEX

# INDEX

Abdul-Hamid II, sultan of Turkey (1876–1909), 32, 41, 122, 125, 126, 166, 188, note, 199, 200, note, 201, 202, note, 208, 224, 232, 233, 234, 240 f., 246, 283, 331.
Adam, Madame Juliette, 162, note, 226, note, 295, note, 300, 301, 302, note, 305, note.
Adriatic, the, 121, 154.
Aegean, the, 121, 154.
Afghanistan, 13, 18, 21, 43, 62, 89, 247.
Africa, 63, 154, 155, 201, 274.
*Agents provocateurs*, 161.
Albania, 155.
Albedyll, General, 260, note, 284, note.
Albert, archduke of Austria (b. 1817, d. 1895), soldier and military writer, 163.
Aleko Pasha, governor general of Eastern Rumelia (1879–84), 193.
Alexander I, prince of Battenberg, prince of Bulgaria (1879–86), 18–27, 29, 32–35, 42–49, 53 f., 63–65, 69–74, 76, 83, 85, 89, 94, 95, 107, 127, 146, note, 168–170, 187, 195, 205, 207, 283.
Alexander II, tsar of Russia (1855–81), 8, 20, 162, note, 292.
Alexander III, tsar of Russia (1881–94), 3, 8, 10, 16, note, 17 f., 20, 23 f., 25, 32, 43, 56, 57, 70, 71, 86, 102, 113, 117, 118, 126 f., 129, 135, 145, 159, 160 ff., 168, 180, 181, 186, 187, 189, note, 190, 191, 195, 198, 231, 236, 237, note, 241–271, 273, 276, 283, 292, 293, 296, 297, 298, note, 299, 301, 302, 306, 308 f., 311, 313, 320, 322.
Alexandra, queen of Edward VII of England, 299, note.
Alsace, 58, 157.
Alsace-Lorraine, 58, 119, 137, 143, 171–184, 200, note.
*Alter Kurs*, 3, 324.

Andrássy, Count Julius, Austro-Hungarian minister of foreign affairs (1871–79), 84, 109–113.
Anglophile theory, 12.
Anglo-Turkish convention (May 22, 1887), fails of ratification, 198–201, 204.
Apponyi, Albert, Count, leader of the Opposition in Hungary, 87 f.
Arbitration, 55.
Armed Neutrality, the, 12.
'Armed peace,' 131.
Armenia, 201, note.
Ars, 176.
Asia, 9, 14, 89, 97, note, 119, 250, 289 f., 291, 294, 318, 320, 323.
Aunay, Count d', French consul general and diplomatic agent at Cairo (1885–87), 100, 106.
Austria-Hungary, 141, 147, note, 317; Balkan interests of, 76, 78 f., 80 ff., 133, 150, 151, 153, 164, 165 f., 187, 189, 194, 197, 205, 207–224; Bismarck supports, 6, 7, 9, 13, 88, 110 f., 122 f., 129, 133 f., 135 f., 156, 163 ff., 191, 193, 195, 197, 198, 316, 318, 331, 333; League of the Three Emperors, 6 f., 9, 56, 123, 136, 186, 190; Triple Alliance, 65, 67, 77, 121, 122, 124, 150-166, 185, 196, 348; relations with foreign countries: Bulgaria, 17, 20–53, 72, 83–129, 134, 135, 192, 233–292, 306, 312, 318; England, 50 ff., 63, 80, 91, 102, 107 ff., 112, 113, 120, 123 f., 124; Germany, *see* Austro-German Alliance, Triple Alliance; Italy, *see* Triple Alliance; Russia, 83, 111, 128, 129, 135 f., 156, 164, 180 f., 188, 189 f., 196, 278, 304, 323; Serbia, 39, 40, 41, 42, 44–47, 49. *See* Andrássy, Francis Joseph, Kálnoky, Rudolf.

355

## 356  INDEX

Austro-German Alliance of 1879, the, 16; 64, 85, 87, 108, 109, 110, 111 ff., 189 f., 191, 193, 195, 197, 250, 262, 272, 278, 293, note, 316 f., 334; basis of Germany's dominant position, 75; publication of (February 3, 1888), 306 ff., 312.

Baden, 172.
Balkan states, 36, 38 f., 43, 51, 52, 54, 63, 76 f., 87, 93, note, 101, note, 110, 112, 119, 122, 129, 151, 153, 155, 169, 170, 187, 189, 190, 193, 195, 197, 217, 234, 246, 279, 287, 297, 318, 323, 333 f. See Eastern Question; Near East.
Baranov, General, governor of Nizhni Novgorod, 243.
Batum, 62.
Bavaria, 172.
Beaconsfield, Earl of, British premier (1874–80) 8, 14, 89, 97, note.
Bebel, Ferdinand August, a leader of the social-democratic party in Germany, 161, note, 183.
Belgium, 142 f., 226, note, 239, 274 f., 291, 295, 301, 304 f.; attitude of England toward violation of Belgian neutrality, 142 f.
Berchem, Max, Count von, German under secretary of state for foreign affairs (1886–90), 216, 221 f.
Berlin, interview of Bismarck and Giers at (Sept. 7, 1886), 86; visit of Alexander III to (Nov. 18, 1887), 247–251, 253, 255–264.
Berlin, congress of (1878), 6, 7, 17, 22, 62, 80, 108, note, 110, 180, note, 193, 312 f., 319.
Berlin, treaty of (1878), 23, 25 f., 28–31, 34 f., 36, 62, 63, 93, note, 103, 107, 109, note, 112, 122, 126, note, 134, 152, 205, 207, 218, 219, 222, 263, 303.
Berlin stock exchange, 141.
Bethmann-Hollweg, Theobald von, German imperial chancellor (1909–17), 316.
Beyens, Baron, Belgian minister at Paris, 145, note.

Biegeleben, Rüdiger, Baron von, Austro-Hungarian diplomatic agent and consul general at Sofia (1881–87), 168.
Bismarck, Count Herbert, German secretary of state for foreign affairs (1886–90), 33, 34 f., 38, 46, note, 52, 61, note, 100, 104, 120, 124, 126, 145, 171, 176, 179, 182 ff., 192, 195, 200, note, 215, note, 223 f., 225, note, 234, 239, 255, 256, note, 259, note, 264, note, 283, 288, note, 294, 299 f.
Bismarck, Prince Otto von, German imperial chancellor (1871–1890), and the army, 115 f., 121, 127 f., 130, 141, 148, 150, 156, 273, 277 f., 282, 284, 306 f., 330; speech on army bill (January 11, 1887), 131–134, 145; great speech (February 6, 1888), vii, 309–316; and colonies (1884–85), 11, 12, 62 f., 100 f., 133, 316; 'Continental system' of, 12, 21; diplomacy criticised, 316–325; foreign policy continued by William II, 3–16, 322–325; fundamental principles, 75 f.; League of the Three Emperors and, 16, 17 f., 55, 185–189; the Pope and, 55, 175, note; preventive war and, 137, 138, note, 315; on treaties, 215; Triple Alliance and, 149–156, 196; policy toward other countries: Austria, support of, 6, 7, 9, 13, 88, 110 f., 122 f., 129, 133 f., 135 f., 156, 191, 193, 195, 197, 198, 316, 318, 331, 333; Austro-German alliance (1879), 189 f., 262, 272, 312; interview with Crown Prince Rudolf (November 17, 1887), 163 ff.; Balkan Peninsula, 19–23, 28, 30–33, 46 f., 53, 69–129, 131, 134, 139, 313 f.; 'Bulgarian documents,' 212 ff., 225–228, 241, 245, 260, 275 f., 292–302, 306; correct Austrian policy in Balkan Peninsula, 52 f.; lack of sympathy for Balkan aspirations, 38, 54, 133; misconception of situation during the Bulgarian crisis, 42 f., 48 f., 51 f.; indirect blocking of Russia in Bulgaria, 80, 129, 134, 156–170, 192, 205–265; the triple entente (December, 1887), 266–288,

314, 318, 329–335; war scare of December, 1887, 276–292, 304, 311; favors Balkan spheres of influence, 51 ff., 79, 86, 104, 110, 123, 125, 129, 187, 188, note; England, advances to, 4–8; an Anglo-German alliance and, 50 f., 59, 62 f., 81, 89; change of policy toward, 10 ff.; 'Continental system,' 12, 21; desires friendship of, 13–16, 114, 120 f., 123, 124; entangles in Triple Alliance through triple entente (December, 1887), 149, 151–154, 156, 157, 163, 164, 187, 199, 205, 234, 249 ff., 253 f., 266–276, 280, 281, 288, 314–318; France, uses against England, 11, 77, note, 99–103; hostility to, 6, 10, 11, 12, 13, 16, 38, 78, 80, 90, 188, 195, 200 f., 281, 303 f., 331; widening breach with, 57–63; war scare of January-February, 1887, 129–149, 151, 153, 160, 171 f.,; war scare of April, 1887, 157 f., 165, 167; unrest in Alsace-Lorraine, 171 f.; Schnaebele incident, 171–184, 185, 247, 304; Italy, 66 f., 120 ff., 155; military convention with (1887), 304; Russia, 4–9, 13, 14 ff., 19, 21, 50, 75, 117, 120, 121, 145 ff., 148, 318–323; anti-Polish measures and, 55 f.; attempted assassination of the Tsar (March 13, 1887) and, 160 ff., 181; attacks Russian credit, 201–204, 229, 255, 257, 259, 320; dictates to Russia, 68; distrusts French approaches to Russia, 120 f., 158–163, 313, 331, 332; keeps tie with Russia, 65, 110, 126, 129, 133 f., 135 f., 139, 144, 185, 304–314, 317; the Reinsurance Treaty, 186–198, 200, 203, note, 204.

Black Sea, the, 154.
Blanc, Albert, Baron, Italian ambassador at Constantinople (1887–91), 246.
Bleichröder, German financier, 144.
Blowitz, Henry Georges Stephan Adolphe Opper de, Paris representative of the London *Times*, 140 f.
Bôcher, representative of the Orleans family in France, 296 f.
Booth, John, forester, 157, 340.

Bosnia and Herzegovina, 7, 20, 24, 26, 30, 31, 79, 151.
Bosphorus, the, 333.
Boulanger, Georges, French general and politician, minister of war (1886–87), 60, 114, 130, 132, 137, 139, 140 f., 143 f., 145, 147, 157 f., 164, 177, 180, note, 187, 191, 204, 235, 262.
Bourse of Paris, 137, 140, 141.
Brest-Litovsk, visit of Prince William of Germany to the Tsar at (Sept., 1886), 86.
Brignon, French beater, 236.
Brisson, Eugène Henri, French premier (1885–86), 57, 59.
Bronsart von Schellendorf, Paul, Prussian minister of war (1883–89), 128, note, 130, 282, 284, 340.
Brussels, 226, 297.
Bucharest, treaty of, between Serbia and Bulgaria (March 3, 1886), 53.
Bucher, Lothar, official in the German foreign office (1864–86), 13, note, 19, note.
Bülow, Bernhard von (prince from 1905), counsellor and first secretary of the German embassy at St. Petersburg (1883–88), 117, 187, 246, 278.
Bulgaria, unification of, 17–54; supported by England, 40; by Turkey, 41; by Russia, 43; temporary settlement, 53 f.; forced abdication of Prince Alexander, 63–65, 69–74; the powers and, 76–129, 133, 134, 135, 147, 151 f., 159, 162 f., 165 ff., 168 ff., 185, 188, 192 f., 194 f., 197, 198, 199, 204, 246, 313, 318, 319; and Prince Ferdinand of Coburg, 205–302.
'Bulgarian documents,' the, 212 ff., 225–228, 241, 245, 260, 275 f., 292–302, 306, 346 f.
Busch, Moritz, Bismarck's literary assistant, 13, note, 19, note, 47, 48, 63, 172, note, 340.

Cabinets (English), Bismarck's distrust of, 14.
Caffarel, 244.

## 358 INDEX

Calice, Heinrich, Baron von, Austro-Hungarian ambassador to Turkey (1880–1906), 26, 41, 233, 239.
Canossa, Bismarck's journey to, 55; Alexander III's journey to, 242, 251.
Caprivi de Caprara de Montecucoli, Georg Leo von, chancellor of the German empire (1890–94), 196, note, 256, note.
Carnot, *see* Sadi-Carnot.
Caroline Islands, 55.
Cartuyvels, Belgian consul general at Sofia, 226 f.
Catacazy, Russian minister at Washington, 297, 300.
Central Powers, 18, 30, 64, 65, 245, 253, 258, 278, 290, 294, 305, 307, 308, 318. *See* Austria-Hungary, Germany.
Charlemagne, 172, note.
Charles, prince of Rumania (1866–81), king (1881–1914), 213.
Chaudordy, Count de, employed by Flourens in approach to England, 162 f., 235, 236, note, 340.
Cherevin, General, aide to Alexander III of Russia, 260, note, 264, note.
Chiala, Luigi, 340; cited, 25, note.
Chimay, Joseph, Prince de, Belgian minister of foreign affairs (1884–92), 226, note, 305.
Christian, Princess, *see* Helena.
Christian communities in the Balkans, 152, 312.
Churchill, Lord Randolph, 50, 89 f., 92 ff., 95–103, 107, 123 f., 151, 152, 268, 293 f., 340.
Clémenceau, Georges Eugène Benjamin, French radical politician, cited, 59, note, 119, note.
Clémentine, princess of Bourbon-Orleans, widow of Prince August of Coburg, 206.
Colonies, German efforts to establish, 11, 12, 62 f., 100 f., 133, 316.
Constantinople, 9, 77 f., 86, 90, 92, 94, 95, 133, 151, 164, 187, note, 192, 193, 194, 199, 201, 202, note, 240, 243, 246, 260, 284, 290, 318; Bismarck's view of a Russian occupation, 52, 76, 237, note, 238.
'Continental system,' Napoleon's, 12; Bismarck's, 12, 16, 21; William II's, 323 f.
Copenhagen, 43, 226, note, 228, 229, 241, 242, 247.
Corsica, 155.
Corti, Count L., Italian ambassador at Constantinople (1875–85), 24, note, 25, 33, note.
Courcel, Alphonse, Baron de, French ambassador at Berlin (1882–86), 341 f.; cited, 10, note, 61, note.
Crimean war, 94.
Crispi, Francesco, prime minister of Italy (1887–91, 1893–96), 215–220, 222 f., 228, note, 234, 254, 261, 296, 304, 309, 318; interview with Bismarck (October 2, 1887), 237 ff., 240, note, 241, 245, 249, 251.
Cronstadt, 248.
Cyon, Élie de, journalist, 145, note, 146, note, 186, note, 203, note, 290, note, 300 f., 341.

Damé, Frédéric, Rumanian editor, 298 f.
Danube, 51, 155.
Dardanelles, the, 13, 155, 285, 333.
Darmstadt, retreat of Prince Alexander of Battenberg, interviews of 1887 at, 168.
Dartford, Lord Randolph Churchill's speech at (1886), 92, 96.
Debidour, Antonin, historian, 301.
Decazeville, labor unrest at, 60.
Deines, Major von, German military attaché at Vienna, 282.
Delbrück, Hans, 3, 198, 324, 342, 351.
Delcassé, Théophile, French minister of foreign affairs (1898–1905), 144.
Denmark, 247.
Depretis, Agostino, Italian premier (1876–77, 1877–78, 1878–79, 1881–87), 215.
Déroulède, Paul, chief of the French 'League of Patriots,' 243.
Dieppe, meeting of Lord Salisbury and Chaudordy at, 235.

## INDEX

Dilke, Sir Charles, English radical politician and author, 102, 103, 142, 167, 342.
'Diplomaticus' letter in London *Standard* (February 4, 1887), 142 f.
Dogali, defeat of Italian force by Abyssinians at (Jan. 26, 1887), 151, note.
Dongorita, 153.
Dual Alliance, the, of Germany and Austria-Hungary (1879), 16, 64, 75, 85, 87, 108, 109, 110, 111 ff.; basis of Germany's dominant position, 75. *See* Austro-German Alliance.
Dunkirk, 242.

Eastern Question, the, vii, 6, 26, 44, 63, 66, 69, 90, 108, note, 111, 118, 123, 133, 134, 204, 231, 252, 258, 267, 311 f., 317, 319, 322. *See* Balkan states, Near East.
Eastern Rumelia, 18, 20, 21, 23, 25 f., 32, 34, 37, 46, 48, 53, 54, 63, 64, note, 103, 125, 193, 223, note, 241, 246.
East Prussia, 225, 229.
Ebenthal, 212, note.
Eckardstein, Hermann, Baron von, 4-6, 197, note, 228, note, 270, note, 271, 299 f., 342.
Edward VII, king of England (1901-1910), 330.
Egypt, 43, 89, 99 ff., 102, 106, 114, 118, 119, 121, 130, 151, 153, 154, 155, 235 f., 249; Egyptian convention (October 24, 1886), 101, 199; failure of Anglo-Turkish convention of May 22, 1887, 198-201, 204.
England, 192, note; attitude toward violation of Belgian neutrality, 142 f.; Bismarck's policy toward, 4-8, 10 ff., 50 f., 59, 62 f., 81, 89; 'Continental system,' 12, 21; Bismarck desires friendship of, 13-16, 114, 120 f., 123, 124; Bismarck entangles in Triple Alliance through triple entente (December, 1887), 149, 151-154, 156, 157, 163, 164, 187, 199, 205, 234, 249 ff., 253 f., 266-276, 280, 281, 288, 314-318, 329-335; relations with foreign countries:
Austria, 50 ff., 63, 80, 81, 102, 107 ff., 112, 113, 120, 123 f., 124, 334; Balkan Peninsula, Bulgarian crisis, 22, 27 f., 28, 32, 34 ff., 40, 42 f., 45 f., 47 ff., 53, 62, 123 f., 151 f., 162 f., 164, 170, 192 f., 197, 207 f., 217-224, 234, 240, note, 241, 251, 253, 294; support of Prince Alexander, 71 ff., 78-81, 88-104, 107; Egypt, 99-102, 106, 114, 121, 151, 153, 154, 249; Anglo-Turkish convention, 198-201; France, 162, 235, 244 f., 247; irritated at France, 153, 201; refusal to enter agreement specifically against France, 153; France used by Bismarck against England, 11, 77, note, 99-103; Germany, 13-16, 50 f., 59, 81, 89, 323, 324, note; colonial agreements with Germany, 62 f., 316; Italy, 66, 81; Russia, Afghan boundary difficulty, 18, 193, 197; boundary protocol (September 10, 1885), 21; boundary convention (July 10, 1887), 199; hostility to Russia, 9, 62, 113, 123, 129, 134, 151, 152, 153, 154, 191, 199, 245, 247, 272, 294. *See* Churchill, Gladstone, Salisbury.
Ernest II, duke of Saxe-Coburg (1844-93), 298.
Ernroth, Russian general, Bulgarian minister of war (1880-81), 194, 211, 217, 220, note, 221, 222, 231, 232.
Errembault de Dudzeele, Count G., Belgian ambassador at St. Petersburg (1866-88), 191, note, 246, note.
Erzerum, 220, note, 221.
Eugénie, widow of Napoleon III of France, 299, note.
Euxine Sea, the, 154.

Ferdinand, prince of Saxe-Coburg-Kohary, prince of Bulgaria (1887-1908), tsar (1908-18), 206-224, 226, 230, 233, 240, note, 241, 245, 246, note, 252, 260, 264, note, 283, 292-302, 319, 323.
Ferry, Jules, French premier (1880-81, 1883-85), 11, 12, 57, 58, 59, 98, 119, 130, 277, 321.

Finland, 248.
Fischer, captain of Zurich police, 161, note.
Floquet, Charles Thomas, French premier (1888–89), 186, note, 292.
Flourens, Émile, French minister of foreign affairs (1887–88), 130, 139 f., 143, 144, 145, 159, 162 f., 175, note, 176, 177, 214, 226, 228, 235 f., 244 f., 247, 249, 343.
Foucault de Mondion, spy in the French service, 226, 227, 293, 299, 300, 301, 346.
France, 6, 58, 59 f., 81, 99, 103, 118, 119, 121, 123, 135, 191, 201, 204, 229 f., 235 f., 237 f., 257, 266, 268, 278, 280, note, 306, 317, 333 f.; Bismarck uses against England, 11, 77, note, 99–103; Bismarck's hostility to, 6, 10, 11, 12, 13, 16, 38, 78, 80, 90, 188, 195, 200 f., 281, 303 f.; Bismarck's widening breach with, 57–63; war scare of January–February, 1887, vii, 129–149, 151, 153, 160, 171 f.; war scare of April, 1887, vii, 157 f., 165, 167; unrest in Alsace-Lorraine, 171 f.; Schnaebele incident, vii, 171–184, 185, 247, 304; Triple Alliance and, 150–156; war of 1870–71, 303 f.; war scare of 1875, 136, 138, 140, 144, 148; Balkan Peninsula, 118, 159, 162 f., 202, note; attempted compromise in Bulgarian crisis, 36, 42; Egypt, 99–102, 106, 114, 153, 199, 200 f.; approaches England, 162, 235, 244 f., 247; irritates England, 153, 201; Germany desires a free hand against, 9, 188; relations with Italy, 67, 251; rapprochement with Russia, 56 f., 61, 68, 102, 110, 118 f., 127, 128, 129 f., 144–147, 157, 158–163, 167, 185, 186, 191, 199, 200, 204, 241, 243 f., 247, 249, 258, 261, 264, 280, 285, 290 ff., 300, 304, 313, 316, 320–323. See Boulanger, Ferry, Freycinet.
Francis Joseph I, emperor of Austria (1848–1916), 17, 20, 39, 109, 111, 136, 189 f., 196, 206, 212, note, 279 f.

Frankfort, treaty of (May 10, 1871), 7, 58, note, 303.
Franzensbad, conference of Prince Alexander of Battenberg and Giers at (1885), 21, 22, 24; visit of Bismarck to Giers at (1886), 69 f.
Fredensborg, castle in Denmark, 225.
Frederick I, grand duke of Baden, 284, note.
Frederick III, German emperor and king of Prussia (March–June, 1888), 78, 138, 187, 225, note, 229, note, 330.
Freycinet, Charles de, French minister of foreign affairs (1885–86), 56, note, 58, note, 59, 60, 102, 106, 114, 118, 119, 130, note, 132, note, 177, note, 199, note, 343.
Friedrichsruh, Giers's visit to Bismarck at (Oct. 7, 1885), 31; home of Bismarck, 182, 209; Crispi's visit to (Oct. 2, 1887), 237 ff., 245, note, 251 f.
Friis, Aage, Danish scholar, cited, 7, note.

Galicia, 285, 288.
Gastein, conference of (August 9–10, 1886), 64, 65, note; meeting between William I and Francis Joseph at (August 6, 1887), 196.
Gautsch, German police commissioner, 176, 178, 182.
*Gedanken und Erinnerungen*, 4, 310, 339 f.
Geneva, 161.
German Empire, 5, 6, 86, 114, 230, 273, 303–325, 331. See Germany.
German foreign office, archives, 8, 344.
Germany, 6, 7, 12, 15, 55, 199, 242; army increase, 114 f., 127 f., 130, 131, 135, 141, 148, 150, 156, 273, 277 f., 282, 284, 306 f., 309 f., 314 ff.; colonial enterprises, 11, 12, 62 f., 100 f., 133, 316; League of the Three Emperors, 8, 9, 11, 13, 16, 34, 136, 158, 185; Germany arbiter of the League, 34, 42, 46, 49, 54; Socialist Law of 1878, 161; Triple Alliance, 65, 67, 124, 149–156, 196; unity of foreign policy, 3, 4, 303–325; secret pacts; vii; relations with foreign countries: Austria, alliance of 1879, 16,

64, 75, 85, 87, 108, 109, 110, 111 ff., 133 f., 135 f., 156, 189 f., 193, 197, 262, 272, 308 f., 312, 334; Balkan Peninsula, 16; Bulgarian crisis, 17, 19, 21, 28, 33, 39, 47, 51 f., 73 f., 77–82, 84, 86, 87, 89, 95, 101, note, 103, 104, 108, 112, 127, 133, 134, 135, 156, 202, note, 205–265, 313 f.; triple entente of December, 1887, 266–288, 294; war scare of December, 1887, 276–292, 304, 311; England, 13–16, 50 f., 59, 62 f., 81, 89, 316, 324, note, 330–335; France, free hand against, 9, 188; hostility to France, 12, 13, 14, 57 f., 114 ff., 188, 195, 200, 277, 281, 288, 310, 316, 320, 333; war scare of January–February, 1887, vii, 57–63, 119, 120, 121, 126, 127, 129–149, 150, 151, 153; Schnaebele incident (April, 1887), vii, 157, 160, 165, 167, 171–184, 185, 247, 304; Italy, military convention with (1887), 304; relations with Russia, 13, 14, 15, 56 f., 68, 127, 133, 134, 135, 139, 144, 147, 242 f., 304, 318; attempt on Tsar's life (March 13, 1887), 160 ff., 181; German colonization of West Russia discouraged, 56; attack on Russian credit, 201–204, 229, 255, 257, 259, 290 ff.; 'Reinsurance Treaty' (1887), 186–198, 200, 203, note, 204. *See* Austro-German Alliance, Bismarck, League of the Three Emperors, Reinsurance Treaty, Triple Alliance, William I, William II.

Giers, Nicholas de, Russian minister of foreign affairs (1882–95), 17, 18, note, 20 f., 31 f., 33, 45 f., 46, note, 48, 56, note, 57, note, 68, 69, 70, note, 71, 86, 102, 117, 134, note, 145, 146, 159, 166, 180, 186 f., 188, 195, 209, note, 220, 221, 226, note, 228, note, 243, 246, 248, 257, note, 278, 283, 285, 291, 293, 295 f., 298.

Gladstone, William Ewart, British premier (1868–74, 1880–85, 1886, 1892–94), 8, 11, 12, 53, 62, 268.

Goblet, René, French premier (1886–87), 130, 177, 199, note.

Golden Horde, pilgrimages of Muscovite princes to, 68.

Golden Horn, the, 202, note.

Gontaut-Biron, Vicomte de, French ambassador at Berlin (1873–77), 10.

Gorchakov, Alexander, Prince, Russian imperial chancellor (1870–92) and minister of foreign affairs (1856–82), 6, 180, note.

Goriainov, Serge, archivist of the Russian ministry of foreign affairs, 138, note, 144, note, 145, note, 159, note, 189, note, 344.

Greeks, the, 32, 36 f., 46, 54.

Greppi, Count Giuseppe, Italian ambassador at St. Petersburg (1883–87), 220.

Grévy, François Paul Jules, president of the French republic (1879–1887), 114, 143, 145, note, 160, 177, 277.

Guildhall speech of Lord Salisbury (November 9, 1886), 97, 106 ff., 114, 121.

Guinea Coast, 63.

Hamlet, 133.

Hammann, Otto, 4, 77, note, 324, note, 344 f.

Hansen, Julius, private counsellor of the Russian embassy at Paris, 144, 174, note, 228, 236, 299, 345.

Hatzfeldt-Wildenburg, Paul, Count von, German ambassador at London (1885–1901), 50, 70, note, 89 f., 159, note, 217, 221, 250, 251, 267, 329, 333.

Haupt, secret agent of the Prussian police, 161.

Hecuba, 133.

Helena, daughter of Queen Victoria of England, wife of Prince Christian of Schleswig-Holstein-Sonderburg-Augustenburg, 169, note.

Herbette, Jules, French ambassador at Berlin (1886–96), 88, 100, 114, 130, 139 f., 160, 177, note, 178, 180, 200, note, 320, note.

Herzfeldt, Hans, 138, note.

Hofburg, the, 281.

Hofmann, Hermann, 345; cited, 197, note.

Hohenlohe-Schillingsfürst, Chlodwig, Prince von, German ambassador at Paris (1874-85), 12, 57 f., 77, note, 114; governor of Alsace-Lorraine (1885-94), 58, 137 f., 172, 179, note, 345.
Hoiningen, Ernst, Baron von, named Huene, German captain, military attaché at London (1882-85) and at Paris (1886-88), 177, note.
Holland, 239, note, 274, 304, note.
Holstein, Baron Fritz von, actual privy councillor in the political and diplomatic section of the German foreign office, 21, 196, note, 259, note, 267, note, 345.
Holy Alliance, 162.
Honveds, 206.
Horvath, Balthasar, Hungarian politician, 87, note.
Hungarians, 73, 84 f., 99, 104-108, 111, 185, note, 232, 252, 306; suspicious of plots against Dual Monarchy, 24; opposition to government, 30 f., 86 f.
Hupka, 300.

Iddesleigh, Lord, British secretary of state for foreign affairs (1886-87), 70, note, 91 f., 206, note.
Iranyi, Hungarian politician, 87, note.
Ischl, 296.
Italy, 41 f., 50, 53, 65 ff., 71, 78, 81, 98 f., 101 f., 103, 104, 119, 120-123, 124, 129, 141, 149-156, 164, 185, note, 192, 196, 200, note, 205, 208 f., 215-224, 233-241, 251 f., 254, 261, 265, note, 266-272, 274, 275, 277, 280, 281, 291 f., 304, 307, 309, 314, 317, 318, 333 f.; pivotal position in Bismarck's diplomacy, 155. See Crispi, Triple Alliance.

Japan, 323.
Jews, 56.
Joint-Stock Land Credit Company of St. Petersburg, 186, note.
Jomini, Henri, Baron, official in the Russian foreign office, 71, 157.
Jonghe d'Ardoye, Count de, Belgian ambassador at Vienna, cited, 200, note.

Kálnoky, Count Gustav, Austro-Hungarian minister of foreign affairs (1881-95), 17, 20, 23, 26 f., 33, note, 34 f., 37-41, 44, 47, 51, 53, 64 ff., 70 ff., 79, 81, 83 f., 86, 94, note, 95, 96, 98 f., 104, 105, 106, 108-113, 120 ff., 123, 124, 125 f., 136, 141, note, 146, 150 f., 154, 156, 163, 168, 169, 188, 194, 196, 208, 210, 211, 217 f., 221, 222, 223, 237, 241, 245, 249, 252 f., 254, 257, 279, 281, 286, 287, 289; his 'middle course,' 109.
Karavelov, member of the Bulgarian council of regency, 65, note, 71.
Karl Ludwig, archduke of Austria, brother of Francis Joseph I, 68, note.
Károlyi, Alois, Count, Austro-Hungarian ambassador at London (1878-88), 35, 275.
Katkov, Mikhail, Russian journalist, 57, 68, 117, 135, 146, note, 157, 160, 180 f., 186, 341, 351; cited, 8, note, 147, note.
Kaufmann, German forest guard, 236.
Kaulbars, Alexander Vasilevich, Baron, Bulgarian minister of war (1882-83), 91.
Kaulbars, Nikolai Vasilevich, Baron, Russian representative in Bulgaria (1886), 91, 95, 103, 104, 117, 118, 166, 187, 188.
Kazan, 311.
Khevenhüller-Metsch, Count von, Austro-Hungarian ambassador at Belgrade (1881-86), 44 f., 46.
Khitrovo, Russian ambassador at Bucharest (1886-90), 298.
Kinsky, Count, attaché to the Austrian embassy at London, 94, note.
Kissingen, conference of (July 22-24, 1886), 64, 65, note.
Klein, Tobias, trial of, 173, 178, note.
Klepsch, Lieutenant Colonel, Austro-Hungarian military attaché at St. Petersburg, 278.
Knorring, 300.
Köchlin, French spy, conviction and pardon of, 200, note.
*Kölnische Zeitung*, 113, 116, 158, note, 206, note, 212, 219, 229, 230, 231, 236,

241, 248, 255 f., 261, 265, 272, note, 283, note, 293, 296 ff., 299, note, 351.
Krasnoiarsk, 289.
Kremsier, meeting of Francis Joseph and Alexander III at (August 25, 1885), vii, 17, 20, 22, 24.
Kropotkin, Prince Peter, Russian anarchist, 57.
Krüger, police director of Prussia, chief of the secret police abroad, 161.

Labouchère, questions of, on adherence of England to the Austro-German Alliance, 294, note.
Laboulaye, Antoine de, French ambassador at St. Petersburg (1886–91), 144.
Länderbank, the, 39.
Landsturm, 273, 278, 284, 306.
Landtag, the, of Prussia, 141, 174 f.
Langenbuch, Professor, German physician, 168 f.
Lappenberg, Hamburg banking house of, 305, note.
Lascelles, Sir Frank, British diplomatic agent and consul general at Sofia (1879–87), 206, note.
Launay, Eduardo, Count di, Italian ambassador at Berlin (1867–92), 66, 98, 121, note, 126, note, 209, note, 215, note, 218.
Lavino, William, correspondent of the London *Times* at Vienna, 256 f., 285, 324, 350.
League of Patriots (French), 173, 243.
League of the Three Emperors, the, informal (1872), 6; (1881), 8 ff., 13, 16, 17 f., 21, 26, 29 f., 75, note, 80, note, 108, 113, 136, 158, 162, 171, 179 ff., 192, 193, 195, 196, 197, note, 236 f., 317; Germany arbiter of, 34, 42, 46, 49, 53, 54; weakening of, 55, 56, 63, 64, 65, 185–190.
Lebel rifle, 114.
Leckert-Lützow trial (December, 1896), 181.
Leipzig, imperial court at, indictments and trials for treason, 173, 175, note, 181, 200, note.

Lemberg, Prince Alexander taken to, 69, 70.
Leo XIII, pope (1878–1903), 55.
Leopold II, king of Belgium (1865–1909), 213, 239, 246, note, 295, 304 f.
*Le prince de Bismarck démasqué*, 226, note, 301, 346 f.
Lesseps, Ferdinand de, French engineer, 159 f., 163.
Leyden, Count von, German chargé d'affaires at Paris (1887), 136 f., 174, 175, note.
'Lichnowsky school,' 4.
Lobanov, Prince, Russian ambassador at Vienna (1882–94), 286, 287, 289, 311, 313.
Lorraine, 137, 173, 236. See Alsace-Lorraine.
Louis XIV, king of France (1643–1715), 331.
Lowe, Charles, Berlin correspondent of the London *Times*, 175, note, 346.
Lublin, 278.
Lucius von Ballhausen, Robert, Baron, Prussian minister of agriculture, domains, and forests, 346; cited, 56, note, 61, note, 62, note, 80, note, 113, note, 128, 140, note, 141, 165, note, 169, note, 187, note, 261, note, 264, note, 269, note, 274, note, 284, note, 305, note.
Lüttichau, Count Conrad, cited, 300.
Lyons, Richard, Earl, British diplomat, ambassador to France (1867–87), 62, note, 145, note, 153, 159, note, 163, 176 f., 191, note, 199, note, 200, note, 347.

Macedonia, 26 f., 30, 36, 65, note, 222.
Maffei, Marquis, Italian diplomat, 239.
Magyars, the, 84, 95, 104, 308. See Hungarians.
Malet, Sir Edward, British ambassador at Berlin (1884–95), 141, 152 f., 250, 271, 272, 334.
Malvano, J., director general of political affairs in the Italian ministry of foreign affairs, 209, note.

Marie, countess of Flanders, sister-in-law of Leopold II of Belgium, sister of King Charles of Rumania, 213, 226 f., 241, 245, 294, 295 ff., 298, note.

Marie, princess of Bourbon-Orleans, wife of Prince Waldemar of Denmark, 228.

'Maurel, Charles de,' 226, note, 301, 346.

'May Laws,' 55.

Mediterranean, the, 81, 101, 122, 150, 238, 272, note, 274; Mediterranean agreement (February–March, 1887), 151–154, 156, 166, 187; second Mediterranean agreement (December 12-16, 1887), 274 f.

Melinite, 114 f., 165.

Menges, private secretary to Prince Alexander of Battenberg, 168.

Metternich, Prince, 331.

Metz, 183.

Meuse, the, 142.

Milan II, prince of Serbia (1868–82), and king (1882–89), 36, 37 f., 40, 44.

Mingrelia, Nicholas Dadian, prince of, 198.

Mittnacht, Hermann, Baron von, minister-president of Württemberg, 47, 165, 172, note, 347.

Mohrenheim, Arthur, Baron de, Russian ambassador at Paris (1884–98), 33, note, 56, note, 144 f., 159, 228, note, 292, 345.

Molden, Berthold, biographer of Kálnoky, 196, 347.

Moltke, Count Hellmuth von, Prussian field-marshal, 131, 158, 164, 281, 283, note.

Montebello, Count de, French ambassador at Constantinople (1886–91), 201, note.

Montenegro, 51.

Moravia, 17.

Morier, Sir Robert, British ambassador at St. Petersburg (1884–93), 221, 285.

Morocco, 121, 153, 155.

*Moscow Gazette*, 43, 57, 68, 135, note, 147, note.

Münster, Georg Herbert, Count zu, German ambassador at London (1873– 85), 5, 8, 11; at Paris (1885–1900), 130, 143, 145, note, 174, note, 228, note.

Mutkurov, Bulgarian nationalist leader, member of the council of regency (1886), 71.

Napoleon I, 331; Continental system of, 12.

Napoleon III, emperor of France (1852–1870), 132.

Near East, 16, 18–54, 63–74, 81, 96, 99, 122, 127, 129, 134, 135, note, 139, 147, note, 150, 152, 153, 155, 156, 157, 164, 166, 168, 171, 185, 238, 251, 269, 274, 288, 290, 304, 311, 329, 331, 332. *See* Balkan states, Eastern Question.

Nelidov, Alexander, Count, Russian ambassador at Constantinople (1883–97), 30, note, 118, 201, note, 241, note.

*Neuer Kurs*, 3, 182, note, 324.

Neujean, interpellation of, 305, note.

Newfoundland fisheries, the, 153, 201.

New Hebrides, the, 153, 201, 235, 244.

Nice, 155.

Nicholas II, tsar of Russia (1894–1917), 322, note, 323.

Nicholas Mikhailovich, Russian grand duke, 242 f., 244.

Nieter, George, official connected with the Belgian foreign office, 226, 227, 259, note, 299, 301, 346.

Nigra, Count Costantino, Italian ambassador at Vienna (1885–1904), 208, note, 210, note, 211, note.

Nihilists, 161, 225.

Nile, the, 155.

Nizhni Novgorod, 243.

*Nord* of Brussels, 297.

*Norddeutsche Allgemeine Zeitung*, 85, 106, 137, 143, note, 178, note, 180, 202, 219, 229 f., 231, 232, 257, 351.

Obolenski, Prince, director of the chancery in the Russian ministry of foreign affairs (1887–90), 228.

Obruchev, General, chief of the Russian general staff, 134, 180, note.

Old Serbia, 38.

## INDEX

Oncken, Hermann, 77, note, 197, note.
Orleans, house of, 206, 212, note, 228, note, 261, 292, 296 ff., 300.
Ostend, significant meeting of diplomats at (September, 1887), 239.
Ottoman debt, 246.

Paget, Sir Augustus, English ambassador at Vienna (1884–93), 23, 26, 27, note, 34, 72, 106, 208, note.
Pagny-sur-Moselle, 173, 176, 181.
Pagès, Georges, 177, note, 347.
Panslavism, 5, 6, 24, note, 37, 43, 77 f., 113, 117, 134, 147, 181, 225, 241, 243, 268.
Paris, 226, 228, 297.
Paul, duke of Mecklenburg (b. 1852), 283.
Pest, 232, 297.
Petrovsk, 290.
Philippopolis, *coup d'état* of (Sept. 18, 1885), 22, 46, 48, 54, 63, 69.
Pilsen, 20.
Plehn, Hans, 7, note, 348.
Poland, 165, note, 203, 237, note, 258, 287, 292.
Poles, the, 56, 237.
Posen, 172, note.
Prague, peace of (August 23, 1866), true date of revision, 7, note.
'Preventive war,' 137, 138, note, 315.
Prussia, 55, 135, 141, 161, 172, 260.
Puttkamer, Robert von, Prussian minister of the interior (1881–88), 161, 162, note.

Rachfahl, Felix, cited, 7, note, 270, note, 322, note.
Radowitz, Joseph, Count von, German ambassador at Constantinople (1882–92), 8, note, 157, 202, note, 260, 283.
Rakhova, Prince Alexander taken to, 69.
Rantzau, Cuno, Count zu, counsellor in the German foreign office (1880–88), 203, note.
*Reichsanzeiger*, the, publishes the 'Bulgarian documents,' 294 ff., 299, 300, 302.

Reichsbank, 255, 256, note.
Reichstadt, pact of (July 8, 1876), 180 f., 189 f.
Reichstag, 115 f., 121, 128, 130, 131, 135, 136, 137, note, 141, 142, note, 145, 156, 161, 171 f., 183, 209, note, 273, 277, 282, 284, 306, 309 f.
'Reinsurance Treaty,' the (1887), 3, 185–198, 200, 202, 203, note, 204, 205, 209, 237, 247, 257, 286, 318 ff., 321, 322.
Reni, Prince Alexander taken to, 69.
Reuss, Prince Henry VII of, German ambassador at Vienna (1878–94), 47, 86, 124, 150, 151, note, 213, 214, 223, 234, 260, 281, 289, 293, 294, 296, 298 f., 302.
Rhine, the, 147, 155, 168, 172, note.
Robertson, C. G., 321, 348.
Robilant, Count Carlo Felice Nicolis di, Italian minister of foreign affairs (1885–87), 41 f., 65–68, 98, 99, 103, 104, 121 f., 123, 124, 150 ff.
Rosebery, Earl of, British foreign secretary (1886, 1892–94), prime minister (1894–95), 21.
Rothfels, Hans, 270, note, 348.
Rothschild, house of, 186, 204.
Rothschild, Alphonse, Baron de, 200, note.
Rouvier, Maurice, French premier (1887), 191, 199, 235.
Rudolf, crown prince of Austria (b. 1858, d. 1889), 141, note, 155, 163 ff., 169, note, 237, 239, note, 317.
Rumania, 16, 48, 51, 52, 65, note, 79, 123, 213, 273, 280, 298.
Rushchuk, 70, 232.
Russia, 5, 6; Bismarck and, 4–9, 13, 14 ff., 19, 21, 50, 75, 117, 120, 121, 145 ff., 148, 318–323, 331 f.; Bismarck's anti-Polish measures, 55 f.; attempted assassination of the tsar (March 13, 1887), 160 ff., 181; credit attacked by Bismarck, 201–204, 229, 255, 257, 259, 320; Bismarck's dictation to, 68; in League of the Three Emperors, 9, 11, 13, 56, 127, 136, 158, 162, 179 ff., 184 f.; relations with foreign countries: Austria, 83, 111,

128, 129, 135 f., 156, 164, 188, 196, 278, 304, 323; pact of Reichstadt (1876), 180 f., 189 f.; Bulgarian crises, 18–37, 40–49, 51–55, 63, 69, 70, 72 f., 76–81, 83–129, 134, 135, 139, 147, 151, 156, 159, 162 f., 164, 189, 193, 197, 202, note, 205–265, 333 f.; blocked by triple entente (December, 1887), 266–288, 304, 318, 323; England, Afghan boundary difficulty, 18, 193, 197; boundary protocol (September 10, 1885), 21; boundary convention (July 10, 1887), 199; hostility of England, 9, 62, 113, 123, 129, 134, 151, 152, 153, 154, 191, 199, 245, 247, 272, 294; France, rapprochement with, 56 f., 61, 68, 102, 110, 118 f., 127, 128, 129 f., 144–147, 157, 158–163, 167, 185, 186, 191, 199, 200, 204, 241, 243 f., 247, 249, 258, 261, 264, 280, 285, 290 ff., 300, 304, 313, 316, 320–323; Germany, Bismarck keeps tie with Russia, 65, 110, 120, 126, 129, 133, 134, 135, 139, 144, 145 ff., 185, 304; Bismarck's disloyalty to Russia, 156–170; 'Reinsurance Treaty,' 186–198 200, 203, note, 204. See Alexander III, Giers, Shuvalov.

Sadi-Carnot, Marie François, president of France (1887–94), 277.
Saint-Vallier, Charles, Comte de, French ambassador at Berlin (1877–81), 77, note.
Salisbury, Marquis of, British premier (1885–86, 1886–92, 1895–1900, 1900–02), and foreign secretary (1885–86, etc.), 12, 22 f., 28, note, 35, 40, note, 41, note, 48 f., 62, 63, 72 f., 89, 90, 92, 93, note, 94, 95, 97, 100, 106 ff., 114, 121, 123, 124, 142, note, 146, note, 152, 153, 154, note, 156, 159, note, 170, 191, note, 192, 193, 197, note, 199, note, 200, note, 201, 208, note, 217, 221, 223, 235, 236, note, 245, note, 247, 249 ff., 254, 267 f., 271 f., 275, 279, 293, note, 294, note, 329–335.
Salonica, 31, 290, 318.

San Stefano, treaty of (March 3, 1878), 26.
Schiemann, Theodor, 187, note, 349.
Schnaebele, French police officer, 173–184, 236.
Schnaebele, *fils*, 236.
Schröder, secret agent of Prussian police, 161, note.
Schweinitz, Hans Lothar von, German ambassador at St. Petersburg (1876–93), 56, note, 146, 147, note, 202, 209, 226, note, 243, 258.
Scott, Sir Charles, first secretary to the British embassy at Berlin (1883–88), 71, note.
Serbia, 16, 26, 27, 28, 30, 32, 34, 36–47, 51 f., 79, 81, 86, 112, 123, 246, 273, 280; declares war on Bulgaria (November 13, 1885), 36, 40, 42, 43, 81; Austrian support, 36, 37 f., 39, 40, 41, 42, 49.
Seven Years' war, 268.
Shuvalov, Paul, Count, Russian ambassador at Berlin (1885–94), 140, 188–196, 198, 204, 209, 218, 219, note, 220, note, 221, 225, 248, 256, note, 259, 263, 283, 284, 293, 300, 308.
Shuvalov, Peter, Count, Russian diplomat, 54, note, 117, 125, 127, 145, 146, 147, 157, 167, 186, 228, note, 293, 320, note; ambassador at London (1874–79), 339; plenipotentiary at the congress of Berlin (1878), 339.
Silistria, *coup d'état* attempted at by Russian partisans (March 3, 1887), 166.
Singer, deputy to Reichstag, 161, note, 162, note.
Skierniewice, interview between the emperors of Russia, Germany, and Austria at (1884), 24, note, 30; treaty of (so-called), 236 f.
Slivnitsa, battle of (November 17–19, 1885), 43.
Smolka, Dr., cited, 105, note.
Sobranie, Bulgarian legislature, 116 f., 205, 208, 209, note, 212, note, 234, 241.
Socialism, 55, 60; German Socialists, 161.

Sofia, Prince Ferdinand goes to (August 9, 1887), 211, 213, 215, 233.
Somaliland, 201.
Spain, 55, 58, 224, 274.
Staal, de, Russian ambassador at London (1884–1903), 41, note, 91, 223, note.
Stambulov, Stephen, Bulgarian nationalist leader, president of the Sobranie (1884–86), member of the council of regency (1886–87), premier (1887–94), 71, 91, 205, 207, 208, 220, 287.
Statthalter, see Hohenlohe.
Steininger, Lieutenant-Colonel von, Austrian military attaché at Berlin, 283.
Stettin, proposed interview between Alexander III and William I at, 225, 229, 230, note, 236, 241, 242, 255.
Stoilov, representative of Bulgarian council of regency at Vienna (1887), 168 f., 205, 207, note.
Straits, the, 9, 127, 146, 188, 195, 240. See Bosphorus, Dardanelles.
Stranski, Bulgarian minister of foreign affairs, 206, note.
Straten Ponthoz, Count van der, Belgian ambassador at Berlin, cited, 131, note, 137, note, 139, 160, note, 201, 202, 203, 256, 259, note, 264, note.
Suez Canal, the, 235, 236, note, 244, 249.
Sweden, 248, 305.
Switzerland, 161.
Széchényi, Emeric, Count, Austro-Hungarian ambassador at Berlin (1878–92), 52, 158.
Szögyény-Marich, Ladislas, first chief of section in the Austro-Hungarian foreign office (1883–92), 65, note.

Tausch, von, Prussian police commissioner, 178, note, 181 ff.
Thielmann, Baron von, German consul general at Sofia (1886–87), 94, note, 216.
*Times*, London, 17, note, 92, note, 108 f., note, 138, 140, 174, note, 175, note, 177, note, 179, note, 182, note, 254, note, 256, 285, 308, 350.

Tirard, Pierre Emmanuel, French premier (1887–88), 277.
Tisza, Koloman, Count von, Hungarian premier (1875–90), 30, 31, 37, note, 87, 93, 95, 105, note.
Tomsk, 289.
Tonkin, 59.
Transylvania, 52, 237, note.
Trentino, the, 151.
Triple Alliance, the (1882–1915), 10, 15, note, 16, 42, 52, 64, note, 65 ff., 81, 93, 98, 104, 107, 120 f., 122 f., 124, 125, 150, 185, note, 196, 199; renewal (February 20, 1887), 149–156, 166, 215, 237, 239, note, 240, note, 241, note, 245, note, 247, 249 ff., 257, 261, 272, note, 273 ff., 292, 304, 314, 317, 318, 323.
Triple Entente, the, of December, 1887, 266–302.
Tripoli, 98, 101, note, 121, 154, 155.
Tunis, 10.
Turin, utterances of Crispi at (October 25, 1887), 251.
Turkey, 9, 13, 26, 28 f., 30 f., 32, 36, 39, 41, 46, 52, 53, 63, 64, note, 72, 76, 77, 79, 83, 84, 87, 90, 106, 107, 109, 118, 121, 125 f., 151, 155, 167, 191, 192, 194, 198–201, 208, 210, 211, 212, note, 220, 221, 222, 224, 230, 231, 233, 234, 239 f., 245, note, 246, 249, 266, 271, 272, note, 275, 280, 281, 283, 285, 304, 312, 320, 334. See Abdul-Hamid II, Eastern Question.
Tyrnovo, assembly of, 116 f.

Ursel, Duke d', 295, note.
*Uruguay*, steamer, 242.
Urussov, Prince Leo, Russian ambassador at Bucharest (1881–86) and at Brussels (1886–98), 298.

Varna, Bulgarian port, 103 f., 220, note, 221.
Varzin, retreat of Bismarck, 17, 211, note, 266; Kálnoky's visit to (August, 1885), 17, 20; Churchill not invited to, 96, note, 97.

'Vasili, Comte Paul,' 238, note, 301, note.
*Verjudete Geldmenschen*, 164.
Vexaincourt, French commune, 236.
Victoria, queen of England (1837–1901), 19, 146, note, 154, 170, 201, note, 299, note.
Victoria, princess of Prussia, 19, 95, 187.
Vienna, conference between Prince Alexander and Kálnoky at (1885), 20; conferences on recall of Prince Alexander by the Bulgarians (1887), 168 f.
Villaume, Lieutenant-Colonel von, German military attaché at Paris (1882–87), 115, 174.
Vladikavkaz, 289.
Vladimir, Russian grand duke, 167, 237.
Vlangali, aide to the Russian minister of foreign affairs, 71.
Vogüé, Melchior, Viscount de, employed by Flourens to approach the Tsar, 159.
Vosges, the, 172, note, 236.
Vyshnegradski, Russian minister of finance (1887–90), 256.

Waldemar, Prince, son of King Christian IX of Denmark, 116 f.
Waldemar, Princess, *see* Marie, princess of Bourbon-Orleans.
Waldersee, Alfred, Count von, German quartermaster general (1882–88), acting chief of the general staff, 115 f., 127, 138, note, 164, 282, 284, note.
Wedel, Count, German military attaché at Vienna (1877–87), 141, note.
Welschinger, Henri, French biographer of Bismarck, 173, 350.
Wertheimer, Eduard von, 350.
White, Sir William, British envoy extraordinary to Turkey (1885–86), 29, 45.
Wilhelmstrasse, 5.
William I, German emperor (1871–88), 17, 32, 126, 130, 165, 168, 178, 179, 183, 187, 196, 200, note, 210, 225, 229, 238, 257, 258 f., 261, 264, note, 273, 283, note, 284, 306, 322, note.
William II, German emperor (1888–1918), 3, 86, 250, 267, 268 f., 272, 283, note, 322 ff., 329 f., 334; criticised by Hammann, 324, note; "Memoirs of the Ex-Kaiser," 86, note, 350.
Wilmowski, 179, note.
Windthorst, Ludwig, German politician, 133.
Wolff, Sir Henry Drummond, special commissioner to Turkey and Egypt for arranging affairs of Egypt (1885–87), 101, 151, 200, 202, note, 350.

Zanzibar, 63, 100 f.
*Zur europäischen Politik*, 349.
Zurich, 161, note.

**DATE DUE**

GAYLORD • PRINTED IN U.S.A.